Real Social Science

Real Social Science presents a new, hands-on approach to social inquiry. The theoretical and methodological ideas behind the book, inspired by Aristotelian phronesis, represent an original perspective within the social sciences, and for the first time this volume gives readers a set of studies exemplifying what applied phronesis looks like in practice. The reflexive analysis of values and power gives new meaning to the impact of research on policy and practice. *Real Social Science* is a major step forward in a novel and thriving field of research. This book will benefit scholars, researchers, and students who want to make a difference in practice, not just in the academy. Its message will make it essential reading for students and academics across the social sciences.

PROFESSOR BENT FLYVBJERG is Founding Chair of Major Programme Management at Oxford University's Saïd Business School and Director of the Oxford Centre for Major Programme Management. He works for better planning and management of megaprojects and cities, plus he writes about phronetic social science and case study research. Bent Flyvbjerg has served as adviser to the United Nations, the EU Commission, and government and companies in many countries.

PROFESSOR TODD LANDMAN is Director of the Institute for Democracy and Conflict Resolution at the University of Essex. He is a political scientist and has carried out numerous projects on the analysis and synthesis of data and complex governmental information, as well as being the author of several books and articles.

Visiting Professor SANFORD SCHRAM has taught social theory and social policy at the Graduate School of Social Work and Social Research, Bryn Mawr College since 1997. He is an affiliate to the National Poverty Center at the University of Michigan, Ann Arbor. As well as being the author of ten books he sits on the editorial boards of a number of journals, including the *Social Service Review*.

Real Social Science

Applied Phronesis

Edited by

Bent Flyvbjerg

Oxford University

Todd Landman

University of Essex

Sanford Schram

Bryn Mawr College

CAMBRIDGE
UNIVERSITY PRESS

CAMBRIDGE UNIVERSITY PRESS
Cambridge, New York, Melbourne, Madrid, Cape Town,
Singapore, São Paulo, Delhi, Mexico City

Cambridge University Press
The Edinburgh Building, Cambridge CB2 8RU, UK

Published in the United States of America by Cambridge University Press,
New York

www.cambridge.org
Information on this title: www.cambridge.org/9780521168205

First published 2012

Printed in the United Kingdom at the University Press, Cambridge

A catalogue record for this publication is available from the British Library

Library of Congress Cataloging in Publication data
Real social science : applied phronesis / [edited by] Bent Flyvbjerg, Todd
Landman, Sanford Schram.
    p. cm.
ISBN 978-1-107-00025-4 (hardback)
1. Social sciences – Research – Methodology.   2. Social sciences – Philosophy.
I. Flyvbjerg, Bent.   II. Landman, Todd.   III. Schram, Sanford.
H62.R355   2012
300 – dc23   2012002647

ISBN 978-1-107-00025-4 Hardback
ISBN 978-0-521-16820-5 Paperback

Contents

Figures

Tables

Contributors

GIOVANNI ATTILI, Department of Architecture and Urban Studies, University La Sapienza, Rome.

RANU BASU, Associate Professor, Department of Geography, York University, Ontario, Canada.

STEWART R. CLEGG, Professor, School of Management, University of Technology, Sydney, Australia.

VIRGINIA EUBANKS, Assistant Professor, State University of New York at Albany, New York.

BENT FLYVBJERG, First BT Professor and Founding Chair of Major Programme Management at Oxford University's Saïd Business School and Director of the Oxford Centre for Major Programme Management, University of Oxford.

ARTHUR W. FRANK, Professor of Sociology, Department of Sociology, University of Calgary, Alberta, Canada.

STEVEN GRIGGS, Reader in Local Governance, Local Governance Research Unit, De Montfort University.

DAVID HOWARTH, Reader in Government, Co-Director, Centre for Theoretical Studies, Department of Government, University of Essex.

TODD LANDMAN, Professor of Government and Director, Institute for Democracy and Conflict Resolution, University of Essex.

TRICIA D. OLSEN, Assistant Professor of Business Ethics and Legal Studies, University of Denver.

LEIGH A. PAYNE, Professor of Sociology and Latin America, St Antony's College, University of Oxford.

TYRONE S. PITSIS, Associate Professor of Strategy, Organization and Society, Newcastle University Business School, University of Newcastle.

ANDREW G. REITER, Assistant Professor of Politics, Mount Holyoke College, Massachusetts.

LEONIE SANDERCOCK, Professor, School of Community and Regional Planning, University of British Columbia, Vancouver, Canada.

SANFORD SCHRAM, Visiting Professor, Graduate School of Social Work and Social Research, Bryn Mawr College, Pennsylvania.

COREY SHDAIMAH, Assistant Professor, School of Social Work, University of Maryland.

WILLIAM PAUL SIMMONS, Associate Professor of Political Science, Social and Behavioural Sciences, Arizona State University.

ROLAND STAHL, Assistant Professor, School of Social Work, Lucerne University of Applied Sciences and Arts.

Acknowledgements

This volume represents the efforts of a good many people. The editors first want to acknowledge our contributors; without their excellent contributions there would be no *Real Social Science*. All our contributors took the project seriously, responded to our numerous requests punctually and never at any time posed any challenges to our project. We thank them all for their fine work. We would also like to acknowledge the support of the Political Science Department at Bryn Mawr College. We also want to acknowledge the excellent work of the folks at Cambridge University Press, not just for their meticulousness but also their cordiality. John Haslam, our editor, took a keen interest in our project and advised us effectively throughout. Gillian Dadd helped make sure our final manuscript was as good as it could be. Last, the editors want to thank each other. We learned that we make a good team.

1   Introduction: new directions in social science

Bent Flyvbjerg, Todd Landman and Sanford Schram

There is ferment in the social sciences. After years of sustained effort to build a science of society modelled on the natural sciences, that project, long treated with suspicion by some, is now openly being rethought. A critical intervention in this period of reflection was *Making Social Science Matter* (MSSM) by Bent Flyvbjerg, published in 2001. In that book Flyvbjerg challenged the very idea of social science as a science modelled on the natural sciences. Flyvbjerg argued that, as the social sciences study human interactions that involve human consciousness, volition, power and reflexivity, attempts to build generalizable, predictive models such as those for the natural world are misplaced and even futile.

MSSM offered a pointed argument about what is wrong with the social sciences today, and enumerated examples of how what it saw as an alternative social science is possible and already happening. The book provided a thorough analysis of how its alternative social science is dedicated to enhancing a socially relevant form of knowledge, that is, 'phronesis' (practical wisdom on how to address and act on social problems in a particular context). Significantly, MSSM reinterpreted the Aristotelian concept of phronesis to include issues of power and explained that building on this new version of phronesis is the best bet for the relevance of the social sciences in society. Intelligent social action requires phronesis, to which the social sciences can best contribute and the natural sciences cannot with their emphasis on 'episteme' (universal truth) and 'techné' (technical know-how). This Aristotelian tripartite distinction of 'intellectual virtues' was critical in MSSM for highlighting the comparative advantage of social science. Even in Aristotle's original interpretation, phronesis is seen as the most important of the intellectual virtues, because it is needed for the management of human affairs, including the management of episteme and techné, which cannot manage themselves. Phronesis, in this sense, is knowledge that is sensitive to its application in specific settings and is therefore able to manage itself (and more), which is what gives it prominence in social thought and action.

MSSM argued that, given their subject matter, the natural sciences are better at testing hypotheses to demonstrate abstract principles and law-like relationships, while the social sciences are better at producing situated knowledge about how to understand and act in contextualized settings, based on deliberation about specific sets of values and interests. Such deliberation about values and interests is central to social, political and economic development in any society, and it is something to which the social sciences are particularly well suited while the natural sciences are not. The natural sciences excel at conducting decontextualized experiments to understand abstract and generalizable law-like relationships, while the social sciences can conduct contextualized studies involving field research that produces intimate knowledge of localized understandings of subjective human relationships, and especially in relationship to the values and interests that drive human relationships.

MSSM put the emphasis not on particular research methods or types of data (it emphasized that both qualitative and quantitative data and methods are pertinent to phronesis), but on producing research that can help develop phronesis by increasing understanding and effecting change in specific contexts rather than questing after the ghost of an abstract knowledge of law-like processes. MSSM called for social scientists to revise their standards for acceptable research methodologies, giving up fruitless attempts to emulate the natural sciences and instead reincorporating context-sensitive research, such as case studies, narratives, and datasets that help social actors learn to appreciate the complexities of social relations and practise various social crafts, including policy and change, more effectively.

MSSM emphasized that social sciences can distinctively produce the kind of knowledge that grows out of intimate familiarity with practice in contextualized settings. These are local knowledges, even tacit knowledges and skills, that cannot be taught *a priori* but that grow from the bottom up, emerging out of practice. Add a sense of praxis, seeking the ability to push for change, leaven it with an appreciation of the ineliminable presence of power, and this phronetic social science can help people involved in ongoing political struggle question the relationships of knowledge and power and thereby work to produce change.

MSSM was followed by a volume edited by Sanford Schram and Brian Caterino, *Making Political Science Matter* (2006), which explored the academic debate generated by MSSM, including a spirited dispute – the so-called 'Flyvbjerg Debate' – between Bent Flyvbjerg and Stanford University political science professor, David Laitin, over what phronesis is and can be in social and political science. Both books were mainly about the theoretical and methodological issues involved in justifying and doing phronetic social science, with only two illustrative case studies of applied phronesis, one in each book (Flyvbjerg 2001: 141–61; Shdaimah and Stahl 2006). Yet in the intervening years, the advantages of the phronetic approach have been demonstrated in many specific studies. Commentators, including one of the co-editors of the current volume, Todd Landman (2008), have pointed out that compiling cases of the phronetic approach would be an important and much needed next step in the development in this alternative to mainstream social science.

The current book responds with case studies demonstrating specific instances where researchers have actively worked to implement a phronetic social science, that is, phronesis used to deliberate and act in relation to substantive issues in social science and policy. In what follows, the book (1) presents a number of outstanding examples of applied phronesis at the nexus of social science and policy studies, (2) examines these examples in the context of the evolving theory and methodology of phronetic social science and (3) teases out the implications and next steps in this new field of policy-oriented social science research. The book is therefore the first systematic attempt to bring together a set of case studies exemplifying what phronetic social science actually looks like in practice.

Part I includes four chapters designed to provide context for the case studies. In Chapter 2, Sanford Schram provides a brief history of phronetic social science, its key concepts and distinguishing features, including how it contrasts practical versus theoretical knowledge, positivistic versus interpretivist methodologies, qualitative versus quantitative data collection efforts, phronetic research versus action research, and the various ways in which research can be of relevance to policy.

In Chapter 3, Todd Landman argues that narrative analysis provides a particularly apt set of methods for phronetic social science, since it allows for stories, intersubjective meanings and experiences with power to be uncovered and analysed in ways that other methods cannot. But narrative analysis is still very much a loose collection of methods ranging from the deep analysis and interpretation of single stories to more systematic approaches that deconstruct and compare different elements of multiple stories. The chapter defines and delineates narrative analysis, establishes its methodological links with phronetic social science and illustrates its main lines of argument with examples from empirical research on human rights, in particular research on the more than thirty 'truth commissions' around the world.

Arthur Frank in Chapter 4 provides an in-depth examination of the relation between phronesis in doing social science and what Frank calls 'everyday phronesis'. Frank accepts that a core topic of social scientific study is the dependence of human action on phronesis, which he understands as people's practical wisdom in dealing with both routine decisions and unexpected contingencies. This practical wisdom seems to have three aspects: it is content, a quality of persons and a form of action. As content, phronesis is a resource – a stock of experiential knowledge. As a quality of persons, it is what enables acquisition and appropriate use of that knowledge – a capacity. And as action, phronesis necessarily involves doing something – a practice in which experiential knowledge is both used and gained. 'Having phronesis' is iteratively dependent on 'practising phronesis'. This chapter discusses social theories in which the study of everyday practical wisdom works to enhance their readers' capacity for phronesis. The chapter revisits the work of Pierre Bourdieu and Michel Foucault to show how, not only to describe, the human condition is dependent on phronesis. Frank shows that each theorist's texts are pedagogical in the sense of being written to equip the reader for what the texts require from him or her: doing the research each theorist recommends, but more generally, appreciating the limits of those recommendations, and, on that basis, taking a newly realized form of responsibility for one's life. Bourdieu and Foucault call on readers to learn what can only be implied, never specified as direct advice, about how to live. Frank argues that social science phronesis has to be more than a topic; it is what social scientific study requires from researchers and what social science seeks to enhance in its audience. *Real* social science is when studying the world has the effect of changing it, by means of what Machiavelli calls *verita effettuale* (effective truth). Real social science that contributes to phronesis grows out of experience and, in turn, contributes to that experience. It cannot be theorized *in toto* in advance.

Chapter 5, the last chapter in Part I, by Stewart Clegg and Tyrone Pitsis, clarifies how three key 'power questions' are handled in phronetic research: (1) how are the specific problematics of power enacted and constituted by the different agents engaged (and not engaged) in social (and non-social) relations in the substantive field studied?; (2) what are the mechanisms by which observers might analytically determine which of the different agents make claims about winning or losing and how they do it?; and (3) what are the social consequences of specific power relations and how can we determine desiderata for calculating them? Phronetic social science is often conducted in collaboration with partners from outside the academy, for example, from industry, government or civil society. The chapter argues that phronetic research views relations between academic researchers and outside partners, as well as relations between outside partners, as matters of power. Such a perspective begs the question of how the phronetic researcher should act in the field of power in which they are themselves implicated. The chapter answers this question specifically and explores issues of power and phronesis in the act of doing research with a point of departure in the authors' own decade-long experience as researchers studying megaproject alliances.

Part II of the book includes the case studies. Each chapter focuses on a specific instance of how the phronetic approach was applied in practice to a substantive problematic in social science as input to practice (policy, planning, management) in what we call 'applied phronesis'. Further, each chapter is a self-contained case study of the chosen problematic, that is, an in-depth analysis stressing developmental factors in relation to context. Each chapter also shows how four phronetic key questions, originally emphasized by MSSM, were asked and answered for the problematic at hand: (1) where are we going with this specific problematic?; (2) who gains and who loses, and by which mechanisms of power?; (3) is this development desirable?; and (4) what, if anything, should we do about it? Each chapter reflects on the phronetic dimension of the research being discussed.

Part II begins with the story of how Bent Flyvbjerg and his associates tried to change conventional megaproject policy and management by taking a phronetic approach to their work and working with mass media to increase impact, first in Denmark and later internationally. Megaprojects are big infrastructures, large ICT systems, megaevents, etc., each of which typically costs over a billion dollars and impacts millions of people. Chapter 6 systematically answers the four key questions of phronesis for megaproject policy and management. The first question – 'where are we going with megaprojects?' – is answered by documenting a dismal performance record for megaprojects in terms of systematically undelivered promises. A true paradox is uncovered: more and larger projects are being built at the same time as their poor performance is becoming increasingly clear. In answering the second phronetic question – 'who gains and who loses, and by which mechanisms of power?' – a Machiavellian formula for project approval is uncovered, which is widely used by promoters to construct a reality on paper that secures funding for their projects: (cost underestimation) + (revenue overestimation) + (overestimation of development effects) + (underestimation of environmental impacts) = funding. The third question – 'is this development desirable?' – is answered by a clear and easily justifiable 'No!'. Finally, the answer to the fourth phronetic question – 'what, if anything, should we do about it?' – is, first, we should problematize conventional megaproject development, including individual projects, to a degree where current practices become indefensible, and, second, we should constructively help develop methods, incentives and legislation that will help to curb the fraud and error that are typical of megaproject development. The chapter shows how Flyvbjerg and his associates do this, with particular emphasis on how they work with mass media, and how it has changed policy and practice for megaprojects.

The second case study in Chapter 7, by Corey Shdaimah and Roland Stahl, focuses on power relations between researchers and advocates fighting for an affordable housing trust fund in Philadelphia. The production of social science knowledge is intimately related to issues of power. This is one of the core aspects of phronetic research, as Flyvbjerg has shown in MSSM. Power permeates all dimensions of the research process. Power issues are at the core of the production process of knowledge relating to everything from the alleged special standing of academic researchers in knowledge production to their relationship to their funders and other key institutional actors. Power perhaps most explicitly permeates the social sciences in their often important and visible role in the political arena. Another dimension of the research process that is suffused with power is the relationships among those who fund projects, those who conduct research and those who are the so-called subjects of social science research. In this chapter, the researchers analyse and theorize how power has played an integral role in the collaborative process between academic researchers and community advocates in a participatory action study they conducted in 2004 in Philadelphia. The researchers used data from retrospective interviews conducted with those involved with the project and participant observations to situate their findings in the broader literature of the collaborative research field. As have other authors before them, Shdaimah and Stahl argue that power has to be reflected and acted upon continuously during the entire research process. The authors find that phronesis provides a particularly effective framework for collaborative social science projects, because it puts power at the core of social science knowledge production. Phronesis is also based on a praxis-oriented epistemology, theory of science and methodology which makes it particularly effective in dealing with issues of power in collaborative work. This chapter shows how.

Chapter 8, by Leonie Sandercock and Giovanni Attili, provides an innovative focus on stories and storytelling. The authors see the focus on storytelling as part of an emergent, post-positivist paradigm of inquiry that goes by various names, including phronetic social science. New information and communication technologies today provide the opportunity to explore storytelling through multimedia, including video- and film-making as a form of digital ethnography. This chapter reports on a three-year, three-stage research project in which the authors experimented with the use of film as a mode of inquiry, a form of meaning making, a way of knowing and a way of provoking public dialogue around planning and policy issues (in this case, the question of the economic and social development of Canada's First Nations and the bridging of the cultural divide between Native and non-Native Canadians). The site of the research is the north-central interior of the province of British Columbia, Canada's westernmost province, and the last to be colonized. The focus is on two subtribes of the Carrier Nation: the Burns Lake Band and the Cheslatta Carrier Nation. The authors see the struggle there as a microcosm of a much bigger problem that exists right across Canada. The authors explore the expressive as well as the analytical possibilities of film in conducting social research and provoking community engagement and dialogue, taking advantage of the aesthetic and involving dimensions of film as narrative. The research question of this chapter is a sociopolitical one: given the historic and ongoing conflict between First Nations and the European colonizers who dispossessed them, is there a way forward that can both provide justice for Native people and begin to bridge the 'two solitudes', the cultural distance that is the legacy of racism and oppression? The chapter concludes with critical reflections on the successes and limitations of the first part of the project, which is still a work in progress.

Chapter 9, by Steven Griggs and David Howarth, is a case study of the 'wicked issues' thrown up by UK aviation policy and especially the plan to build a third runway at London's Heathrow airport. 'Wicked issues' in policy-making are informed by competing problematizations, where each problematization articulates rival and often irreducible demands that privilege different 'scientific' facts and evidence. Such endemic conflict around competing demands presents particular challenges for policy-makers seeking to construct policy 'solutions' that can respond adequately to various social demands and claims voiced across policy sectors. Indeed, appeals to evidence, to science and to technical cost–benefit analysis often backfire in the face of such ambiguity, and the competing values and practical judgements made by stakeholders. This chapter demonstrates how a 'phronetic' approach in social science, coupled with post-structuralist discourse theory, offers an alternative understanding of critical policy analysis, especially with respect to the way in which policy-makers and practitioners can begin to address such 'wicked issues'. The chapter pursues a phronetic approach to emphasize power practices implicit in policy analytical techniques, highlighting their implications for constructing identities associated with urban boosterism in the case of an airport expansion conflict. This particular empirical case study explores the way in which successive Labour governments in the

United Kingdom have sought to address the 'wicked problem' of aviation expansion, where the dominant logic has been accompanied by increasing dislocation and political contestation, as different groups have articulated competing demands and problematizations to tackle the issue as they conceive it. The problem of aviation expansion in the UK context constitutes an exemplary case for exploring the growing clash between the logics and values of economic growth, on the one hand, and environmental sustainability on the other. Particular emphasis is placed on the recent decision by the UK government to approve the building of a third runway at Heathrow airport. The chapter concludes by establishing how such an approach leads us to a different understanding and evaluation of 'wicked issues' like aviation policy, while also addressing the clash between the values of economic growth and environmental sustainability.

Chapter 10, by Tricia Olsen, Leigh Payne and Andrew Reiter, describes as an instance of phronesis research that helps transitional countries and policy-makers promote strategies that reduce human rights violations and improve democracy. The term 'justice cascade' is employed in transitional justice scholarship to describe the existence of an international justice norm that has diffused throughout the world. International non-governmental organizations, it is argued, promote the norm; international treaties, covenants and laws institutionalize it; and international and national courts enforce it. The justice cascade suggests that, today, few countries can transition from authoritarian rule or civil war without putting perpetrators of human rights violations or war crimes on trial. The argument further contends that the implementation of domestic and international justice deters future human rights violations. The justice cascade, however, poses a particular problem for the authors of this chapter. While the authors are sympathetic to the idea behind the justice cascade – seeking justice for past violations and deterring future ones – their research in the end challenges the justice cascade as practised. It questions its existence both methodologically and empirically. The chapter brings new evidence to the discussion. It finds, for example, that countries emerging from authoritarian rule and civil war continue to use amnesties, not trials, to deal with the violent past. Further, evidence shows that a combination of trials and amnesties are more likely than trials alone to bring improvements in democracy and human rights. The chapter builds these findings on the construction of a Transitional Justice Database that includes all countries of the world and focuses (for the justice cascade) on ninety-one transitions from 1970 to 2007. The chapter shows that careful empirical work can often contradict scholars, scholarship and normative approaches that may have influenced previous work. It includes considerations on how to use research that contradicts other's findings, while still working towards the same political goals. By utilizing a cross-national database, the authors aim to help transitional countries and policy-makers to deliberate phronetically about and to promote the strategies that will reduce human rights violations and improve democracy in specific contexts most effectively. In that process, the analysis traverses a fraught, normative terrain in ways that conventional research is less likely to do.

Virginia Eubanks provides Chapter 11. The chapter is framed to address one aspect of phronetic social science that has been largely overlooked, that is, its close links to feminist epistemology and methodology. These links were mentioned in MSSM (Flyvbjerg 2006: 104–7, 163–4), but had been lying dormant until Eubanks' treatment. This chapter gives an overview of how to undertake situated practical reasoning in the real world, highlighting the contributions that feminist thinking and action can make to phronetic social science. The chapter suggests that a uniquely feminist phronesis would follow five precepts: (1) begin by grounding your analysis in the subjectivities and everyday/everynight experience of the people being studied (Dorothy Smith's sociology for people); (2) recognize that different individuals and groups inhabit different social locations in relationship to the phenomena being studied, locations shaped by their relationship to power along the lines of race, class, gender, sex, ability and nationality (Kimberlée Crenshaw's intersectional analysis); (3) uncover how this social location shapes how individuals and groups understand the world, developing different 'situated knowledges' (Donna Haraway's feminist epistemology); (4) put these specific situated knowledges in conversation with each other in the context of collaborative, action-oriented practice in order to develop better accounts of the world, accounts that are both more true and more just (Sandra Harding's strong objectivity); and (5) therefore, produce knowledge that is useful for praxis and social movement. Feminist phronesis is explored through two case studies, based on eight years of work with the grassroots organizing groups, Women at the YWCA Making Social Movements (WYMSM) and Our Knowledge, Our Power: Surviving Welfare (OKOP), both of which attempted to contribute to a high-tech equity agenda that protected the economic human rights of women struggling to meet their basic needs in the Capital Region of New York.

Chapter 12, by William Paul Simmons, asks us to imagine that Bent Flyvbjerg in his quest for a model for teaching phronetic social science turned to Paulo Freire's pedagogy of the oppressed instead of Hubert and Stuart Dreyfus' stage theory of skill acquisition. Flyvbjerg would have been confronted with a much more radical and nuanced theory of power than Foucault's, one that would call for a different kind of phronetic social science, perhaps tentatively labelled anti-hegemonic phronetics. Phronesis – grounded in praxis – would still be privileged over techné and epistemé and it would still require a deep understanding of context and power, but it would stress a host of new questions such as: who is *aneu logou* (without a voice in Aristotle's words) in the political community?; what does it mean to speak for the Other?; and are attempts at empowerment actually perpetuating hegemonic discourses? Teaching phronetic social science would also be expanded from producing virtuoso social actors proficient in understanding sociopolitical contexts and adept at marshalling political power to include working with marginalized populations to develop anti-hegemonic discourses based on indigenous knowledges. Virtuoso teachers and practitioners of phronesis would now be those who can learn to learn from below through what Gayatari Spivak (2004: 207–8) has called a 'no holds barred self-suspending leap into the other's sea'. This chapter first briefly develops the need to expand our understanding of phronetic social science and then considers two case studies of teaching anti-hegemonic 'phronetics' in relation to current controversial issues at the United States–Mexico border. First, the chapter discusses the author's use of problem-based learning in working with victims' families in seeking innovative legal remedies for the feminicides in Ciudad Juárez, Mexico. It discusses the teaching of action research in a new Masters programme in Social Justice and Human Rights especially studying the sexual victimization of migrant women crossing the United States–Mexico border. In each case, the students and instructors rely on phronetics in the sense of working with affected communities to achieve empowerment.

The last case study, by Ranu Basu (Chapter 13), provides a work in spatial phronesis. It examines the role of research in confronting the challenges in the wake of rapidly deteriorating conditions of Ontario schools. The Learning Opportunities Grant was established in 2006 to provide funding for schools in dire need. In Toronto, similar reports such as the *Poverty by Postal Code* and *Model Inner City School Initiative* have become guiding doctrines for poverty recognition and alleviation. Localized spaces of poverty and marginality in such documents are efficiently identified and labelled as 'at risk' and 'priority areas' where resources and opportunities to support the needs of the most vulnerable populations should be directed. With its progressive and pragmatic discourse, attention is strategically diverted from underlying structural factors and the neoliberal strategies that had originally led to problems in the first place. Instead, attention is focused on measuring and labelling communities that have failed, and to the further sifting and sorting of vulnerabilities. Neighbourhood identities very rapidly translate into the politics of stigmatization, individuation and stern accountability. Yet this kind of policy reform, readily received by social planning and general public discourse, lacks a fundamental self-critical dimension that would reflect how technologies of social policy may generate the very problems they were designed to solve. The redistributive system rapidly develops into a strategy of geosurveillance relying on scientific rational planning models. The chapter asks how, then, can the techniques of identification reflect a spatially contingent redistributive justice system that can coherently combine with the social politics of equality? The chapter is a case study in spatial phronesis as a transformative methodology that builds into its foundation a critical spatial dimension and relational dynamics. Using the case study of the *Model Inner City School Initiative* adopted by the Toronto District School Board in 2006–7, the logics, politics and ethics of a re-distributional funding allocation process is traced and explored.

The chapters that follow respond to the call for examples of phronetic research in practice. They demonstrate that this alternative social science has much promise that is constantly growing. The book ends with a concluding chapter that summarizes the major implications of the foregoing chapters for phronetic research as an emerging alternative social science. In particular, the concluding chapter emphasizes the importance of phronetic research focusing on the 'tension points' in social and policy struggles. These tension points are weak spots in any struggle where disagreement creates an opening for research to sway opinion and move a decision in a particular direction. By exploiting these tension points, phronetic research can prove its relevance in specific settings and influence outcomes so as to improve social action and policy-making. In this way, phronetic social science can deliver on the promise of mainstream social science to speak truth to power, to inform society, improve decision-making and enhance social life. As the book demonstrates, phronetic social science has moved beyond its formative stages, past initial critiques of mainstream social science, while returning social science to society and demonstrating that social science can and does already play a meaningful role in efforts to make the world a better place.

REFERENCES

Flyvbjerg, B. 2001. *Making Social Science Matter: Why Social Inquiry Fails and How it can Succeed Again.* Cambridge University Press.

Landman, T. 2008. 'Paradigmatic Contestation and the Persistence of Perennial Dualities', *Political Studies Review* 6: 178–85.

Schram, S. F. and Caterino, B. (eds.) 2006. *Making Political Science Matter: Debating Knowledge, Research, and Methods.* New York University Press.

Shdaimah, C. S. and Stahl, R. W. 2006. 'Reflections on Doing Phronetic Social Science: A Case Study', in Schram and Caterino (eds.), *Making Political Science Matter.* New York University Press.

Spivak, G. C. 2004. '"On the Cusp of the Personal and the Impersonal": An Interview with Gayatri Chakravorty Spivak by Laura Lyons and Cynthia Franklin', *Biography* 27: 203–21.

Part I

Theory and method

2 Phronetic social science: an idea whose time has come

Sanford Schram

Some critics of mainstream social science argue that the very idea of a social science is an oxymoron, at least when it is done in ways that strictly mimic the most prominent versions of science: that is, the natural sciences. Part of this critique stems from the realization that, given their respective subject matters, the natural and social sciences are entirely different enterprises. The natural sciences are focused on prediction and control of the natural world, making them the wrong place to look for a model about how to produce scientific knowledge that can inform social relations. Rather than mimicking the natural sciences, social science is arguably practiced best when it produces knowledge that the people being studied can themselves use to address better the problems they are experiencing.

It turns out that there is good news on the social science front these days. Some critics who do not entirely dismiss the idea of a social science as a science have gone beyond their criticisms to not only offer viable alternatives but to actually implement them, demonstrating that an alternative science that is more consistent with and relevant to the social nature of its subject matter is in fact entirely possible. In recent years, a confluence of alternatives has been developing that to varying degrees embrace this ethic. Interpretive approaches in particular feature the study of social relations from the perspective of the people being studied and have gained more visibility in recent years (Yanow and Schwartz-Shea 2006), as has participatory action research that involves active collaboration of researchers and the researched (Naples 2003). 'Phronetic social science' is one prominent example of this renewal in social science. It, however, has so far existed mostly in theory, with only a few examples of application to practical issues in policy, planning and management. The aim of *Real Social Science* is to rectify this deficiency in the literature by bringing together case studies illustrating phronetic social science in practice.

To help frame these case studies, this chapter provides a brief history of phronetic social science, outlining its key concepts and distinguishing features, including how it contrasts practical versus theoretical knowledge, positivistic versus interpretivist methodologies, qualitative versus quantitative data-collection efforts, phronetic research versus action research, and the various ways in which research can be of relevance to policy.

Phronetic social science: its own form of praxis

Bent Flyvbjerg's *Making Social Science Matter* (2001) coined the term 'phronetic social science'. Since then, the term has entered into the lexicon of the social sciences. It has obtained its own entries in Wikipedia, the *Blackwell Encyclopedia of Sociology* and the *Sage Dictionary of Qualitative Management Research*, among other reference works. According to the *Blackwell Encyclopedia of Sociology*, phronetic social science 'has had considerable influence in recent years'. The 'phronetic' in phronetic social science is based on a contemporary interpretation of the Aristotelian concept of phronesis. Phronesis for Aristotle and Flyvbjerg refers to practical reasoning or practice wisdom. Phronetic social science is designed not to substitute for, but instead to supplement, practice wisdom and to do so in ways that can improve society.

Making Social Science Matter (MSSM) caused quite a stir when it was published. Within a few short years, it had been reviewed by more than a hundred journals and magazines, including *Science* (by the late Clifford Geertz, a leader in promoting interpretive approaches to social science) and also subsequently the *Times Literary Supplement*. With ten printings to date, Flyvbjerg's book has found a wide readership and has become central to a new line of social science inquiry and teaching in the United States and Europe. The book eventually became known as a 'manifesto' for the Perestroika movement to open Political Science to alternative approaches (Caterino and Schram 2006).

MSSM provided a detailed analysis of how its alternative social science is dedicated to enhancing phronesis. MSSM explained that phronesis is what the social sciences have to offer that the natural sciences cannot, with their emphasis on episteme and techné. This Aristotelian tripartite distinction is critical in MSSM for highlighting the comparative advantage of social science. Phronesis is, as Aristotle termed it, the practical wisdom that comes from an intimate familiarity with the contingencies and uncertainties of any particular social practice. Episteme, however, is knowledge that is abstract and universal; and techné is the know-how associated with practising a particular craft. Social sciences, for Flyvbjerg, are better situated to conduct research that can inform and thereby enhance phronesis. Given their subject matter, the natural sciences are better at testing hypotheses to demonstrate abstract principles and law-like relationships, while the social sciences are better at producing situated knowledges about how to understand and act in contextualized settings. While the natural sciences excel at conducting decontextualized experiments to understand abstract and generalizable law-like relationships, the social sciences can conduct case studies involving field research that produces intimate knowledge of localized understandings of subjective human relationships.

MSSM offered a devastating critique that social science was hopelessly lost if it persisted in seeking to emulate the natural sciences with a quest for theory-driven abstract knowledge of universal rationality. It joined others in compelling fashion to show that there is no symmetry between natural and social science in that natural science's interpretive problems are compounded by what Anthony Giddens (1976) called the 'double hermeneutic' of the social sciences. By virtue of its distinctively human subject matter, social scientists are inevitably people who offer interpretations of other people's interpretations. And the people being studied always have the potential to include the social scientists' interpretations in theirs, creating an ever-changing subject matter and requiring a dialogic relationship between the people doing the studying and the people being studied. For MSSM, this situation unavoidably meant that there can be no theory for social science in the sense that social science needs to forgo the dream that it can create time-tested theories of a static social reality. As a result, the social sciences should not seek to emulate the natural sciences. In such a comparison the social sciences will always fare very poorly, being seen as inferiors incapable of producing knowledge based on tested theories that can evince prediction of the worlds they study. Instead, MSSM concluded that the social sciences are better equipped to produce a different kind of knowledge – phronesis, practical wisdom – that grows out of intimate familiarity with practice in contextualized settings. Local knowledges, even tacit knowledges, cannot be taught *a priori* and are grown from the bottom up. They emerge out of practice, forgoing the hubris of seeking claims to a decontextualized universal rationality stated in abstract terms of false precision. Add a sense of praxis, seeking the ability to push for change, leaven it with an appreciation of the presence of power, and this phronetic social science can help people involved in ongoing political struggle question the relationships of knowledge and power and thereby work to change things in ways they might find more agreeable and even satisfying.

MSSM went beyond critique to offer a positive programme; it demonstrated it in detail, pointing to a rich variety of contemporary work from that of Pierre Bourdieu, to Robert Bellah, to Flyvbjerg's own work.

Flyvbjerg's initial phronetic research project is detailed in the book. It spanned fifteen years and focused on a major redevelopment project initiated by the city of Aalborg, Denmark, where Flyvbjerg previously taught urban planning before his recent move to Oxford. His research on the project evolved over time, quickly becoming more phronetic as he came to appreciate how social science could make real contributions to the ongoing dialogue over the city's redevelopment efforts once his research was retrofitted to the specific context in which the issues of development were being debated.

Flyvbjerg focused on producing research on understanding how power constrained decision-making in the Aalborg context. In the process, power relations were not just analysed but challenged in a very public way, the framing of the development agenda was successfully revised to include more grassroots concerns, an ongoing dialogue with participants in the redevelopment process was richly elaborated and social science research that gave up an interest in proving grand theories became critical to a very robust discourse on urban planning. As a result, the Aalborg planning project gained increased visibility as a successful project that went out of its way to democratize its decision-making, in part by allowing social science research to help keep it honest, open and collaborative. Phronetic social science such as this would be very different from the social science that predominates today. In his analysis in his co-authored book *Megaprojects and Risk*, Flyvbjerg has since demonstrated the real potential of phronetic social science to make a real difference (Flyvbjerg, Bruzelius and Rothengatter 2003; also see Flyvbjerg, Chapter 6, below).

Therefore, we can suggest four inter-related reasons for promoting phronetic social science over the mainstream variety:

(1) Given the dynamic nature of human interaction in the social world, social inquiry is best practiced when it does not seek general laws of action that can be used to predict courses of action, but instead offer a critical assessment of values, norms and structures of power and dominance. Social inquiry is better when it is linked to questions of the good life, that is, to questions of what we ought to do.

(2) While the social world is dynamic, social research is best seen as dialogical. Social inquiry is not a species of theoretical reason but of practical reason. Practical reason stays within an horizon of involvements in social life. For Flyvbjerg, this entails a context-dependent view of social inquiry that rests on the capacity for judgement. Understanding can never be grasped analytically; it has a holistic character. Understanding also has intrinsic subjective elements requiring researchers to forgo a disinterested position of detachment and enter into dialogue with those they study.

(3) As the study of dynamic social life, dialogical social inquiry is best practiced when we give up traditional notions of objectivity and truth and put aside the fact–value distinction. Instead, we should emphasize a contextual notion of truth that is pluralistic and culture-bound, further necessitating involvement with those we study.

(4) Dialogical social inquiry into a dynamic and changing social world provides a basis for emphasizing that interpretation is itself a practice of power, one that if conducted publicly and in ways that engage the public can also challenge power and inform efforts to promote social change.

Phronetic social science puts the emphasis not on particular research methods or types of data, but on producing research that can enhance phronesis by increasing understanding in specific contexts as opposed to questing after the ghost of an abstract knowledge of law-like processes. Therefore, phronetic social science calls for social scientists to revise their standards for acceptable research methodologies, re-incorporating context-sensitive research, such as case studies that help social actors learn to appreciate the complexities of social relations and practice various social crafts more effectively. Phronetic social science emphasizes that social sciences can provide an important research supplement to the kind of knowledge that comes from an intimate familiarity with practice in contextualized settings. This is research in aid of local knowledges, even tacit knowledges, that cannot be taught *a priori* but which grow from the bottom up, emerging out of practice. Add a sense of praxis, seeking the ability to push for change, leaven it with an appreciation of the inevitable presence of power, and phronetic social science becomes the kind of research that can help people in ongoing political struggle question the relationships of knowledge and power and thereby work to produce change.

Phronetic social science, therefore, is centrally about producing research that has relevance to decisions about what can and should be done, and also how to do it. It differs from either philosophical or scientific knowledge (episteme) and from technical knowledge or know-how (techné). In contrast to the first, it is practice-focused; in other words, it is not just about what is true, but also about what it would be good to do in given circumstances. It differs from technical knowledge in that it is concerned with evaluating and prescribing goals as well as with selecting means. Equally important, and more fundamentally, it is not equivalent to grasping some theory or having command over a set of skills; it is actually closer to a virtue, or a set of virtues, that is part of the character of the person.

Phronetic social science, therefore, rejects the fact–value distinction prevalent in mainstream social science and focuses its efforts on answering four critical questions related to enhancing practice wisdom: (1) where are we going?; (2) who gains, and who loses, by which mechanisms of power?; (3) is it desirable?; and (4) what should be done? (Flyvbjerg 2001: 162). These questions suggest that phronetic social science is concentrated on producing research that helps make a difference in people's lives by focusing on what it would really take to make that difference on the issues that matter to them most and which most crucially affect them.

Phronetic social science is not detached but engaged, and engaged in a way that is designed to empower change. In this it shares some features in common with various forms of action and participatory research, including even what has been called 'action science' (see Argyris 1983; Reason and Bradbury 2001; Whyte 1991). Yet phronetic social science is different in that it does not privilege collaboration with the people being studied as much as some forms of participatory action research; instead, it privileges producing knowledge that improves the ability of those people to make informed decisions about critical issues confronting them (regardless of whether that research is done in collaboration with those people or not). Phronetic social science is ultimately about producing knowledge that can challenge power not in theory but in ways that inform real efforts to produce change. Phronetic social science, therefore, combines an Aristotelian concern for phronesis with a Marxist concern for *praxis*. Phronetic social science produces research that can inform practical wisdom about how to conduct affairs in a particular setting and is infused with a sense of challenging power to improve the conduct of those affairs.

The question is not 'which method?' but 'what matters?'

As the foregoing suggests, phronetic social science has its own ontological and epistemological commitments that are based on an understanding of the distinctive nature of the subject matter of the social sciences. Yet it is important to note that phronetic social science is not organized around specific methods of data collection. It is open to relying on a diversity of data collection methods in order to best inform attempts to promote change related to the issues being studied. Depending on how they are conducted, mixed-methods projects are entirely consistent with phronetic social science (cf. Landman, Chapter 3, below). In this respect, phronetic social science provides an opportunity to move beyond the debates between positivists and interpretivists about how to organize social science in terms of method.

The debate has ground on for years now between positivists, who champion emulating the natural sciences, and interpretivists, who side with approaching the study of politics along the lines of more human-istic forms of inquiry. Competing positivist and interpretivist epistem-ologies have spawned distinctive methodologies with separate logics of inquiry, varying preferences for different methods of data collection and debates about a number of other issues including, most commonly, the value of quantitative versus qualitative data. Most recently, debates between positivists and interpretivists have been complicated by inter-ventions by others who do not situate their investigations in either camp. This group has included a growing number of scholars who refuse to accept that they must limit their research to either a positivist or inter-pretivist methodology. Mixed-methods researchers have been joined by others who stress the importance of 'problem-driven' over 'theory-driven' research (Shapiro 2005). These researchers want to focus on real-world problems and then use however many different methods of study and forms of data collection necessary to study those topics as best they can. It might be tendentious to call this a debate of relevance versus rigour, but that framing harkens back to the *Methodenstreit* that wracked the fledgling social sciences in Europe during the late nineteenth cen-tury. One prominent intervention was by Max Weber, who came to be a major influence in both what today are the positivist and interpretivist factions. One prominent commentator on the history of political science has written:

Max Weber published his 1904 essay on 'The "Objectivity" of Knowledge in Social Science and Social Policy' in the newly created *Archiv für Sozialwis-senschaft und Sozialpolitik*, which he shared in editing. Weber's argument was in part a response to the failure of the *Verein [für Sozialpolitik]* and the ideo-logical and methodological disputes that had characterized its history. Although he presented his essay as an intervention in controversies about the nature of social scientific explanation, he also explicitly addressed it to a wider public audience with the aim of vouchsafing the cognitive authority of academic social science. He stressed the commitment of the journal was to the scientific pursuit of 'the facts of social life,' but it was also concerned with 'social policy' and 'the training of *judgment* in respect of *practical problems* arising from these social circumstances' . . . Weber . . . emphasized various ways in which social scientific knowledge could, in principle, constrain and direct policy decisions as well as the extent to which scientific investigation necessarily proceeded from the perspective of value-laden premises. The authority of social science nevertheless depended, he argued, on acceptance of the autonomy of empirical claims and on the profes-sional status and independence of those who made such claims. (Gunnell 2006: 480–1)

In his famous 1904 essay, Weber was simultaneously doing what he would often do – take two sides of the argument at once: he was for social science being practised in an objectively scrupulous way that would enable it to inform decisions regarding the most pressing public issues. For years, both positivists, who strove to make social science more like a natural science, and interpretivists, who worked to make it more like the interpretive investigations of the humanities, would draw upon Weber, each in their own selective ways, to suggest the direction for social science.

The debates that preoccupied Weber and his colleagues were framed in terms of whether social science ought to be more about *erklären* (explanation) or *verstehen* (understanding) (see Von Wright 1971). The interpretive approaches emphasize that it is more important to try to arrive at understanding how the social world is subjectively experienced and interpreted by people than it is to provide an explanation of what caused social phenomena to happen. The 'interpretive turn', as it came to be called in the social sciences, had many sources, including, perhaps, most prominently Clifford Geertz and his leadership in the School of Social Science at the Institute for Advanced Study in Princeton, New Jersey. Geertz (2000), to be sure, saw interpretive approaches as providing important perspectives for understanding whatever was being studied. Yet Geertz resisted the idea that researchers had to choose either an interpretive or positivist approach as a distinct logic of inquiry. Nonetheless, over time, the main thrust of the interpretive turn has been to insist that interpretive social science implied a distinct logic of inquiry that prevented mixing methodologies. Positivism and interpretivism became the oil and water of social science research. While researchers might be able to mix different methods of data collection, they were increasingly discouraged from mixing the methodologies on the ground that positivism and interpretivism implied distinct logics of inquiry that could not be sensibly combined in the same analysis. Over time, the separate logic of inquiry argument has undoubtedly contributed to a fracturing in the social sciences where different researchers employing different approaches talk to each other less and less (Almond 1988).

Yet this may be changing. In recent years, with the flowering of a diversity of approaches, it might be that we are finally able to move beyond this stale debate. Social science is now arguably increasingly non- or post-paradigmatic in the sense that the field is moving away from the idea that research should be according to one unifying methodology or distinctive logic of inquiry. In fact, the changing currents associated with social science research indicate that perhaps it was always best seen as non-paradigmatic both in terms of what it ideally should be in theory as well as what it actually was in practice. It is perhaps only now with Minerva's Owl that we can look back to see the value of the diversity that was present in social science research throughout its history. And with perspective, it might be that we are now able to see how choosing one method of inquiry over another is not so much the critical issue as whether the research, however conducted, is designed to address the issues with which people are concerned.

Yet embracing the non-paradigmatic nature of social science means not only giving up the idea that the social sciences can be unified around a particular method; it also means that we must give up the idea that the social sciences produce generalizable scientific truths that are affirmed by a growing body of empirical research. Phronetic social science recognizes that social scientific knowledge is neither transcontextual nor cumulative. At a minimum, this involves a repudiation of the main tenets of the positivist model of social science as composed of the following hierarchy of assumptions:

(1) social science exists to help promote the understanding of the truth about social relations in general;

(2) social science research contributes to this quest by adding to the accumulation of an expanding base of objective knowledge about social relations;

(3) the growth of this knowledge base is contingent upon the building of theory that offers explanations of social relations;

(4) the building of theory is dependent on the development of universal generalizations regarding the behaviour of social actors;

(5) the development of a growing body of generalizations occurs by testing falsifiable, causal hypotheses that demonstrate their success in making predictions;

(6) the accumulation of a growing body of predictions about social relations comes from the study of variables in samples involving large numbers of cases; and

(7) this growing body of objective, causal knowledge can be put at the service of society.

Yet from the perspective of phronetic social science, this paradigm excludes much valuable research. For instance, it assumes that the study of a single case is 'unscientific', provides no basis for generalizing, does not build theory, cannot contribute to the growth of political knowledge and, as a result, is not even to be considered for publication in the leading journals and is to be discouraged as a legitimate doctoral dissertation project. While there have always been dissenters to the drift toward 'large-n', quantitative research in service of objective, decontextualized and universally generalizable truth about social relations, there is a good case to be made that the dissenters have been increasingly marginalized as the centre of gravity of the social sciences has drifted more and more towards reflecting these core assumptions about science.

However, as fate would have it, with the continued quest for a scientific discipline, increased challenges were put forward by proponents of alternative logics of inquiry. In other words, rather than move from the methodological purity of the positivist paradigm to a methodological pluralism, the most common response has been instead to push for more 'interpretive' approaches in social science. Yet a growing number of social scientists have challenged the idea that the separate logics of inquiry forces researchers to choose to pursue positivist or interpretive approaches to the exclusion of the other. There is now a growing interest in mixed-methods research in the social sciences today, including books and whole journals dedicated to promoting the idea. While the idea of mixed-methods research itself can be contained within either the positivist or interpretivist paradigm, other versions cross those boundaries more freely. Even though mixed-methods research is a growing trend in the social sciences, such research still constitutes the minority of projects and is even less represented in journal articles. Given the format and space constraints of most academic journals, the tendency is to present findings associated with one particular data-collection effort even if it was part of a mixed-methods project. These constraints may need to change if mixed-methods research is to get a full hearing. The possibilities that come with electronic publishing of journals over the Internet may well help in this regard.

Mixed-methods research fits nicely with the call for problem-driven research, where a researcher starts with a specific problem in the world of politics and then employs multiple approaches to study it as best he or she can. The power of such combined approaches needs to be assessed by researchers on both sides of the positivistic and interpretive divide. The upsurge in mixed-methods, problem-driven research might then prove to be better able to deliver on the founding promise of the social sciences to connect science and democracy, leading to the improvement of both, not just in theory but in practice as well.

Phronetic social science has been undoubtedly influenced and emerges out of this ferment and offers an explicit programme for realizing these goals. Phronetic social science, however, builds on this diversity and goes further. Phronetic social science understands the importance of case studies (Flyvbjerg 2006). Given its critique of the quest for transcontextual and cumulative empirical knowledge that validates social scientific truths, phronetic social science understands that social science is best equipped to offer contextualized knowledge appropriate to particular settings and focused on specific problems. The case study becomes not just an acceptable alternative, but central to conducting phronetic research. Further, phronetic social science stays true to its principles and allows for a diversity of data-collection methods to help produce relevant contextualized knowledge. Case studies need not be limited to ethnography. Phronetic social science understands that the main issue is not method, but whether the research is designed consciously to answer the questions Flyvbjerg originally proposed in *Making Social Science Matter*: (1) where are we going?; (2) who gains, and who loses, by which mechanisms of power?; (3) is it desirable?; and (4) what should be done? Phronetic social science, in fact, explicitly calls for answering these questions in a way that is relevant to the particular situation in which the people being studied find themselves. Therefore, the key questions need to be answered in a contextually sensitive fashion. Case studies, using whatever methods help them address the issue being studied, are no longer a marginal form of social science research.

Given the foregoing, it could be that the future includes a more optimistic assessment of the idea of social science. It may be that the social sciences are more amenable to putting aside debates about method to focus on what matters most. From problem-driven research to phronetic social science, social science may be now more open to putting aside its own science wars in favour of centring research on addressing critical social issues using whatever set of diverse methods of data collection that best help address those issues. It could be that a preoccupation with method is giving way to a more committed effort to make social science matter. Only once we begin to practise contextually sensitive phronetic social science will social science research be living up to its potential as *real* social science that informs efforts to enhance practical wisdom and does so in ways that promote positive social change.

REFERENCES

Almond, G. 1988. 'Separate Tables: Schools and Sects in Political Science', *PS: Political Science and Politics* 21(4): 828–42.

Argyris, C. 1983. 'Action Science and Intervention', *Journal of Applied Behavioral Science* 19: 115–40.

Caterino, B. and Schram, S. 2006. 'Introduction. Making Political Science Matter: Debating Research, Method and Knowledge', in S. Schram and B. Caterino (eds.), *Making Political Science Matter*. New York University Press.

Flyvbjerg, B. 2001. *Making Social Science Matter: Why Social Inquiry Fails and How it can Succeed Again*. Cambridge University Press.
  2006. 'Five Misunderstandings about Case-study Research', *Qualitative Inquiry* 12(2): 219–45.

Flyvbjerg, B., Bruzelius, N. and Rothengatter, W. 2003. *Megaprojects and Risk: An Anatomy of Ambition*. Cambridge University Press.

Geertz, C. 2000. *Available Light: Anthropological Reflections on Philosophical Topics*. Princeton University Press.

Giddens, A. 1976. *New Rules of Sociological Method: A Positive Critique of Interpretative Sociologies*. London: Hutchinson.

Gunnell, J. 2006. 'The Founding of the American Political Science Association: Discipline, Profession, Political Theory, and Politics', *American Political Science Review* 100(2): 479–86.

Naples, N. 2003. *Feminism and Method: Ethnography, Discourse Analysis, and Activist Research*. New York: Routledge.

Reason, P. and Bradbury, H. (eds.) 2001. *The Sage Handbook of Action Research: Participative Inquiry and Practice*. London: Sage.

Shapiro, I. 2005. *The Flight from Reality in the Human Sciences*. Princeton University Press.

Von Wright, G. H. 1971. *Explanation and Understanding*. London: Routledge & Kegan Paul.

Whyte, W. 1991. *Participatory Action Research*. Thousand Oaks, CA: Sage.

Yanow, D. and Schwartz-Shea, P. (eds.) 2006. *Interpretation and Method: Empirical Research Methods and the Interpretive Turn*. Armonk, NY: M. E. Sharpe.

3 Phronesis and narrative analysis

Todd Landman

Introduction

The phronetic approach includes an attention to method; the ways in which evidence is collected, coded and analysed; and the ways in which the inferences that are drawn from that analysis of evidence inform larger questions of appropriateness and the challenge to existing power relations with respect to the research topic area at hand. I think it is incorrect to cast the phronetic approach as somehow antithetical to strong method, or some form of 'method-light' that can be adopted by those who are more interested in the *substance* of social science research (see Landman 2008: 307–11; and Schram, Chapter 2, above). Indeed, Flyvbjerg (2006: 68–74) argues that he has been set up as a straw man for those who opposed the so-called 'perestroika' movement in the American Political Science Association, and argues forcefully (and with examples) why method sits squarely within the phronetic approach. His argument is that we as social scientists have spent perhaps too much time focusing on epistemé and techné to the neglect of phronesis.

I endorse this view, while at the same time wanting to make sure that we do not lose sight of the importance of the whole triumvirate of concepts that form the phronetic approach. As a comparative methodologist and scholar of human rights, I have argued over the years for the use of systematic methods that address otherwise normatively informed and value-based questions (see, e.g., Landman 2002, 2005). I see no contradiction in this perspective, especially if the careful and systematic analysis of human rights evidence can bring about their greater protection; a position that is consistent with a larger Weberian 'value-rational' tradition in the social sciences (see Landman 2005: 553–4; and Olsen, Payne and Reiter, Chapter 10, below). Quality systematic value-oriented research can and should contribute to incremental gains in knowledge. Contextually informed knowledge based on a phronetic approach can move beyond the cases under investigation and provide generalizations that are helpful for solving political problems in other contexts. In my own field, and as will be demonstrated in this chapter, learning about the struggle for and against human rights in particular political contexts is valuable for advocates in other contexts.

Narrative analysis is a method (or group of methods as we shall see) that in my view is particularly apt for phronetic social science. It is one of many different kinds of methods available to social scientists, and in some ways it is in its nascent phases of development, since many of its practitioners are committed to getting close to the narrative and preserving its meaning and authenticity (Frank 2002), while struggling with how to make it useful for adding to our knowledge of the social world alongside more established methods (see, e.g., Chase 2005). Narrative analysis can illuminate the ways in which individuals experience, confront and exercise power in ways that are useful if one adopts the phronetic approach outlined in this volume, as well as in *Making Social Science Matter* (Flyvbjerg 2001) and *Making Political Science Matter* (Schram and Caterino 2006). Yet there remain significant tensions within narrative analysis itself, and between narrative analysis and the phronetic approach. This chapter examines these two different sources of tension in several important ways. First, it outlines the main methods currently used in narrative analysis, the tensions between and among different narrative approaches, and the types of research questions for which it has been used. Second, it shows how narrative analysis is useful for the phronetic approach by showing the connections between epistemé, techné and phronesis, on the one hand, and narratives, on the other; the ways in which narratives address questions of power relations; and how a phronetic approach can bring value to narrative analysis itself. Third, the chapter shows how different forms of narrative analysis have featured in the work of truth commissions around the world, which have had to collect a large number of narrative accounts of human rights abuse during periods of authoritarian rule, conflict and/or foreign occupation; collate, code and analyse them; and use their published findings to challenge institutionalized power, reserve domains of authority and deeply embedded social and political hierarchies that have tended not to be eroded through otherwise 'transitional' periods. Finally, the chapter concludes by arguing that narrative analysis has much to offer the phronetic social scientist; however, like any method, it has its own strengths and weaknesses, as well as its own trade-offs between the depth and breadth of knowledge about the social world it provides.

Methods of narrative analysis

Narratives are at a base level 'stories' that people tell about things that they have experienced directly or indirectly, as well as the evaluative impressions that those experiences carry with them (e.g., the subjective experience and registering of emotions, feelings and insights connected to such experiences). Such stories are often complemented with other items that can form the universe of data and evidence for the researcher, including journals, field notes, letters, conversations, interviews, photos and other artefacts, and videos and film (see Clandinin and Connelly 2000: 98–115; Reissmann 2008; Sandercock and Attili, Chapter 8, below). Typically, narratives are of 'events', which in the social world include large occurrences or 'macro' events and small personal or 'micro' events. In my own discipline of political science macro events include such things as elections, military coups, transitions to democracy, social revolutions, international and civil wars, foreign interventions and invasions, social protests and labour strikes, government crackdowns (i.e., the 1989 Tiananmen Square massacre or the Burmese military's response to the 2007 'Saffron' revolution), and significant market crashes (e.g., the 1929 market crash, the 1982 'debt crisis' or the 1997 Asian financial crisis). Micro events include such negative things as village skirmishes and raids, personal and organized crimes, public lynching, looting, sexual violence, bribery and other corrupt acts, denial of access to services, consumer and commercial firm choices, among countless others. But they can also include positive things such as agreements and compromises, bargains and deals, resolution of conflict and public displays of support. Both macro and micro events can be the subject of narrative analysis as the narrator recounts the event, the meanings and feelings associated with it, and any larger implications that the event may have had in their life and those of others.

At a more methodological level, such events carry with them other analytical features, such as a start date and time (also known as an *onset*) and an end date and time, where the difference between the two is understood as the event *duration*. They also have various dimensions of *magnitude* and *size*, including the number of actors involved (e.g., individuals, groups, regions, countries, organizations, etc.), the types of things that actors do and the types of things that happen to them (e.g., violence, liberation, suppression). The narratives themselves also contain a variety of analytical features that may be of interest to the researcher, including the themes that are addressed, the structure of the narrative, its use of particular constructions and ideas, as well as the use of complementary materials. Indeed, as Reissmann (2008: 11–14) argues, there is a continuum of approaches in narrative analysis that ranges from the single and long narrative of one individual to the category-centred and thematic analysis of multiple narratives, where there are varying degrees to which one can focus on detailed and unique forms of interpretation or make more general statements across many subjects and themes.

The tradition of narrative analysis has typically been one that focuses on individual stories, life histories, autobiographies and the lived experiences of particular individuals whose stories serve as the bulk of the empirical material for a study. Known as the 'Chicago School', the tradition allowed the narrative in many ways to speak for itself, but as the field has developed, methods are being pursued that allow for attention to dimensions *across* narratives, while at the same time not losing the richness of the various dimensions *within* narratives (Chase 2005). Narrative analysis has featured in psychology (life experience and psycho-social development), sociology (the construction of identity and meaning), anthropology (ethnography and long-term research within specific communities), and auto-ethnography, or the study of the researcher's own life history through narrative (see Chase 2005: 658–60). I would add to this list of disciplines that of political sociology and discourse analysis. For example, Richard Fenno's (1978) *Homestyle* is a classic study of eighteen members of the US House of Representatives in their own districts, which combined participant-observation with narrative analysis. Bellah *et al.*'s (1985) *Habits of the Heart* captures what it means (or not) to be American with reference to Tocqueville's understanding of American community through a series of in-depth interviews that are analysed for the meanings of words as they are used by respondents. David Howarth's work on apartheid and black consciousness in South Africa and airport protest in the United Kingdom and Europe has developed a particular form of narrative analysis that in many ways elides action and words, and analyses them through the lens of post-modernist deconstruction and the discourse analytic approach developed by Ernesto Laclau (Howarth 2000; Howarth, Norval and Stavrakakis 2000; Glynos and Howarth 2008; see also Griggs and Howarth, Chapter 9, below).

Stories and narrative accounts of events provide a fundamental form of empirical information for social scientists that have different levels of analysis. First, there is the *linear level* of the basic structure of the narrative – the subject, verb and object of a story – which relates the basic 'facts' as they are understood by the storyteller, and will include the sequential nature of the story. Second, there is the *relational level*, in which the story can reveal relationships between the storyteller and other actors, as well as the temporal, spatial and other contextual dimensions that are related to the event that is being recounted. Third, there is the *emotional level*, which conveys the feelings (e.g., love, hate, fear, warmth, coldness, alienation, acceptance, rejection, etc.) and subjective understanding of the event as it has unfolded and been experienced by the storyteller (e.g., the sense of who was really responsible and why, what really happened, what features of the story are considered 'right' and 'wrong', etc.) (see, e.g., Riley and Hawe 2005: 229–30). Fourth and finally, there is the analytical level, which involves the social scientist adding a layer of meaning by drawing connections across different narratives of the same or similar events for a sample of stories that have been collected through qualitative interviewing, participant observation and other ethnographic research techniques. These four levels are not necessarily mutually exclusive, and the different degrees to which the researcher involves his- or herself in the narrative, as well as the different degrees of authority with which the analyst communicates the narrative evidence vary greatly across different research projects (see Chase 2005: 660–7).

There may not be a direct connection between events *per se* and narratives, since a narrative can involve a story told about feelings, emotions, evaluations of particular ongoing events, conditions, institutions, contradictions, inequalities, injustices and other perceptions that are of a more general nature, but are nonetheless rich for the social scientist to analyse. Narratives thus float between those that are directly connected and experienced by the narrator and that are tied to quite specific events (trauma, loss of a job, illness, a discriminatory act, etc.) to those that are much broader, longer and deeper impressions of an individual's life experiences. Moreover, the recollection and memory work that form part of a narrative suggest that many narratives involve a creative process that embellishes, hides, enhances and otherwise alters that account in ways that make it less connected to the facts of the event itself. As has been shown in work on truth processes in transitional countries, physical reminders such as diaries, calendars, news clippings and/or objects associated with events can help in recounting them, as they pin down dates and trigger associated memories.[1]

In what ways is the analysis of narratives made systematic to move beyond the oft-heard charges that it is nothing more than 'storytelling' and/or 'journalism'? Efforts over the past few decades have sought to sharpen the ways in which narrative analysis can be used in a more systematic fashion in order to harness the empirical information that is gathered. The tools and methods that have been developed are the function of the types of research questions that have been posed (see below), the types of narratives that have been gathered and the type of individuals from whom they have been gathered. Narratives can range from short and

---

[1] In 2003, I carried out an assessment of information-processing and management within truth commissions for the International Center for Transitional Justice in New York (www.ictj.org), and in my interview with Alex Boraine, former commissioner with the South African Truth and Reconciliation Commission (TRC), he emphasized this point that many deponents to the TRC brought with them physical items that were in some way related to the events about which they were issuing a statement.

discrete accounts of well-defined events (at least in terms of timing and duration) to life histories spanning decades of experience. The individuals whose narratives have been collected can range from senior political and historical figures, to professionals within private and public organizations, to highly marginalized and 'hidden' populations. Moreover, some narratives feature as 'found data', since it may be that a researcher discovers personal diaries or official diaries and archival documents from which rich narratives emerge (instances of which have proved crucial in uncovering the abuse of human rights, for example).[2] Building on these base materials, there are different approaches to narrative analysis that have different understandings of what constitutes narrative analysis, how that understanding is represented in text, the basic units of analysis and the variable attention to contexts, while the different approaches today primarily include *thematic analysis, structural analysis, dialogic and performance analysis* and *visual analysis* (see Reissmann 2008: 53–182).

There are many distinct advantages to narrative analysis. First, it provides a close reading of events with detailed and often times unique accounts from which larger impressions can be drawn. Second, the sequencing and action of a story as it interacts with larger impressions and feelings can provide rich insight into a range of substantive topics of interest to social scientists. Third, it allows for subjective and inter-subjective understandings to be captured in ways that are not available through other methods, particularly those that rely on large sample populations, closed response survey instruments and quantitative analysis of respondent choices to predetermined questions. Fourth, it maintains the social, political and human elements to the ways in which individuals interact and behave towards one another, as well as the ways in which they interact with their larger environments. While each of these advantages is closely related to the phronetic approach (close readings, sequencing, intersubjectivity, interactions), its final advantage is central to phronesis; namely, it allows the social scientist to uncover perceptions, experiences and feelings about power, power relations and institutionalized constraints as they are confronted (or not) through social and political engagement (see below).

But despite these advantages, there are also many distinct disadvantages to narrative analysis. First, any move to transcend the individual

---

[2] The Human Rights Data Analysis Group (HRDAG) at the Benetech Initiative in Palo Alto, CA, assisted in the coding and analysis of such found data in a former prison used by the Hisséne Habré government in Chad. The archival records were discovered by Human Rights Watch and subsequently used to paint a picture of systematic violence and abuse from 1982 to 1990, as well as the flow of documentation of that abuse through the various ministries of the government (see Silva, Klingner and Weikart 2010).

and unique nature of the narrative will involve losing some of the meaning of the narrative as the analyst looks for logical equivalences, shared meanings and intersubjective understandings. Indeed, there is an upper limit for the number of narratives that can be collected and analysed where the whole story is maintained and where the analyst starts to lose control over the information. Category-oriented and thematic narrative analysis can accommodate some of this problem, but will also reach a natural limit as the number of narratives increases. Second, and related to the first disadvantage, there are large questions of representativeness in narrative analysis, since the samples of narratives that are collected are rarely random and necessarily biased in some way. The frequent retort to this problem is to claim that narrative analysis does not aspire to the goal of inference and generalizability and seeks a different 'way of knowing' that is opposed to the positivistic spirit of the natural science model. But surely, the word 'analysis' suggests at a minimum level the desire to make inferences beyond the original source information and, once that step is made, narrative analysis (like many other forms of analysis) needs to address this problem of representativeness.

Narrative and phronesis

These different methods, dimensions, strengths and limitations of narrative analysis suggest that there are significant methodological issues within the field that need to be addressed and that relate directly to its utility for a phronetic approach to social science. First, there is a large question over the *authenticity* and *veracity* of the account that is provided by the narrator. Bias can be introduced at any moment in the narrative in ways that can distort, misrepresent and mislead the audience. Second, there is the issue of *interpretation* carried out by the narrative analyst, where the degree of separation between the original account from the narrator to the analysis of meaning can vary depending on the subject position, presuppositions, epistemology and disciplinary background of the analyst. That is to say, what is the degree of *faithfulness* of the analysis and how close does it follow the original narration? Third, there is the issue of *representativeness*. Are the narratives that have been collected typical of the population of interest? Are they representative? Are the narratives extreme cases, typical cases and/or confounding cases? Fourth, and related to the third issue, is one involving levels of analysis, number of observations and the desire for *generalizability*. There is undoubtedly a trade-off between the specificity and uniqueness of the account in all its richness and the ability to make inferences to a larger set of questions or population of individuals (see Chase 2005: 666–7; on a similar trade-off in comparative politics, see also Landman 2000, 2003, 2008).

These issues are in many ways inter-related and can be addressed in different ways. The research question or the purpose of the research, including the theory that is being developed, supported and/or tested, will in large part determine what kind of narrative analysis is conducted. For example, if the study is to reveal the inner thoughts, perceptions and experiences of a great figure from history, then the narrative analyst may want to let the narrative speak for itself and the study will be more biographical in nature. It may have great authenticity and varying degrees of veracity, however, the object of the study is not to establish 'truth' in any objective fashion but to let the words flow and speak for themselves. If the study is a life history of a particular historical figure and his or her struggle against oppression (e.g., the account of Nobel Laureate Rigoberta Menchú), then it is likely that it will focus on that particular individual and use his or her narratives to access and examine larger questions of oppression, resistance, emancipation and liberation. Such a study might illuminate these questions, but the inferences will remain relatively limited to the narrative account that is provided and analysed. In contrast, if the research question is to examine the different ways in which social movement activists conceive of their struggle against power and the obstacles that prevent them achieving their goals, then the number of narratives and the ways in which they are analysed will necessarily be much different from the first two examples.

The analysis could be modified even more radically to use statistical techniques to code and count particular words, clauses and themes within the narrative (see, e.g., Franzosi 2004). Such thematic analysis has been used in political science since the behavioural revolution and the first applications of statistics to content analysis of newspapers (see, e.g., Eulau 1996). Beer and Balleck (1994) code debates in the US Congress on foreign policy and Budge *et al.* (2001) code political party manifestos over time across a sample of advanced industrial democracies to map policy preferences over the same period. These examples are not normally labelled narrative analysis since the content and text that is coded are not 'stories' *per se*, but the method has been adopted to analyse narratives in other studies. Williamson *et al.* (2001), for example, provide an example of a statistical narrative study of the mechanisms of fatality in New Zealand, Australia and the United States. The individual nature of the narratives is completely lost given the large number of observations, while the analysis focuses on common words used to describe and identify the main reasons for fatality in the three countries. As outlined above, many researchers located within the larger linguistic and narrative 'turn' reject the idea that narratives must be (or can be) generalizable to a particular population, and that any such move to compare across multiple narratives is overly positivistic (see Chase 2005: 667), nevertheless, as we shall see with reference to the work of truth commissions, such techniques have been adopted in ways that seek to balance the quantitative and qualitative aspects of narrative.

The second major way in which to address the problems of veracity and representativeness is to rely on multiple narratives of the same event. While risking the label of being 'overly positivistic', I do believe that there is great value in collecting multiple stories of the same event, since each individual will recount the event differently and each will have different impressions, experiences and feelings about the event. Methodologically, the use of multiple sources provides other gains for the analyst. Recollections can often be incorrect about dates, times and the other contextual details of an event, while multiple accounts can narrow down ranges for these variables and provide greater clarity on the veracity of different accounts. Multiple sources can also provide a 'mean' account of an event and what have been called 'reporting densities' (the number of individuals reporting the same event). As we shall see below in the discussion of truth commissions, the American Association for the Advancement of Science and the Benetech Initiative have been pioneers in developing methods for coding and analysing multiple sources of information about human rights events in ways that have been crucial in challenging dominant accounts of particular historical periods of authoritarianism, conflict and civil war, and occupation (see Ball, Spirer and Spirer 2000; Ball *et al.* 2003; and also Landman 2006: 107–25, Landman and Carvalho 2009: 45–63). In the language of statistics, narrative accounts within truth commissions represent 'convenience' samples, the biases of which can be overcome through the use of multiple sources. The benefits of this approach can be seen in the Williamson *et al.* (2001) study on fatality in which common factors that contributed to fatality were identified across multiple narratives.

There are thus strategies for overcoming some of the inherent limitations to narrative analysis that are useful to take into consideration if narrative analysis is to be used for phronetic social science. Indeed, Chase (2005: 667–9) argues that narrative inquiry can lead to social change, and she is motivated by questions of democratic reform, social justice and dignity. Her argument is very much in line with the one developed in this volume, but ours goes further in articulating a position that challenges power through research and then looks for ways to redress power imbalances that are revealed through the research process. Flyvbjerg outlines in this volume and elsewhere (see

2006: 76) the four value-rational questions that motivate the phronetic approach:

(1) Where are we going?
(2) Who gains and who loses, and by which mechanism of power?
(3) Is this development desirable?
(4) What, if anything, should we do about it?

It is clear that these motivations are broader than a concern over democracy and social justice, and are geared towards social change that assesses relative gains and losses (as shown through empirical analysis), the desirability of outcomes and ongoing conditions (the application of moral reasoning and phronesis to the empirical record), as well as our ability as researchers to do anything about it (providing solutions to challenge the demonstrated problem). If narrative analysis is to be useful for this approach, then it needs to tackle the problems of authenticity, faithfulness, representativeness and generalizability. Social research that is vulnerable to methodological attack weakens its ability to challenge mechanisms of power, since the beneficiaries and defenders of the status quo look for possible avenues to discredit the findings of research that undermine their position or systems that maintain their position (see Clegg and Pitsis, Chapter 5, below).

Typically, the first of these two challenges – authenticity and faithfulness – can be addressed through the phronetic approach, since the analyst's practical wisdom is born of his or her 'expert' status in Flyvbjerg's (2001: 17) terms (i.e., the analyst who has achieved the level of being *unconsciously competent* within a chosen social science discipline). The expert applies holistic and intuitive decision-making in studying a problem and can readily discern important distinctions between and among narrative accounts in ways that draw out the important elements of any inquiry.[3] Moreover, the expert can detect authenticity and maintain faithfulness to a narrative account that is provided. But if we draw on Schram's argument in the previous chapter and combine it with my own insistence on strong method, then it seems to me that with a fully developed phronetic approach (i.e., one that pays equal attention to epistemé, techné and phronesis) the challenges associated with representativeness and generalizability can also be addressed. Despite having a well-developed capacity to discern, the expert also relies on systematic evidence that obeys basic rules of inquiry relating to the fairness of a sample population from which

---

[3] In my view, this idea of the expert is not reserved to qualitative analysis only. I have seen the most positivistic quantitative analysts look at a data set and intuitively know the best ways to model the relationships of interest in ways that move beyond any simple application of 'rules' for data analysis.

narratives are drawn. The greater representiveness of such a sample, the greater the ability to make generalizations, and when combined with the expert's additional capacity for intuitive and holistic interpretation, it seems to me the fuller the account that is provided. These challenges and the ways in which they can be overcome through a phronetic approach are illustrated through a discussion of the social scientific work on truth commissions.

Narrative, phronesis and truth

One key feature characterizing post-conflict, transitional and democratizing societies has been the establishment of a formal body that investigates past wrongs, patterns of gross human rights violations, atrocities and/or crimes against humanity. These formal bodies have included: (1) international tribunals such as those used in Nuremberg after the Second World War, the International Criminal Tribunal for the Former Yugoslavia (ICTY) in the Hague and the International Criminal Tribunal for Rwanda (ICTR) in Arusha; (2) domestically-based truth commissions, commissions for historical clarification, truth and reconciliation commissions, and community-based justice programmes (e.g., the *gacaca* system in Rwanda); and (3) larger projects on historical memory and lustration processes for former agents of the authoritarian state apparatus. In each case, the establishment of such a formal body fundamentally puts down a marker to acknowledge that past wrongs must be addressed in some way and to recognize that ignoring such past wrongs is to leave open the possibility of them happening again (see also Olsen, Payne and Reiter, Chapter 10, below).

These formal bodies range in the degree to which they establish criminal liability, accountability, legal justice, financial compensation, public acknowledgement and reconciliation (Hayner 1994, 2002: 24–31). Truth commissions have been a popular type of investigative body that has been used across a wide range of such transitional societies. For post-conflict situations, truth commissions represent a formal institutional mechanism for establishing a public record of violent events and gross violations of human rights, such as those that have been held in Guatemala, El Salvador, Haiti, Peru and Sierra Leone. For those societies undergoing democratic transition, truth commissions are a product of accommodation between dominant political forces that have taken part in the transition and often involve a careful negotiation over the different roles for truth, justice, amnesty and impunity (Skaar 1999; Skaar, Gloppen and Suhrke 2005). Such commissions include those used in Argentina after the military regime (1976–82), in Chile after the Pinochet regime

(1973–90) and in South Africa after the apartheid regime (1960–94). In other countries, truth commissions have been set up to provide a record of human rights abuses for multiple periods of authoritarian government (e.g., in Ghana 1966–9, 1972–9, 1981–93; and South Korea and Panama), while others have been set up to investigate human rights abuses during prolonged periods of foreign occupation, as in the case of East Timor (1974–99).

To date, there have been more than thirty such commissions that have spanned the regions of Central and South America, the Caribbean, Africa, Europe and Southeast Asia and the Pacific. While these commissions have been established for different purposes with different legal mandates and under the auspices of different authorities, they share a number of common features: (1) they focus on the past; (2) they do not focus on specific events, but seek to discover a broader picture; (3) they are temporary; (4) they have the authority to access all areas to obtain information (see Hayner 1994: 604, 2002: 14); and (5) they have a legal mandate to 'clarify', 'establish the complete picture', 'investigate serious acts of violence', 'establish the truth' and 'create an impartial historical record'. The proliferation of truth commissions and the similarity in their basic features, purpose and work has led to a burgeoning social science literature that examines their establishment, impact and the 'essentially contested' (Gallie 1956) nature of the truth that they uncover (see, e.g., Hayner 1994, 2002).

At a fundamental level, such commissions have engaged in narrative analysis of some kind, and they have used their findings in different ways to contest past and existing power structures that resist the impulse for justice of whatever kind. But they face huge challenges in developing and implementing their research strategies, as once such commissions are opened they tend to be flooded with deponents who want to come forward and present their stories. To understand the scale of the problem, consider South Africa and Peru. The Truth and Reconciliation Commission in South Africa took roughly 22,000 statements, while the *Comisión de la verdad y Reconciliación* (CVR) in Peru took close to 17,000 statements. The challenge that such a volume of statements poses is how can any truth process use the richness of the material that is collected and balance that against the need for systematic methods for collection and analysis? Legal epistemologies that had dominated earlier truth processes in Argentina and Chile, for example, led to very simple forms of data collection using word-processing software, where the richness of the detail was recorded but a large bulk of it was in a form that could not be analysed in any meaningful way. Later processes developed increasingly sophisticated statistical methods for deconstructing the 'grammar' of human rights events, analysing narratives across different sources of information, estimating the nature and extent of gross human rights abuses, and then complementing their efforts with qualitative narrative methods. For example, in Peru the CVR collected, coded and analysed the 17,000 statements it received, combined these data with other significant data sources, and then complemented the quantitative narrative data with over thirty *estudios en profundidad* (in-depth case studies) on the communal-level impact of the conflict over twenty years and over 150 elite in-depth interviews with political party leaders, senior figures in the military and leaders from the two main rebel groups, the *Sendero Luminoso* ('Shining Path') and *Movimiento Revolucionario Túpac Amaru* (Revolutionary Movement Túpac Amaru or MRTA) (see Ball *et al.* 2003; Landman 2006; Landman and Carvalho 2009; Landman and Gohdes 2010).

The approach that has been developed by the Human Rights Data Analysis Group[4] involves a moment of grammatical deconstruction of a narrative about what can often be very complex human rights events. The complete statement is taken from the deponent, and then the structure of the narrative is deconstructed into what has become known as the 'who did what to whom' model of analysis (Ball, Spirer and Spirer 2000). This model sees any such narrative comprising many different individuals and organizations as having 'roles' in the human rights event (e.g., victim, perpetrator, witness, etc.), which commit different acts of violation (e.g., torture, unlawful killing, arbitrary detention, etc.) across a variety of different contexts (e.g., urban setting, rural setting, morning, night time, season, etc.). In this way, the narrative statement reveals a cycle of information that will contain details about one or many victims, who suffer one or many violations, which happened at particular times and places, and which were committed by one or many perpetrators who belong to different sectors, organizations and institutions within the society (see Ball, Spirer and Spirer 2000: 29; Landman 2006: 112). This style of analysis fits squarely in Reissmann's (2008) notion of thematic or category-based analysis, since the goal of the analysis is to identify common things or common sets of things that can be identified across narratives, while at the same time preserving the precise identifying information from the narrative.

In its application to truth commissions, the 'who did what to whom' model of analysis proved to be a major leap forward, since most

---

[4] The Human Rights Data Analysis Group developed its early models at the American Association for the Advancement of Science in Washington, DC and then moved to the Benetech Initiative in Palo Alto, CA, where they are based today.

commissions were taking such a large number of statements and yet they wanted to harness as much information as possible from the statements they collected. In Peru, the CVR wanted to preserve as much detail as possible, while at the same time make a statistical estimate of the probable number of people who had been killed throughout the twenty years of conflict between 1980 and 2000. They thus adopted the model and processed over 17,000 statements. The final report included a listing and narrative of events surrounding the death or disappearance of each of the approximately 24,000 people whose accounts emerged from the statements. The CVR also carried out thirty in-depth case studies on the impact and effects of the conflict on community life, as well as over 150 elite interviews with political leaders, military officers, and rebels and guerrillas. The final statistical estimate of the total number of people killed relied on additional sources of narrative data collected by other organizations. Using the 'capture-tag-recapture' technique common in statistical studies that estimate unknown populations (e.g., see Bishop, Feinberg and Holland 1975; Ball *et al.* 2003; Zwane and van der Heijden 2005; Landman 2006; Landman and Carvalho 2009), the data team in Peru matched records across multiple sources, and then estimated the total number of killed and disappeared based on the ratio of probabilities of narrative accounts being reported in one or more of the sources. The final estimates showed that between 61,007 and 77,552 people died or disappeared in the armed conflict (see Ball *et al.* 2003);[5] a number, as it turned out, that was significantly higher than any previous estimates. Moreover, the analysis showed that *Sendero Luminoso*, the main guerrilla group, was the perpetrator responsible for the largest proportion of killings and disappearances, and that a disproportionate number of victims were indigenous people living in the highlands. There was shock at all three findings while Peruvians came to terms with the fact that they lived in such a divided society.

The 'who did what to whom' model used in Peru was based on earlier precedents set in the cases of El Salvador, Haiti, South Africa and Guatemala, and was then exported to the cases of Sierra Leone and East Timor. Peru, Guatemala and East Timor were all able to find enough additional sources for narrative accounts to be able to use the 'capture-tag-recapture' method of estimation, where the analysis in Guatemala, like the case of Peru, showed that indigenous people were six times more likely to be killed than those who were not indigenous (see Landman 2006: 111). But across all these cases, it is important to stress that the

---

[5] The point estimate was 69,280 with a 95 per cent confidence interval comprising roughly ±7,000 killings and disappearances.

goal of the work of the truth commissions was not solely focused on getting the correct number of gross human rights violations, and in all cases complementary forms of narrative analysis were carried out. The South Africans and Peruvians had public hearings, and both projects combined narrative and qualitative analysis alongside the use of statistics, which drew on the processing of a large number of narrative statements. Interestingly, in the case of South Africa, the public hearings were a way of engaging the general public with the work of the Truth and Reconciliation Commission and allowed Archbishop Desmond Tutu at the time to claim that apartheid had affected all South Africans; however, the selection of the individuals for the public hearings relied on quota samples and not random samples, such that the public hearings were hugely *unrepresentative* of the true nature and extent of human rights abuse against black South Africans, since the sample under-represented that social group (see Chapman and Ball 2001).

These experiences across truth commissions show the full range of narrative analysis that includes the kind of thematic and category oriented analysis identified by Reissmann (2008). The experiences also show that such projects will have competing goals, and the specification of their work programme, funding and results are necessarily a function of the epistemological and disciplinary composition of truth commission personnel. In my interviews with the team in Peru, Executive Director Javier Ciurlizza was keen to have a statistical component to the work of the CVR. As the work of the commission got under way, it became apparent that the number of statements to be collected was going to far exceed the initial expectations and required the adoption of the 'who did what to whom' model. The large number of statements also had cost and resource implications, which created competition within the commission for scarce resources between the data team and those working on the case studies and in-depth interviews. The complexity of the data capture and then capture-tag-recapture techniques and subsequent statistical estimations meant that the data team did not have 'results' for long periods of time, thereby causing resentment from teams that perceived the data team to be getting more financial support. Ciurlizza thus had to balance the demands and attenuate the conflicts between these different groups within the commission.

Beyond these practical complexities of running a large-scale project within a short period of time, what are the lessons for narrative analysis and phronesis? First, the narrative accounts collected across the truth commissions yield unbelievably detailed stories about interpersonal violence, abuse of power and human tragedy, so much so that researchers and coders involved in this work experienced their own forms of trauma and burn-out. These accounts have a Foucauldian feel to them as they focus on the intimate details of violence that has been directly experienced or witnessed in some way. Second, the public acknowledgements of past wrongs created through these commissions challenge past power relations and seek to break down deeply embedded power structures in ways that can help to build a new future for the country in which the work has been done.[6] Even if a particular truth commission used an amnesty for truth policy, as in the case of South Africa, the perpetrators of human rights violations either gave account for their actions or their victims were able to name them publicly. Third, the narrative accounts, the publication of descriptions of human rights events as in the case of Peru, as well as the statistical estimations provide a means for the restoration of victim dignity. The narrative account gives voice to the victim and provides a sense of participation and inclusion, while the statistical analysis shows that the individuals were part of something much bigger and that their story was an important part of a larger event. Finally, the public record of past abuse becomes something that empowers new generations of people, who can use the conclusions and recommendations of the official reports as leverage for mobilization against individuals, groups and institutions in an effort to hold them accountable for their actions.

As I see it, these different elements of the truth process inform and are informed by the phronetic approach. There are strong elements of epistemé and techné surrounding the design and implementation of the information management system, as well as the subsequent statistical analysis. Data capture, processing and analysis all contribute to the story that is then told in the final reports of the commissions. I would also argue that there is an awful lot of phronesis in these aspects of truth work, especially in knowing how to analyse the data, as in the case of Peru, where analysts needed in-depth and expert knowledge about the structure of Peruvian society, tendencies of racial and ethnic discrimination and the culture of violence that characterized the conflict. More directly, the qualitative elements clearly have a strong relationship with phronesis in the recounting and interpretation of the many stories that emerge in any truth process. But a real phronetic approach would have avoided some of the pitfalls as happened in South Africa with biased samples used for the public hearings, since the voice that was heard over-represented certain sectors and strengthened the impression that all segments of South African society were affected equally by apartheid when in fact they were not. Phronesis is also crucial in understanding what is important in a narrative statement in order to move beyond the mere utterances

---

[6] For example, the 'myth' of one Peru was deeply challenged by the findings regarding violence against indigenous groups, particularly those living in Ayacucho.

within a statement and tease out the dimensions of power, impunity and abuse in ways that identify practical routes to justice, reparation and, in some cases, reconciliation.

Conclusion

This chapter has provided an overview of the main issues surrounding narrative analysis and how it relates to the phronetic approach that has been developed here and elsewhere. The chapter is part methodological and part applied, as it sought to delineate the main contours, strengths and weaknesses of narrative analysis, make the links with phronesis, and then provide an illustration through a discussion of the work of truth commissions. Throughout, I have tried to stress the methodological trade-offs associated with narrative analysis and the importance of good method for phronetic research and practice. Much narrative analysis is vulnerable to problems of authenticity, veracity and representativeness, particularly if it is to be used to challenge power in the ways articulated in the phronetic approach. These vulnerabilities arise from the different research traditions from which narrative analysts come, but the analysis itself must be cautious in the claims it makes depending on the ways in which the narrative accounts are obtained, the ways in which they are analysed and interpreted, and how many have been collected and from whom. The discussion of truth commissions showed that they faced a daunting challenge of providing an accurate and representative account of the 'truth' about past wrongs, but had to manage large numbers of statements that were based on unrepresentative samples of people coming forward. To date, there have been only a handful of truth commissions that have sought to overcome the limitations associated with convenience samples, but they have all had to rely heavily on some form of narrative analysis to do their work. Narrative analysis thus offers a good method for real social science, but, like any method, comes with its own limitations of which all phronetic practitioners must remain aware.

Far from providing a comprehensive framework for the phronesis of narrative analysis, it does seem sensible to conclude this chapter by offering a modest set of steps (in the form of key questions) for anyone interested in conducting real social scientific research that uses narrative analysis as its primary method for establishing its evidentiary base:

Definition of research problem

(1) What do you want to know?
(2) What is the key research question?
(3) What kind of universe of people does it involve?

(4) Are your goals for particular knowledge or to make generalizations?
(5) If you seek generalizability, what are the limits to your contribution to knowledge about your topic of research?

Research design and methods

(1) What is the ideal population to which your question is directed? Is your selection of a sample of that population representative?
(2) If you have used a non-random method of selection, how can you best overcome the inherent biases in that sample?
(3) What kind of narrative analysis will you adopt?
(4) Is your narrative analysis more grounded and interpretative analysis more categorical and thematic?
(5) Will you use content analysis software, such as AtlasTi, NVivo, NUD*IST, QDA Miner or QDA Max?

Value added of the phronetic approach

(1) Is your research question one that focuses on problematic issues that are of real concern to the public?
(2) Have you thought about your own degrees of epistemé, techné and phronesis?
(3) What aspects of your epistemé and techné are important for this project?
(4) Is this a new area of research or one born of a long career of working in this area?
(5) In what ways will your own *expert status* have a bearing on what you do from the definition of the research question through the analysis and interpretation of the results?
(6) How will your own sense of phronesis inform the way you gather narrative evidence for your research question?
(7) How will that phronesis help you in understanding the narratives you collect?
(8) How confident and satisfied will you be with the results of your analysis?
(9) Does your analysis of the narratives uncover and/or challenge dominant modes of power?

These are fairly straightforward questions, but ones that are rarely asked or answered explicitly from the outset of a particular project. They are 'meta' questions that shape any new inquiry and ask for justification and clarification of the choices that are made when engaged in real social scientific research in the ways outlined in this volume. I leave open the possibility of different forms of narrative analysis (as I have shown, there are many), but for me such analysis must always be connected back to the primary research question and will be ultimately related to types and the strength of analytical statements that can be made about the social world.

REFERENCES

Ball, P., Asher, J., Sulmont, D. and Manrique, D. 2003. 'How Many Peruvians have Died? An Estimate of the Total Number of Victims Killed or Disappeared in the Armed Internal Conflict between 1980 and 2000', American Association for the Advancement of Science, Washington, DC.

Ball, P., Spirer, H. and Spirer, L. 2000. *Investigating Large Scale Human Rights Violations Using Information Systems and Data Analysis*. Washington, DC: American Association for the Advancement of Science.

Beer, Francis A. and Balleck, Barry J. 1994. 'Realist/Idealist Texts: Psychometry and Semantics', *Peace Psychology Review* 1: 38–44.

Bellah, R. N., Madsen, R., Sullivan, W. M., Swidler, A. and Tipton, S. M. 1985. *Habits of the Heart: Individualism and Commitment in American Life*. New York: Harper & Row.

Bishop, Y. M., Feinberg, S. E. and Holland, P. H. 1975. *Discrete Multivariate Analysis: Theory and Practice*. Cambridge, MA: MIT Press.

Budge, I., Klingemann, H. D., Volkens, A., Bara, J. and Tanenbaum, E. 2001. *Mapping Policy Preferences: Estimates for Parties, Electors, and Governments 1945–1998*. Oxford University Press.

Chapman, Audrey R. and Ball, Patrick 2001. 'The Truth of Truth Commissions: Comparative Lessons from Haiti, South Africa, and Guatemala', *Human Rights Quarterly* 23: 1–43.

Chase, S. E. 2005. 'Narrative Inquiry: Multiple Lenses, Approaches, Voices', in N. K. Denzin and Y. S. Lincoln (eds.), *The Sage Handbook of Qualitative Research*. Thousand Oaks, CA: Sage, pp. 651–79.

Clandinin, D. Jean and Connelly, F. Michael 2000. *Narrative Inquiry: Experience and Story in Qualitative Research*. San Francisco, CA: Jossey-Bass.

Eulau, H. 1996. *Micro–Macro Dilemmas in Political Science: Personal Pathways through Complexity*. Norman, OK: University of Oklahoma Press.

Fenno, R. F. 1978. *Home Style: House Members in Their Districts*. Longman Classics Series, New York: Longman.

Flyvbjerg, B. 2001. *Making Social Science Matter: Why Social Inquiry Fails and How it can Succeed Again*. Cambridge University Press.

   2006. 'A Perestroikan Straw Man Answers Back: David Laitin and Phronetic Social Science', in Schram and Caterino (eds.), *Making Political Science Matter*, pp. 56–85.

Frank, A. 2002. 'Why Study People's Stories? The Dialogical Ethics of Narrative Analysis', *International Journal of Qualitative Methods* 1(1): 1–20.

Franzosi, R. 2004. *From Words to Numbers: Narrative, Data and Social Science*. Cambridge University Press.

Gallie, W. B. 1956. 'Essentially Contested Concepts', *Proceedings of the Aristotelian Society* March: 167–98.

Glynos, J. and Howarth, D. 2008. *Logics of Critical Explanation in Social and Political Theory.* London: Routledge.

Hayner, P. B. 1994. 'Fifteen Truth Commissions – 1974–1994: A Comparative Study', *Human Rights Quarterly* 16: 597–655.

2002. *Unspeakable Truths: Facing the Challenge of Truth Commissions.* London: Routledge.

Howarth, D. 2000. *Discourse.* Buckingham: Open University Press.

Howarth, D., Norval, A. and Stavrakakis, Y. (eds.) 2000. *Discourse Theory and Political Analysis: Identities, Hegemonies and Social Change.* Manchester University Press.

Landman, T. 2000. *Issues and Methods in Comparative Politics: An Introduction.* London: Routledge.

2002. 'Comparative Politics and Human Rights', *Human Rights Quarterly* 24(4): 890–923.

2003. *Issues and Methods in Comparative Politics: An Introduction*, 2nd edn. London: Routledge.

2005. 'Review Article: The Political Science of Human Rights', *British Journal of Political Science* 35(3): 549–72.

2006. *Studying Human Rights.* London: Routledge.

2008. *Issues and Methods in Comparative Politics: An Introduction*, 3rd edn. London: Routledge.

Landman, T. and Carvalho, E. 2009. *Measuring Human Rights.* London: Routledge.

Landman, T. and Gohdes, A. 2010. 'Principals, Agents, and Atrocities: The Case of Peru 1980–2000', Paper prepared for a meeting on casualty recording and estimation in conflict and post-conflict situations, hosted by Carnegie Mellon University and the University of Pittsburgh, 23–25 October 2009, Pittsburgh, PA.

Reissmann, C. K. 2008. *Narrative Methods for the Human Sciences.* Thousand Oaks, CA: Sage.

Riley, T. and Hawe, P. 2005. 'Researching Practice: The Methodological Case for Narrative Inquiry', *Health Education Research* 20(2): 226–36.

Schram, S. and Caterino, B. (eds.) 2006. *Making Political Science Matter: Debating Knowledge, Research, and Method.* New York University Press.

Silva, R., Klingner, J. and Weikart, S. 2010. 'State Violence in Chad', Palo Alto, CA: Benetech Initiative, available at: www.hrdag.org/about/downloads/State-Violence-in-Chad.pdf.

Skaar, E. 1999. 'Truth Commissions, Trials – or Nothing? Policy Options in Democratic Transitions', in I. Kolstad and H. Stokke (eds.), *Writing Rights: Human Rights Research at the Chr. Michelsen Institute 1984–2004.* Bergen: Fagbokforlaget, pp. 149–71.

Skaar, E., Gloppen, S. and Suhrke, A. (eds.) 2005. *Roads to Reconciliation.* Lanham, MD: Lexington Books.

Williamson, A., Feyer, A-M., Stout, N., Driscoll, T. and Usher, H. 2001. 'Use of Narrative Analysis for Comparisons of the Causes of Fatal Accidents in

Three Countries: New Zealand, Australia, and the United States', *Injury Prevention* 7: 15–20.

Zwane, E. and van der Heijden, P. 2005. 'Population Estimation using the Multiple System Estimator in the Presence of Continuous Covariates', *Statistical Modelling* 5: 39–52.

4   The feel for power games: everyday phronesis and social theory

Arthur W. Frank

> The higher the human intellect goes in discovering more and more purposes, the more obvious it becomes that the ultimate purpose is beyond comprehension.
>
> <div align="right">Leo Tolstoy, <i>War and Peace</i> ([1868–9] 2005: 1270)</div>

This chapter explores the relation between phronesis in doing social science and what I will call everyday phronesis. A core topic of social scientific study is the dependence of human action on phronesis, understood as people's practical wisdom in dealing with both routine decisions and unexpected contingencies. This practical wisdom seems to have three aspects: it is content, a quality of persons, and a form of action. As content, phronesis is a resource – a stock of experiential knowledge. As a quality of persons, it is what enables acquisition and appropriate use of that knowledge – a capacity. And as action, phronesis necessarily involves doing something – a practice in which experiential knowledge is both used and gained. Having phronesis is iteratively dependent on practising phronesis.

For social science phronesis has to be more than a topic; it is what social scientific study requires from researchers (Flyvbjerg 2001), and what social science seeks to enhance in those whom I will call readers. *Real* social science is when studying the world has the effect of changing it. This chapter discusses social theories in which the study of everyday practical wisdom works to enhance their readers' capacity for phronesis.

I will revisit the writings of Pierre Bourdieu and Michel Foucault to show, first, how each describes the human condition as being dependent on phronesis, and, second, how studying their texts enhances readers' capacity for phronesis. Each theorist's texts are pedagogical in the sense of being written to equip the reader for complementary capacities that the texts require from him or her: becoming able to do the research each theorist recommends, but also appreciating the limits of how much is pedagogically justifiable to recommend. Bourdieu and Foucault call on readers to learn what can only be implied about how to live, because

48

phronesis, as a quality of persons, can be acquired only by changing oneself, not by following directions. This chapter thus begins by showing what I understand exemplifies phronesis, because phronesis can only be shown in part, never fully specified in abstract descriptions.

Exemplifying phronesis

I seek not to define phronesis, but to exemplify it *in practice*. Because I believe that people acquire their sense of practice by hearing and then telling stories, I leave the Aristotelian origins of phronesis to others and turn instead to two very different stories: one literary and the other folklore.

Near the end of *War and Peace*, Tolstoy's description of the maturity of one of his central characters, Nikolay Rostov, shows phronesis as an everyday practice. The novel follows Nikolay's development from youth to maturity. The young Nikolay is never malicious, but he is impulsive, vain and easily led into trouble by companions on whose opinion he is too dependent. In selecting those companions, he shows little discrimination. In particular, he incurs gambling debts beyond that which his family's considerable wealth can sustain. But at the end of the book, the Rostov fortunes now dissipated, Nikolay assumes responsibility for the massive debts of his deceased father. He supports his mother as best he can, sacrificing the military career that he loves. Then he marries Princess Marya, heiress to the Bolkonsky fortune, and assumes management of her estates. He pays his debts without drawing upon his wife's property; he brings increased prosperity to her estates; and buys property, including his family's former estates. Tolstoy describes in some detail how Nikolay achieves such success. 'Nikolay was a farmer of the old school,' Tolstoy writes, 'he didn't like new-fangled ideas, especially the English ones that were coming in at the time. He laughed at the theoretical studies of estate management . . . ' ([1868–9] 2005: 1277).

Phronesis begins with turning away from ideas and theory, and depending instead on the observation of *practice* that can be trusted. What Nikolay studies are peasants whose knowledge of the land is grounded in their daily labour:

When Nikolay took up farming, and began to investigate its different branches, it was the peasant that claimed most of his attention. He saw the peasant as something more than a useful tool; he was an end in himself and a source of good judgement. He began by closely observing the peasants in an attempt to understand what they wanted, and what they considered good and bad practice. He went through the motions of making arrangements and giving out orders, but what he was really doing was learning from the peasants by following their methods, their language and their notions of what was good and bad. And it was only when he came to understand the peasants' appetites and aspirations, when he had learnt their way of speaking and the hidden meaning behind their words, when he felt a kind of kinship with them, that he began to manage them with confidence, in other words to fulfil the obligation towards them that was demanded of him. And Nikolay's management produced the most brilliant results. (Tolstoy [1868–9] 2005: 1277)

This passage might be read as an allegory for an author's relation to his characters and the phronesis required for writing fiction. But my interest is in how Nikolay's practice exemplifies the attainment of phronesis. His phronesis is both a prerequisite for his close observation of the peasants, and it is the outcome of those observations.

Nikolay's disinterest in what is called 'theory' clears a space for his interest in the peasants. He becomes an ethnographer of their judgements and knowledge, studying 'what they consider good and bad *practice*' (Tolstoy [1868–9] 2005: 1277, emphasis added). Nikolay's attitude towards the peasants can be expressed in research terms by saying that he regards them not as subjects of research, but as research participants in the fullest sense: 'as something more than a useful tool; he was an end in himself and a source of *good judgement*' (Tolstoy [1868–9] 2005: 1277, emphasis added). Nikolay goes through the motions of giving orders – much like a qualitative researcher must go through the motions of claiming to know in advance of the research what the project is fundamentally about, exactly how it will be carried out and even what its results will be – but in actuality he is 'learning from the peasants', in particular 'their notions of what was good and bad' ([1868–9] 2005: 1277). Whatever 'confidence' Nikolay comes to feel is based on his sense of 'kinship' with the peasants, including knowing 'the hidden meaning behind their words' ([1868–9] 2005: 1277). Although he manages the peasants, he understands his relation to them as an 'obligation'.

In this allegory of Nikolay as ethnographer, the basic principle of study is to *learn from the participants*. What counts is not what the social scientist thinks she or he already knows – by virtue of the accumulated wisdom of the social scientific literature – but what the participants can teach. Phronesis lies in looking to participants' judgements; research involves doing whatever makes those judgements available to the researcher. That does not mean that the researcher stops at passively recording what participants already know, accepting that knowledge as the sum of all that can be said. Nikolay does not leave the peasants to manage themselves; in social scientific terms, he keeps open a space for analysis of them. But he understands the limits of what he can contribute to their practices and their 'good judgement' (Tolstoy [1868–9] 2005: 1277).

Nikolay Rostov is one exemplar of phronesis as a practice of learning from those whose lives represent the wisdom of accumulated practice. His good judgement is reflexively dependent on the peasants' good judgement. Of course, not all the peasants are wise, and part of what Nikolay must learn through observation is how to tell whom to learn from – that requires *discrimination*, which emerges as a crucial aspect of phronesis. A second exemplar brings out a different aspect of phronesis. Here I turn to folklore and one of its stock characters, the trickster.

Lewis Hyde's magisterial study of tricksters describes the particular intelligence of these characters in terms that explain when phronesis is needed in life and in research:

While [tricksters] are often smart, they have a sort of 'rudderless intelligence', responding to situations as they arise but unable to formulate any coherent, sustainable, long-term plan . . . It might be right to say that the trickster, like the psychopath, has a 'rudderless intelligence', but if so, it is a useful intelligence, for it continues to function when normal guidance systems have failed, as they periodically will. (Hyde 1998: 158)

Nikolay Rostov's intelligence is not exactly 'rudderless', but it is tacit and comparatively unaccountable, in the sense that he could not articulate exactly what he learns from the peasants or how he translates that into his management of his estates – he could not write a 'handbook for masters of estates' and would find the idea of such a book silly. Nikolay's work is coherent and sustainable at any moment, but his 'long-term plan' seems to be mostly to respond to 'situations as they arise' (Tolstoy [1868–9] 2005: 1277).

The 'new-fangled' agricultural theories of scientific soil analysis that Nikolay rejects (Tolstoy [1868–9] 2005: 1277) probably emphasize long-term planning, with science as the rudder. But battle has taught Nikolay – and *War and Peace* has taught the reader – the truth of Hyde's contention that 'normal guidance systems' will inevitably fail. A recurring tension in *War and Peace* is between those military officers who believe that battles can be fought according to plans (e.g., Tolstoy's satirical depiction of Carl Maria von Clausewitz, who in 1833 would write *On War*) and those who realize that battles can perhaps be prepared for, but they cannot be planned (the Russian Field Marshal Kutuzov). Tolstoy's sympathies clearly lie with the latter, and according to Isaiah Berlin, he was not above rewriting history in order to assert those sympathies (see Berlin [1952] 1978).

Throughout *War and Peace*, characters confront situations for which their normal guidance systems are inadequate, and they either have a 'rudderless intelligence' to fall back upon or they do not, to their peril. These characters are not necessarily tricksters, but those who succeed are capable of at least the trickster capacity for shape-shifting; thus, Nikolay reinvents himself as a farmer, for which little in his former life seems to prepare him, except perhaps a generalized capacity to adapt to necessity.

These two accounts of Tolstoy and Hyde hardly exhaust what might count as phronesis – it is, in principle, inexhaustible – but they bring the idea into the sphere of practical action. Phronesis in these accounts is acquired through training – Nikolay *studies* the peasants and their subtle and generally inarticulate knowledge – but even if it could be formulated in principles, those who act on phronesis realize what would be contradictory about such formulation. The refusal of explicit formulation enables the singular virtue of adaptability. When intelligence systems dependent on principle confront unforeseen situations to which their principles are not readily applicable, their circuits jam. Phronesis continues to function, in part because such intelligence does not try to make present circumstances conform to long-term plans. Unencumbered by obligation to follow a predetermined plan, phronesis can respond to whatever requires response, seeing exactly what is at hand and using the resources at hand.

This chapter now turns to theory, but not the sort that Nikolay disdains. That kind of theory claims to prescribe action based on knowing the essence of things (soil, in the theories Nikolay ignores). Most practitioners of contemporary social theory would either flatly refuse, or at least be made nervous by, the label of theorist. Bourdieu and Foucault present inter-related concepts that indicate directions of inquiry, but not *theory* as a self-contained scheme of logically related explanatory propositions. My highly selective emphasis is how each theorist (a word I continue to use for want of a better descriptive term, and because I believe they indicate the shape and *modus operandi* of theory-to-come) offers a *performative description* of the practical wisdom of everyday actors: the theory *enacts* a version of what it describes, and that enactment is a form of pedagogy. On a descriptive level, each theorist shows how people utilize a mostly tacit knowledge as a way of confronting life's challenges. But neither Bourdieu nor Foucault is only studying others, and their respective reflexive practices lead readers towards each theorist's own practical wisdom, much of which is probably tacit. As the reader attempts to view the world through the theory, utilizing the conceptual toolkit that it provides, she or he realizes that the theory is not a rudder guiding inquiry – much less a 'framework' – but it can be a form of intelligence informing inquiry. Bourdieu and Foucault exemplify theorists who do not tell their readers how to do research, but they offer sufficient tools that readers can use, and they write in a style that teaches how to use these tools.

Bourdieu: the capacities and limits of practical wisdom

Bourdieu depicts people as wise but limited; capable but not fully equipped. His sociology seeks a balance between respecting the practical wisdom with which people make the most of their circumstances, but also demonstrating and attempting to teach the limitations of people's practices and the extensive consequences of those limitations.

Discussion of Bourdieu cannot avoid beginning with his most notable concept, *habitus*, even if the multiple meanings of this idea exceed the scope of this chapter.[1] Habitus is, first, *embodied*; it is a disposition of the body to feel comfort or discomfort with certain ways of being (eating this or that, wearing certain clothes) and to entertain as possible *for me* certain action possibilities (finishing school, holding one or another kind of job, enjoying familiarity of association with certain people). Second, habitus is not fixed but it is *durable*; acquired early in life, it changes but only slowly. Third, while habitus does not determine action, it does *dispose* the actor to feel the rightness and even the necessity of particular ways of acting.

Habitus provides the embodied practical wisdom that guides decisions made in conditions of inevitable uncertainty. David Swartz describes Bourdieu's recognition 'that action involves *uncertainty* even in normative situations and that actions occur *over time* rendering the outcomes seldom clear to the actors involved' (1997: 99, emphases in original). In these conditions, strategy can never be entirely rational in the sense of calculated. Actors are strategic, but their guidance system is closer to phronesis than to rational choice. Swartz summarizes what Bourdieu learned in his research on the Kabyle in Algeria:

> The sense of honor derives from the sets of dispositions that internalize in practical form what seems appropriate or possible in situations of challenge, constraint, or opportunity. Thus, choices do not derive directly from the objective situations in which they occur or from transcending rules, norms, patterns, and constraints that govern social life; rather, they stem from *practical dispositions* that incorporate ambiguities and uncertainties that emerge from acting *through time and space* . . . Actors are not rule followers or norm observers but strategic improvisers who respond dispositionally to the opportunities and constrains offered by various situations. (1997: 100, emphases in original)

Swartz underscores Bourdieu's interest in emphasizing 'the *inventive* as well as habituated forms of action' (1997: 101, emphasis added). Habitus is not simply habit; it is the improvisational capacity that overrides and corrects the force of habit in conditions of uncertainty. This

---

[1] For extensive discussions of *habitus* see Maton (2008) and Swartz (1997: 95–116).

improvisational capacity of action seems to be Bourdieu's version of phronesis. Dependence on 'rules, norms, patterns, and constraints' (Swartz 1997: 100, quoted above) involves what Hyde describes the trickster showing as inadequate: belief that a single rudder can steer action. Sociologists search for *the* rudder as an explanatory principle. The intelligence of the habitus is not rudderless, but it does comprehend the limitation of how well any fixed rudder can steer.

Habitus may be the cornerstone of Bourdieu's thinking, but most relevant to phronesis are his recurring metaphor 'feel for the game' and his concept of *illusio*. Underpinning both ideas is Bourdieu's recognition that an actor's habitus does not convey equal advantage in all fields of action – a *field* most briefly understood as being a bounded set of positions defined by access to capital, as well as an area in which certain forms of capital are valued and those values are contested.[2] Bourdieu's theory of inequality depends on his observation that habitus provides differential chances of success in any field. Some actors' feel for the game played in a particular field will be more conducive to capital accumulation than others' guidance systems. Bourdieu describes the affinity between habitus and field as 'being born in a game', implying the primacy of early childhood experiences. This fit conveys a distinct advantage:

> One of the privileges associated with the fact of being born in a game is that one can avoid cynicism since one has a feel for the game; like a good tennis player, one positions oneself not where the ball is but where it will be; one invests oneself and one invests not where the profit is, but where it will be. Reconversions, through which one moves toward new genres, new disciplines, new subjects, etc., are experienced as *conversions*. (Bourdieu 1998: 79, emphasis added)

The practical wisdom of this feel for the game requires what Bourdieu calls *illusio*, or 'the fact of being caught up in the game, in the *illusio* understood as a fundamental belief in the interest of the game and the value of the stakes which is inherent in that membership' (Bourdieu 1998: 11). Success in a field thus has two essential prerequisites: knowing what the stakes are in that particular game; and – related, but by no means the same – having the capacity to take the stakes seriously:

> Taking part in the *illusio* – scientific, literary, philosophical or other – means taking seriously (sometimes to the point of making them questions of life and death) stakes which, arising from the logic of the game itself, establish its 'seriousness', even if they may escape or appear 'disinterested' or 'gratuitous' to those who are sometimes called 'lay people' or those who are engaged in other fields (since

---

[2] To amplify this perilously brief statement, see Thomson (2008) and Swartz (1997: 117–42).

the independence of the different fields entails a form of non-communicability between them). (Bourdieu 1998)

War and Peace provides a good example of *illusio* in the gambling of young Nikolay Rostov. Nikolay goes to a party attended by his peers, finds them gambling and, despite his misapprehensions, feels compelled to join them. He loses but he cannot withdraw from the game, even as his losses become massive. Later, he asks his father for money to cover his debt, and their dialogue exemplifies a shared *illusio* that others outside their field might find absurd:

'I promised to pay tomorrow,' said Nikolay.

'Oh, no!' explained the count, throwing his arms in the air as he flopped down helplessly on to a sofa.

'Can't be helped! Everyone does it,' said his son, outwardly brazen and breezy but feeling in his heart of hearts that he was an unspeakable cad and his crime could never be redeemed in a lifetime.

Count Ilya lowered his eyes at these words from his son, and began fidgeting as if he were looking for something.

'Yes, yes...' he managed to say. 'It will be difficult, I'm afraid, difficult to raise... but it happens to everybody! Yes, it happens to everybody...' (Tolstoy [1868–9] 2005: 371)

Father and son share a conviction of what is at stake: the dependence of honour on demonstrating an aristocratic disdain for money and willingness to risk. They take these stakes *seriously*, to the point of assuming unaffordable debt to stay in the game. Their continued position in the field depends on acting as they do, even as their action undermines sustaining their position. 'When we deliberate on entry into the game,' Bourdieu writes (1998: 11), 'the die is already more or less cast.'

The Rostovs illustrate how actors' feel for the game is in one sense their practical wisdom, but it can equally be their undoing. What enables them to be members of what Bourdieu (1990: 133) calls 'the dominant class with a "theodicy of its own privilege"' paradoxically risks their continuing membership in that class. Or in Bourdieu's other terms, their investment in symbolic capital imperils their maintenance of sufficient economic capital.

Bourdieu thus suggests a crucial qualification of phronesis. Practical wisdom is generally specific to a particular field – it predisposes strategies that work in that field, but not necessarily elsewhere – and even in that field, practical wisdom can indicate lines of action that incur losses as well as benefits. Practical wisdom – *illusio* as investment and taking the stakes seriously – involves a willingness to lose as well as a disposition to see where profit will be. As Bourdieu emphasizes, action unfolds over time. Over time, and in different fields, aspects of the dispositions that precipitate Nikolay's gambling will bring him eventual success in the military, sustain his class position and, in the very long run, lead to the rebuilding of his family's fortunes on a more secure foundation of economic capital. Judged over a sufficiently long duration, Nikolay's gambling losses can be understood as a high-risk reconversion of capital that eventually, and in utterly unanticipated ways, pays off.

Bourdieu never allows his academic readers to forget that they, in the academic field, are just as affected by habitus, feel for the game and *illusio* as actors in other fields. His work constantly reflects on the academic field that he and his readers occupy. He begins *Pascalian Meditations* (2000), which I understand as the most complete summation of his ideas, by discussing the 'scholastic disposition' and how it risks confusing the imperatives of its gaze with the practical realities of life as it is lived in other fields: scholastic worlds 'offer positions in which one can feel entitled to perceive the world as a representation, a spectacle, to survey it from above and from afar and organize it as a whole designed for knowledge alone' (2000: 21). The academic risks developing what Bourdieu quotes John Dewey as calling 'a spectator's theory of knowledge', in which the researcher projects 'his theoretical knowledge into the heads of acting agents' (2000: 51).

For Bourdieu, the practical wisdom necessary to play the scholastic game – to do real social science – involves recognizing both the continuities and the profound discontinuities between the academic field and non-academic fields. All fields have their characteristic forms of capital, their stakes, and the necessity of taking those stakes seriously. Bourdieu writes autobiographically (in what he insists is *not* an autobiography) of his own *illusio*: 'my total, slightly crazed, investment in research' (2007: 69). And he accounts for his relationship with the senior academic Georges Canguilhem: 'He took a liking to me, in one of those movements of sympathy obscure to itself that are rooted in the affinity of habitus' (2007: 27). But Bourdieu is equally at pains to elaborate the distinctive separateness of the academic field, especially its possibility for a leisure that 'inclines its possessors to suspend the demands of the situation, the constraints of economic and social necessity, and the urgencies it imposes or the ends it proposes' (2000: 12).

Real social science, as I understand Bourdieu, requires the capacity for sustaining the respective *illusio* of both the academic and the everyday fields, while remembering the differences between them. To understand the everyday fields of non-scholastic life, the scholastic suspension of demands must be set in brackets, lest actors who operate with quite different necessities and stakes be misunderstood. But for Bourdieu to claim to do science, he must be scholastic, beginning with that field's allowing and requiring a delayed response. The point is having the practical wisdom to recognize which field one is in and what the distinctive features of that field are.

Feel for the game is one level of phronesis in Bourdieu's thinking, adequate for actors who remain in whatever field has the closest affinity to their initial habitus. Actors who try to understand other fields, either academically or to enter and compete in those fields, must move to a different level. Bourdieu's writing teaches the capacity to suspend the *illusio* of one field in order to perceive the stakes of another, and then suspend those stakes in order to return to the original field. On first reading of Bourdieu's *Pascalian Meditations* I was confused about why it opens with an extended discussion of the scholastic disposition; I wanted to get straight to habitus, field and capital. Bourdieu is teaching academic readers to begin with our own field and to recognize how its principles of vision and division affect our capacity to observe other fields that operate on different principles. Practical wisdom begins in asking how the field to which our habitus is most suited conditions the observations – which are too often projections – of other fields.

The practical wisdom of social science includes perceiving the comparative 'non-communicability' between different fields (2000: 11) and recognizing that the scholastic disposition is as non-communicable as any other. Phronesis for the social scientist is having – unlike Nikolay Rostov, who can be caught up in only one game at a time – sufficient reflective control over which stakes are taken seriously for what purposes. The game for which the scholastic must develop a feel involves this *movement between* fields, becoming caught up in one field's stakes and then suspending that engagement. There is a profound ethics and a politics in this capacity for alternating engagement, if one understands the world today as fraught between groups incapable of grasping what is at stake for other groups. Each group's investment is the measure of its *inability* to communicate. *Illusio* is what makes living possible, but also what makes living together dangerous.

Foucault: danger and practical wisdom

Bourdieu understands that actors' lives become dangerous when there is a mismatch between their habitus and the field in which they seek capital. Such actors have no feel for the game they are in; they fail either to recognize the stakes or to take the stakes seriously. Bourdieu names this condition *hysteresis* (Hardy 2008).

Foucault, quoting from a newspaper account of a court hearing in 1840, provides a dialogue in which a vagrant, Béasse, is brought before a judge. The judge might describe Béasse's condition as a mismatch between habitus and field, but this mismatch is not exactly hysteresis because Béasse is fully aware of what the field demands of him, and he resists its distribution of capital:

'The judge: One must sleep at home. – Béasse: Have I got a home? – You live in perpetual vagabondage. – I work for a living. – What is your station in life? – My station: to begin with, I'm thirty-six at least; I don't work for anybody. I've worked for myself for a long time now. I have my day station and my night station. In the day, for instance, I hand out leaflets free of charge to all the passers-by; I run after the stage-coaches when they arrive and carry luggage for passengers; I turn cart-wheels on the avenue de Neuilly; at night there are the shows; I open coach doors, I sell the pass-out tickets; I've plenty to do. – It would be better for you to be put into a good house as an apprentice and learn a trade. – Oh, a good house, an apprenticeship, it's too much trouble. And anyway the bourgeois . . . always grumbling, no freedom. – Does your father wish to reclaim you? – Haven't got no father. – And your mother? – No mother neither, no parents, no friends, free and independent.' Hearing his sentence of two years in a reformatory, Béasse 'pulled an ugly face, then, recovering his good humour, remarked: "Two years, that's never more than twenty-four months. Let's be off, then."' (Foucault 1978: 290–1)

This scene is notable as the only occasion in *Discipline and Punish* when the one being punished and the one who punishes are quoted speaking to one another. It is a rare, perhaps singular, moment of actual dialogue in Foucault's published works.

Béasse is one of those whom Foucault calls 'infamous men' who live lives characterized by 'disarray and relentless energy' (2000: 158). Foucault's most definitive commentary on Béasse may occur not in *Discipline and Punish*, but rather in his 'Lives of Infamous Men':

Is it not one of the fundamental traits of our society, after all, that destiny takes the form of a relation with power, of a struggle with or against it? Indeed, the most intense point of a life, the point where its energy is concentrated, is where it comes up against power, struggles with it, attempts to use its forces and to evade its traps. The brief and strident words that went back and forth between power and the most inessential existences doubtless constitute, for the latter, the only monument they have ever been granted: it is what gives them, for the passage through time, the bit of brilliance, the brief flash that carries them to us. (2000: 161–2)

Perhaps Foucault brushes the dust from this archival newspaper report so that Béasse can once again enjoy

the chance that enabled these absolutely undistinguished people to emerge from their place amid the dead multitudes, to gesticulate again [Béasse's ugly face, hearing his sentence], to manifest their rage [or their wit], their affliction, or their invincible determination to err – perhaps it makes up for the bad luck that brought power's lightning bolt down upon them, in spite of their modesty and anonymity. (2000: 163)

Béasse has the practical wisdom to have survived doing his odd jobs, collecting tips, working for no man, living without a fixed residence. We do not know what bad luck led to his arrest. Seeing him in court, we might ask, following Bourdieu, whether he recognizes the field he is in, the game he is playing and the stakes of that game – doesn't he realize he is before a judge who will sentence him? 'At times,' Foucault writes of infamous men, 'they remind one of a poor troupe of jugglers and clowns who deck themselves out in makeshift scraps of old finery to play before an audience of aristocrats who will make fun of them. Except that they are staking their whole life on the performance: they are playing before powerful men who can decide their fate' (Foucault 2000: 171).

Yet Foucault's question is not so much *why* Béasse and other infamous men court danger as they do. Rather, I understand Foucault to be confronting the rest of us – those who lead safe lives, not challenging power – with what is dangerous in our lives; how do we sort out these dangers? And if that is at least one salient question, it addresses why Béasse acts as he does. He realizes life is dangerous *whatever* his action, and his habitus disposes him to confront power, knowing the risks, lest he become the subject that power calls upon him to become: an apprentice, a person of fixed station, even a bourgeois. Becoming that subject is the real risk for Béasse.

Continuous with the practical wisdom that allows Béasse to survive on the streets of Paris until his arrest and then to survive the attempt of the court to turn him into its model of a productive subject, Foucault proposes to his readers the need for a practical wisdom for living freely – the choice of that adverb being probably the most complicated word selection in this chapter – in the face of multiple dangers. I suggest three levels of life's danger, each requiring wisdom to negotiate. The core text in this elaboration is Foucault's frequently quoted statement: 'My point is not that everything is bad, but that everything is dangerous, which is not exactly the same as bad' (Rabinow and Rose 2003: 104). This sentence best exemplifies the need for phronesis, both in everyday life as Foucault depicts it, and also in Foucauldian social science. What, then, are the dangers to which Foucault refers?

First, a danger of acting on truth in a world in which 'men govern (themselves and others) by the production of truth' (Foucault 2000: 230). That truth is *produced* is not, however, to disclaim the practical adequacy of most truths. The problem of finding a relation to truth is that produced truths *are* true, in the sense of being efficient. Jeffrey Nealon writes: 'Power's intensity most specifically names its increasing *efficiency* within a system, coupled with increasing *saturation*. As power becomes more intense, it becomes "more economic and more effective"' (2008: 32, emphases in original; Foucault quoted from *Discipline and Punish*). Truth delivers the goods, which is what complicates resistance. Norms – the understanding and self-understanding of the subject by means of a statistical distribution of what is considered normal – 'introduce a vast and intense new productivity into the regimes of truth, or what Foucault calls the ways of truth-telling' (Nealon 2008: 50). As some commentators have noted, it was not ironic but consistent that, when Foucault became ill, he went to a hospital. Seeking medical care exemplified phronesis as balancing; in this instance, balancing the recognition of the danger in how hospitals constitute medical truths against their efficacy and productivity in repairing bodies.

When the judge offers Béasse the possibility of an apprenticeship, power remains comparatively inefficient and unproductive, insofar as that offer may not be worth much more than jail. The *intensification* of power – to use Nealon's important phrase – occurs as the offers improve. The greater the practical benefits of acceding to truth, the greater the dangers of truth-telling, and the greater the need for the practical wisdom necessary to live in an intensified regime of power. Again, the danger of truth is greatest not when its assertions are untrue, as Marxists claim that capitalist ideology is untrue, but precisely when they are most true in the efficiency of their immediate effects. Foucault seeks to teach his readers the practical wisdom of thinking beyond those effects and asking *what productivity produces*. Especially, what kind of subject is being produced at the cost of being constituted by such truths; for example, with reference to different norms.

Second, and already anticipated in the danger of truth, is the danger of how each person becomes a subject, which is one of the densest words in Foucault's writing. 'There is literally no such thing as unconstrained subjective action in Foucault,' Nealon 2008: 102) writes. Given that the subject is always constrained, inquiry shifts away from the common-sense question of 'where's the "real" agency in Foucault – subjective agency that is "free", not "merely" an effect of power?' (Nealon 2008: 102). That question is mistaken for reasons already evident in the case of Béasse. This infamous man becomes visible to us, 150 years later, only because of his encounter with power. That confrontation is 'the most intense point' of Béasse's life and what Foucault calls its 'monument' (2000: 161–2, quoted above) because it offers Béasse's *possibility of becoming a subject*, and thus his greatest freedom. His life – his visibility to himself as a subject – *is* his coming up against power, struggling with it, and attempting to use its forces and to evade its traps. And this is the dilemma within which all of us become visible to ourselves as subjects. The issue is not *whether* we confront power; the only question is how we do so: *how well* we use its force and evade its traps.

The matter of *how well* suggests enumerating criteria for success in an encounter with power, and that raises the third danger: the seduction of the solution, which in this instance would be specifying criteria for *how well* and then a method – a way of reflecting upon and changing one's life – for systematically implementing those criteria. At times Foucault's ethics seem to point towards such criteria – he admires the criteria of certain Greek philosophies – but then he vehemently rejects that approach. Here we return to the context for Foucault's famous statement about life's dangerousness, quoted earlier. The full quotation is from the interview with Foucault by Hubert Dreyfus and Paul Rabinow in 1983. They are discussing his research on ancient Greek ethics:

Well, I wonder if our problem nowadays is not, in a way, similar to this one, since most of us no longer believe that ethics is founded in religion, nor do we want a legal system to intervene in our moral, personal, private life. Recent liberation movements suffer from the fact that they cannot find any principle on which to base the elaboration of a new ethics. They need an ethics, but they cannot find any other ethics than an ethics founded on so-called scientific knowledge of what the self is, what desire is, what the unconscious is, and so on. I am struck by this similarity of problems.

Q: Do you think that the Greeks offer an attractive and plausible alternative?

M. F.: No! I am not looking for an alternative; you can't find the solution of a problem in the solution of another problem raised by another moment by other people. You see, what I want to do is not the history of solutions – and that's the reason why I don't accept the word *alternative*. I would like to do the genealogy of problems, of *problématiques*. My point is not that everything is bad, but that everything is dangerous, which is not exactly the same as bad. If everything is dangerous, then we always have something to do. So my position leads not to apathy but to a hyper- and pessimistic activity.

I think that the ethico-political choice we have to make every day is to determine which is the main danger. (Rabinow and Rose 2003: 104–5)

That last line expresses what I understand to be Foucault's version of phronesis: the capacity to make choices every day as to which is the *main* danger, because no course of action will ever be without danger. Solutions or alternatives offer the seductive possibility of delegating such choices to some ethical algorithm for choosing some truth. Subjects may have no sphere of unconstrained subjective action, they may live with truths that seek to govern them, but they can still choose, and therein lies freedom.

Foucault's perpetual struggle, most evident in his interviews and perhaps one reason he sought to express himself in that format, is his refusal to become the Law Giver that others press him to be, and, to be fair, that his own work sometimes seems to lead towards. When Dreyfus or Rabinow ask Foucault if the Greeks provide an alternative, that's a fair question following the problem that Foucault has just posed. To return to Hyde's 'rudderless intelligence' metaphor, Foucault offers his work as a guide to living lives that cannot be utterly rudderless, but the effects of steering with any particular rudder must always be interrogated.

Foucault may show us most about choosing among dangers in his 1983 interview, 'The Risks of Security', the latter term understood then as referring primarily to state health and social insurance benefits. Foucault is at pains not to deprecate the real need for such benefits, but he also wants to underscore their risks. The interview presents repeated instances of the need to make practical choices that balance need against risk.

'Our systems of social coverage impose a determined way of life that subjugates [*assujettit*] individuals,' Foucault says (2000: 369; brackets in original). 'As a result, all persons or groups who, for one reason or another, cannot or do not want to accede to this way of life find themselves marginalized by the very game of the institutions.' Therein lies the need for choice: to accept the benefit that subjugates or risk marginalization. Yet this expression of what seems almost a binary dilemma is too simple. Later, Foucault rejects what he calls 'a sort of Manicheism, afflicting the notion of state with a pejorative connotation at the same time as it idealizes society as something good, lively, and warm' (2000: 372). Foucault then reasserts that there is no existence outside relations of power: 'We evolve in a world of perpetual strategic relations' (2000: 372). The subject comes to be only in power relations that 'are not bad in and of themselves, but it is a fact that they always entail certain risks' (2000: 372).

Foucault concludes, when he is asked to summarize, by situating his ethics – such as they are – as the posing of questions: 'I would say that social security contributes to an ethic of the human person at least by posing a certain number of problems, and especially by posing the question about the value of life and the way in which we face up to death' (2000: 380). The value I find in such a response – which many readers might consider an evasion on Foucault's part – is that the social theorist refuses to be the subject who knows. Foucault affirms that people will choose, and history is a genealogy of different idealizations of what counts as choosing *well*. History is emphatically not a teleology of humanity aspiring towards some ultimate perfection always already set in place as its immanent goal and final resting place. 'If everything is dangerous, *then we always have something to do*,' Foucault affirms (Rabinow and Rose 2003: 104; quoted earlier, emphases added). That *something to do* is, at minimum, making choices about what is dangerous and also reading Foucault. Because in reading Foucault, we are shown how to think about what the main danger may be. If Foucault does not offer principles of choosing, his writing is full of examples of choices. Phronesis is tolerating the understanding of life and theory as projects-in-process – *there is always something to do* – and Foucault offers his work as potentially helpful in this project. Foucault has no aspiration to make decisions for us, but his writing can clarify the terms of what is at stake in our decisions. In Bourdieu's terms, our *illusio* becomes less a matter of accidents of birth and more an on-going problem that we become better equipped to work on, even if that work never ends.

Conclusion: theory and practical wisdom

The goal of theory as exemplified by Foucault and Bourdieu is not to provide a logically unified conceptualization of what society is and how it works. The theorist continues to struggle very much in the world, never above it. This location of struggle may be clearest in Bourdieu's emphasis on the limitations imposed by the scholastic disposition as structurally similar to other fields, which means having its own distinctive stakes and distribution of capital. Reflexive theory is not the opposite of making the self of the theorist the perceptual locus from which all else is made visible. Bourdieu makes that clear in his refusal to call his *Sketch for a Self-analysis* (2007) an autobiography. He writes about his life by situating it within the fields in which he found himself; his *self* is the possibility of choices delimited by those fields, conducted by a habitus with its characteristic *illusio*. Except, of course, Bourdieu's *illusio* was in many ways not characteristic if that means either predictable or rational, as he notes: 'But all these causes and reasons are not enough truly to explain my total, slightly crazed, investment in research' (2007: 69, quoted earlier).

To broaden what can explain his particular investment in the stakes of research, Bourdieu turns first to the activity itself – 'the enchanted, perfect world of science' (2007: 69) – and then to relationships with colleagues: 'my own belief producing in others the belief capable of re-inforcing and confirming my belief' (2007: 69). The crucial point is that phronesis is not an inherent quality of isolated individuals. Phronesis is always already relational or dialogical. Half of that relation is with a world that invites and resists consciousness; in Bourdieu's example, the activity of science is what it is in itself.[3] The other half of the relation comprises other people who reinforce and confirm Bourdieu's choices and investments, but who might at another moment discourage and disillusion him.

Phronesis, then, is much like power as imagined by Foucault. The subject comes to be through a series of occasions – most explicitly *confrontations* – requiring phronesis. In these confrontations, the subject uses knowledge to confront knowledge. Practical wisdom becomes visible only at moments of confrontation when something significant is at stake. The history of such moments guides future choices, less as specific precedents and more as gradual shifts in the feel for the game. But however rich any individual history may be, no self ever chooses by itself; all choices are expressions of relationships with the world and with other people.

The most developed phronesis guides action *before* the moment of choice, in the prior choices of which relationships and forms of capital to invest in with what degree of seriousness. If Nikolay Rostov's gambling suggests a lack of wisdom on his part, the significant moment of choice was not in putting down the final and unaffordable wager. The wager was only the inevitable product of prior choices to invest in those friendships and to go to a party where such wagers would be unavoidable. The young Nikolay lacks that feel for the game that would allow his anticipation of where to place himself with respect to profits to be gained or losses to be incurred. Through a series of other relationships, and by running up against the world when it is most resisting, in war, Nikolay increases in phronesis. Others approve his judgements, and he approves of himself. 'And long after he was dead and gone his rule was reverently preserved in folk memory. "What a master 'e was . . . Put the peasants first and himself second, 'e did. Didn't stand no nonsense neither. Right good master 'e was!"' (Tolstoy 2005: 1279).

REFERENCES

Berlin, Isaiah [1953] 1978. *The Hedgehog and the Fox: An Essay on Tolstoy's View of History*. Chicago, IL: Ivan R. Dee.
Bourdieu, Pierre 1990. *The Logic of Practice*. Stanford University Press.
  1998. *Practical Reason*. Stanford University Press.
  2000. *Pascalian Meditations*. Stanford University Press.

---

[3] Of course, never entirely in itself. Bourdieu remains enough of a phenomenologist that he would have agreed that the scientific world is 'perfect' only in its relational intentionality with his consciousness. But – and here phenomenology is not at all the purely subjective stance that it is sometimes mischaracterized to be – Bourdieu's consciousness is what it is only in relation to a world that exists outside that consciousness and resists it, even while always in relation to it.

2007. *Sketch for a Self-analysis*. University of Chicago Press.

Flyvbjerg, Bent 2001. *Making Social Science Matter: Why Social Inquiry Fails and How it can Succeed Again*. Cambridge University Press.

Foucault, Michel 1978. *Discipline and Punish*. New York: Vintage.

2000. *Power*. ed. James D. Faubion. New York: New Press.

Hardy, Cheryl 2008. 'Hysteresis', in M. Grenfell (ed.), *Pierre Bourdieu: Key Concepts*. Durham: Acumen Publishing, pp. 131–48.

Hyde, Michael 1998. *Trickster Makes This World*. New York: North Point Press.

Maton, Karl 2008. 'Habitus', in Michael Grenfell (ed.), *Pierre Bourdieu: Key Concepts*. Durham: Acumen Publishing, pp. 49–65.

Nealon, Jeffrey T. 2008. *Foucault beyond Foucault: Power and its Intensifications since 1984*. Stanford University Press.

Rabinow, Paul and Rose, Nikolas (eds.) 2003. *The Essential Foucault*. New York: New Press.

Swartz, David 1997. *Culture and Power: The Sociology of Pierre Bourdieu*. University of Chicago Press.

Thomson, Patricia 2008. 'Field', in Michael Grenfell (ed.), *Pierre Bourdieu: Key Concepts*. Durham: Acumen Publishing, pp. 67–81.

Tolstoy, Leo [1868–9] 2005. *War and Peace*, trans. Anthony Briggs. London: Penguin.

5   Phronesis, projects and power research

Stewart R. Clegg and Tyrone S. Pitsis

Introduction

This chapter will not be an account of hard research in the time hon-
oured way: big theory; general hypotheses; specific propositions; general
models; survey data collection; and sophisticated quantitative analysis.
Lest this sound like a caricature, let us note that hard political science
has been characterized by Kasza (2006) as a combination of quantitative
analysis and formal modelling and an omission of political philosophy.
Ranged against this, he argues, is something known in political science
circles in the United States as the Perestroika movement, which offers a
radical critique of hard science, for which Flyvbjerg's (2001) book has
become a beacon. We shall consider some of the issues that Kasza raises
in relation to the central topic of Flyvbjerg's (1998) work on power. In
recent years, much of this work has been conducted in collaboration
between the authors, looking at power and human relations in the context of megaproject alliances (Clegg *et al.* 2002; Pitsis *et al.* 2003; Pitsis,
Kornberger and Clegg 2004; van Marrewijk *et al.* 2008; Bjorkeng, Pitsis and Clegg 2009). Ontologically, we have to admit that few of these
papers, if any, were the working out of an *a priori* research design or
theory and that there was precious little rational choice involved, features
that characterize, as Kasza suggests, a 'hard science' model.[1]

---

[1] An opportunity presented itself to gain funding and do research and was seized. In accord
with Kasza's version of soft science, there were certainly personal politics involved. The
researchers were seduced by the prospect of an engagement with a commercially important organization. An Australian Government Commonwealth Grants scheme sought
to enrol academics in industry in order to mutually implicate academic knowledge and
organizational practices in industry. As such, it was a local instantiation of a more general
theory of knowledge: the Mode II model that Gibbons *et al.* (1994) had developed. In
Foucauldian terms, this model of how knowledge should be produced underscored
the research framework through which the mutual relation between the researchers
and the industry partner was consummated, albeit around an agenda that was more
a matter of convenience than conviction. The researchers' major strategic thrust was
to secure funding support, maintain good industry partner relations, and collect data

Research is as much a process of power as any other sphere of social life. In our experience social science research certainly is not a sphere characterized by the elegant theory-driven abstract rationalities of the hard science model. We do not believe this is because our experience indicates that we are particularly inept researchers. Nor do we believe that we became entangled in power relations almost from the outset of the project because we were operating in a field that is somehow pre-paradigmatic (as Dreyfus 1991 suggests) or post-paradigmatic (as Schram 2003 suggests). We agree with Flyvbjerg (2006: 64) that, in fact, social science is non-paradigmatic: there have clearly been periods when in specific fields it *appears as if* there is a dominant paradigm but, we would argue, the mechanisms of its maintenance are, above all, political: they have to do with sponsorship, enrolment, journal editorships and board composition, and nationality. Most prestigious journals are invariably dominated by North Americans who share much *habitus* in common, such as graduate school, training and cognitive maps of the field of production of knowledge.

Against Kasza (2006: 223–4), as researchers we have found that knowing intimate details of the lives of others is rare – and unnecessary. When we consider examples of phronetic work, such as Flyvbjerg's (1998) study of planning in Aalborg, its truth is not based on intimate personal knowledge, but on a narrative based on many thousands of hours, over many years, of dedicated empirical enquiry in official documents, media reports, unofficial enquiries, surveys and whatever sources of information could be accessed. And, no doubt, there were predilections, epistemologically, that were premised on an intimate knowledge of Foucault's work and the roots that sustained it.

---

and make interpretations that would result in inscriptions that might eventually be published – hopefully in those journals whose cover and title implied their truths were more forceful than many other journals. There were points of much intersection between the power games that were being played by the industry partner and the researchers.

Not all the power games were immediately evident. When the industry partner nominated two people to be seconded as researchers to the project we assumed that they were the individuals that the organization best considered likely to accomplish the research. Many years later, at a cocktail function, we learnt that this had been an erroneous impression. The industry partner was playing power games that were so subtle that we had not grasped them. The people they selected suited their convenience as a way of redeploying resources rather than filling the research needs. Such an outcome was a fairly blunt use of power as an instrument. We had been made power subjects, placed in a fairly onerous subject position, in order to resolve political issues in the partner organization.

Researching power

The research we did on power had a theoretical prehistory. Epistemologically, the major debates about power were rooted in a specific time period that unfolded from the 1950s onwards. For most of the twentieth century it was hard science models of power that dominated the literature and the research agenda. From the late 1920s the American Political Science Association had turned increasingly away from political philosophy in favour of a more behavioural and model-based conception of science. The epitome of the approach was to be found in several articles written by Robert Dahl, of which his 1957 article was probably most influential. In this article the analytical foundations of what Steven Lukes (1974) was to characterize as the one-dimensional view of power were laid. Power was to be regarded as an observable, causal mechanism, limited in scope to specific domains, and measurable through its effects on a directly coupled actor who was the recipient of precedent attempts to get them to do something about a specific issue of decision-making that they would not otherwise do.

In many ways the dominant model was an elegant account of ideas whose genesis was to be found in Hobbes' ([1651] 2007) *Leviathan*. It was not without its critics, as Bachrach and Baratz (1962) indicated when they developed what Lukes (1974) referred to as second-dimensional view of power in which agenda setting, limiting the scope of issues and refraining from action were brought into focus, arguing that power has two faces. One face concerns the outcomes of decisive battles between different actors over specific issues. The other face is more subtle, however. It concerns the 'mobilization of bias' (Schattschneider 1960: 71) that can result in 'non-decision-making'. Some things never make the political agenda; they are, either implicitly or explicitly, ruled out of bounds, hence, they are not raised. To adapt Haugaard's (2003: 94) terms, the existing elites do not collaborate in the reproduction of these new issues as phenomena to be taken seriously rather than ignored, disdained or dismissed. Only those issues that conform to the dominant myths, rituals and institutions of politics will be admitted. Hence, important issues that challenge these dominant ideas will not be heard. Their exclusion from consideration signals a neglected face of power. If analysis is restricted merely to those issues that elites sanction, we miss the power-shaping and restricting agendas, and we miss the way in which, anticipating the likely reaction to what are perceived to be contentious issues, these issues are never raised (Friedrich 1937).

Lukes' (1974) book, *Power: A Radical View*, was a major landmark in the conceptualization of power. It sought to bring what had hitherto been a largely liberal and individualist tradition of theorizing about power as a causal relation into a fruitful dialogue with broader traditions of thought. He shows that each dimension of power rests on a different set of moral assumptions: the one-dimensional view of power is premised on liberal assumptions; the two-dimensional view of power is premised on a reformist view; while it is the moral assumptions of radicalism that underlie the three-dimensional way of seeing power.

The *one-dimensional view of power* pivoted around an account of the different preferences that actors might hold and how these will be settled empirically. It concentrated on observable behaviour and concrete decisions that are expressed in overt conflict concerning specific issues, revealed in political participation. The *two-dimensional view* added some features to the primary view. It did not focus on just observable behaviour, but sought to make an interpretative understanding of the intentions that are seen to lie behind social actions. These come into play, especially, when choices are made concerning what agenda items are ruled in or ruled out; when it is determined that, strategically, for whatever reasons, some areas remain a zone of non-decision rather than decision. What is important is how some issues realize their potential to mature, while others do not; how some become manifest, while others remain latent. Given that an issue may remain latent then conflict is not merely overt; it may also be covert, as resentment simmers about something that has yet to surface publicly. One may address these two-dimensional phenomena not so much through discrete political participation as through express policy preferences embodied in subpolitical grievances.

From Lukes' point of view, the two-dimensional position is an improvement on that which is one-dimensional – but it could be improved further. Hence, he provides what he calls a *three-dimensional view* – a radical view to be contrasted with liberal and reformist views. While the previous views both define their field of analysis in terms of policy preferences, with the second dimension relating them to subpolitical grievances, the radical view relates policy preferences to real interests. Real interests are defined as something objective, as distinct from the interests that people think they have and express themselves as having through their preferences. He summarizes the distinctions that he is making in the following terms:

Extremely crudely, one might say that the liberal takes men as they are and applies want-regarding principles to them, relating their interests to what they actually want or prefer, to their policy preference as manifested by their political participation. The reformist, seeing and deploring that not all men's wants are given equal weight by the political system, also relates their interests to what they want or prefer, but allows that this may be revealed in more indirect and sub-political ways – in the form of deflected, submerged or concealed wants and preferences. The radical, however, maintains that men's wants may themselves be a product of a system which works against their interests, and in such cases, relates the latter to what they would want and prefer, were they able to make the choice. (Lukes 1974: 34)

With the three-dimensional view of power the concept has shifted into a radical interiority: it is tied up with what people find themselves able to articulate and say, what their consciousness, defined in terms of normal discourses and language, enables them to think and feel. In other words, what we have is a kind of negative account: rather than shaping consciousness positively, through discourse, radical theorists such as Lukes (1974) see power as prohibitory, negative and restrictive. If it were more radical it would have to be about what people are *able to articulate and say* and what *language enables them to think and feel*.

In the second edition of his book, Lukes (2006: 9) cites Przeworski (1985) approvingly to argue a slightly different tack: hegemony '*does not consist of individual states of mind but of behavioural characteristics of organizations*' (emphasis in original), noting that when wage-earners 'act as if they could improve their material conditions within the confines of capitalism' they are consenting to capitalism (Lukes 2006: 9, citing Przeworski 1985: 145–6). It is a long bow. If there is only one game in town then one has to play it. Lukes (2006: 10–11) also relates his position to that of Tilly (1991: 594) and, in so doing, shows that his fundamental views of 'real interests' have not changed in the intervening thirty years since he first wrote *Power: A Radical View*. In Tilly's (1991: 594) words, with which Lukes concurs, 'subordinates remain unaware of their true interests' because of 'mystification, repression, or the sheer unavailability of alternative ideological frames'. In Marxist terms, they suffer from false consciousness – an inability to realize their real interests.

To suggest that someone is in a state of false consciousness presupposes that there must be a correct or true consciousness as its counterpart, which is theoretically problematic (Haugaard 2003: 101). The theoretical consequences of a radical three-dimensional position might seem insignificant. Theoretically, some Marxist or feminist scholars might insist that the people about whom they theorize simply do not really know their own interests. The practical consequences can be considerably more serious, however. Theoretical positions that presume to know the real interests of others despite the views that others articulate are deeply dangerous, because they engage only with an abstract world of theory and do not engage with the material reality of those about whom they theorize.

In order to avoid these theoretical pitfalls, while still attempting to retain the essence of three-dimensional power, Haugaard (2003: 102) suggests that 'undermining power relations' may be 'a matter of facilitating individuals in converting their practical consciousness knowledge into discursive consciousness knowledge'. This is not a question of some enlightened theorist presenting subject actors with some external truth. Social life presupposes a large tacit knowledge of everyday life and in routine social interaction this knowledge remains practical consciousness. The moment of insight is that moment when what they *already know* in terms of their lived experience and their practical consciousness of it, that what is articulated discursively for them as an adequate and true account of this experience, is, in fact, false. It doesn't ring true. When this occurs people are facilitated in critically confronting their everyday social practices as part of a system of relations of domination, which are reproduced, with their complicity, through everyday interaction. Practical consciousness is a tacit knowledge that enables us to be competent and capable actors in our everyday lives, while discursive consciousness comprises knowledge that we can put into words. These two forms of knowledge are not entirely separate. The relative separateness of the two types of social knowledge is an important element in the maintenance of systemic stability. If practical consciousness has never been critically evaluated, never formed part of discursive consciousness, then it will be reproduced virtually as a reflex. Marx and Engels argued that for most people, lacking the critical education to see through the fancy words of political economy that held them captive, they could nonetheless grasp enough of them to know that their everyday life contradicted these words and, once they are provided with an alternative way of interpreting their reality, these intuitions become the departure for social critique.

As Haugaard (2003) argues the case, the radical feminist and the Marxist do not dispense true consciousness. However, they may make actors aware of aspects of their practical consciousness, knowledge that they have never previously confronted in a discursive fashion. In consequence, they can see things differently. There are parallels here with what Schutz (1967) refers to as 'shocks' or glimpses into alternative realities. Typically, such shocks are only temporary and have no pragmatic value, but sometimes shocks provide impetus for change as new social realities are opened up. Thus, social critique entails converting practical consciousness into discursive consciousness in a pragmatic way. Once knowledge of structural reproduction becomes discursive, actors may reject it or they might simply shrug and accept that this is how things are and there is little they can do to make them otherwise, or, of course, they may seek to change the situation. As such, it may become apparent that certain structural practices contribute to relations of domination and/or are inconsistent with other discursively held beliefs. What is useful about this approach to the matter of consciousness is that it accommodates arguments about the definition of the situation (Clegg, Courpasson and Phillips 2006: 216). On balance, as the adage has it, if people define situations as real they are real in their consequences, and while interlocutors may try to argue different definitions with different consequences, they rarely have any fulcrum outside the consciousness of the people whose definitions they are to do so. Theorizing Lukes' third-dimension of power in terms of a form of consciousness-raising through the conversion of practical consciousness knowledge into discursive consciousness knowledge is theoretically consistent and avoids the chief pitfalls of Lukes' analysis: that it requires the theorist to adopt a transcendent position.

Enter phronesis

> The strongest and most effective force in guaranteeing the long-term maintenance of power is not violence in all the forms deployed by the dominant to control the dominated, but consent in all the forms in which the dominated acquiesce in their own domination.
>
> Robert Frost, American poet

Inherent in Frost's words is the idea that domination and control maintain power through the unwitting self-subjugation of those dominated. We do not wish to imply that those who are being dominated are allowing themselves to be so because of some dysfunctional thought processes. We do believe, however, that Frost's idea reflects the idea that freedom from domination requires at least some level of reflexivity about one's role and place in the circuits of power. Phronesis is a pragmatic tool that allows one to both make sense of the study of power in organizations, and free one from an assumption that power is necessarily a bad thing, or necessarily about entrapment. To be sure, the position we have outlined thus far is entirely consistent with the agenda of phronesis as Flyvbjerg (2001) outlines it. Phronetic research focuses on many aspects: know-how (skill, art and competence), context and judgement, 'the particular', dialogue, incorporated knowledge and the narrative aspect. It is 'the narrative or storytelling aspect' that is more and more widespread. The phronetic and narrative approaches have been seen to be especially appropriate for analysis of power (Flyvbjerg 2001: ch. 10; Landman, Chapter 3, above).

What are the implications of phronesis for the analysis of power? Well, following Foucault, power should be seen as productive and positive, not merely as restrictive and negative; it should be seen not only in terms of sovereign centres of power, such as boardrooms or Cabinet offices, where on many occasions it may be said to reside; it should also be seen as constituted in dense networks and entanglements that comprise the normalcy of everyday life – what we may refer to as the governmental rationalities of specific situations (Clegg and Haugaard 2009). Thus, it is not really sufficient to analyse who has power without analysing how and why such attribution makes sense (Flyvbjerg 2006: 76). Power is not merely episodic, but also facilitative and dispositional; it moves through various circuits rather than being confined to a world of causality that seeks mimesis with that of hard science (Clegg 1989). Power is constitutive (Haugaard 1998): because it is constitutive it is irremediably wrapped up in what knowing counts as knowledge; counts as truth; counts as rationality. Such terms have meaning only in context and all contexts are marked by power relations, oftentimes entangling distinct contexts in reciprocal and similar circuits. Analytically, we should work from the specificities of contexts outwards rather than assume that those sovereign points that dominate the landscape are necessarily the loci of power. They may be – but we should work to them, not from them.

The narrative approach can be related to Geertz's (1973: 6) 'thick descriptions' when he writes that those facts 'that we call our data are really our own constructions of other people's constructions and what they and their compatriots are up to', something that 'is obscured because most of what we need to comprehend a particular event, ritual, custom, idea, or whatever is insinuated as background information before the thing is directly examined . . . ethnography is thick descriptions' (Geertz 1973: 9). Phronesis does not constitute a form of social enquiry that seeks to construct general causal law-like covering statements. It does enquire into the critical assessment of values, norms and structures of power and domination. Theoretical reasoning is not privileged over and above practical reasoning: we can only really grasp the nature of interests through deep involvement in practical contexts of everyday life and engagement in the dialogues that constitute these. The basis for grasping social reality is not so much the construction of elegant and internally coherent models of action, but an understanding that the social world has a historical and narrative structure: the one is understood through the other.

Flyvbjerg arrives at these conclusions, interestingly, without much consideration of the central one-, two- and three-dimensional debates. The crucial resources from power theory that he draws on come from the work of Michel Foucault. Foucault teaches us that, rather than being a resource that can be held or exercised – a capacity inanimate but potential – power is inseparable from its effects. The focus for analysis is the play of techniques, the mundane practices that shape everyday life, structuring particular forms of conduct and, more especially, structuring the ways in which people choose to fashion their own sense of self, their dispositions and those devices with which, through which, by which, they are shaped and framed:

A thoroughly heterogeneous ensemble consisting of discourses, institutions, architectural forms, regulatory decisions, laws, administrative measures, scientific statements, philosophical, moral and philanthropic propositions – in short, the said as much as the unsaid. Such are the elements of the apparatus [*dispositif*]. The apparatus itself is the system of relations that can be established between these elements. Secondly, what I am trying to identify in this apparatus is precisely the nature of the connection that can exist between these heterogeneous elements. Thus, a particular discourse can figure at one time as the programme of an institution, and at another it can function as a means of justifying or masking a practice which itself remains silent, or as a secondary re-interpretation of this practice, opening out for it a new field of rationality. In short, between these elements, whether discursive or non-discursive, there is a sort of interplay of shifts of position and modifications of function which can also vary very widely. Thirdly, I understand by the term 'apparatus' a sort of – shall we say – formation, which has as its major function at a given historical moment that of responding to an *urgent need*. The apparatus thus has a dominant strategic function. (Foucault 1979: 194–5, emphasis in original. See also Deleuze 1989: 157–8)

These are techniques of power insofar as they induce appropriate forms of conduct in those others whom they target. Hence, power is only visible in its effects. However, these effects are not at all mechanistically related to some initiating prime mover. Instead, technologies of the self work initially by inducing people to regulate their own behaviour and actions in accord with idealized representations that are institutionalized in specific contexts: the worker who strives for excellence; the manager who strives to be enterprising; the service worker who aims to leave every client delighted. This is only one of the three ways relations of power unfold. In the first unfolding, the subject is constituted as a particular body/soul in relation to others – an enterprising worker, for instance; second, the subject is constituted in relation to those social bodies or populations defined in relation to authoritative categorizations – the official employee of the month, for instance; in the third unfolding, the subject constitutes knowledge of itself, in relation to itself and in relation to others – the employee as coach and mentor (Ibarra-Colado 2001). These are rarely pure forms, but a complex mixture of articulations that, together, form specific local regimes of governmentality – how power is constituted locally in specific organization settings (Clegg *et al.* 2002).

Power produces its own truths – which is why, occasionally, epochal and seismic shifts occur, some more perceptible than others, in what is taken to be true: as power shifts, so do those truths held to be self-evident. The analytic interest is not in adjudicating between different truths – such an activity seems utterly pointless if one rejects the transcendent position; we should be more interested in the conditions of different truths' existence and possibility. The key element for the production of contemporary discourse is the understanding of current practices. When practices change, then there is an opportunity to re-produce (produce again and in a different way) that knowledge that characterizes them. In an immanent view, 'Power does not show itself because it is implicated in all that we are and all that we inhabit' (Allen 2003: 65). The immanent idea of power is not dependent on an analytical claim to omnipotence, to a pure form of knowledge that stands apart from and outside power, and which legislates on what power is and is not. At its core, Foucault's view of power seeks to dissolve any sense of some privileged and transcendent position from which the truth of power is visible. Such positions, he argues, can only ever be constituted within specific discursive practices. Within some institutionalized forms of these, some representations will achieve dominance: for instance, power may be registered as an overwhelmingly mechanical and causal relation between people who possess differential access to differential resources. What one might say is that, discursively, some representations of the world, which of necessity have a historical specificity (ways of seeing the world are always diachronically shifting and contested language games) become fixed in usage, are normalized, become the common currency of thought and conceptualization. Specific discursive practices become institutionalized and thus have common currency among other discursive practices, even as they are resisted. Discourses are always in permanent dispute; there is no meta-discourse of/for everyday life. The tactical polyvalence of discourses indicates the unstable, contingent articulation between knowledge and power in discourses, marking possible displacements and re-utilizations (Foucault 1980: 98–102; Ibarra-Colado 2001); they denote the possibilities of appropriation of some discourses (the discourses of the opposition, for example), changing their meaning. Some discourses may become temporally and temporarily ontologized; that is, taken for granted as a necessary aspect of (thinking about) being. Hence, part of the task of analysis is to provide a history of the present: how are the ways of thinking and conceptualizing the world that have become normalized possible? What are the grounds of what passes for reason in any given epoch? And what concordance and dissonance does this buried history prepare? These are questions raised by Foucault. Foucault's analysis of the 'present' refers to 'modernity', the present within which we produce our existence as 'modern subjects', a production about which we need to become reflexive, by asking what actor networks sustain the truths that maintain specific elements of this modernity?

Allen (2003) notes that different modalities may be engaged in the construction of complex actor networks; they may be networks of domination; they may achieve legitimacy and be accorded authority; they may eschew the necessity for authority and seek to operate wholly through coercion, be induced to do something, perhaps through fear of the alternatives or expectation of the rewards, or they might seek to manipulate or seduce the other. When manipulated the others are misled; when seduced, they are intrigued, sensually involved and emotionally ready to be compromised. There is thus great freedom in contemporary forms of power: our present is a complex reality with a large and varied set of materials and technologies to constitute individuals, a relational palette with plenty of options for composition. While all these may be examples of power, they are also examples of different modalities.

Power is not a force that intrudes on a stable situation from the outside so much as a way of talking about the structuring of social action in normal ways (Falzon 1998; Heiskala 2001). The general idea is that rather than power being something exercised between two or more conflicting combatants or adversaries divided over some issue, one to the other, it is 'more a question of ongoing and active structuring of the possible field of action of the others – a process that is always open to resistance, transformation and renegotiation', as Peltonen and Tikkanen (2005: 275) put it. From this perspective, the common view of power as a negative phenomenon can be relaxed.

Power and wisdom at work

Construction projects are not necessarily places in which good ends routinely occur (Kasza 2006: 225). As Flyvbjerg, Bruzelius and Rothengatter (2003) argue, nine out of ten construction projects do not come in on time or budget – indeed, in the most spectacular case, that of the Sydney Opera House, the actual budget was at variance by 1,000 per cent in terms of the projected cost. Our experience has been fortunate, however; we have had the inestimably valuable experience of working on two major projects that have been occasions in which good ends routinely occurred. We would argue that this was not merely a matter of luck, but of specific and unusual but well thought-out modalities of power being instituted in these projects.

Typically, power relations in construction projects afford an opportunity to see a governmental combination of fiction and testing at work. The fictional element is expressed in the normal mode of contracting on a competitive tendering basis. The fiction here is that the lowest price tendered actually bears some relationship to the costs that the project will finally incur. First, it is noticeable that this can hardly be the case, given the findings of Flyvbjerg, Bruzelius and Rothengatter (2003) that 90 per cent of megaprojects exceed times and cost specifications so dramatically (see also van Marrewijk *et al.* 2008). More to the point, why do they do so?

Earlier studies have established the important indexical role played by contractual documents in the construction context, specifically the role of the competitively tendered contract. The types of behaviour and commitments that are needed to win a tender are quite distinct from those typically used to deliver it. For the former, when in public competition to win a tender, it is the least costly bid that wins, all other things being equal. However, as Clegg (1975) demonstrated, the delivery of the contract is situationally contingent on the ability for the contractual and associated documents to be indexed when interpreted by self-interested and highly skilled actors such as project managers, clients' architects and so on. All such documents have to be interpreted, and have to be related to each other, even when they are the product of many diverse hands, skills and contractors. The key power relations in delivering on a contract in the construction phase relate to making certain indexical interpretations stick, those favouring one's side of the contractual relations, against those of others engaged in the process. This applies in relations between head contractor and subcontractors, between project managers and clients, as well as between management and labour. Typically, these are negative power and zero sum relations: I win, you lose. In such a context, if it appears that a losing hand has been dealt, interpretively, the rational actor will proceed to a testing game, organized either through arbitration or other juridical devices, where the outcome of contested claims is the outcome of conflict: 'lawyers at ten paces', as we have heard it called. The establishment of judicial truth regarding contested claims is always a matter of assigning responsibility for judgements made. As in other battles, the outcomes often relate more to who is strongest in terms of legal resources (expert barristers and deep pockets), rather than the truth of the competing claims about the matters at hand. The procedure is one that constitutes truth about contests through the event of the competing claims being heard and decided. It 'can only be brought about at a specific moment, in a given location, by determined actors' (Macmillan 2009: 160). These specify not a method for producing truth so much as enforceable interpretations whose veracity owes much to power relations. It is for this reason that so many construction projects are riven by conflict and appear to be marked by ambiguity and miscommunication; however, it should be evident that the latter are only apparent causes of the former. In fact, the appearance of miscommunication, ambiguity and conflict are skilfully produced performances situated to extract additional value over and above whatever has been formally contracted.

In the contracts that we have investigated the contractual form of making alliances displaces the power of indexical interpretation, contest and conflict away from contractual documentations *per se*, and on to features much more integral to the construction process. If, in the competitively tendered contract, the politics are oriented towards seeking to impose a particular disciplinary reading of the contractual documents, such as the architects over the project managers, the engineering subcontractors over the project managers and so on, under alliancing the politics shift from being largely disciplinary, interorganizational and contestable to a more positive mode. What is crucial to making alliances and their delivery is the power of the norm 'and the particular way in which knowledge that revolves around the virtual – instead of actual facts – is produced' (Macmillan 2009: 158).

These virtual facts are produced through key performance indicators, which create 'a field of objects on which power will be able to intervene in order to control production' (Macmillan 2009: 158). Key performance indicators construct specific forms of knowledge as a strategic ideal: if performance on a project always accorded with the strategic ideal the project would always rate 100 per cent on any performance indicator. Rarely will this be the case, however. The point of the performance norms is to create virtual objects around which reality can be related normatively, in terms of the distribution of outcomes according to measures that can be represented in terms of means and standard distributions around the virtual norm. What the key performance indicators do is to construct a series of virtual realities represented in the norms that are actually recorded around those measures constructed. The measures construct the environment of the project, one in which community, safety or environment, as well as costs and schedule, can be talked into being. They take on a life independent of the project through their projection and measurement of behaviour in accord with these projections. The point is not to make behaviours accord with some pre-established norm, such as those that might be specified in a quantity survey, but to start from the given state of affairs in the project as seen through the key performance indicators. These constitute the norms as the average of the performance measured. Such a politics of power does not require exhaustive and continuous control of the particulars of the project in its minute execution. On the contrary, all that is required is the registering of an actual range of performances, its inspection in terms of the norms established, and the communication of these norms to those whose performance is being reg-ulated so that they may maintain the targets or try harder, as the case may be. Aligning the final project averages with a 'risk and reward' scheme in which all parties to the contract are implicated does the rest: there is an evident self-interest in registering outstanding performances across the board. To ensure that this is the case the specific key performance indicators are made non-negotiable with each other: each establishes its own norm and it is only outstanding performance across all norms that will generate rewards. The regulation of behaviour is achieved through an increasing appeal to norms and not disciplines, *per se*.

In such a system, the most important criteria for managing power rela-tions positively are the actual measures used, since the tendency will be for on-site managers to manage the measures, because reward is related to establishing high performance-related norms. A great deal of care thus has to go into the construction of the measures, which, ideally, should be constructed from a broad-based perception of who the stakeholders are in any project. These can include, for example, government or one of its agencies as the client, an array of specialist service contractors com-prising the alliance, and contexts valuing diverse phenomena, such as the environment, occupational health and safety, and community satis-faction. Indeed, both the major projects we have studied have excelled in most of these key performance indicators.

The power of value

> Wherever the relevance of speech is at stake, matters become political
> by definition, for speech is what makes man a political being.
>
> Hannah Arendt (1958)

One might assume that excellent outcomes in major projects delivered between public and private partners would be a welcome change from the conflict-ridden and underperforming traditional mode of competitive contractual arrangements. Indeed, it is established that alliances, in cer-tain forms, offer innovation in managerial and organizational practices that enable organizations to operate in highly uncertain and complex environments (Huxham and Vangen 2004; Josserand *et al.* 2005; Pitsis 2007; van Marrewijk *et al.* 2008; Bjorkeng *et al.* 2009). While there are a number of reasons as to why organizations choose to engage in alliances, for instance, where organizations come together because each organiza-tion provides complementary and much needed skills, knowledge and resources currently unavailable to individual parent organizations, it is uncertainty that is the driving-force behind alliances. Often alliance projects are significant in scope and size, and are typically delivered as collaborations between public–private organizations in highly uncertain and complex contexts. Increasingly, such alliances are referred to as megaprojects to denote their scale, complexity and cost (van Marrewijk *et al.* 2008). Flyvbjerg and his colleagues (2003) consider megaprojects a particularly risky form of venture for those agencies whose capital is at stake. Politically, authorities and contractors are only too willing to fudge the figures in order to secure the contract, because contractors are confident that they can claw back any losses or discrepancies later.

Recent economic events have motivated political leaders globally to respond through large-scale macro-economic policy initiatives, including the allocation of several billions of dollars towards public infrastructure programmes. The motives for doing so are often to off-load debt from public accounts in order to ensure that these accounts appear more credible to ratings agencies than might otherwise be the case. One effect is that public management have progressively stripped themselves of the capabilities for design and construction that were once a generic part of their structural repertoire. Instead, these are contracted out to the private sector. As such, public–private megaprojects will increasingly become the norm rather than the exception.

Notwithstanding the growth of megaproject alliances, there is a growing body of research and theory that is concerned with the issue of 'value' in public–private partnerships (Bovaird 2004; Hogget 2006; Weber and Khademian 2008). The issue of *value* in megaproject alliances is a fruitful and important area for debate, theory and research, and so it is to value we wish to focus our gaze – specifically our role as researchers studying organizations where the idea and demonstration of value is implicated in the idea of phronesis, especially in Aristotelian terms. Value in many senses of the word refers to the end state or the result of 'good action' that has a sense of value to society (Aristotle 1934). In this case we take 'value' to mean both 'the public value' in terms of Moore's (1995) idea of public value as improved government as an asset to society, and also to the value that is accrued to individuals, groups and societies from the delivery of services, infrastructure and so on. While the notion of value has been typically dominated by economic value, theory and research on value in megaprojects has slowly permeated into administrative sciences, and more recently management and organization studies – as such the understanding and sense-making around value is changing to include less conventional, functional notions of value, such as 'community benefit, sustainability, legacy, process innovation' (van Gestal *et al.* 2008).

One cannot speak of phronesis without its relative concept of *poiesis*, which Aristotle conceptualized as having an end other than of itself.

Earlier we argued that phronesis enquires into the critical assessment of values, norms and structures of power and domination, and an understanding that the social world has a historical and narrative structure. Power is not only restricted to boardrooms and in the upper echelons of organizations, but also in the tapestry of networks, human relations that exist in organizations. In power research, the intended actions and interactions we study in the production of good value (phronesis) will often produce something that might not be interpreted or experienced as 'value' (poiesis). Researching power not only has implications for the organizations, groups and individuals under investigation, but those doing the research are also subject to the values, norms and structures of power and domination; in both positive and negative ways. It would be ludicrous to assume that we, as researchers, can operate or exist outside the system we are trying to make sense of. We are all, as Clegg (1989) states, enmeshed in circuits of power.

To elaborate further and clarify the points we are making we will now introduce a vignette (or more precisely a collection of integrated vignettes) that we believe important for a number of reasons. First, they illuminate the subtlety of power in organizational life through a phronetic/narrative approach. Second, they show how being a phronetic researcher requires one to be more cognizant of the power political implications inherent in researching 'real-life' organizations, which both problematize the life of researchers, while also being a generative process. Before we consider the vignette, it is appropriate to provide a brief background to the research.

Background

From 2003 until 2009, we studied a megaproject alliance between a major public and several private organizations, which we shall call 'The Programme Alliance' (PA). We were funded under an Australian Research Council (ARC) scheme known as the Linkage Grant, whereby an industry partner and a research team conjointly develop a project and the ARC funds it on the basis of matching contributions in-cash and in-kind from the industry partner. It should be made clear that the scheme is not intended to support consultancy and the project had no elements of consultancy about it. The PA was designed to deliver upgrades to the sewerage system across the outer greater Sydney region (an approximate radius of 80 km) through seven distinct projects. The original aim of our research project, after negotiation with our industry partners, was to make sense of the learning and process improvement that occurs across and between consecutive projects. The alliance evolved out of a previous project which ran from 1999 to 2001, the North Side Tunnel Project Alliance (NSTP) (see Clegg *et al.* 2002; Pitsis *et al.* 2003; Pitsis, Kornberger and Clegg 2004), on which we were involved as researchers funded by the Australian Government through the ARC Discovery grant scheme (which, unlike Linkage grants, do not involve partner support). The leaders of that NSTP had invited us to continue our research and so we applied for and were awarded another ARC grant. As with the NSTP, the PA was governed by an alliance leadership team (ALT) that sanctioned decisions and provided guidance, governance and leadership. The alliance management team (AMT) managed the pragmatic day-to-day operations of the PA. The ALT and the AMT oversaw all seven original projects, as well as all subsequent projects.

Value for money?

Towards the latter part of our research into the PA, we were asked to no longer attend meetings because, we were advised, some very sensitive issues were going to be dealt with; once these were dealt with, we could rejoin the leadership team. It was also felt that the alliance members had been surveyed to death by us as researchers, by consultants who had been engaged and even by internal auditors, so it would be good to stay away for a while in order to give people a break. We did as we were asked, but during that time a number of the leadership team left, including successive programme managers. About six months later the team was asked to sign-off on some university research they were funding – at which point the current members of the team, with little continuity with those with whom we first negotiated and liaised, having no idea what this research was, who was doing it and what the point of it was, quite reasonably asked what our purpose was and why the university and ARC were asking them to support us.

We received a phone call to meet with the team; however, before that meeting Tyrone arranged to see a couple of people within the client organization. It was an uncomfortable conversation: 'we have these invoices, and we have not really gotten any value from this research'. Tyrone's nervous response was, 'well, we have given several feedback workshops, and helped you refine your key performance indicators in a full-day workshop, and we have some research papers on the project here for you to read and comment on'. The public organization middle manager, one that we did not recognize, replied, 'Well, I don't know, but my view on research is it's a waste of time.' It is difficult to respond to a statement such as this, so Tyrone asked, 'well, what would be of value?', his response was something to the effect of 'that's not for me to decide, it's the alliance team'.

Three days later, we met with the alliance team and we explained what we were doing, why we were doing it, explained how we were asked to stay away, and that obviously due to no one's fault we assumed the data collection part of the research was over. The team discussed and then decided that it would 'still be of value' for us to research their project, but added that what they were really interested in was its value, 'there are some within the client organization that are not convinced of the value for money that this alliance is providing', so they decided that it would be good to know how the alliance is perceived in relation to creating value and, more importantly, whether the value they are adding is important or even relevant to the key power players in the client organization. In one short conversation the entire aims and intentions of our research was transformed from a study on alliance learning to one on alliance value-creation and sense-making.

There is an important lesson about research, project and power relations here. Research is a slow process and the creation of academic materials, such as research papers, especially in a form that passes through the review process of top-tier journals, takes considerable time. It is also conducted in the interstices of busy professional careers centred on publication, teaching, conferences and students. Researchers are occasional visitors and observers of most of the scenes that they research; very occasional if survey researchers, less occasional if they are phronetic researchers. One advantage of using a survey instrument, of course, is that you do not get noticed so easily as a presence and thus do not build potentially political relations with those being studied.

Where those being researched are a complex formal organization, then their enrolment is critical for maintaining access. While complex formal organizations are never marked by stasis, they are often as pools of tranquillity when compared with complex project organizations where people cycle in and out of different positions with great frequency. Project life in construction is essentially mobile and peripatetic for senior project managers, especially in times of a booming resource-based economy where there are many attractive project management options available. On this project none of the people, bar one (who at the time in question was absent with a serious medical condition), with whom we had initially formulated and contracted the project still remained on the project. Putting this together with the fact that we had been 'warned off' the project for a lengthy period, social relations were broken and power relations were frayed in consequence.

Doing phronetic research necessarily entails a power relation between researchers and researched. Essentially, as researchers we were relatively weak in terms of power relations: we needed access and could not guarantee it; only the project leaders could do that and as they had changed we were not a part of their sense-making of the project. Meanwhile, as the request to shift our focus to the value of alliance projects suggested, the broader power relations were changing as well. The lead organization had a new CEO who, while positive and supportive of the early achievements of the alliance, was very sceptical about the value of alliance projects. When we started the research alliance projects were seen as very much 'flavour of the month' by the senior executives and the state government to whom they reported: this was no longer so certain. There had been several well-publicized cases of such projects that on delivery had failed to live up to the projected value that had been embedded in them to get the projects authorized. Of course, Flyvbjerg and his colleagues (2003) would not be surprised. Value projections seem so often to be inflated as to be normal. Hence, being asked to switch focus was hardly negotiable: we felt that we either did that or the research would not be supported. Researchers, even if they are well-respected academics in their field, are relatively powerless compared with the gatekeepers of the organizations they research. When these organizations are project-based organizations, for all the reasons outlined, these issues are amplified.

We were redirected, and we had to accept our new direction even though it meant we would have difficulty reporting to the ARC on what we were doing. So, off we went, designed new interview schedules, and made appointments to interview some of the key power players and decision-makers in the organization. Despite what had seemed initially as if it were hostility from the new managers on the project – which later we could reinterpret as anxiety and uncertainty – we found that our path to the senior portals of power was not rough. All of the senior people proved to be surprisingly accessible – including the CEO and other very senior executives. We explored their understanding and sense-making of value at the personal level, at the organizational level and beyond. We explored how they judged value, what they expect and what needs to be demonstrated. We analysed our data, designed our workshop and delivered our findings, which were as follows:

(1) The value the alliance is adding is perceived as important, but it is also a 'Minimum Condition of Satisfaction'. In other words, it is an expectation, not something that differentiates the alliance from any other mode of organizing. As such, it would need to perform some amazing feats to be perceived as a standout.

(2) Some of the most senior people, including the CEO, believed the particular alliance should cease operating because, while it definitely added value in terms of the original seven projects, it no longer added value in terms of 'public good, safety and environment' – in fact, it

was perceived as a tool being used by politicians to sway the vote in marginal electorates more so than being primarily a programme designed to deliver value.

The first finding was not too surprising, even though the PA had achieved some exceptional results in terms of innovations in process and practice, outstanding results in terms of connecting customers, award-winning project management in highly uncertain and ambiguous environments, significant project success in terms of budget, schedule, safety, community and environmental outcomes. The reason this finding was not surprising to us is that the client organization had spent a great deal of time and effort in learning from other alliance projects over the past fourteen years. Thus, many of the benefits of making alliances were captured and integrated within how the organization collaborated with other organizations, and in identifying the value they expected. The result, however, was that if the value being added was beyond that expected, where these expectations had been shaped progressively by the added value of prior projects, it was not 'of value'.

The second point, however, in the phenomenological sense of the word, was a shock for members of the alliance as professional practitioners. As stated earlier, Schutz (1967) conceives of shocks as momentary glimpses into an alternative reality, where our taken-for-granted assumptions and ideas are disturbed. These shocks are an ideal moment for reflexivity because they can serve as nodal points that enable learning, questioning and re-evaluating one's position. The shock uncovered the reality that in the end organizational life is all about power: be it power over, power to or power with. While we were not surprised to find that this was the case, having invested a great deal of writing in support of that proposition, its starkness was a major blot on the cognitive landscape of the project professionals for whom pride in the project was paramount, and, indeed, they had much to be proud of in terms of safety, innovation, community building, and so on. The reality here was that, irrespective of its history, and its present, in generating and demonstrating value, if those in the most powerful relations of power perceive you as an instrument of power and politics, your value, and values, will be negated. Under such conditions it is probably prudent to ensure that values are aligned: that is, that those in power, and those who use you as a tool of power are aligned in their interests, for what we know is that it is power and interest that dominates rationality in sense-making (Flyvbjerg 1998; Flyvbjerg, Bruzelius and Rothengatter 2003). Indeed, in such cases power determines rationality.

All of this prudence in the face of power flies in the face of both formal professional and managerial rhetoric. There the stress is on people being empowered to do their best with the resources available to them; there is little discussion of the need to compromise value and values in the face of power.

Back to phronesis

In the natural science model of social research one would not consider adapting one's approach to incorporate the structures and systems of power underpinning the possibilities of research. Yet if we had not done so there would have been no further research, and no further access. Moments of shock from those being researched, rather than destroying projects and relationships, caused us to question 'where we are going with our research, what power relations are relevant as we do our research, and what practical actions are required for us to do our research'. The vignette above describes a very pragmatic response to events that occur in social science research projects that echo, if not amplify, Flyvbjerg's contributions to the phronetic debate (2001).

From the vignette, it is important for us to revisit the mid-level manager who claimed that research was a waste of time. The man was no fool, he had thirty years of experience and was highly pragmatic and the guy was honest by his own lights, but he also typifies one of the challenges researchers can face in the Australian research environment. Australian managers, when compared globally, are not as academically curious as their Danish, German or Swiss counterparts. They are extremely unlikely to have postgraduate qualifications, and PhDs are as rare as hen's teeth. Typically in Australian industry innovation lags, investment in R&D lags, as does the academic skill-formation of managers (Green 2009). Viewed from a position where a lack of familiarity with research is fairly normal, then speaking ill of that with which one is not overly familiar might not seem surprising.

The manager in question may be correct: perhaps research is a waste of time, but our experience and record of research collaboration with industry suggests otherwise. Nonetheless, the reality facing us was one in which research scepticism about the question of what value we are adding to the industry partner through this research could be articulated relatively easily and without relation to any contractual relations entered into in the project's name by people long since gone from the project. Enveloped within such a question is the idea that the role of the researcher is to add value to industry, which is an important issue considering that the current funding structures and arrangements within universities necessitate industry research collaboration. Implicitly, there is a midwife view of research: the researcher, working in conjunction with the partner(s) will deliver value.

On the one hand, there is the question of what value is inherent in university research and in the taken-for-granted assumptions of how research is conducted by academics. On the other hand, there is the commercial value of the research to industry. As we pointed out earlier, researching organizations implicates the researcher in multiple levels of power relations. The study of alliances are further complicated because the multiple actors, from an array of organizations, both exacerbate and mask the inherent and complex power relations. Without sounding overly dramatic, our situation was further complicated in that not only were we studying multiple organizations trying to work together, we were also studying a combination of private and public organizations. Concomitant with the public organizations is *government* and all that that entails; particularly in relation to the demonstration of public and private value relative to project execution and realization through public–private relationships.

There is a subsequent layer of complexity in research with partners such as ours that complicates the role, identity and even the well-being of researchers that is a reality irrespective of whatever type of research the researcher does. In government–industry funded university research, there are multitudes of masters underpinning the performativity of the academic researchers. Industry, be it public or private, has a distinct sense of what 'valuable' research means.

We have learnt some lessons from our career as project researchers. Our experience suggests that funding research is a way for industry to make sense of what they are doing. When we do this then our terms for making sense get to be adopted by the industry partners. It is this recursive relation that validates social science. Essentially, what most project managers want to hear is that they can do better in a couple of areas, but all in all they are doing OK. Governments also have expectations: they want to know that taxpayers' money spent on research is demonstrating value for money, and power research is seldom seen as valuable because it cannot be quantified, it questions taken-for-granted assumptions and realities within organizations, and, even where it occurs as an unanticipated consequence of the turn that project power relations take, enquiry into power relations is not seen as an integral part of progressing society economically or socially. Power relations, much as the furniture, are too often taken for granted and there are many for whom the lack of problematicity is just fine. As such, questions of power relations must be covertly rather than overtly stated.

Government want neat packages of research outcomes and policymakers tend to deal almost exclusively with hard, evidence-based, usually quantitative, data. At the same time, government imposes measures of 'quality' upon university research and researchers. In terms of the ERA in Australia, the Research Assessment Exercise (RAE) in the United Kingdom,[2] and all the like-minded policies anywhere else in the world, the 'good' academic researcher publishes in top journals, does research, makes an 'impact' and attains research grants. It is a game that we know how to play, but, as with all games, there are rules. The institutional environment for research today demonstrates that there is a further power consideration at play: 'normal science' is increasingly being normalized and intensified as a result of journal-ranking exercises associated with national research evaluations. A limited range of journals, mostly those most accepting of normal science orthodoxy, are valorized; hence, not only is power research itself less than encouraged, but if you are studying power using other than dominant approaches and methods – surveys, resource-dependence theory, exchange theory – if you are using approaches such as phronesis, for example, the chances of acceptance will not be as great. Of course, the situation is never hopeless and resistance can change the circuitry of power – moves such as ensuring that phronesis was included in the second edition of *The Handbook of Organization Studies* (Flyvbjerg 2006) for instance, do a lot to position the legitimacy of the approach in the gaze of the institutionalized field.

Added to the mixture of industry and government, when we add in university expectations, we can uncover another layer of complexity. The rhetoric of universities is that all research is valued and academic promotion is assumed to be based on merit demonstrated through publication in peer-reviewed journals and outlets. Output rather than process is king. Phronesis is about process, yet little concern is shown with process beyond assessing the level of the individual researcher. Every researcher, especially field researchers in the social sciences, exists within the fabric of the broader social system within which they practise their craft. The upshot is that all the aspects of doing qualitative research discussed in this chapter should never be seen in isolation from political realities and analysis. The organizational structures, the funding mechanisms, the power/political games, and the support systems and frameworks that enable good research to be done cannot just be taken for granted or passed over in silence. In the laboratory or the library these may not seem evident issues: in the field they certainly are. We were lucky – we managed to get our feet back in the door by bending to the will of others and, doing other than that which we had intended to do, we maintained

---

[2] This is now called the Research Excellence Framework and will assess the research quality and impact for all disciplines across all qualified 'units of assessment' (UoA) in 2013–14.

social and power relations and thus were able to complete our project. Yet the pitfalls we encountered are common in our experience of the research process – so how come we read about them so infrequently?

REFERENCES

Allen, J. 2003. *Lost Geographies of Power*. New Malden, MA: Blackwell.

Arendt, H. 1958. *The Human Condition*. University of Chicago Press, p. 3.

Aristotle 1934. *Nicomachean Ethics*, trans. H. Rackham. Cambridge, MA: Harvard University Press.

Bachrach, P. and Baratz, M. S. 1962. 'Two Faces of Power', *American Political Science Review* 56(4): 947–52.

Bjorkeng, K., Pitsis, T. S. and Clegg, S. R. 2009. 'Becoming a Practice: The Act of Project-based Interorganizational Management', *Management Learning* 40(2): 145–59.

Bovaird, T. 2004. 'Public–Private Partnerships: From Contested Concepts to Prevalent Practice', *International Review of Administrative Sciences* 70(2): 199–215.

Clegg, S. R. 1975. *Power, Rule and Domination*. London: Routledge.

    1989. *Frameworks of Power*. London: Sage.

Clegg, S. R. and Haugaard, M. 2009. *The Sage Handbook of Power*. London: Sage.

Clegg, S. R., Courpasson, D. and Phillips, N. 2006. *Power and Organizations*. London: Sage.

Clegg, S. R., Pitsis, T., Rura-Polley, T. and Marosszeky, M. 2002. 'Governmentality Matters: Designing an Alliance Culture of Inter-organizational Collaboration for Managing Projects', *Organization Studies* 23(3): 317–37.

Dahl, R. A. 1957. 'The Concept of Power', *Behavioral Scientist* 2(3): 201–15.

Deleuze, G. 1989. 'What is a Dispositif?', in T. J. Armstrong (ed.), *Michel Foucault, Philosopher*. London: Routledge, pp. 159–68.

Dreyfus, H. 1991. 'Defending the Difference: The Geistes/Naturwissenschaften Distinction Revisited', in *Akademie der Wissenschaften zu Berlin, , Internationale Kolloquium der Akademie der Wissenschaften zu Berlin, Bonn, 25–27 June 1990*. Berlin: Walter de Gruyter.

Falzon, C. 1998. *Foucault and Social Dialogue: Beyond Fragmentation*. London: Routledge.

Flyvbjerg, B. 1998. *Rationality and Power: Democracy in Practice*. University of Chicago Press.

    2001. *Making Social Science Matter: Why Social Inquiry Fails and How it can Succeed Again*. Cambridge University Press.

    2006. 'Making Organization Research Matter: Power, Values, and Phronesis', in S. R. Clegg, C. Hardy, T. B. Lawrence and W. R. Nord (eds.), *The Sage Handbook of Organization Studies*, 2nd edn. Thousand Oaks, CA: Sage, pp. 370–87.

Flyvbjerg, B., Bruzelius, N. and Rothengatter, W. 2003. *Megaprojects and Risk: An Anatomy of Ambition*. Cambridge University Press.

Foucault, M. 1979. *Discipline and Punish*. Harmondsworth: Penguin.

1980. *Power/Knowledge: Selected Interviews and Other Writings 1972–1977*, ed. C. Gordon. New York: Pantheon Books.

Friedrich, C. 1937. *An Introduction to Political Theory*. New York: Harper.

Geertz, C. 1973. 'Thick Description: Toward an Interpretive Theory of Culture', in *The Interpretation of Cultures: Selected Essays*. New York: Basic Books.

Gibbons, M., Limoges, C., Nowotny, H., Schwartzman, S., Scott, P. and Trow, M. 1994. *The New Production of Knowledge: The Dynamics of Science and Research in Contemporary Societies*. London: Sage.

Green, R. 2009. 'Innovation Capability in the Economy and Workplace', Presentation to the Training & Skills Commission, Adelaide, 17 June.

Haugaard, M. 1998. *The Constitution of Power: A Theoretical Analysis of Power, Knowledge and Structure*. Manchester University Press.

2003. 'Reflections on Seven Ways of Creating Power', *European Journal of Social Theory* 6(1): 87–113.

Heiskala, R. 2001. 'Theorizing Power: Weber, Parsons, Foucault and Neostructuralism', *Social Science Information* 40(2): 241–64.

Hobbes, T. [1651] 2007. *Leviathan*, available at: http://ebooks.adelaide.edu.au/h/hobbes/thomas/h68l.

Hoggett, P. 2006. 'Conflict, Ambivalence, and the Contested Purpose of Public Organizations', *Human Relations* 59(2): 175–94.

Huxham, C. and Vangen, S. 2004. 'Doing Things Collaboratively: Realizing the Advantage or Succumbing to Inertia?', *Organizational Dynamics* 33(2): 190–201.

Ibarra-Colado, E. 2001. 'Considering "New Formulas" for a "Renewed University": The Mexican Experience', *Organization* 8(2): 203–17.

Josserand, E., Clegg, S. R., Kornberger, M. M. and Pitsis, T. S. 2004. 'Friends or Foes? Practicing Collaboration – An Introduction', *Management* 7(3): 37–45.

Kasza, G. J. 2006. 'Unearthing the Roots of Hard Science: A Program for Graduate Students', in S. Schram and B. Caterino (eds.), *Making Political Science Matter: Debating Knowledge, Research, and Method*. New York University Press.

Lukes, S. 1974. *Power: A Radical View*. London: Macmillan.

2006. *Power: A Radical View*, 2nd edn. London: Palgrave Macmillan.

Macmillan, A. 2009. 'Foucault and the Examination: A Reading of "Truth and Judicial Forms"', *The Journal of Power* 2(1): 55–172.

Moore, M. H. 1995. *Creating Public Value Strategic Management in Government*. Cambridge, MA: Harvard University Press.

Peltonen, T. and Tikkanen, H. 2005. 'Productive Power, Organized Markets and Actor–Network Theory', in B. Czarniawska and T. Hernes (eds.), *Actor–Network Theory and Organizing*. Malmö: Liber.

Pitsis, T. S. 2007. 'Management Networks', in G. Ritzer (ed.), *The Blackwell Encyclopaedia of Sociology*. Malden, MA: Wiley-Blackwell, pp. 2742–4.

Pitsis, T. S., Clegg, S. R., Marosszeky, M. and Rura-Polley, T. 2003. 'Constructing the Olympic Dream: Managing Innovation Through the Future Perfect', *Organization Science* 14(5): 574–90.

Pitsis, T. S., Kornberger, M. M. and Clegg, S. R. 2004. 'The Art of Managing Relationships in Interorganizational Collaboration', *Management* 7(3): 47–67.

Przeworski, A. 1985. 'Capitalism and Social Democracy', in *Studies in Marxism and Social Theory*. Cambridge University Press.

Schattschneider, E. 1960. *The Semi-Sovereign People*. New York: Holt, Rinehart & Winston.

Schram, S. F. 2003. 'Return to Politics: Perestroika, Phronesis, and Post-Paradigmatic Political Science', in S. F. Schram and B. Caterino (eds.), *Making Political Science Matter: Debating Knowledge, Research, and Method*. New York University Press.

Schutz, A. 1967. *The Phenomenology of the Social World*. Evanston, IL: Northwestern University Press.

Tilly, C. 1991. 'Domination, Resistance, Compliance, Discourse', *Sociological Forum* 6(3): 593–602.

van Gestel, N., Koppenjan, J., Schrijver, I., van de Ven, A. and Veeneman, W. 2008. 'Managing Public Values in Public–Private Networks: A Comparative Study of Innovative Public Infrastructure Projects', *Public Money and Management* 28(3): 139–45.

van Marrewijk, A., Clegg, S. R., Pitsis, T. S. and Veenswijk, M. 2008. 'Managing Public–Private Megaprojects: Paradoxes, Complexity, and Project Design', *International Journal of Project Management* 26(6): 591–600.

Weber, E. and Khademian, A. M. 2008. 'Managing Collaborative Processes: Common Practices, Uncommon Circumstances', *Administration & Society* 40(5): 431–64.

Part II

Applied phronesis

6   Why mass media matter and how to work with them: phronesis and megaprojects

Bent Flyvbjerg[1]

The purpose of the present chapter is to demonstrate how social scientists may engage with mass media to have their research impact public deliberation, policy and practice. Communicating research to practice is part and parcel of applied phronesis and not something external to it. Even in Aristotle's original definition of phronesis, laid down more than two millennia ago, the knowledge–action relationship is clear. A defining characteristic of phronesis is, in Aristotle's words, that it is 'reason capable of action' (*The Nicomachean Ethics*, 1976: Bk VI, 1140a24–1140b12). Phronetic research results ('reason') are therefore results only to the extent they have an impact on practice ('action'). In public affairs, reason is made capable of action by effectively having reason enter the public sphere and public deliberation. It is reason times exposure in the public sphere that matters, not reason alone.[2] Today, mass media dominate the public sphere in liberal democracies. The relationship of research with media therefore needs to be reflected. However, to my knowledge no study exists that describes in detail this aspect of phronetic research. Even in social science as a whole, studies of how scholars work with mass media to secure public impact of their research seem rare (Bagdikian 2004; McCombs 2004; Bryant and Oliver 2009). This, then, is the purpose of the present chapter: to begin to close this gap in our knowledge

---

[1] The author wishes to thank the following for valuable comments on earlier versions of this chapter: Alexander Budzier, Arthur Frank, Martyn Hammersley, John Haslam, Todd Landman, Maxwell McCombs, Linsey McGoey, Sanford Schram, Martin Wachs and an anonymous Cambridge University Press reviewer.
[2] A North American colleague commented on the phronetic reliance on the public sphere for public deliberation: 'In North America right now, the "public sphere" looks too much like the Tea Party in the US and the paralyzing California referendum system. It's enough to send us back to Plato, longing for some Guardians.' However understandable such longing is, history shows that opting for Plato's Guardians spells disaster. As observed by Hirschman (1994: 208), democracy and the public sphere will not work in a society until various groups that are at each other's throat finally come to recognize their mutual inability to gain dominance and the need for some accommodation. The alternative to such accommodation is variations on totalitarianism, including Plato's Guardians, or to keep at each other's throat.

of social science and phronesis. Because the field is underexplored, it was found to be prudent to start with a phenomenological case study. The study shows how a group of phronetic social scientists, including the author, engaged with media, including world-leading titles such as *The New York Times*, in order to place their research results on the public agenda and initiate change in their chosen field of interest: megaproject policy and management.

Media as magnifier

My first experiment with applied phronesis was like throwing a stick of dynamite. What I had read by Machiavelli, Nietzsche and Foucault proved to be true: you can effectively transform specific social and political practices by writing what Machiavelli calls the *verita effettuale* (effective truth) and Nietzsche *wirkliche Historie* (real history) of such practices. I published my carefully researched real history of corrupt city management in my hometown, Aalborg, Denmark. This created a media storm, and this in turn stopped the management practices I had studied dead in their tracks, to be replaced by a more democratic and modern type of city governance. The latter was designed along lines I had proposed, and it won the European Union's 'European Planning Prize' for innovative and democratic urban policy and planning, carrying the day in Brussels over 300 nominees (Flyvbjerg 1998a, 2001: 141–61, 2003; Hansen 2002, 2006). The experience was almost too good to be true. If this was how applied phronesis worked I wanted to do more. I also wanted to test whether the success in Aalborg was just beginner's luck.

Without the media exposure, the Aalborg study would not have had the impact on practice that it did. To be sure, the exposure did not happen by chance. My university and I helped it along with press releases, a news conference and by being available to media for interviews. But the fact that the media picked up the story across the board, locally and nationally, was the single most important factor in making change happen. The media magnified a thousandfold the transparency created by the study and thus brought the problems uncovered to the attention of voters and the general public. Voting is taken seriously in Denmark, with an 80–90 per cent turnout at most elections, so public opinion matters to officials. Confronted with a study and a strong public opinion that depicted officials and politicians as ineffective and corrupt, those responsible quickly decided to change their ways.

This is not to say that the media were the only game changer. Other parts of civil society were important as well, as was government. But in contemporary liberal democracies mass media play a key role, because more than any other factor they structure and dominate the public sphere, for better and for worse (Calhoun 1992; Croteau and Hoynes 2006). Today's mass media are seriously called the 'fourth power' of government, expanding on Montesquieu's three classic powers: the legislature, the executive and the judicial. Therefore, concerned citizens and organizations bring their issues to the attention of the media in order to be heard and to effect change. So do concerned social scientists involved in applied phronesis.

The main means of communication for academics is the scholarly text. The impact of a scholarly text in public debate depends on both its publication and exposure, apart from content. Without publication there can be no impact. But equally, with zero public exposure there will also be zero public impact. Most scholars are concerned mainly with academic exposure and typically do not focus on public impact. Their focus is on publication and citations in academic media, because the culture and incentives of academic institutions encourage this. Thus, it is unsurprising that most academic work has little impact in the public sphere.[3] In contrast, phronetic social scientists are explicitly concerned about public exposure, because they see it as one of the main vehicles for the type of social and political action that is at the heart of phronesis. Even so, phronetic social scientists are fully aware that other social scientists may not share the view that such action should be a goal for social science. Phronetic social scientists are also aware that their research may have impacts which are at odds with those they aimed for. Phronetic researchers therefore actively try to manage the impact of their work.

The importance of tension points

One day, while I was pondering what research to do after the Aalborg study, disaster struck at a major underwater rail tunnel that was being built between East and West Denmark. The Great Belt Tunnel, as it is called, would be the second longest underwater rail tunnel in Europe, after the Channel Tunnel, and would link Scandinavia with continental Europe across the entrance to the Baltic Sea. In addition to the tunnel, two bridges were being built across the Belt, one of which was the world's longest suspension bridge at the time of completion. With a cost in the multibillion-dollar range, seventeen times that of the largest project built

---

[3] By a combined use of Google Scholar (or the ISI Web of Knowledge) and Google News, it is easy to establish that most academic publications have little or no impact in both mass media and academic media. Publications may have other important impacts, needless to say, for example, in teaching students. Here, the focus is on impact via mass media.

in Denmark until then, the Great Belt project (1987–98) signified a giant leap in the scale of construction projects in Denmark. It was, in effect, the first Danish megaproject.[4] Now seawater was flooding the near-completed tunnel due to an error in managing the tunnel boring process.

A leading engineer on the project later told me that damage to the tunnel was so complete that it would have been cheaper to bore a new tunnel rather than to rescue the existing one. But the loss of face this would entail – leaving an unused, flooded, multibillion-dollar tunnel sitting permanently under the seabed as a negative monument to politics and engineering – was unacceptable to those in charge. So the flooded tunnel was emptied out, repaired and boring completed. And, sure enough, when the tunnel finally opened to traffic, the cost overrun was 120 per cent in real terms and the venture proved financially non-viable. The government had paid for more than two tunnels but got only one, with revenues from the tunnel insufficient to cover the escalated costs.

The events at Great Belt got me interested in answering the following specific research question: 'Was Denmark just unfortunate with the Great Belt megaproject, as its promoters argued, or are cost overruns and disasters like those observed for this project common for megaprojects in general?' To my amazement, when I did a comprehensive survey of the world literature on megaprojects, I found that no one had done a systematic *ex post* study of performance in large-scale infrastructure projects. Worldwide, hundreds of such projects had been built and trillions of dollars spent. I thought that surely someone must have had the idea or need to study whether these projects were in fact performing as promised in terms of costs, benefits, and social and environmental impacts. But no. A few case studies existed and studies of small samples of projects (Hall 1980; Morris and Hough 1987; Fouracre, Allport and Thomson 1990; Pickrell 1990; Wachs 1990), but not a study that could be called systematic that would give a valid and reliable picture of this costly field of policy and management. I decided to do such a study and to document the *verita effettuale* of megaprojects. I applied for, and was awarded, a large research grant.

---

[4] Megaprojects are multibillion-dollar public infrastructure projects, each with the potential to transform cities, regions and the lives of millions. Ever more and larger megaprojects are currently being built around the world, in what *The Economist* (7 June 2008, p. 80) has called the 'biggest investment boom in history'. Enormous amounts of money are at stake in potential waste of citizens' money, as are massive social and environmental impacts and due democratic process.

Then something *really* interesting happened, something I had never experienced before.

I was asked whether the next time I was in Copenhagen would I kindly have lunch with the highest-ranking government official in infrastructure planning in Denmark. I had met the official several times at professional meetings and liked him, so I gladly accepted. As far as I could judge, we were on the same side of things in working for an improved version of the welfare state – a favourite pastime in Scandinavia – including better and more democratic policy and management for cities, infrastructure and the environment. He took me to a nice restaurant on the canal close to his ministry, where we had lunch and pleasant conversation, until towards the end of the meal, when he congratulated me on my new research grant and told me in no uncertain terms that if I came up with results that reflected badly on his government and ministry he would personally make sure my research funds dried up.

I froze. I could not believe what I heard. Was I in Denmark or some banana republic, or were the two the same? And why the threat? I figured it must be because I had publicly criticized management at the Great Belt project for misinforming Parliament and the public about cost overruns on the project. Management said costs had overrun by 29 per cent in total for the tunnel and two bridges combined. My research showed the figure to be 55 per cent, a difference of several billion kroner. Every time management publicly mentioned their 29 per cent figure, I would just as publicly point out that the real overrun was 55 per cent. This happened over and over until management did an opinion poll asking the public which of the two figures they thought was right. The public said 55 per cent, and this forced management to give up on postulating their 29 per cent and acknowledge my 55 per cent, a figure later verified by the National Audit Office of Denmark (1998). For a scholar, a poll seems a strange way to decide the truth value of data, but it taught me the lesson that it is possible to inject research results into and influence the often highly manipulated public discourse on megaprojects. Now it also taught me that blowing the whistle repeatedly on the management of the largest and most prestigious project in Danish history may have miffed people in high places.

Then a rush of blood and excitement shot through my body. My colleagues and I had hit pay dirt even before properly beginning the research! If the Danish government found it worth their while to send their Chief Planner to threaten me over a piece of research, this was the best demonstration that the research must be done and was likely to produce interesting results. So that is what I told the official before I got up and left, incredulous but happy about this backward endorsement of the work my colleagues and I were just starting.

The Chief Planner inadvertently alerted us to the type of power relation we call a 'tension point' and which Foucault calls 'virtual fractures'. These are 'lines of fragility in the present . . . which open up the space of freedom understood as a space of concrete freedom, that is, of possible transformation' (Foucault 1998: 449–50). This type of power relation is particularly susceptible to problematization and thus to change, because it is fraught with dubious practices, contestable knowledge and potential conflict. Thus, even a small challenge – like problematization by scholars – may tip the scales and trigger change in a tension point. Problematizing tension points may be compared with hitting a rock with a hammer. If you hit the rock at random it seems unbreakable, even if you hit it hard. If you hit the rock more strategically at the small, near-invisible fault lines that most rocks have, the rock will fracture, even if you hit it gently. Tension points are the fault lines that phronetic researchers seek out; this is where researchers hit existing practices to make them come apart and create space for new and better ones.

Tension points have the added advantage that with their focus on power and dubious practices they tend to make good stories and thus to be of interest to media and the public. Chapter 14 expands on the use of tension points in phronetic social science. Here it is enough to say that the Chief Planner made us aware of the acute tension between the *image* that he and the government wanted to project for megaproject development and the *reality* of such development. This tension point proved to be an important lead for our research and got us off to an effective start in problematizing megaproject policy and management.

Working with tension points in practice

During the time my colleagues and I were busy collecting data around the world for our study on megaprojects, the Danish government approved two more such projects in addition to the Great Belt link. The two new projects were the Øresund bridge between Denmark and Sweden (1991–2000), the world's longest combined cable-stayed bridge for road and rail, and the Copenhagen metro (1992–2007), one of the first driverless metros in Europe. We decided to test our methodology, described in Flyvbjerg (2001), on the three Danish projects before going global. Both the Øresund bridge and the Copenhagen metro were under construction and, like the Great Belt link, the two new projects quickly ran up billion-dollar cost overruns that threatened their viability.

The project promoters, including the Danish government, had now made the same error three times straight on three different megaprojects. They had underestimated costs by billions of dollars and thereby placed large sums of citizens' money at risk. We pointed this out in public. We also told Parliament, who approve megaprojects in Denmark, and citizens, who underwrite projects financially, that they might want to consider the idea that an error made three times over was perhaps not a random error. Maybe the 'error' was better understood as either incompetence, that is, not learning from experience, or intentional misrepresentation, that is, lying, the latter being unlawful in Denmark for this type of situation.

The public and the media quickly became interested in our work and since then we have never lacked outlets for, or interest in, our problematizations of Danish megaproject policy and management, including on national TV, radio, newspapers and the web, plus endless invitations to lecture on our research. Literally hundreds of newspaper articles have covered and quoted our research in Denmark, as have dozens of TV and radio programmes – some of them with hour-long coverage of our work – on both national and local media. We spend time working with the media and the public, because phronesis is aimed at public debate, and in modern society public debate takes place in the media to a large extent. As a result we have made it more difficult for promoters to get away, unproblematized, with the delusions and deceptions that are at the core of conventional megaproject policy and management (Flyvbjerg, Garbuio and Lovallo 2009).

While the public and the media liked our work, this was not the case for the powers that be. We had actively generated the type of situation that the government's Chief Planner had wanted to avoid when he threatened me to not do research that reflected badly on his government. In fact, as we gained momentum with our critique, I was called on the carpet in Copenhagen once again, this time by the Chief Planner's boss, the Minister of Transport. At the meeting, the Minister complained that our research was making front-page news in the papers, placing the Ministry in a bad light. The Minister also assured me that the repeated errors in the budgets for the Danish megaprojects were honest mistakes; the Minister's own planners had told the Minister so. Maybe the meeting was designed to intimidate my colleagues and me by reminding us that those in power were watching us, but my main take-away was, again, that if our work got this kind of top-level attention from government it must be because we were on to something and because our problematizations were working.

The megaproject promoters tried to undermine us. When we problematized their actions they would try to problematize us right back. Each of the government-owned multibillion-dollar public corporations that were running the three Danish megaprojects now had their own well-staffed PR offices. They, with their top brass, got on our case. This is fair enough, of course, as critique is what makes scholarship and democracy work. Except sometimes the PR people's critique would be as deceptive as the cost–benefit analyses used to justify their projects. That happened, for instance, when a former mayor of Copenhagen, who had become CEO of the Copenhagen metro through a controversial political appointment, tried to publicly label me as 'anti-rail' and as generally 'holding animus' towards the metro. He did this despite the fact that I was on record as stating that a metro was good for Copenhagen and more metro should be built, just not in the mismanaged way it was then being done.

Top management at the metro became particularly agitated when – during a week where Lego, the Danish toymaker, and the Copenhagen metro both discovered billion-kroner holes in their budgets due to mismanagement – I pointed out on national TV that the CEO of Lego had been sacked, whereas the metro CEO again got an extra billion and stayed on, and perhaps this was why mismanagement at the metro continued year after year. The fact that the metro CEO had to resort to name-calling, like 'anti-rail' against someone who supports rail, showed to my colleagues and I, and to many others, that the metro leadership had no real arguments to counter our critique. This strengthened both the critique and our predictions that without changes the metro would most likely end up as financially non-viable (Flyvbjerg 2007b: 19–24). In fact, the Copenhagen metro later became insolvent and was saved only through further subsidies and financial restructuring. Lego made a spectacular turnaround with a new CEO.

More problematically, the PR people on the megaprojects did not fight fairly and in public. Out of the public eye, some of them would routinely contact journalists and editors who covered our research and try to undermine our credibility. This is one of many ways in which power tries to subvert knowledge that does not suit its purposes. And if you do not counter, knowledge will be weak (Flyvbjerg 1998a: 227–34). Fortunately for us, many journalists and editors were on our side and tipped us off. Serious journalism and serious research share and work for the same basic values: namely, truth and democracy. Moreover, both tend to see PR people as working in the less dignified world of spin, which may also be important to society, but which we tend to see as a target to expose and attack.

So when media were contacted by PR people who tried to put a nega-tive spin on our research, the media would often alert us. The PR people were clearly peeved when a 'personal' email they had sent to a journalist or editor stating that our work was faulty had been forwarded to us and now reappeared in the PR people's inbox with our request for them to kindly document the postulated faults. When they could not do so, which was every time, we would report it back to the journalists who had tipped us off and they would have a news item. This went on for years, and still does. It is work that needs to be done to protect the power of knowl-edge and to make debate transparent. If the work is not done, knowledge and public deliberation suffer. I believe it has gained us much credibility with the media and the public that we are willing to chase misinfor-mation about megaprojects and abuse of power wherever they appear, even in 'personal' emails to journalists and editors from promoters of megaprojects.

Our research seemed to strike a chord with the general public. People were tired of the repeated cost overruns, benefit shortfalls and the endless excuses and false promises made by project promoters. To illustrate just how widespread negative public sentiments were, consider that when a popular Danish financial magazine asked their readers to choose the most wasteful person in Denmark among ten nominated for their misuse of citizens' money, the readers unambiguously chose the chairman of the Copenhagen metro, a former treasurer for Denmark and vice-president of the European Commission. The chairman was nominated for 'having no control whatsoever over costs for the Metro, as regards both operating and construction costs, not to speak of ridership' (*Penge og Privatøkonomi* 2004, 2005). The public seemed delighted that somebody was doing research that exposed and explained this type of behaviour and called for accountability.

Members of Parliament also picked up on the research. They used it to ask questions in Parliament of those responsible for megaprojects, typically the ministers of transport and finance, in order to hold them accountable. Staff with the Auditor General of Denmark told us our research had triggered decisions by the Auditor General to audit first the Great Belt link and later the Øresund bridge and Copenhagen metro. I consulted for the Auditor General on some of these audits and made our data available to them, so the audits could be more effective. Fur-thermore, I was invited by an independent government body to head an expert group that did a year-long study on how to design a decision-making process – nicknamed 'megaprojects without tears' by the media – for the next multibillion-dollar project in Denmark, the Fehmarn Belt rail and road link, which is one of the biggest infrastructure projects in the world, crossing the Baltic Sea between Denmark and Germany (Flyvbjerg, Bruzelius and Rothengatter 2003: 143–51). The idea was to design a process that would explicitly try to avoid the problems that had beset Great Belt, Øresund and the Copenhagen metro. It was, in effect, an early example of 'Black Swan' prevention (Taleb 2007) and incorporated the type of practical knowledge that Scott (1999) calls *metis* and identifies as crucial for avoiding project failure. Later, the Parliament Treasury Committee and the Treasury passed government regulation that made mandatory methods that we had developed for estimating more accurately the costs and risks of major projects (Danish Ministry of Transport 2006, 2008). Finally, a new Minister of Transport appointed me to a policy-proposing national infrastructure commission (Danish Infrastructure Commission 2008). Thus, my colleagues and I had other avenues of impact for our research than the media. But media exposure was crucial for getting the research known in the first place to policy-makers and the public and thus for gaining practical import.

We found that government was not monolithic, as any Foucauldian and other true pluralists know. Government was beginning to fracture and to work against itself regarding megaprojects. By strategically doing our research on tension points, that is, the dubious practices of conventional megaproject development, we had deliberately contributed to this fracturing. The fracturing spread to those parts of government that were responsible for developing the four Danish megaprojects. Some staff began to change sides and to act as 'guerrilla employees', that is, working against the wishes of their superiors, because the employees were dissatisfied with the superiors' actions. Such staff began to see that conventional megaproject policy ran against the basic values of economic efficiency, truth-telling and due democratic process. They wanted to help remedy the situation. For strategic reasons, the guerrilla employees typically chose not to go public with their concerns. They moved clandestinely behind the scenes, leaking information from the inside to us and others, as 'salmon swimming against the current of power' (O'Leary 2010: 8).

For instance, when the Danish government began planning in earnest the Fehmarn Belt megaproject, the government's Chief Planner was so fed up with public debate, and with our problematizations, that meetings about the new project were planned to be held outside the borders of Denmark, in secret. In this manner the Danish Freedom of Information Act would not apply and nosy journalists, researchers and citizens would be unable to find out what was going on. But unfortunately for the Chief Planner, guerrilla employees – his own colleagues – leaked his Machiavellian scheme to the media and to me, among others. A major scandal ensued. The Chief Planner's boss, the Minister of Transport, was summoned to Parliament to be questioned by MPs, for them to consider whether the Minister should be fired. The MPs took offence that the country's laws of freedom of information were being circumvented. The Minister apologized profusely and explained that the Chief Planner had gotten carried away and that the Minister had not known what was going on. The Minister survived, but the Chief Planner did not. After a period of leave he returned to a less demanding position.

The four phronetic questions answered for megaprojects

While researching the Danish projects mentioned above, my colleagues and I had also collected data on projects worldwide, eventually covering twenty nations, five continents and seven decades. Our data documented that the problems with cost overruns and benefit shortfalls, first identified for Denmark, were global. So were the causes. Our data basically showed that the promoters and professionals behind megaprojects had to be either fools or liars to keep underestimating costs and risks, and overestimating benefits and viability, on project after project, decade after decade.

Following the four questions at the core of phronetic social science (see Chapter 1), our research showed, in brief:

Question 1: Where are we going with megaprojects?

The answer to this question is: astray. Never have more or bigger megaprojects been built, but, ironically, this happens despite their dismal performance record in terms of cost overruns and benefit shortfalls. This is called the 'megaprojects paradox' (Flyvbjerg, Bruzelius and Rothengatter 2003: 1–10). Nine out of ten projects have cost overruns. Overruns of over 50 per cent are common, while overruns of over 100 per cent not uncommon. Standard deviations are large, indicating risk to the second degree, that is, risk of cost overrun *and* risk of the overrun being much larger than expected. Most interesting of all, overruns have been constant for the seventy years for which data are available, indicating that no improvements in estimating and managing costs have been made over time (Flyvbjerg, Holm and Buhl 2002).

Benefit shortfalls generally mirror cost overruns. A majority of projects have benefit shortfalls. Shortfalls of around 40–50 per cent are common, 75 per cent is not uncommon, and again the standard deviations are large. Thus, benefit shortfalls compound the risk that projects end up being non-viable, as happened with the Channel Tunnel, the Great Belt Tunnel and the Copenhagen metro. For benefits, as for costs, historical data indicate no improvements over time in estimation and management skills (Flyvbjerg, Holm and Buhl 2005).

A distinct effect of establishing the first large dataset with valid and reliable information on cost overruns and benefit shortfalls in megaprojects, has been that project promoters can no longer, as was their habit, explain away overruns and shortfalls in specific projects as one-off instances of bad luck that are unlikely to happen again. We now know that a new project has more than a 90 per cent risk of having either cost overruns, benefit shortfalls or both. Cost overruns and benefit shortfalls are inherent to megaprojects. National audit offices and MPs concerned about government overspend, community groups fighting specific projects, banks whose money is at risk, government officials serious about curbing wasteful projects and media who know a good story when they see one have all been quick to seize on these data for their own purposes.

All we had to do was collect the data (which was difficult enough and took several years) and communicate the results effectively to media around the world, and immediately the results got an army of feet to walk on. This alone has helped to change discourse and policy for megaprojects and is an important first step in the problematization that is at the core of phronetic research. The new data have changed the power balance in megaproject deliberation and decision-making by giving ammunition to stakeholders who had little or no influence before. Decision-making has become less closed, undermining the dominance of project promoters who had a virtual monopoly on information until our data came along.

Today it is basically impossible for project promoters to postulate certain costs, benefits or risks for their projects without taking our data into account. If they try to ignore the data, other stakeholders – with an interest in exposing the real costs, benefits and risks of projects – will bring them up, or we will. That is how decision-making should work in a pluralistic democracy.

Question 2: Who gains and who loses, by which mechanisms of power?

The chief winners in megaproject development are promoters who profit from the large amounts of money and prestige involved in megaproject building. Most obviously, contractors who negotiate multimillion-dollar contracts and politicians who get to build monuments to themselves are winners. Typically, there is also a complex coalition behind each megaproject of MPs whose constituencies will gain, local authorities, developers, land owners, labour unions and consultants, who all stand to profit from the project and therefore support it. Engineers and technologists also often see themselves as winners, since megaprojects offer rich opportunities for pushing the boundaries for what technology can do, like building the tallest building, the longest bridge, the largest aircraft and so on. There is even an academic concept for the rapture engineers and technologists get from megaprojects, the 'technological sublime' (Frick 2008).[5]

The main losers in megaprojects are the funders of projects, primarily present and future taxpayers, banks and other investors, who cover the large losses often incurred by megaprojects when costs overrun, delays, revenue shortfalls and other mismanagement hit projects, which happens in more than nine out of ten cases, as said. Losers are also people who are negatively impacted by the social and environmental effects of projects, which are often substantial and unevenly distributed socially and geographically. Users of megaprojects may be winners or losers, but are typically left with considerably fewer benefits and higher costs than originally promised (Flyvbjerg 2007a).

The main mechanism of power that megaproject promoters use to get their projects approved and funded – and to define themselves as winners and others as losers – is the following formula:

> (Underestimated costs)
> + (Overestimated revenues)
> + (Overestimated development effects)
> + (Underestimated or omitted environmental impacts)
> = Project approval and funding.

The formula denotes an unusually clear mechanism of power and it is well understood by the actors involved in megaproject development. The formula is used so pervasively that it may be considered a main business model in megaproject development. But its use has the unfortunate effect of leading to an inverted Darwinism: that is, survival of the *un*-fittest, because projects that have falsely been made to look good on paper, at approval, tend to be the worst performers in reality, at implementation. Thus, promoters' self-serving use of the Machiavellian formula for project approval is a key explanation of the poor performance of projects and of the megaprojects paradox (Flyvbjerg 2009).

---

[5] Three other sublimes are relevant to understanding the drivers of megaproject development: (1) the political sublime, that is, the rapture politicians get from building monuments to themselves and their causes; (2) the economic sublime, that is, the delight business people get from making lots of money from megaprojects; and (3) the aesthetic sublime, that is, the pleasure designers get from building something very large that is very beautiful, like the Golden Gate bridge in San Francisco. All four sublimes are important drivers of megaproject development.

After developing our explanations of cost overruns and benefit short-falls, we were invited to test them against other theories of bias in decision-making, including Kahneman's and Tversky's (1979a, 1979b) Nobel Prize-winning theories. The tests showed that our theories chart a new domain of biases and that they supplement existing theories in important ways where these lack explanatory power, that is, in situations where biases are not cognitive, as they are in Kahneman's and Tversky's theories, but instead political and organizational (Flyvbjerg 2003; Flyvbjerg, Garbuio and Lovallo 2009).

Question 3: Is this development desirable?

The answer to the third question is: No! The third phronetic question is the most value-laden of the four questions, and therefore the one closest to Aristotle's (1976: 1140a24–1140b12) original definition of phrone-sis as reasoning that is 'capable of action with regard to things that are *good or bad for man*' (italics added). Importantly, my colleagues and I did not need ideals of strong democracy, radical economics or diehard environmentalism to arrive at the conclusion that the way megaprojects are developed, as summarized above, is undesirable, that is, 'bad for man'. Not that we have anything against strong democracy, radical economics or diehard environmentalism. But such ideals would almost certainly be rejected by the mainstream as being idiosyncratic or marginal, which would be counterproductive to our purposes.

In contrast, most informed persons who subscribe to the standard values of liberal democracy would have to agree that the misinformation that feeds decisions on megaprojects violates central and long-held norms of democracy and is thus neither desirable nor justifiable. After all, truth-telling is written into the constitutions and laws of most liberal democracies. For instance, in most democracies it is unlawful for a civil servant to knowingly misinform a minister, and for a minister to misinform parliament. Similarly, most people who subscribe to the standard values of the market economy and effective resource allocation would have to agree that the inefficiencies imposed on society by the multibillion-dollar cost overruns and benefit shortfalls, which we documented to be common for megaprojects, are also neither desirable nor justifiable. Thus, our analysis could not be easily rejected on grounds of being idiosyncratic. This was strategically important, because as we moved on to answering the fourth question – What should be done? – we wanted to have as broad popular support as possible for our conclusions and suggestions for action, in order for them to have as much impact as possible.

Question 4: What should we do, if anything?

According to the Nietzschean–Foucauldian interpretation of phronesis described in Flyvbjerg (2001), the first thing to do is to problematize dubious social and political practices. According to Foucault (1981), the purpose of such problematization is:

> precisely to bring it about that practitioners no longer know what to do, so that the acts, gestures, discourses that up until then had seemed to go without saying become problematic, difficult, dangerous.[6]

Problematization exposes dubious practices so they become problematic and difficult to continue. This is also a basic mechanism of accountability in liberal democracies. Exposure leads to public attention and public attention to accountability. Our studies showed that the way decisions are made for megaprojects is highly dubious and we tried to help change things for the better by calling public attention to our results. For someone who takes scholarship and democracy seriously, problematization is among the finest things one can do. Open and constant critique is *the* core idea of scholarship and democracy and must be vigorously practised to keep them alive, effective and improving. Those who practise such critique are part of a millennia-long tradition that, although it has had its setbacks and is not perfect by any means, is remarkably successful. However, problematization is only a first step in phronetic social science. Problematization is good at stopping things, and many things in conventional megaproject policy and management indeed need to be stopped. But a singular focus on problematization runs the risk of becoming overly negative. And phronetic social science is emphatically not negative.

Political action requires constructively getting things started again, and this is the second step in phronetic social science after problematization. As social scientists, my colleagues and I problematize and deconstruct megaproject policy and management. As planners, we constructively design proposals for improvements to what we problematize. Thus, we are not satisfied with only writing the *wirkliche Historie* of what we study and with problematizing it, although we see problematization and critique as the most important drivers of progress. Examples of our constructive work may be found in Flyvbjerg, Bruzelius and Rothengatter (2003: 73–151); Flyvbjerg (with COWI) (2004); Flyvbjerg (2006, 2008, 2009); and Flyvbjerg, Garbuio and Lovallo (2009).

[6] Here quoted from Miller (1993: 235).

Going global

Our first problematizations and constructive proposals, for Danish megaproject policy and management, seemed to work well. Now – after having researched and answered the four phronetic questions for projects in twenty nations on five continents – we were ready to go global. We resolved to aim for publication of our first batch of international results in the leading academic journal in our field, the *Journal of the American Planning Association* (*JAPA*). We did this as *JAPA* has the most rigorous review process we know of, and at our suggestion the editors made it even more exacting for our article by appointing referees who were known to be particularly critical of our findings. We wanted possible errors and questionable interpretations to be found by the referees, not by readers after being in print. Moreover, *JAPA* has the widest readership of academic planning journals. It is read by both scholars and practitioners and it is read all over the world, not just in the United States, which was important to our phronetic objective of spreading the word and having an impact. Finally, we wanted the credibility and prestige of *JAPA* behind our results, as, given our experience from Denmark, we figured this might come in handy if project promoters decided to attack our findings as they had at home.

It turned out, however, that we were hedging against the wrong opponent. This time, our main adversary would initially not be project promoters, but – much to our surprise – the American Planning Association (APA), the parent organization of *JAPA* and the biggest and most powerful professional organization for planners in the world. By choosing to publish with *JAPA*, we unwittingly triggered censure by APA, who tried to suppress our study, because they saw it as presenting planners and planning in a bad light.[7] What follows is a brief summary of what happened (for a more complete analysis, see Flyvbjerg, forthcoming).

The first article from our global study was called 'Underestimating Costs in Public Works Projects: Error or Lie?' (Flyvbjerg, Holm and Buhl 2002). During the months before publication, *JAPA* and I discussed the newsworthiness of the study and we agreed that it might generate substantial media interest. *JAPA* therefore contacted APA's Public Affairs

---

[7] Here and elsewhere in the text, when I talk about APA's suppression of our study, I specifically mean APA's attempts to suppress exposure of the study by (1) suppressing media coverage of the study and (2) glossing over and misrepresenting the study in APA's communications about the study. Both points are dealt with in detail in Flyvbjerg (forthcoming). As mentioned, the impact of a text depends on both publication and exposure. Thus, impact may be suppressed by suppressing publication or suppressing exposure. APA's efforts were focused on suppressing exposure.

Coordinator to enlist professional support in promoting the article with the media. He agreed to help and developed a comprehensive publicity strategy for our study, including the following items:

(1) Place an exclusive with *The New York Times*, or, if unsuccessful, with *The Wall Street Journal*, *Time* magazine, *Newsweek*, *US News & World Report*, *The Economist* or *USA Today*, in prioritized order.
(2) Try to get a major US television network interested or CNN.
(3) Hold a press conference.
(4) Write eight to twelve regionalized press releases for the largest US metropolitan areas, including New York City, Los Angeles, Chicago, Boston, Philadelphia, Washington, DC, Atlanta, Houston, Phoenix, Seattle, St Louis and Detroit.
(5) Keep Associated Press and Reuters in the loop.
(6) In Europe, place an exclusive with *The Sunday Times* in London.
(7) The APA's Public Affairs Coordinator would implement the media strategy for the United States. We and our university would cover Europe and the rest of the world.[8]

This looked good, and familiar, to my colleagues and me. It was the kind of thing we were used to doing with the Public Affairs Office at Aalborg University for our Danish research, this time only on a much larger scale. But while we were busy collaborating with APA on the press releases, their Public Affairs Coordinator let me know that he needed to discuss the media strategy for our study with APA's Executive Director. The publicity operation had evidently grown to a size where the Public Affairs Coordinator felt uncomfortable by continuing it without approval from top management. He asked me to wait until he heard from the Executive Director before we contacted media. After a week, the Public Affairs Coordinator got back to me and let me know that the APA Executive Director 'does not want me to do anything in terms of promoting, whether as an exclusive story or on a regional basis, the results of your infrastructure cost underestimation study as appearing in the Summer issue of *JAPA* . . . I'm sorry I can't be of further help.'[9] This was a 180-degree turnaround in both tone and content, compared with APA's previous enthusiasm for the project and our extensive correspondence and comprehensive publicity strategy.

At first, *JAPA*'s Managing Editor decided that *JAPA* would assert their independence of APA by facilitating media coverage of our study in the United States, no matter what APA said. However, the Managing Editor quickly came under pressure from his editors, who decided to follow

---

[8] Source: emails from the APA Public Affairs Coordinator to the author, 29–31 May 2002.
[9] Quotes are from the author's communications with those quoted; author's archives.

APA's stance, and the Managing Editor thus had to retract his decision. He explained that 'APA has particular political reasons not to spotlight your findings' and that APA's Executive Director 'is worried that the spin will be that planners are liars, even though this is not what you say in your article, and he is trying to protect the profession from that bad press'. Instead of APA openly acknowledging that (1) planners are doing an exceptionally poor job at costing major public works projects, sometimes perhaps intentionally, (2) this results in large-scale waste of public money, and (3) APA, as the main professional organization for planners, has a responsibility to help rectify this situation, APA decided to gloss this over and suppress the unpleasant facts. APA's idea of protecting member interests was apparently to cover up malpractice in planning, thus defending the status quo. Our idea was to improve planning by problematizing malpractice and demonstrating how it may be avoided.

Alarmingly, we also learned that APA had decided to write their own news release about our study and that they would try to 'track and monitor all reporter requests for copies of [the study]'. To achieve this, APA's Public Affairs Coordinator instructed *JAPA* to not get involved with media contact and instead 'direct reporter inquiries to me [the APA Public Affairs Coordinator] and we [APA] will follow-up [sic] . . . We are doing this so that if we want to talk to a reporter about the study, we don't give him or her a copy of the study until we've had a chance to talk with them.' According to APA's plan, neither we nor *JAPA* would have a say in what the media were told about the study, and APA had decided to gloss over its real content in order to protect APA members from bad press. Generally, if you are not in control of the press releases and publicity strategy for your research you are not in control of its public impact. Phronetic social scientists therefore make a point of being in control on this point. APA now threatened this control by their attempt to take over all media contact and eliminating both us and *JAPA* from this important stage of research communication and impact.

JAPA accepted APA's machinations, we did not. We were less than three weeks from publication of the study when this happened and we quickly decided to try to beat APA to the media. First, we personally pitched our story and offered exclusives to the editors of *The New York Times* and *The Sunday Times*. We reasoned that if two prominent newspapers like these would cover our study, then the rest of the media would follow. This proved to be correct. At the time we had no experience with major international media, but we did have experience from Denmark. Here we had found that media contact for new work is simple: if you have a newsworthy story – and a good press release – you float; if not, you sink. We expected that the same would hold true for international media. This also proved to be correct. *The New York Times* and *The Sunday Times* both accepted the offer to run exclusives on our study. We realized that we did not need PR people to get in touch with the media. In fact, editors and journalists seemed to prefer to deal with us directly. Second, while *The New York Times* and *The Sunday Times* were printing their exclusives, we emailed copies of the study and a press release written by us to every other main media in the English-speaking world, including the United States. Many of these media covered the study. Distributing news like this is amazingly fast and efficient with modern information and communication technologies. Anyone who thinks they can control this process is seriously out of touch with the times.

We experienced a minor, but potentially ruinous, hiccup in our contact with *The New York Times*. I mention it here to illustrate how you have to be prepared for anything and for thinking on your feet when dealing with media. A few days before publication, I learned that *The New York Times* reporter who had been assigned to write the story about our study, and who had interviewed me at length over the past weeks, had unexpectedly dropped everything and rushed to the hospital where his wife was giving premature birth to their first child. I contacted the reporter's editor, who said it was too late to place someone else on the story. He was sorry, but they had to abandon it. It was just one of those things that happen at a big, busy newspaper. He hoped I understood.

I did understand, of course, why the reporter had to drop everything. But I also understood that our strategy of gaining impact for our research through the public sphere would be seriously set back. As we had offered an exclusive to *The New York Times*, no other media were in place to cover the story in the United States. We would lose the whole country, the biggest and most important one. We could not let this happen. But what to do? Somehow the thought struck me that maybe we could play on the American fear of litigation. I got the idea from the *Times* editor himself. He had demonstrated this fear just a few days earlier, when he had our study checked for legal liabilities. I now explained to the editor that he had actually agreed, in writing, to run an exclusive on our study, and because of this agreement we had sacrificed opportunities with other media. If he dropped the exclusive this would incur substantial costs on us in terms of not achieving one of the key objectives of our work, namely, making it public. Then I mentioned, as gently as possible, that in my view an agreement like ours was legally binding. I did not say I would sue, but I did make it clear that I thought if someone wanted to sue, they could, and that they would have a good chance of winning. I was improvising and this was clearly a long shot on my part that I feared might somehow backfire. I had no experience in dealing with media of this size and calibre, or any media in the United States for that matter, and certainly not regarding legal issues. But I felt I had no choice other than letting our strategy for going public, so central to phronesis and thus to our work, collapse. This, to me, would be equivalent to not taking our work seriously. After I made my spiel, the editor went quiet for a while. Then he said he would run the story, and he had it pieced together from the unfinished work of the reporter who had to withdraw.

The coverage of our study in *The New York Times* and *The Sunday Times* proved to be invaluable, both in itself and in getting the study picked up by other media. It also proved an effective first step in establishing a role for ourselves globally, like the one we already had in Scandinavia, as the scholars who know about megaprojects, and especially about cost over-runs, benefit shortfalls, risks and deception in such projects, and who are therefore often heard when these issues are deliberated about in new policies and projects. In this role we would eventually help to reform policy and practice in the United Kingdom, the United States, the Netherlands, Switzerland and Denmark, plus our work is used *ad hoc* in many other countries (Dutch Commission on Infrastructure Projects 2004; Flyvbjerg (with COWI) 2004; Swiss Association of Road and Transportation Experts 2006; UK Department for Transport 2006a, 2006b; Transportation Research Board 2007; Simpson 2008).

Working with media like this is what transforms the research from results sitting in academic journals and books to what Aristotle called 'reason capable of action' and Machiavelli *verita effettuale* (effective truth). Aristotle and Machiavelli both emphasized that this type of truth must be at the heart of social science if it is to matter to society. Machiavelli sought out princes to have an effect; such were his times. We seek out the public. Like princes, the public sphere is fallible and often lacks virtue. But it is key to public deliberation in modern democracies and thus inescapable for anyone who hopes to influence public decisions. With our research, comments and analyses, we try to make it harder for the many opportunists, who invariably converge where billions of dollars and political monument-building are at stake, to hijack the public debate, policy and projects for their own purposes.

This is not to say that you need media like *The New York Times* or *The Sunday Times* to do applied phronesis. If you are researching local issues, as I was when I did phronesis in Aalborg, and as my colleagues and I are today with individual megaprojects, then the relevant media are typically local newspapers and local TV and radio stations. However, my colleagues and I have deliberately taken the phronetic approach from first local to national issues and then to global ones. This was done out of scholarly curiosity, as a methodological experiment, to test whether phronesis works at all three levels. We found that it does. In our experience, there is no substantive difference between doing phronesis at the local, national or global level. The only difference is scale, and the methodology scales well.

Lessons of mass media and phronesis

This chapter may give the impression that my colleagues and I spend a lot of time on media contact. That is not the case. While we think working with the media is crucial to doing phronetic social science, and while we may spend more time than most academics on media contacts, it is really only a few hours here and there, typically weeks and months apart, but we have done it consistently over the years of doing phronesis. Working with media is intense and results are immediate and practical. As such, it is a stimulating break from the slow data collection, analyses and theory-building that are at the core of academic research. Compared with the vast number of hours that go into the research, the hours spent on media are negligible; probably less than 1 per cent. The difference that this minuscule effort makes to the impact of the research on public debate, policy and practice may be large, nevertheless, which is why the effort needs to be made from a phronetic point of view.

It should be mentioned again that mass media are not the only way to influence practice when doing phronetic social science. Other parts of civil society, government and markets are important as well, including community groups, social and environmental movements, political parties, trade unions, business associations, coalitions, advocacy groups, professional associations, audit offices, guerrilla employees and more. But in contemporary liberal democracies mass media play a key role, because more than any other factor they structure and dominate the public sphere, for better or for worse. And the public sphere is where public deliberation takes place, that in turn influences policy and practice.

My colleagues and I have learned the following from our engagements with mass media and the public sphere in doing phronesis:

(1) *In liberal democracies, working with mass media is crucial to doing phronetic social science.* This is because in liberal democracies the public sphere is dominated by mass media, and the public sphere is the main vehicle for phronetic research results to enter into public deliberation, policy and practice. Mass media are dominated by commercial interests and raw political power, which limits and biases access. This is a danger that needs to be managed, as pointed out by Frank in Chapter 4, but it is not a game stopper. If, as a

phronetic researcher, you have produced research results that you can stand by and that media think are newsworthy, then you and the media have joint interests on this particular point in spreading the word and gaining phronetic impact. That is how media exposure worked for the studies described in this chapter.

(2) *Problematization of tension points is particularly well suited for generating change and for producing research results that are of interest to the public and media.* Rule number one for gaining exposure and impact with phronetic research is to study things that matter in ways that matter. Here, problematization of social and political tension points has proved to be particularly effective. This is because such problematization focuses on power and on dubious practices, both of which are attractive topics to both the public and the media, and both of which are often difficult to justify when exposed to the hard gaze of scholars and investigative journalists. This ensures that the combined efforts of research and journalism are likely to have an impact, which, too, is attractive to the public and to media. As an example, consider the practice described above of megaproject promoters routinely underestimating costs and overestimating benefits in their proposals for new projects in order to have them approved and funded. This is a dubious practice that has proved to be difficult to justify once it had been problematized in our research and exposed in the media. How to work with tension points is further discussed in Chapter 14.

(3) *Phronetic research and phronetic impact is replicable across different problematics, geographies and time periods.* The initial concern that the impact of the Aalborg study on practice was perhaps just beginner's luck proved to be unfounded. My colleagues and I were able to replicate the same type of impact with, first, our research on megaprojects in Denmark and, later, similar research globally. Other researchers have achieved similar impacts, as demonstrated by several of the chapters in this book.

(4) *Phronesis scales well.* My colleagues and I deliberately took the phronetic approach from, first, local to national issues and, then, to the global level. This was done as a methodological experiment to test whether phronesis works at all three levels. We found that methodologically there is no difference between doing phronesis at the local, national or global level; phronesis is equally relevant and effective at each. The only difference is scale, and the methodology scales well. For mass media, the effort it takes to get a relevant piece of research covered by *The New York Times* is approximately the same as it takes to get research covered by *The Aalborg Stiftstidende*, that is,

the local paper in Aalborg that was the main vehicle for exposing the results of the Aalborg study. The economies of scale are therefore substantial regarding exposure and impact.

(5) *Tension points bite back.* When you publicly problematize dubious practices and propose alternatives to replace them, do not expect a smooth ride. The people and organizations who benefit from the practices you problematize are likely to bite back. But you do not do this type of work for the smooth ride, you do it to change things. If your research triggers change, this is likely to gain you both friends and enemies. If nobody is against a specific piece of phronetic research, most likely the research is unimportant as regards its implications for practice. Phronetic researchers are power researchers, and as such they do not expect consensus for their work, but conflict. Consensus cannot be ruled out and is desirable where possible, but *a priori* consensus is considered dubious, because too often it is an illusion created by disregarding power, as in Habermasian discourse ethics or by marginalizing groups who are inconvenient to the supposed consensus (Flyvbjerg 1998b). In our experience, true consensus is rare in matters of policy, planning and management.

(6) *Dissemination of research results via mass media is unstoppable.* If your research results are newsworthy – and results of phronetic research often are – no one can stop you from spreading the word via mass media. This is particularly true today with the Internet and social media. Not even top management in the biggest and most powerful professional organization in our field, the American Planning Association, could stop exposure of our research results when they tried. This is encouraging. When someone tries to stop you, guerrilla employees may come in handy and they can be found in most organizations.

(7) *Press releases matter.* Media contact for research is simple: if you have a newsworthy story – and a good press release – you float; if not, you sink. We found that if you are not in control of the press releases about your work, you are not in control of its possible impact on public debate. We also found that it is a bad idea to make yourself dependent on PR people for writing and disseminating press releases. It is better to write your own releases, with feedback from professional journalists, and to distribute the releases yourself. Most media are inundated with PR people and like to deal with researchers directly, so you can cut out the middleman. Press releases are more effective for communicating research results than are op-eds and the like. Generally, it is more effective for scholars

to help journalists do their work by feeding journalists important and newsworthy research results they can write about than it is for scholars to try to do the work of journalists by writing journalistic articles about their own research.

(8) *Working with mass media is an extremely cost-effective way to increase the impact of research on policy and practice, and thus to meet the phronetic imperative that research should make a difference to action.* Media contact takes little time, compared with the time it takes to do research; in our experience less than 1 per cent of the total time involved. The difference that this minuscule effort makes to the impact of the research on public debate, public deliberation, policy and practice is large, which is why the effort needs to be made.

(9) *Recent developments in information technology have made phronetic research even more effective.* For phronetic research to have an impact, it must reach people. With the Internet and social media such reach has grown dramatically. The instruments for problematization and for opening up alternative courses of action that are the key results of phronetic research may be uploaded to the Internet and social media, to be downloaded and used by anyone with a computer or smartphone.

(10) *Research results take on a life of their own.* After being published and exposed via the mass media and the Internet, phronetic research results take on their own life as instruments in the struggle for a better life for specific communities and individuals. This is an effect for which phronetic researchers deliberately aim.

I suspect many social scientists would prefer not to have to deal with the media in the manner described above and not to have to jump into the fray of public debate, risking public critique of their work and sometimes even attempts at vilification. When it comes to the media, most social scientists seem to be wisely living according to the ancient Latin motto *bene vixit qui bene latuit* (they who live unnoticed live well). I also suspect that this is one of the main reasons why social science matters so little in society today.

In contrast, imagine that a majority of social scientists decided to (1) do research that matters to the communities in which we live and (2) make sure that the research results are effectively communicated to the public sphere, to be used in public deliberation, policy and practice in those communities. Social science and society would both be transformed for the better, where 'better' is defined by the conventional values of liberal democracies, for example, better informed and more just. In addition, social science would stand a chance of ridding itself of its role as perennial loser in the 'science wars', because it would finally start doing something useful, instead of its fruitless attempts at emulating natural science.

This chapter shows that such an alternative course of action for social science is possible and can be replicated and scaled. The question is not whether it can be done, rather it is whether we social scientists want to do it or not. I suggest we do, in order to strengthen truth and democracy and, not least, to strengthen social science itself.

REFERENCES

Aristotle 1976. *The Nicomachean Ethics*, trans. J. A. K. Thomson, revised with notes and appendices by Hugh Tredennick, introduction and bibliography by Jonathan Barnes. Harmondsworth: Penguin.

Bagdikian, Ben H. 2004. *The New Media Monopoly*. Boston, MA: Beacon Press.

Bryant, Jennings and Oliver, Mary Beth (eds.) 2009. *Media Effects: Advances in Theory and Research*. New York: Routledge.

Calhoun, Craig (ed.) 1992. *Habermas and the Public Sphere*. Cambridge, MA: MIT Press.

Croteau, David R. and Hoynes, William 2006. *The Business of Media: Corporate Media and the Public Interest*, 2nd edn. Thousand Oaks, CA: Pine Forge Press.

Danish Infrastructure Commission 2008. *Danmarks Transportinfrastruktur 2030* (Denmark's Transportation Infrastructure in 2030), Commission Report No. 1493. Copenhagen: Infrastrukturkommissionen.

Danish Ministry for Transport 2006. *Aktstykke om nye budgetteringsprincipper* (Act on New Principles for Budgeting). Aktstykke No. 16, Finansudvalget, Folketinget, 24 October.

   2008. *Ny anlægsbudgettering på Transportministeriets område, herunder om økonomistyringsmodel og risikohåndtering for anlægsprojekter* (New Construction Budgeting for the Ministry of Transport, including Financial Management Model and Risk Management for Construction Projects), 18 November.

Dutch Commission on Infrastructure Projects 2004. *Grote Projecten Uitvergroot: Een Infrastructuur voor Besluitvorming*. The Hague: Tweede Kamer der Staten-Generaal.

Flyvbjerg, B. 1998a. *Rationality and Power: Democracy in Practice*. University of Chicago Press.

   1998b. 'Habermas and Foucault: Thinkers for Civil Society?', *British Journal of Sociology* 49(2): 208–33.

   2001. *Making Social Science Matter: Why Social Inquiry Fails and How it can Succeed Again*. Cambridge University Press.

   2003. 'Delusions of Success: Comment on Dan Lovallo and Daniel Kahneman', *Harvard Business Review*, December: 121–2.

   2006. 'From Nobel Prize to Project Management: Getting Risks Right', *Project Management Journal* 37(3): 5–15.

2007a. 'Policy and Planning for Large Infrastructure Projects: Problems, Causes, Cures', *Environment and Planning B: Planning and Design* 34(4): 578–97.

2007b. 'Cost Overruns and Demand Shortfalls in Urban Rail and Other Infrastructure', *Transportation Planning and Technology* 30(1): 9–30.

2008. 'Curbing Optimism Bias and Strategic Misrepresentation in Planning: Reference Class Forecasting in Practice', *European Planning Studies* 16(1): 3–21.

2009. 'Survival of the Unfittest: Why the Worst Infrastructure Gets Built, and What We can Do about It', *Oxford Review of Economic Policy* 25(3): 344–67.

Forthcoming. 'The Dark Side of the American Planning Association: A Study in Malpractice and Professional Ethics', paper in progress.

Flyvbjerg, Bent, Bruzelius, Nils and Rothengatter, Werner 2003. *Megaprojects and Risk: An Anatomy of Ambition.* Cambridge University Press.

Flyvbjerg, Bent, in association with COWI 2004. *Procedures for Dealing with Optimism Bias in Transport Planning: Guidance Document.* London: Department for Transport.

Flyvbjerg, Bent, Garbuio, Massimo and Lovallo, Dan 2009. 'Delusion and Deception in Large Infrastructure Projects: Two Models for Explaining and Preventing Executive Disaster', *California Management Review* 51(2): 170–93.

Flyvbjerg, Bent, Holm, Mette K. Skamris and Buhl, Søren L. 2002. 'Underestimating Costs in Public Works Projects: Error or Lie?', *Journal of the American Planning Association* 68(3): 279–95.

2005. 'How (In)accurate are Demand Forecasts in Public Works Projects? The Case of Transportation', *Journal of the American Planning Association* 71(2): 131–46.

Foucault, Michel 1998. 'Structuralism and Post-Structuralism', interview conducted by Gérard Raulet, originally published in *Telos* 16(55), 1983, here from Michel Foucault, *Aesthetics, Method, and Epistemology. Essential Works of Foucault 1954–1984*, vol. 2, ed. James D. Faubin, trans. Robert Hurley *et al.*, first published in French in 1994. New York: New Press.

Fouracre, P. R., Allport, R. J. and Thomson, J. M. 1990. 'The Performance and Impact of Rail Mass Transit in Developing Countries', Research Report No. 278, Transport and Road Research Laboratory, Crowthorne.

Frick, Karen Trapenberg 2008. 'The Cost of the Technological Sublime: Daring Ingenuity and the New San Francisco–Oakland Bay Bridge', in H. Priemus, B. Flyvbjerg and B. van Wee (eds.), *Decision-Making on Mega-Projects: Cost–Benefit Analysis, Planning, and Innovation.* Cheltenham: Edward Elgar.

Hall, Peter 1980. *Great Planning Disasters.* Harmondsworth: Penguin.

Hansen, Carsten Jahn 2002. *Local Transport Policy and Planning: The Capacity to Deal with Environmental Issues.* Aalborg University Press.

2006. 'Urban Transport, the Environment and Deliberative Governance: the Role of Interdependence and Trust', *Journal of Environmental Policy and Planning* 8(2): 159–79.

Hirschman, Albert O. 1994. 'Social Conflicts as Pillars of Democratic Market Society', *Political Theory* 22(2): 203–18.

Kahneman, D. and Tversky, A. 1979a. 'Prospect Theory: An Analysis of Decisions under Risk', *Econometrica* 47: 313–27.

1979b. 'Intuitive Prediction: Biases and Corrective Procedures', in S. Makridakis and S. C. Wheelwright (eds.), *Studies in the Management Sciences: Forecasting*, vol. 12. Amsterdam: North Holland.

McCombs, Maxwell 2004. *Setting the Agenda: The Mass Media and Public Opinion.* Cambridge: Polity.

Miller, James 1993. *The Passion of Michel Foucault.* New York: Simon & Schuster.

Morris, Peter W. G. and Hough, George H. 1987. *The Anatomy of Major Projects: A Study of the Reality of Project Management.* New York: John Wiley.

National Audit Office of Denmark (De af Folketinget Valgte Statsrevisorer) 1998. *Beretning om Storebæltsforbindelsens økonomi*, beretning 4/97. Copenhagen: Statsrevisoratet.

O'Leary, Rosemary 2010. 'Guerrilla Employees: Should Managers Nurture, Tolerate, or Terminate Them?', *Public Administration Review*, January–February: 8–19.

Penge og Privatøkonomi, 2004, No. 11; 2005, No. 1.

Pickrell, Don 1990. *Urban Rail Transit Projects: Forecast versus Actual Ridership and Cost.* Washington, DC: US Department of Transportation.

Schram, Sanford F. and Caterino, Brian (eds.) 2006. *Making Political Science Matter: Debating Knowledge, Research, and Method.* New York University Press.

Scott, James C. 1999. *Seeing Like a State: How Certain Schemes to Improve the Human Condition Have Failed.* New Haven, CT: Yale University Press.

Simpson, James S. 2008. Speech made by the Administrator of the US Federal Transit Administration at the American Public Transportation Association (APTA) Rail Conference, San Francisco, 2 June, available at: www.fta.dot.gov/news/speeches/news_events_8247.html, accessed 15 February 2010.

Swiss Association of Road and Transportation Experts (SARTE) 2006. *Kosten-Nutzen-Analysen im Strassenverkehr*, Grundnorm 641820, valid from 1 August. Zurich: SARTE.

Taleb, Nassim Nicholas 2007. *The Black Swan: The Impact of the Highly Improbable.* London: Penguin.

Transportation Research Board (TRB) 2007. *Metropolitan Travel Forecasting: Current Practice and Future Direction*, Special Report 288. Washington, DC: National Academy of Sciences.

UK Department for Transport (DfT) 2006a. *Changes to the Policy on Funding Major Projects.* London: DfT.

2006b. *Transport Analysis Guidance (TAG), Unit 3.5.9: The Estimation and Treatment of Scheme Costs.* London: DfT.

Wachs, M. 1990. 'Ethics and Advocacy in Forecasting for Public Policy', *Business and Professional Ethics Journal* 9(1/2): 141–57.

7   Power and conflict in collaborative research

Corey Shdaimah and Roland Stahl

Introduction

There are many ways to practise phronetic social science. One way is what social scientists frequently refer to as collaborative research (CR). In this form of phronetic research, the non-academic stakeholders of a research project are integrated into the processes of planning, implementing and interpreting a study. Social scientists who work in the collaborative tradition (Freire [1970] 1999; Addams 2002; Minkler and Wallerstein 2003; Stoecker 2005; Strier 2007) have long insisted that many of the problems of contemporary mainstream knowledge production may be overcome by adopting a collaborative approach to research (Shdaimah, Stahl and Schram 2009). Their ideas have an obvious affinity with Flyvbjerg's theory of phronesis. One primary concern that arises in such collaborations is conflict, which is often a manifestation of power. In this chapter, we examine consensus and engagement approaches to conflict, using our own CR project as a case study.

In *Making Social Science Matter* (MSSM), Bent Flyvbjerg (2001) is careful to point out 'that the methodological guidelines [that he offers] should not be seen as methodological imperatives' (129). Phronetic social science can be practised using a variety of methods as long as it 'effectively deals with public deliberation and praxis' (129); that is, as long as it is done in a manner that invites engagement with issues that matter to the communities and other stakeholders. Collaborative research can be seen as the very model of phronetic research because these components are built into it by design. Collaborative research not only adds a praxis-oriented scientific voice to the public debate, but actively engages debate around issues that matter to stakeholders while developing and carrying out research. Any CR project includes, as Flyvbjerg puts it, a 'polyphony of voices' in all the decision-making stages of research. And it does so 'with no voice, including that of the researcher, claiming final authority' (2001: 139). When knowledge production is grounded in a polyphony of equally authoritative voices, the process by which these voices speak to each other and are negotiated becomes an important aspect of conducting the research project. One consequence of constantly negotiating various stakeholder interests is that power dynamics are more likely to be of immediate importance. How one engages conflict and the power relations in such collaborations is at least as important as the outcome and merits its own analysis.

The intimate relationship between the production of knowledge and the distribution and deployment of power has been well established (Foucault 1972; Rose and Miller 2008; Dean 2009). Power permeates all dimensions of knowledge production: the special standing of academic researchers in knowledge production (Toulmin 2001); the setting of a research agenda; the choice of specific research questions; the relationships between researchers and their research subjects (Fine *et al.* 2000); and the political use of research results by stakeholders such as politicians, policy-makers (O'Connor 2002) or street-level bureaucrats (Stone 1985).

In this chapter we highlight practical consequences that researchers may face once they forgo the position of power conferred on them by universities or colleges. As we have argued elsewhere in more detail, social scientists cannot claim special standing in CR projects, but merely a different role and with it a different perspective. Following the basic premises of phronesis and collaborative research, we argue that collaboration does not mean that stakeholders participate in a research project with researchers. It is the other way around: researchers participate in the larger societal projects (Stoecker 2005) or processes by contributing 'reflective thought aimed at action' (Flyvbjerg 2001: 127). 'Thoughtful reflections', Flyvbjerg argues, are the contribution of intellectuals (and researchers) to the public debate. In the case of a CR project, they are one of the many voices that, like all other positions, must be justified in open debate. Bringing our thoughtful reflections to interactions with stakeholders and negotiating shared actions in the research project is one way in which science is more fully part of praxis.

The need for public persuasion and discussion brings to the fore the fact that ideas and arguments will always be contested. This means that in any phronetic or collaborative research project, power will play an evident and important role. It is thus not surprising that there is a rich CR literature concerned with power (Stoecker 2003). The CR literature addresses the practical 'power problems' that collaborators face in a CR project. We contribute to this literature and to the discussion about Flyvbjerg's phronetic social science by providing conceptual suggestions regarding power debates in collaborative research. We argue that many CR theorists, if often implicitly, adopt a consensus-oriented theory of power. Such a conceptualization of power may lead to a vaguely idealistic approach to solving 'power problems' among researchers and their ostensibly less resourceful partners in CR projects. Refocusing the theoretical analysis of power towards engaging conflict may strengthen both the theoretical analysis and the practice of collaborative research. In the next section, we review Flyvbjerg's discussion of power and then apply this to the CR literature. This is followed by a brief description of our own research. We then draw on data from interviews with collaborators on one of our CR projects in order to connect the theoretical discussion with research practice.

Theorizing power in collaborative research

Flyvbjerg's discussion in MSSM outlines two fundamental approaches to the study of power. The first is Habermas' (1984) theory of communicative action, in which power relations can be viewed as a problem to be solved. Flyvbjerg indicates that Habermas appears to view conflict as 'dangerous, corrosive, and potentially destructive of social order and therefore in need of being contained and resolved' (2001: 108). Here we follow Flyvbjerg who prefers a different approach to power that is concerned with *wirkliche Historie* (real history) told in terms of conflict . . . ' In the tradition of Machiavelli (2005) and Nietzsche (1998) to Foucault (2000), Flyvbjerg suggests that suppressing conflicts may suppress freedom. To be free means that we may, at our own risk, participate in conflicts (Flyvbjerg 2001: 108). Referring to Hirschman's work on the role of conflict in democracies, Flyvbjerg concludes that 'social conflicts themselves produce the valuable ties that hold modern democratic societies together and provide them with the strength and cohesion they need'. This view is compatible with our own experiences, which we use to demonstrate how conflict can be engaged to enrich collaborative relationships and the research that emerges from them. We propose that what is true for modern democracies, and by extension phronetic social science conceptualized as a dimension of democratic practice, is also true for the field of collaborative research.

A close reading of the CR research literature that discusses power suggests that more often than not CR scholars adopt a theory of power that is consensus-oriented (Stoecker 2003). Minkler's and Wallerstein's widely cited *Community-based Participatory Research for Health* (2008) provides an overview of the current discussions on one of the most recent widely practised collaborative research variants. Israel and her colleagues develop a set of key principles for Community-based Participatory Research (Israel *et al.* 2005). The third principle focuses on power-sharing: 'In CBPR all parties participate in and share control over all phases of the research process, including problem definition, data collection, interpretation of results, and application of the results to address community concerns' (50).

Such a conceptualization of 'power-sharing' is characteristic of the writings on power in collaborative research. The claim that CR projects should be structured to enable all parties to participate is similar to Habermas' view that communication must be just in order to be good. In a recent study based on interviews with academics who conducted community-based research, respondents indicated tensions created by an overly idealistic perspective of power in collaborative research (Kennedy *et al.* 2009). One researcher described this as follows:

The power division is very, very important . . . Our ideal goal is really just being in power equally. Sometimes it's hard when you are the one who's going to bring the money and you are the one who is responsible for reporting to the funding agency for the quality outcome and some of your community partners are challenging you. You get frustrated and you often forget that, yes the power has to be equally distributed. (Kennedy *et al.* 2009: 3)

The consensus perspective of power is fraught with a tension between normative goals and what may be achievable in real life, where participants in a communicative process rarely have equal resources. Recognizing the existence of unequal access to public discourse in the real world, Habermas essentially solves the problem by claiming that all participants of a communicative process should have the same resources that are the prerequisite of communicative action (Habermas 1984). Habermas develops a set of rules or prerequisites for communicative action that are designed to neutralize or mitigate unequal access to power and other resources. But since, as Flyvbjerg suggests, participants never have access to equal resources, the goal of communicative action remains elusive.

If one accepts the above conclusion, this would mean that if researchers and their collaborative research partners never have equal access to available resources, then 'fair' collaboration is impossible. This may be one reason why CR scholars have written extensively on the difficulty of sharing power. Much like Habermas' idea of setting a fair process for communicative action, CR theorists have attempted to set up processes to achieve fair distribution of power. We agree that preventing the abuse of power is indeed an important principle of collaborative research (Israel *et al.* 1998). Since academics in CR projects often have superior resources to negotiate the knowledge production process, they need to be careful not to exploit their position of power (Kennedy *et al.* 2009). This is, indeed, a potential risk in any CR project and has been widely discussed in the literature (Hampshire, Hills and Iqbal 2005). However, we maintain that conceptualizing power as a destructive force to be overcome may also prevent collaborators – especially researchers – from engaging in conflicts with their collaborators. If power is conceived only as a negative force, this may lead to the undesirable result that conflicts among collaborators might be suppressed or, as Flyvbjerg frames it, 'controlled' (2001: 108), leading to a false impression of consensus.

Reflecting on and practising power in CR: trust, respect and conflict

We illustrate power processes in CR with data from our own experiences as part of a three-person team of academic researchers. We were hired by a Philadelphia-based non-profit organization, the Women's Community Revitalization Project (WCRP), to conduct CR for their advocacy work around home repair and maintenance needs of low-income Philadelphia homeowners ('the Home Repair Study'). The Home Repair Study was funded by the William Penn Foundation, a private local funder interested in pairing advocates and academics. During the year following the study, we interviewed all members of the research team who participated in the study on an ongoing basis. We taped and transcribed seven interviews and two were recorded in handwritten notes. The nine participants were four members of the WCRP including its executive director, the grant administrator from the funding agency, our fellow academic researcher and a local lobbyist who was hired to 'translate' the research for a political audience. We also relied on our *post hoc* reflections as participant observers. For a detailed discussion on the research methods see Stahl and Shdaimah (2007). We used a grounded theory approach (Charmaz 2006) to analyse data. Power emerged as a central concept related to decision-making processes and control over the production, interpretation and use of data in the Home Repair Study. Due to the contested definitions of power and its centrality to phronetic research (Flyvbjerg 2001; Caterino 2006), we chose to explore the concept further in our data through this particular lens (Sands 2004). Such a reading shored up our initial understanding of power in the relationships and revealed additional manifestations of power in the form of conflicts at different stages in the research process.

In our re-analysis, we identified three main areas where power struggles were manifest in the Home Repair Study. While these were not the only ones, they are illustrative in that they relate to different phases and different relationships. The first power struggle that we identified is political. It shaped perceptions of which arguments and forms of argumentation were considered appropriate in the local political process. The second struggle had its source in funder priorities and how those shaped the collaboration. Finally, we review power struggles between the advocates and academic partners. These three dynamics are intertwined and mutually reinforcing. We start from the 'outside in'; that is, from the larger societal circle that is least controlled by members of the collaborative research team. This is the circle where we individually and collectively wield the least power.

Politics and power

Conflict in the political arena might not arise in obvious ways. Political actors do not explicitly force advocates to act in particular ways or raise particular arguments. However, advocates and researchers alike know that certain arguments are more likely to capture public attention. Political discourse shapes and is shaped by the way in which public problems are framed. Advocates can tap into frames in order to popularize their causes and make them palatable to politicians (Gusfield 1980). Savvy researchers can also influence the framing of causes (Lakoff 2004).

The current political arena shaped the substantive and methodological frame for our project. As we have discussed elsewhere (Stahl and Shdaimah 2007; Shdaimah, Stahl and Schram 2009), the focus on home repair was shaped by the perception of a receptive policy climate. Support for asset-building strategies for low-income families meant that policymakers were receptive to the concerns of homeowners. Methodologically, we knew that in the current local political arena, our study had to include quantitative data. The Women's Community Revitalization Project did not have the in-house expertise to perform quantitative analysis. In order to be heard by the City Council, the WCRP needed to rely on outside experts to present a certain form of knowledge, produced according to certain procedures; that is to say, the politicians wanted numbers. The advocates understood what mattered to decision-makers, despite the fact that most of them found this frustrating. They believed that their own knowledge-gathering would be de-legitimized, both because it was 'anecdotal', that is, derived from their own work with community members, and because they were activists and therefore considered to be biased:

You know it's just legitimacy . . . I mean I don't know if this is really the case but let's say with this report; if we had gone in and said 'the waiting times seem really long, we don't know exactly what they are but we know they're really long . . . ' So I think there is a thing about anecdotal information and I think that the players are already known and I think that people might respond more to their preconceived idea of who the players are than to what actual information they have.

The advocates understand that their assertions lacked credibility in the eyes of policy-makers. The need for research (and researchers) was, to large extent, a result of the political forces. This frustrated advocates because it required use of their limited resources on the research, despite the sense that these resources might be better spent on organizing. Wrangling with data collection and analysis meant that time was spent on tasks that seemed irrelevant to their day-to-day work. One WCRP community organizer, who had ongoing contact with constituents, told us:

I felt that the concern for accuracy or data was taking energy out of doing organizing or talking to people or making change in the arena. That the amount of time that was spent at what, at times, seemed very small details, and I think it was frustrating and I think that it's why I stopped going to the meetings because I didn't have time.

Advocates resented the devotion of precious energy and resources to research. The executive director reported that during the time the WCRP was spending money on our research, they needed to fire a staff member due to resource constraints. Even though the funding for our participation came from an outside source, she used this as an illustration that these resource utilization choices are very real, and may be more frustrating when they are driven by strategic political considerations rather than by the substantive priorities of advocates.

Funding and research agendas

The second focus of our power-analytic lens is on funding for the Home Repair Study. Funding shapes research content, design and implementation. Our advocate partners told us that the substantive content of the collaboration was, at least in part, shaped by the knowledge that home repair problems faced by homeowners would be funded by a local funding agency with which they had enjoyed a good relationship. The desire for funding forced the WCRP to focus the research on home repair, which was tangential to the advocates' mission that had focused on providing low-income rental housing for women. While home repair concerns of low-income homeowners were not incompatible with their mission, it was not the advocates' priority:

In reality so much of what gets done is what gets funded and so in reality I think WCRP would have liked to have done something that was more grass-rootsy . . . not to be going out and surveying people about homeownership. We work with a lot of homeowners in the community but our housing is rental. I think we made a choice based on that we could, the thing that was important and get funded to do, and also get some money to do organizing even if it's around a specific issue – it allows us to get out and talk to people, to get to know more people.

Another organizer told us that she 'didn't know if the research was that flexible really' and so she worried that it might not serve the WCRP's larger goals. However, she also noted that the dearth of resources presents an ongoing struggle for organizers that necessitates compromise:

But that's always something that we – I don't know, as organizers, we struggle. We get money to do something and by the way . . . we got the money to do the [neighborhood] survey – but heck there's no funding to do organizing by itself so you can use any tool, any excuse, to do organizing.

The need for funding may limit researchers as well as activists. In discussing their choice of the Bryn Mawr research team, our advocate partners told us that they chose to invest in our learning curve rather than hire researchers with more expertise on housing. Among the reasons for their choice was the concern that available housing researchers had closer ties to the city. This meant that they might be beholden to city agencies for funding, and therefore may be less likely to critique city government:

They get funding from the City and we were fighting the City. So they couldn't really stand up – they were uncomfortable saying in the research document – putting the City first as the place where the change needed to happen – they only wanted to say the federal government. Yeah, those things are very real. And yeah, that's what has to change. Yeah, there has to be a revolution. They could put that too.

The leadership of the WCRP did not worry that the other researchers more closely tied to the city would produce inaccurate research. However, they were afraid that they would not explicitly implicate the city as a source of necessary change and would, instead, provide vague recommendations aimed at the federal government or other actors far removed from local politics. They contracted with us due to their awareness of how the power dynamics of the relationships between the other researchers and the city might negatively impact their advocacy efforts. In this case they did not outwardly challenge the other researchers by engaging in discussion and conflict, but made an internal decision that recognized potential conflict and avoided it. Similar to their own reliance on funding and the way it shaped our advocates' agenda, our partners at the WCRP were aware that the city of Philadelphia, as a provider of funding to researchers, might shape the work and goals of researchers who regularly work with the city. Academics' reliance on funding, which is growing with the increasing pressure on academics to bring in grants, is a form of power and source of conflict that shapes decisions of researchers in much the same way that it shapes the decisions of activists.

Power and the research team

Researchers generally have tools that provide them with the means to produce knowledge that lay people do not have at their disposal. Resources that academic researchers bring include skills and training. They may also include data analysis software, time and the ability to leverage student contributions through courses and graduate assistantships. Recognized less often is the way that organizers or advocates may control resources, such as access to funders (and funding) and access to constituents, policy-makers or other stakeholders who may be 'research subjects'.

In discussing the Home Repair Study, the WCRP's executive director told us how she viewed our collaboration as different from the approach of other researchers in her description of a panel discussion where she presented the study:

The idea that we would raise money and define the research questions based on some ideas we had, some things we needed to figure out on a campaign related to housing felt backwards to [my fellow panelists]. And I felt like you were so open to that process. You know it's not necessarily the academic or the researcher who's raising the money and creating the questions and then pulling in some folks who are in the neighborhood or folks who are practitioners.

Although the WCRP's executive director often used the term 'sharing power', it was clear that what she means, as this quote suggests, is that we were willing to open up the research process to conflict and acknowledge who had control over the decision-making when consensus could not be achieved. This is where the consensus approach to collaboration diverges from the conflict approach. Collaboration is defined by a willingness to work together or to share power. Consensus assumes that we can always reach a resolution, no matter what conflicts arise. A conflict approach recognizes that collaborators will have conflicting interests and boundaries that cannot be crossed and therefore consensus may not be possible. For researchers, for example, one likely boundary is the integrity of the research. This came up in our collaboration when the advocates wanted us to combine data from two different sources and pushed us to come up with one number of homes requiring repair in the city that would be readily understandable and memorable for policy-makers, a struggle that we have discussed in depth elsewhere (Shdaimah and Stahl 2006; Shdaimah, Stahl and Schram 2011). For advocates, it might be fear that the research process itself could harm constituents. It is in these instances where tension is felt most intensely, and where the power and conflict underlying the collaboration is most often exposed.

Most of our respondents reported tensions at one point or another. When tensions emerged, they brought forth questions concerning control: control of the research and control of the information. The three academic researchers were drawn to this project by what one described as a desire to partner with advocates: 'to be "on tap" rather than "on top"'. This was a priority even in negotiating the research contract: we were paid by the WCRP and our payments were meted out in instalments based upon satisfactory completion of work phases (reviewed by the WCRP's lawyer, who sometimes requested additional information). One of the WCRP organizers told us explicitly that this was an important area of control. They had learned from prior collaborations how important it was to have researchers commit to a project on their terms – it was a way that they leveraged their power in the collaboration. The executive director noted that prior research partners had failed to come through as promised and seemed to attribute this failure to the possibility of unseen and unidentifiable conflicts coupled with the WCRP's lack of power over the researchers:

I don't know if it was political in the sense that they really didn't want to do it or they didn't have the relationships or what, but it never progressed and it never was clear that it wasn't progressing. It was always on hold. That was [why] getting the money and being able to choose somebody and have them sign a contract [laughs] and say that they were going to do certain things was really important for this.

The fact that we were willing to openly address the power struggles and negotiate with our advocate partners around framing research questions and strategies for presenting data means that conflicts were seen and identified. This allowed areas of control to be identified early so boundaries to 'sharing' power were delineated from the outset. This meant open engagement with conflicts and recognition of which compromises would not be acceptable. For example, we did not always receive full information about major components of the work, including what all the components were, who would be carrying them out, what was to be included in the report and how it was to be presented. This raised conflicts around the question of access to constituents. From the outset, we wanted to speak directly to homeowners. The WCRP directed us to interview high-level city and programme officials and community organizations. After repeated requests, we were given the names and contact information for three homeowners whom the WCRP decided would be appropriate for us to interview. At various times, there was also talk of us coming to a neighbourhood meeting, but that never came to fruition. We received notice of these meetings a few days prior, if at all, and were not involved in any planning. This seemed to be a way by which the WCRP minimized our power over the research as they exercised their own and, ultimately, it meant that we were unable to attend any meetings with constituents during the course of the year-long collaboration. We did not reach consensus about whether we could speak directly with constituents, and it was clear that this was an area where the WCRP's power trumped our own.

We later learned that different WCRP team members also had different visions of the project. There, too (as in any organization), was a hierarchy of knowledge and control. Leadership at the WCRP did not want us to speak directly to homeowners, at least initially; they preferred to remain the only direct link:

> I think there's a way that you develop trust. I mean I don't want you talking to the homeowners that I talk to – or I don't even talk to that much – unless I am really clear where you are coming from. And I think there's a process in all of that. And you may think that that's valuable to your research and I may think that may be detrimental to my relationships with people. And so you go through a process to figure out what's worth it. And in this case because we hired you, we had the power.

The WCRP leadership did not want us to act inappropriately. Our research was, in part, an organizing tool for them and so they wanted to ensure that any contact would be compatible with their advocacy goals. In contrast, we heard from some of the WCRP community organizers that our attendance at a community meeting was something they would have desired. The discrepancy between the WCRP leadership and staff organizers revealed another layer of conflict, power and control:

> See that's a breakdown. That's a breakdown. That's something to consider next time. If you had come and done a presentation to the neighborhood group about your findings, oh man they would have loved it. They would have loved it. It would have given them weapons to understand their immediate reality.

This advocate believed that more direct contact with the WCRP's constituents would further their organizing and advocacy efforts. She viewed the surveys that the WCRP had conducted as taking something from the neighbourhood and she desired reciprocity, which such a meeting might have provided. However, she was only made aware of the conflict in our retrospective interview and had little input in shaping the Home Repair Study, even though she carried out some of the advocacy work. There are tensions in the three positions we present here: organizers who wanted us to speak to homeowners; our own desire to talk with the WCRP's constituents; and a reticence on the part of higher-level WCRP decision-makers to bring together the academic researchers with homeowners. This was an area of conflict to which each brought different goals, interests and levels of power. It was the WCRP leadership who prevailed in this arena where they set boundaries that could, partially, be subject to compromise only once trust had been built.

Conclusion

Power struggles and overt engagement with conflicts among participants lie at the heart of collaborative research. Any CR theorist or practitioner would agree that negotiation around power differentials is a difficult and prolonged process, and that a balance of power can be achieved only through trust and mutual respect (Postma 2008). We agree that mutual respect among stakeholders is a prerequisite to productive conflict (Stahl and Shdaimah 2007). What distinguishes phronetic research and, by extension, our view of power in CR, is that engaging in conflict with the various stakeholders of a research project – or with the public at large as in the case of phronetic research – is at least as important as trust and mutual respect. It is only through actively engaging conflicts that stakeholders in knowledge-production processes fully realize the potential of the knowledge–power nexus. We view collaborative research as an expansion of Flyvbjerg's (2001) conceptualization of phronetic social science. We expand on his concept of active engagement rather than prevention of conflict at every step of the research process. Collaborative research requires that conflicts be engaged actively and openly while a research project is carried out. In other words, the conflicts among the scientific, advocacy and public spheres are recognized and negotiated within the collaboration.

It is possible that we were particularly attuned to the possibilities of conflict and power in the Home Repair Study, because we worked with politically savvy organizers who were versed in the tactics of power analysis. Literature also suggests that, with experience, collaborative research partners see an improvement in their ability to conduct collaborative research and address concerns, including 'finding appropriate partners, perceived tokenism, [and] power imbalance' (Savan *et al.* 2009: 786). We were lucky to have been able to learn from our experienced CR partners to acknowledge the importance of power. We respected each stakeholder's differential ability to wield power constructively for the use and production of knowledge. Making power an explicit part of the conversation is hard work (Stahl and Shdaimah 2007), but the dialogue puts conflicts in the open and allows negotiation that does not suppress different interests, goals and boundaries. Such dialogue raises the potential for using power productively, as one of the WCRP community organizers suggests:

WCRP talks about tensions a lot because there are lots of tensions in the agencies. So I think in the last two years I've come to see tension as a really positive thing. I think those tensions exist whether or not people talk about them. In a good group I think they come in to the open and they're worked through in a different way than if one group is working by itself and another group is working by itself.

It would have been absurd (and analytically unfruitful) to ignore the role of power in our collaboration. It also would have been inaccurate and patronizing to view our collaborators as powerless or, indeed, to view our position as 'sharing' power, since it implies it is ours to give. Even as they were constrained by some power dynamics, the WCRP used power in other ways to further its goals. Funding sources wielded the power of the purse to dictate collaboration with academic researchers around housing, but our advocate partners simultaneously used their own power to secure grant funds to further their organizing goals, to pursue concrete resources for their neighbourhood constituents, and to dictate the terms of the research to us.

Power and the conflicts in which it manifests are not inherently good or bad. Power is structural and subtle, and is not always an obvious coercion or use of a person's will over another person. Attention to power is subversive and radical when it is not minimized and 'shared', but actively identified and engaged. Our research in its very structure democratizes through allocation of power, even as it sits within a mainstream hierarchy of knowledge development. Researchers must be willing to abdicate privilege and participate in arenas where they do not have as much power and to engage in conflict with their collaborative research partners. Advocates and researchers have to be willing to work together rather than strong-arm one another, and to be clear about the boundaries they cannot ethically cross. Mechanisms for negotiating conflict have to be created and built in to the collaborative research process. But these mechanisms should not suppress conflict and they cannot be viewed as a source of long-term definitions or solutions. Instead, they must allow evolution of trusting, open relationships and create spaces for shared conflict that leads to situational, contextual and mutually beneficial collaborations.

REFERENCES

Addams, J. 2002. *Democracy and Social Ethics*. University of Chicago Press.
Caterino, B. 2006. 'Power and Interpretation', in Schram and Caterino (eds.), *Making Political Science Matter*, pp. 134–51.

Charmaz, K. 2006. *Constructing Grounded Theory: A Practical Guide through Qualitative Analysis*. Thousand Oaks, CA: Sage.

Dean, M. M. 2009. *Governmentality: Power and Rule in Modern Society*, 2nd edn. Thousand Oaks, CA: Sage.

Fine, M., Weis, L., Weseen, S. and Wong, L. 2000. 'For Whom? Qualitative Research, Representations and Social Responsibilities', in N. K. Denzin and Y. S. Lincoln (eds.), *Handbook of Qualitative Research*, 2nd edn. Thousand Oaks, CA: Sage, pp. 107–32.

Flyvbjerg, B. 2001. *Making Social Science Matter: Why Social Inquiry Fails and How it can Succeed Again*. Cambridge University Press.

Foucault, M. 1972. *The Archaeology of Knowledge and the Discourse on Language*, trans. A. M. Sheridan Smith. New York: Pantheon.

2000. *Power: Essential Works of Foucault, 1954–1984*, vol. 3. ed. James D. Faubion, series ed. Paul Rabinow, trans. Robert Hurley. New York: The New Press.

Freire, P. [1970] 1999. *Pedagogy of the Oppressed*. New York: Continuum.

Gusfield, J. R. 1980. *The Culture of Public Problems: Drinking-driving and the Symbolic Order*. University of Chicago Press.

Habermas, J. 1984. *Theory of Communicative Action, Vol. 1: Reason and the Rationalization of Society*, trans. T. McCarthy. Boston, MA: Beacon Press.

Hampshire, K., Hills, E. and Iqbal, N. 2005. 'Power Relations in Participatory Research and Community Development: A Case Study from Northern England', *Human Organization* 64(4): 340–9.

Israel, B. A., Eng, E., Schulz, A. J. and Parker, E. A. 2005. *Methods in Community-based Collaborative Research for Health*. San Francisco, CA: Jossey-Bass.

Israel, B. A., Schulz, A. J., Parker, E. A. and Becker, A. B. 1998. 'Review of Community-based Research: Assessing Partnership Approaches to Improve Public Health', *Annual Review of Public Health* 19: 173–202.

Kennedy, C., Vogel, A., Goldberg-Freeman, C., Kass, N. and Farfel, M. 2009. 'Faculty perspectives on community-based research: "I see this still as a journey"', *Journal of Empirical Research on Human Ethics* 4(20): 3–16.

Lakoff, G. 2004. *Don't Think of an Elephant! Know your Values and Frame the Debate*. White River Junction, VT: Chelsea Green Publishing.

Machiavelli, N. 2005. *The Prince*, trans. P. Bondanella. Oxford University Press.

Minkler, M. and Wallerstein, N. (eds.) 2003. *Community-based Collaborative Research in Health*. San Francisco, CA: Jossey-Bass.

Minkler, M. and Wallerstein, N. (eds.) 2008. *Community-based Participatory Research for Health: From Process to Outcomes*. San Francisco, CA: Jossey-Bass.

Nietzsche, F. W. 1998. *On the Genealogy of Morality*, trans. M. Clark and A. J. Swenson. Indianapolis, IN: Hackett.

O'Connor, A. 2002. *Poverty Knowledge: Social Science, Social Policy, and the Poor in Twentieth-century US History*. Princeton University Press.

Postma, J. 2008. 'Balancing Power among Academic and Community Partners', *Journal of Empirical Research on Human Ethics* 3(2): 17–32.

Rose, N. and Miller, P. 2008. *Governing the Present: Administering Economic, Social and Personal Life*. Cambridge: Polity.

Sands, R. G. 2003. 'Narrative Analysis: A Feminist Approach', in D. K. Padgett (ed.), *The Qualitative Research Experience*. Belmont, CA: Wadsworth/ Thomson Learning, pp. 48–78.

Savan, B., Flicker, S., Kolenda, B. and Mildenberger, M. 2009. 'How to Facilitate (or Discourage) Community-based Research', *Local Environment* 14(8): 783–96.

Schram, S. 2002. *Praxis for the Poor: Piven and Cloward and the Future of Social Science in Social Welfare*. New York University Press.

Schram, S. and Caterino, B. (eds.) 2006. *Making Political Science Matter: Debating Knowledge, Research, and Method*. New York University Press.

Seng, J. S. 1998. 'Praxis as a Conceptual Framework for Collaborative Research in Nursing', *Advances in Nursing Science* 20(4): 37–48.

Shdaimah, C. S. and Stahl, R. W. 2006. 'Reflections on Doing Phronetic Social Science: A Case Study', in Schram and Caterino (eds.), *Making Political Science Matter*, pp. 98–113.

Shdaimah, C. S., Stahl, R. and Schram, S. F. 2009. 'When You Can See the Sky through the Roof: Homeownership Looking from the Bottom Up', in E. Schatz (ed.), *Political Ethnography*. Chicago University Press, pp. 255–74.

  2011. *Change Research: A Case Study on Collaborative Methods for Social Workers and Advocates*. New York: Columbia University Press.

Stahl, R. and Shdaimah, C. S. 2007. 'Collaboration between Community Advocates and Academic Researchers: Scientific Advocacy or Political Research', *British Journal of Social Work* 38(8): 1610–29.

Stoecker, R. 2003. 'Are Academics Irrelevant?: Approaches and Roles for Scholars in Community-based Research', in Minkler and Wallerstein (eds.), *Community-based Participatory Research in Health*, pp. 98–112.

  2005. *Research Methods for Community Change: A Project-based Approach*. Newbury Park, CA: Sage.

Stone, D. A. 1985. *The Disabled State (Health, Society, and Policy)*. New York: Palgrave Macmillan.

Strier, R. 2007. 'Anti-oppressive Research in Social Work: A Preliminary Definition', *British Journal of Social Work* 37(5): 857–71.

Toulmin, S. 2001. *Return to Reason*. Cambridge, MA: Harvard University Press.

Unsettling a settler society: film,
        phronesis and collaborative planning in
        small-town Canada

Leonie Sandercock and Giovanni Attili

Prologue

Five years ago we heard three anecdotes about the small town of Burns
Lake in northern British Columbia that whetted our phronetic research
appetite, as well as our evolving interest in film as a mode of inquiry and
a way of approaching collaborative and transformational planning. This
northern interior town has a population of 3,000 people, almost equally
divided between First Nations (indigenous) and non-Native Canadians,
the latter constituting the 'settler society'.[1] The first anecdote reported a
kind of 'High Noon' conflict between the municipality of Burns Lake and
one of the First Nations bands, the Burns Lake Band (whose preferred
name is Ts'il Kaz Koh First Nation).[2] As part of a dispute over land
and taxation which culminated in the year 2000, the municipality shut
off water and sewer services to the Burns Lake Band's Reserve, in the
middle of winter (in a region where winter temperatures in February are
typically −30°C). To our then innocent ears that seemed like a pretty
shocking situation. How could there be such an apparent affront to basic
human rights, we wondered, in twenty-first-century Canada, a country
with a rather stellar record of defending human rights abroad? How could

---

[1] The official census counts only non-Native residents, so the 3,000 represents that demographic group. In addition, there is an almost equal number of First Nations, most of
whom live on two Reserves within municipal boundaries, so the actual population is
close to 5,000. The term 'settler society' is in widespread use now in discourses around
colonialism and its impacts in countries of the 'New World', which were colonized by
Europeans and which had devastating effects on the indigenous populations.

[2] Under the Indian Act of 1867, formerly sovereign tribes who referred to themselves as
Nations were stripped of their sovereignty, given the identifier of 'band' rather than tribe
or Nation, and their hereditary chief system of governance was replaced by a federally
mandated election process for chief and band councillors. Today, there are 203 bands in
the province of British Columbia, ranging in size from fewer than 100 members to 6,000
members. From the 1850s onwards in British Columbia, Nations were stripped of their
lands and forced to live on Reserves, tiny patches of marginal lands, and thereby reduced
to poverty for lack of a land base to ensure their livelihood.

such injustice and seemingly blatant racism be happening and how could the perpetrator be an arm of the state, namely, local government?

The second anecdote told how in 2005 some of the local youth in the town had gotten together, Native *and* non-Native, and written and performed a song about racism and violence in the town, calling their song 'Leave it Behind'. This raised a second question of whether and how, amid a history of segregation and conflict, some people were struggling to change things, and how well were they faring? And, third, we learned that in the municipal elections of 2005 a member of the Burns Lake Band had been elected to the Village Council, the only Native person ever to serve on that Council. What effect would this have on local politics? Was the local power structure changing or were there more subtle shifts in power occurring, and, if so, how and why? And what potential effect might our research have in aiding this shift towards more equitable economic, social and political relations between Native and non-Native Canadians in this town, and possibly beyond, through the power of their story? These were the questions that prompted us to make an exploratory trip to the town in the summer of 2006.

To be more precise, we were invited to make this visit by one of the local anti-racism activists (Pauline Goertzen), a woman in her late twenties who was born and raised in the town, from a Mennonite family background. She had seen our first film and was hoping that we might think there was a story worth telling, on film, about her small town so far away from where the majority of the Canadian population lives.[3] After that initial trip we, as researchers, were hooked.

This chapter discusses what is, in fact, our second exploration of the potential of multimedia in working with communities on a vexing public policy issue.[4] We have been working now since 2006 on a documentary film *and* action research project titled 'Finding Our Way', which we describe as an investigation of the inconvenient truth of Canada's apartheid, through two detailed case studies of conflict involving two small First Nations communities in northern British Columbia. Our approach is that of phronetic social science. We look at what has happened there, historically and in the present day. Who has gained and who has lost by the historic and current mechanisms of power operating in

---

[3] Most Canadians live in the three large metropolitan areas in the south, Vancouver, Toronto and Montreal, and their concerns are metropolitan-based. There is not much knowledge of life beyond these big city regions.

[4] Our first exploration, working in a culturally diverse immigrant neighbourhood in Vancouver, resulted in the 50-minute documentary 'Where Strangers become Neighbours' (Attili and Sandercock 2007) and the book and DVD package of the same title (Sandercock and Attili 2009). See also Sandercock and Attili (2010c).

this particular socio-cultural landscape? We ask whether this has been fair or desirable according to the espoused values of Canadian society today, values expressed in the 1982 Charter of Rights and Freedoms passed by the national parliament. And we collaboratively explore, with key actors in the town, whether there is a way forward and what that might look like. What should be done, and how might our research contribute to transformational planning (that is, social change), through our research design?

The chapter begins by locating film as a mode of inquiry that is part of an emergent, post-positivist paradigm that draws on the importance and powers of story and storytelling. We outline our initial thinking about the potential of film as a mode of inquiry, a form of meaning-making, a way of knowing, and a way of provoking public dialogue and community engagement around planning and policy issues. We connect our approach, which Attili (2007, 2008) calls 'digital ethnography', with what Flyvbjerg (2001) describes as 'phronetic social science' or value-rational research. We then explain the guiding research question we chose to work on: 'can relations between Native and non-Native Canadians move beyond the oppressive history of colonization to a future of partnership for economic and social development, in this specific region of northern British Columbia?', addressing why this is a research question in planning. (We are also, of course, interested in whether the answer to this question can be generalizable across Canada.) This is followed by a description of power and social relations at our research 'site', the north-central interior of British Columbia, a situation that can be understood only by digging further into the history of colonization in Canada and British Columbia, and its specific technologies of power. In other words, we excavate the 'High Noon' conflict of 1999–2000 through both ethnographic and historical strategies. We describe the political force field into which we were entering and of which we have become an unavoidable part, and how, on completion of filming, our editing process and choices were made with a strategic eye towards helping shape future economic and social development opportunities. Finally, we discuss how our research is contributing to emerging change processes through our communication and dissemination strategies, describing the dialogical and other action processes that the film is now driving.

An emerging paradigm

The beginnings of an epistemological shift in the field of planning were foreshadowed in the early 1970s in the works of Friedmann (1973) and Churchman (1971). Friedmann outlined a 'crisis of knowing' in which he skewered the limitations of 'expert knowledge' and advocated a new approach, which he called 'mutual learning' or 'transactive planning', an approach which could appreciate and draw on local and experiential knowledge in dialogue with expert knowledge. At the same time, Churchman's inquiry into knowing was exploring the value of stories. 'The Hegelian inquirer is a storyteller, and Hegel's Thesis is that the best inquiry is the inquiry that produces stories' (Churchman 1971: 178). Over the next several decades, the termites kept eating away at the Enlightenment foundations of modernist planning, anchored as it was in an epistemology that privileged scientific and technical ways of knowing. Accompanying a broader post-positivist movement in the social sciences (Stretton 1969; Rabinow and Sullivan 1987; Geertz 1988; Bourdieu 1990; Flyvbjerg 2001) that was complemented by feminist and postcolonial critiques (Said 1979; hooks 1984; Kelly 1984; Trinh 1989; Lerner 1997; Sandercock 1998), planning scholars began to see the need both for an expanded language for planning and for ways of expanding the creative capacities of planners (Landry 2000, 2006; Sandercock 2005a, 2005b; Sarkissian and Hurford 2010). There was a wider recognition of the need to acknowledge and use the many other ways of knowing that exist: experiential, intuitive and somatic knowledges; local knowledges; knowledges based on the practices of talking and listening, seeing, contemplating and sharing; and knowledges expressed in visual, symbolic, ritual and other artistic ways. An 'epistemology of multiplicity' (Sandercock 1998) would nurture these other ways of knowing, without discarding or dismissing more traditional forms of scientific or technical reasoning.

The 'story turn' in planning has been one response to this epistemological crisis. In the past two decades a growing number of planning scholars have been investigating the relationship between story and planning (Forester 1989; Mandelbaum 1991; Eckstein and Throgmorton 2003; Sandercock 2003a; Attili 2007). These investigations highlight how planning is performed through stories, how rhetoric and poetics are crucial in interactive processes, how the communicative dimension is central to planning practices, and how story can awaken energies and imaginations, becoming a catalyst for involving urban conversations, for deep community dialogues.

Today, new information and communication technologies (ICTs) provide the opportunity to explore storytelling through multimedia forms, including film/video, which offer a vast repertoire of analytical as well as expressive possibilities. We have been attempting to mesh two forms of inquiry, digital ethnography and phronetic social science, which have turned out to be extraordinarily complementary.

The digital ethnographic approach is a research perspective through which the communicative potentialities of an ethnographic analysis are widened by the use of digital languages. The language of film can give expression to a dense qualitative analysis of social phenomena in a territorial context. It can be used to give thick and complex accounts of a city or community focused on stories, interviews and narration. Qualitative analysis succeeds in expressing what lies beyond the surface of maps, physical objects, classifications and aggregate quantitative data. It intentionally focuses on individual lives in urban settings made up of changing densities, memories, perceptions and aesthetics. It is an attentive, extremely focused analysis of urban space, where existence, intersections, languages and interstitial freedoms delineate controversial and palpitating urban landscapes.

The goal of this kind of analysis is to probe deeply into inhabitants' lived practices, conflicts and modalities of space appropriation, which will reveal principles, rationalities and potential writings that interrogate the ordered text of the planned city. Intercepting these multiform practices means being able to listen to the city's murmurs, to catch stories, and to read signs and spatial poetics, all of which are generative of new meanings. Using film is to research what normally remains invisible in planning (though not in life) and ends by questioning the way planners typically explore, analyse and represent urban space.

Bypassing the ideology of the Archimedean observer who stands outside the observed, the qualitative approach privileges collaborative contexts to produce a collective invention of interconnected stories. In this perspective, there is no longer a single eye that encompasses 'everything' in its vision, but a multiplicity of stories told by the inhabitants of specific neighbourhoods or communities who no longer can be thought of as isolated monads (as, for example, in survey research), and whose stories must be understood as an interconnected web. Through in-depth interviews and the confrontation of diverse visions of the world, this approach becomes a powerful tool for a deeper comprehension of what animates the many souls, conflicts and resources of the city.

The result is an ethnographic narrative that is built on the intersection of multiple narratives captured by the ethnographer. It is a story that does not pretend to represent 'the truth': rather, it is explicitly subjective, even partial (cf. Landman, Chapter 3, above). The key word to comprehend the fulcrum of digital ethnographic analysis is 'to evoke', that is, to create a plausible world – one of many such worlds – taken from everyday life. Assuming this perspective, ethnography rids itself of the obsession of a mimesis rooted in objects, facts, empirical generalizations and ultimately in a single truth. Rather, it becomes an interconnected patchwork of evocative images imbued with ambiguity and indeterminacy. Their full comprehension escapes the researcher's intentionality, as the film creates a dynamic field that is open to diverse interpretations and possibilities. This level of interpretative openness transforms a digital ethnography into a potential catalyst for participatory planning. In other words, digital ethnographies represent a new way of provoking dialogue in decision-making contexts. It is a way of starting a public conversation (Attili 2008: 260–1).

Sandercock's advocacy of the importance of multiple ways of knowing, and particularly of the power of story in planning (Sandercock 2003b), resonated with the approach Flyvbjerg (2001) was forging into 'phronetic social science'.[5] This is an approach that, by explicitly focusing on values, could effectively deal with public deliberation and praxis. Using this approach, the point of departure is a series of classic value-rational questions: where are we going?; is it desirable?; what should be done? For anyone in the planning and policy fields, researchers or practitioners, these questions ought to be central to praxis, along with their obvious companions, 'who gains and who loses, through what kinds of power relations?; what possibilities are there for changing existing power relations?; and is it desirable to do so?' (Flyvbjerg 2001: 130–1). An equally important question for post-modern, self-reflective researchers becomes: 'Of what kinds of power relations are those asking these questions themselves a part?' (Flyvbjerg 2001). Flyvbjerg's mode of inquiry is particularly well suited to investigating contemporary policy or planning issues. It is particularly useful for us as digital ethnographers, committed to immersion in the place and people we are filming, yet also seeking some critical distance. It presents a way of thinking beyond the objectivity–subjectivity divide, recognizing that the researcher becomes part of the phenomenon being studied and can be both insider and outsider:

For contemporary studies, one gets close to the phenomenon or group whom one studies during data collection, and remains close during the phases of data analysis, feedback, and publication. Combined with the focus on relations of values and power, this strategy typically creates an interest by outside parties, and even outside stakeholders, in the research. These parties will test and evaluate the research in various ways. The researchers will consciously expose themselves to reactions from their surroundings – both positive and negative – and may derive benefit from the learning effect which is built into this strategy. In this way, the researcher becomes part of the phenomenon being studied, without necessarily 'going native' or the project becoming simple action research. (Flyvbjerg 2001: 132)

---

[5] *Phronesis* is usually translated as practical wisdom, in contrast to *epistemé* (theoretical knowledge) and *techné* (technical know-how).

Fundamental to phronetic research is a focus on 'thick description', generated out of asking 'little questions'. This requires patience and the accumulation of a vast amount of detail. (In the case of our film, perhaps a hundred hours of our own video footage, along with a massive digital archive that we collected, comprising thousands of photographs, newspaper clippings and so on, all of which had to be edited down to what became a 90-minute film.) Also fundamental to such research is the art of narrative. If the question driving the phronetic research process is the 'how' question (how could this happen?; how did it happen?; through what technologies of power?), then the clearest way to answer such a question is by doing narrative analysis. And film is a very powerful, polyphonic narrative tool:

Narrative is our most fundamental form for making sense of experience. Narratives not only give meaningful form to experiences already lived, but also provide a forward glance, helping us anticipate situations before we encounter them, allowing us to envision alternative futures . . . Narrative inquiries develop descriptions and interpretations of the phenomenon, from the perspectives of participants, researchers, and others. (Flyvbjerg 2001: 137)

Phronetic research then, along with digital ethnography, is dialogical in the sense that it includes and (if successful) is included in a polyphony of voices, with no one voice, including that of the researcher, claiming final authority. It is also potentially liberatory or empowering, in creating the space for people to tell their own stories (Freire 1970). The goal is to produce an input into the ongoing social dialogue and praxis of a society, rather than to generate ultimate, unequivocally verified knowledge.

Such were our epistemological and methodological starting points. But what was the research question through which we were going to test the potential of multimedia/film as a mode of inquiry, a form of meaning-making, and a way of stimulating dialogue in divided communities?

Research questions

We started with a very specific, contextual question. What was the nature of the conflict between the Burns Lake Band and the Village that came to a head with the village shutting off water, fire and sewer services to the houses on the reservation, and the Band taking the Village to the Supreme Court of British Columbia? That specific question led us to a deeper question. What was the hundred-year history of relations between the Village and the Band? And as we developed answers to that question, we realized that we needed to go back even further into an understanding of the very process of colonization by European settlers, which had imposed certain technologies of power on indigenous peoples which had devastating and lasting consequences on those communities. So that question became, what power relations had structured the relationship between Native and non-Native Canadians?

But research processes also take on a life of their own once one is 'in the field'. And, as we spent more time in the region, we discovered another story, equally shocking, about another band, the Cheslatta Carrier Nation, now living 20 miles south of Burns Lake. In the space of one morning's visit to their Band office, where we met their senior policy adviser, Mike Robertson, we were so emotionally as well as intellectually drawn into their tragic history that we committed that very day to telling their story as well. What we learned that morning was that the Cheslatta people (also members of the larger Carrier Nation of which the Burns Lake Band was a part) were evicted from their lands in 1952 by the federal Department of Indian Affairs in association with the province of British Columbia and the Aluminium Company of Canada (Alcan). The province had promised Alcan exclusive rights to the Nechako watershed for the purposes of building a dam to power a hydroelectric plant, which would drive the aluminium smelter which Alcan was building on the coast. As part of the dam-building project, Cheslatta's lands would be flooded. The Cheslatta people were given ten days' notice of the impending flooding and were forced to evacuate their villages (houses, barns, animals, farming equipment, gardens, smokehouses and church) without taking anything with them ('not even a pencil' as one of the Elders said).[6] It was years before Cheslatta received any compensation, and as a community what followed the eviction for them was a descent into social chaos which would take decades to repair. But we also heard a story of a remarkable revitalization among the Cheslatta people and a series of projects in the past decade that were path-breaking in terms of new (Native/non-Native partnership) forms of social and economic development.

We realized immediately that the Cheslatta story could take our narrative beyond an exposé of the structures and dire consequences of colonization and its contemporary effects, and towards a more hopeful story of agency in the present and a new kind of relationship between Native and non-Native people, and we wanted to understand how this apparent transformation had come about.[7]

---

[6] Interview with Abel Peters, June 2007.

[7] In the interests of word length, and at the same time recognizing the importance of thick description to phronetic research, this chapter will focus on the Burns Lake story and draw only sketchily on the Cheslatta story.

As researchers in planning we were drawn to these stories for three main reasons. The conceptualization of 'the dark side' of mainstream planning as that of power trumping rationality and good intentions (Flyvbjerg 1996), and 'the ordering of bodies in space' (Sandercock 1998), that is, as a way of using land use and other spatial regulations as exclusionary practices that denied certain groups their rights to occupy space, seemed to fit very well the historic and ongoing situation of First Nations people, who had been dispossessed of their traditional lands by European 'settlers' (or colonizers) and forced onto marginal patches of land under the nineteenth-century land policy known as the Reserve System of Indian Lands (Harris 1997, 2002). The town of Burns Lake was settled only after the completion of the transcontinental railroad that stretched from Prince Rupert on the west coast to Toronto and Montreal in the east. The town was surveyed in 1916, one year after local First Nations had been forced onto Reserves by the provincial government, and the town site immediately appropriated one-third of that reservation land. Subsequent conflicts between the Village of Burns Lake and the Burns Lake Band (that is, First Nation) all revolved around conflicts over land and land use. That seemed to put the story squarely in planning territory, linking spatial and socioeconomic practices.

As for the contemporary situation of First Nations and non-Native people in this region, both are faced with challenges of economic and social development in a precarious regional economy overly dependent on the lumber industry. And First Nations were living in such relative poverty, having been deprived of their land base, as well as social dysfunction as a result of generations of physical, emotional and sexual abuse at the hands of the Residential School system (RCAP 1998; Molloy 1999), that they seemed to be facing a Sisyphean task of healing as well as of economic and social development. Here was a classic case of uneven development as a result of discriminatory practices, which only in the past several decades were being challenged in the courts and addressed through legislation. But it seemed that many First Nations had been so disempowered by almost two centuries of colonization that it was still difficult for some of them to actually assert their new rights, and equally difficult for the dominant culture to accept this assertion, let alone its material consequences. (This got to the heart of the causes of the shutting off of the water and sewer episode.)

More specifically, there was a major planning conflict bubbling over the town's old high school. After a new school had been built, the old premises were occupied by the Burns Lake Band (on whose former land the school had been situated and who had been granted a 99-year lease) to prevent the buildings from being demolished. They wanted to convert the buildings into a gathering place for First Nations, to replace their former Feast House (which had been burned down by government officials in the 1950s). But the Band now faced major obstacles in terms of financial resources, capacity to plan and programme the new facility, and to get planning approvals from the Village. This seemed to be both a current planning conflict and symbolic of much larger unresolved issues in the relationship between the village and the Band.

Another piece of the puzzle that drew us to this story was the demographic reality of Burns Lake. This small town is divided roughly fifty/fifty between Native and non-Native folks and yet they had been living as 'two solitudes', side by side but segregated, for most of the twentieth century. Now the demographic balance was about to shift in favour of First Nations and it was clear (although not widely accepted in the town) that the two peoples were in fact interdependent and would have to figure out how to carry out future economic and social development planning together. And in this respect, the town could be seen as a microcosm of many such communities across Canada that share the same demographic reality, in the same context of a shift in political thinking at national level about the rights of First Nations.

In this context, our potential story seemed to have both a timeless theme – a people dispossessed, deep historic wounds, and still unresolved conflict, ongoing suffering and a desire for justice – *and* a very specific historic and political setting. This is early twenty-first-century Canada. It is one small town. And events there are unfolding against a larger political, legal and constitutional canvas, together with a larger attitudinal canvas of guilt as well as some denial in the wider society regarding the ongoing effects of colonization. So it became a story with a question mark. Is there a way forward? What can and should be done?

Planning the research: thinking through the ethics and politics

What did we hope to set in motion with our presence and, in particular, with our film? The project was always conceived as an intervention into an already highly charged political force field. Initially, we anticipated two potential contributions. One was that we could provide some fresh eyes through which a polarized community might be able to stand back and see itself in a different light: seeing both its dark past and the potential now being demonstrated by some leaders and in some local institutions to move towards a future based on recognition, acknowledgement and partnership for social and economic development. A second was that the film could assist other northern communities with similar demographics (substantial Native populations, in some cases likely to become local majorities) and politics (histories of the dominance of settler societies, now being unsettled by legal challenges for Aboriginal rights and title at both national and provincial levels) to begin to come to terms with the past and to develop a different collective vision for the future of their communities. A third possibility emerged as we started to screen versions of the rough-cut outside the province of British Columbia and our audiences told us that this was a national problem, not just a northern British Columbia problem, and that our story could make a difference, could open eyes as well as hearts.[8]

Being aware of these objectives from the beginning made a considerable difference to how we conducted ourselves during the research and filming. It would have been easier, and it was always tempting, to make a pure advocacy film on behalf of First Nations, given the scale of historic injustices. But if the larger goal was to encourage healing across the cultural divide, and indicate ways forward together, new forms of relationship, then neither the film process nor the film itself should exacerbate the existing polarization. Nor should it shy away from the ongoing conflicts and injustices. So we needed to maintain good relations with all the 'actors' in the local political landscape, in the hope that they would stay in a process of dialogue. And we needed to walk a rather fine line in exposing the injustices of settler society without completely alienating present-day settlers, many of whom feel that they are being blamed for crimes they have not committed or that they cannot change the past, and thus feel powerless or frustrated about First Nations' apparent attachment to, or reluctance to let go of, the past.

If the politics were complex, so too were the ethical issues embedded in this research. One issue was our responsibility to First Nations. How to avoid the classic anthropological dilemma of capturing their stories and offering nothing in return? Another involved how to present and conduct ourselves as researchers. On the one hand, we could not hide our values. Clearly something was wrong here if the Burns Lake Band had had to resort to challenging the actions of the Village in the Supreme Court of British Columbia, and if that Village had thought it was acceptable behaviour to shut off water, sewer and fire services to the Burns Lake Band Reserve over a taxation dispute. But we were not experts in Native/non-Native relations. We were entering this community

---

[8] Subsequent audiences have told us that the film has international significance and resonance for all colonized peoples, as well as their colonizers. Palestinians, for example, have been very moved by the film and asked us to come to Palestine to screen it and discuss the issues. There has been a similar response from Native Hawaiians when we screened a rough-cut at the Hawaiian Planning Officials Conference in 2008.

as learners, as researchers, and we saw it as our responsibility to gather as many stories as we could from all sides of the community in order to find a larger meaning. And simultaneously, we would have to educate ourselves about the history, contemporary politics and legal complexities of Native/non-Native relations, both locally and on the national scale.

So there were really two main ethical questions: what kind of relationship could and should we develop with First Nations people (would they even want to collaborate with us)?; and what kind of responsibility did we have to the broader community? Our intention to make a film only made ethical sense if the First Nations whose stories we hoped to tell could see for themselves some potential benefit in the telling, and if we could work with them in a deeply collaborative way, yet also retain our independence in terms of making our own sense out of the information that we would be collecting. We asked ourselves (and are still asking) what we could give back to these communities, and we had three initial answers. One instrumental answer was that the film itself could potentially make a difference by assisting them in attracting economic development funding and investment once their story of struggle and cross-cultural bridge-building and initial achievement became more widely known. A second was that many of the Elders were passing and there was a real danger of losing their stories and memories and teachings. So we offered to make a digital archive of their stories. Third, we hoped that the film could potentially contribute to a shift in understanding within the Village, which might result in a less confrontational stance and more willingness to collaborate on projects for economic and social development.

The other branch of the ethical dilemma was our responsibility to the wider community. To put it crudely, were we going to judge and vilify them as 'colonizers', or listen to them and try to empathize with their stories as well as identifying 'tension points' (Flyvbjerg, Chapter 6, above) where change might be possible? We committed in our minds to the latter, which meant being committed to making something other than a pure advocacy film on behalf of Native people. Our commitment was to 'finding a way forward', beyond history's often tragic antagonisms, and that meant not vilifying (as hard and as tempting as that sometimes was, given what we were hearing), but letting each side tell its story in its own words, and for us, appreciating and understanding where relationships were already changing and why and how, and building on that.

Another aspect of this particular ethical dilemma is related to the political issues we faced, of deciding to gather as many sides of the story as possible, and being always alert to the ways in which we might be affecting the unfolding of events in a town in which there is always conflict just below the surface, ready to bubble up and explode. Our political antennae had to be acute, and yet we were neophytes in this town, and somewhat eager to be accepted by everyone. This led to an early mistake, during our first field trip, which could have had damaging consequences on the unfolding of our project. The local newspaper got wind of our presence in town and wanted to do an interview, to which we readily agreed. We thought a lot about what words to choose to describe our project, not wanting to seem like 'ambulance chasers', and also not wanting to be seen as 'biased' (or, as some of the locals would say, as 'Native worshippers'). The interview itself went pretty smoothly. Then the journalist wanted to take our photo, for which he had to send a photographer. By the time the photographer caught up with us, we were spending the afternoon with the chief of the Burns Lake Band, and happened to be sitting outside in the sun with him when the photographer arrived. The photographer suggested that the chief be included in the picture and we readily agreed, not realizing that 50 per cent of the town (the Non-Native half) may well 'read' this picture as indicating that we were working for the Band, or 'in their pocket' in some way. And subsequently, when we were filming we were occasionally stopped by locals, who asked whether this was the film for the Band. It took time to repair this early mis-step, especially in our relationship with the mayor.

We made another false step initially when we began to interview Elders without presenting them with a gift or some form of payment. We were made aware of this by a Band councillor who was quite angry with us, and we proceeded to make amends. But that situation spoke to the importance of developing an ethical awareness from the specificity of the context in which we were working, the need to learn 'other languages' rooted in completely different sociocultural worlds and the uselessness of pre-codified ethical protocols of supposed universal applicability.

We had learned from our first collaborative documentary project the importance of developing a good research protocol with the communities whose stories we would be telling. Accordingly, we spent time talking through how the film might benefit them, and we agreed on an editing process in which we would take each stage of the rough-cut back to the community (Native and non-Native) and get their feedback. We also offered not only to give everyone we interviewed the chance to see how we used their interview, but also to give them the right to withdraw their permission for us to use their words. This is what we have evolved as our collaborative model of film-making with communities.

With these forms of preparation in place, we immersed ourselves in the field work and filming, which were completed by the end of summer 2007. It would take us two-and-a-half more years to edit the 90-minute, three-part film. During that time, through our collaborative process of taking the various stages of rough-cuts back to the communities for viewing, we were collectively making meaning, clarifying and shaping the many layers of our stories through iterative conversations with the communities themselves. And while we were doing this, the words of Alasdair McIntyre were always with us:

I can only answer the question 'What am I to do?' if I can answer the prior question 'Of what story or stories do I find myself a part?' (quoted in Flyvbjerg 2001: 137)

Of what stories then did we find ourselves a part?

Excavating the present, retrieving the past: what is happening here?

What brought relations between the Village and the Burns Lake Band to a crisis point in 2000 and what, if anything, has changed since then? Here is how the film script explains it:

Narrator (Leonie's Voice Over):
The conflict that led to the High Noon confrontation between the Village and the Band began in 1974, when the provincial government granted a large forestry licence to Babine Forest Products, a non-Native timber company, who built a new mill 26 km from the town, on land leased from the BL Band.

At that time, the village of BL was a small, struggling settler community without much industry or commerce to support it. In need of a stable tax revenue base, the village saw the new mill as the proverbial pot of gold. So they asked the provincial government to extend their municipal boundaries, to encompass the reservation land on which the mill was built.

After that, a third of village revenue was derived from taxing this mill.

By the 1990s, changes in federal legislation had made it possible for Bands to tax businesses operating on their land. When the BL Band decided to exercise these powers to tax the mill, the village faced a crisis: the loss of $400,000 of annual tax revenue.

The Band offered to share the revenue, but the village decided that the way to make up for the revenue loss was to charge the Burns Lake Band a $400,000 annual fee to provide water, sewer and fire services to twenty houses on their Reservation.

$20,000 per house, per year![9]

Larry Fast (legal adviser to Burns Lake Band):
At that time, the village was dominated by old-school pioneer stock, elected officials and administrators who didn't see the Burns Lake Band as a legitimate organization and who were quite prepared to exercise their powers to carry out their own objectives.

---

[9] Houses on the Reserve are basic, and worth perhaps $40,000 each.

Narrator:
The Band refused to pay, and in 1999 the conflict ended up in the Supreme Court.

The Court assessed the money owed by the Band for these services at $8,000 per year, not $400,000.

The village, though, continued to insist on their original amount.

The Band was outraged.

The village delivered an ultimatum.

The Band refused to back down.

Now, the question was, would the village shut off water and sewer services to the houses on the Reservation?

Paul Jean (businessman and Mayor at this time):
We'd just been re-elected and we had to make this decision whether to cut off the water. It was a difficult decision, middle of winter, but, well, it had to be done.

Narrator:
In this highly charged situation, pressure was brought to bear on the village by some of the town's churches and businesses to end the dispute.

Eventually, the (federal) Department of Indian Affairs brought in a mediator, and within days the two sides came to an agreement, not only on the service fee, but also, finally, to open a dialogue.

Larry Fast:
As the day for the water cut-off got closer, some marvellous things started happening. A wall was erected between the Reservation and the town and Rob Charlie (the Chief of the BL Band) used it to get out his message, writing slogans on the wall such as 'Injustice anywhere is injustice everywhere' and other sayings from world leaders, and these were visible from the railway and the main highway and it elevated the conflict to the level of basic human rights.

Pauline Goertzen (anti-racism coordinator):
And then the media started showing up, first the local then the national media, and suddenly it was no longer a municipal water and sewer issue, but a basic human rights issue.

Larry Fast:
So the Band did win, and it won in the arenas that counted. The message came through loud and clear that the Band had been unjustly treated for decades. People in Burns Lake started to sympathize with the Band and the village started losing the support of its own people . . . Eventually some churches and businesses started pressuring the Village to settle the dispute. (Sandercock and Attili 2010c)

So here we had an understanding of the conflict itself and how and why it was settled, reflecting a 'tension point' (Flyvbjerg, Chapter 6, above) in power relations in the town, an erosion of support for the 'old pioneer stock'. But this raised two further questions, one about the past, the other about the present and future. If the Band had been treated unjustly for decades, what system of power was undergirding that situation? And, was this now a turning point in race relations in Burns Lake? Our interviews had probed both of these questions, and became part of the script.

Rob Charlie (chief of Burns Lake Band):
We've had a running battle with this municipality for 80 years and it's all about expropriated land . . . 80 years ago the so-called settlers came in here and they had to ask us for permission to do things. Today, it's us going to them almost on a daily basis and it's a juxtaposition completely unreal . . . When I was 4 years old I was forced to watch them burning down our Feast Hall. It made me angry. It made me so angry that three years later I smashed all the stained glass windows in the church, thousands of dollars worth of damage. I thought it was a fair trade.

Narrator:
With the completion of the transcontinental railway in 1914, there was a land rush. The Burns Lake Band was forced onto reserve lands in 1915, but lost a third of their allocation when the town site was surveyed the following year.[10]

By the mid-twentieth century, Burns Lake Village was a typical northern interior town in which two separate worlds, two solitudes, existed side by side, Natives and settlers, each with vastly different life experiences.

Ryan Tibbetts (Burns Lake Band councillor):
When I was a kid growing up here, Natives walked on one side of the street, non-Natives on the other. We were not allowed into certain stores and restaurants. There was no Native employment.

Now we had a portrait of a deeply divided community. And these were structural (that is, land-based) and not just attitudinal divisions. So a further excavation was necessary, into the structures underpinning colonization in nineteenth-century British Columbia.

Narrator:
Thousands of years before Europeans first set foot in the northern part of the North American continent, diverse Native peoples occupied these lands, each with their own tribal territory that provided the resources for survival.

The land now known as British Columbia was home to between 250,000 and 400,000 Native people at that time.

The arrival of European settlers imposed a new story on this landscape.

Europeans brought diseases like smallpox that decimated the pre-contact population by a staggering 90%.

But even more devastating to the Native world was the *process of colonization* that brought into being a European settler society.

ON SCREEN: ASSIMILATION POLICY
The settlers imposed three kinds of control over Native life: the Reserve system of Indian Lands; the Indian Act; and the Residential School system.

---

[10] The Band lost more of its Reserve allocation when it was pressured by the DIA to give up land for Village purposes, such as a hospital and a school, but also for housing developments for non-Natives.

In the eyes of colonizers, Natives stood in the way of progress and development. These settlers, who came with their own dreams of a better life ahead, saw themselves as moving into an empty land. Their right to occupy and own this land, justified by 19th-century ideas of racial and cultural superiority, was the basis for the Reserve system, which confined Natives to tiny patches of marginal land.

Natives were now trespassers on their former lands, and reduced to poverty for lack of a land base...

Under the Indian Act of 1867, independent tribal nations now became dependent wards of the state, not permitted to manage their own reserve lands or money, pushed into a culture of dependence on the Department of Indian Affairs. From the 1880s on, the Department appointed Indian agents, who were sent to every reserve across Canada, to supervise virtually every aspect of Native life...

Indian agents, along with priests and police, went to the Reserves and forced parents to send their children to residential school.

The Residential School System was a partnership between the churches and the state, and the cornerstone of assimilation policy. The intent of these Schools, according to official documents, was to 'kill the Indian' in the Native child.

Their direct attack on Native language and spirituality was pure cultural genocide.[11]

As we excavated this third layer of power relations, we had to make a crucial editorial decision about the structure of the film. We could not simply tell the dramatic story of the water and sewer dispute as an account of present-day injustice. We had to go back into history to demonstrate the systemic nature of this injustice. And although we realized that such exposition could detract from the 'political thriller' approach and slow the narrative pace (making it much harder to get the film selected for screening in film festivals), it was a decision we had to make as scholars/researchers. And equally, we had the enormous challenge of how to make that part of the film visually compelling.

After we'd excavated the past, we turned again to the present, and to the shape of things to come. Was the Court case and the Band's victory an historic turning point? Definitely. Did it transform race relations in Burns Lake? Of course not. In the next elections for the Village Council, some of the old blood, the old racist pioneer stock, were not re-elected and there were new faces, including one First Nations member (from the Burns Lake Band), all of whom were more sympathetic in wanting to address injustices to First Nations.

---

[11] See RCAP (1998); Molloy (1999).

Narrator:
But progress is rarely linear.

This new spirit of reconciliation was severely tested during the planning of a new high school for the village in 2002.

The old high school was on former Burns Lake Band land. The Band wanted that land back, along with all the buildings on it. While negotiations were proceeding, the School District began tearing down the buildings, prompting Band members to occupy the school.

Ultimately, they were granted a 99-year lease for one dollar a year, but conflict with the village continued, rubbing old wounds, as the Band proceeded with its plan to convert the school to a new Gathering Place, replacing the torched Feast House.

We explored some positive steps towards partnership that have emerged, such as the new Community Forest in which the village and First Nations jointly manage a community forest, and it was the Burns Lake Band who insisted on a consensus way of managing this entity. And we documented the coming together of some of the youth, Native and non-Native, to make a video about racism and violence and to record an anti-racism song. But our conclusion to this part of the story was ambivalent.

Pauline Goertzen:
Change is coming about now through a myriad of people leading it: it's the pressure of the community, the moms, and others whom I wouldn't have seen coming out ten years ago, it's the community saying 'We have to Stop This!'

Narrator:
But to stop this, a spirit of trust, mutual recognition and real partnership still needs to be built between the village and the Band, healing the century of antagonism over land and sovereignty.

Robert Charlie (chief of Burns Lake Band):
We're involved in a social rebuilding here, and sometimes we're the learners and sometimes we're the teachers.

Bernice Magee (mayor of Burns Lake since 2004):
We have everything in place . . . we have the tools to work with. Do we know how to use those tools? It's a learning process.

Narrator:
In spite of declared positive intentions on both sides, a decade after the Supreme Court case various attempts at partnerships between the village and the Band have fallen apart. The soil of partnership, like the actual northern soil, is very thin.

A strong sense of the need to move forward does exist, but the village still sometimes uses its economic and political power to thwart the Band, and, in turn, the Band's spirit of forgiveness and letting go continues to be tested.

Pauline Goertzen:
So the challenges are: dialogue, definition, sustainability, real tangible shared partnership. Not tokenism, but shared opportunity, control, resources, not logos . . .

And it's not easy to change your path and think about the Why . . . because the 'I' isn't just 'I' anymore, it's 'we'.

From the politics of film composition to the politics of communication and dissemination: film as catalyst for change

The final question in a phronetic social scientist's project is 'what should be done?' Or more personally and strongly, 'what can we do?' From the very beginning of this project, we had many discussions with each other, as well as with our key informants, including the two First Nations, about the possible audiences for and uses of the film, political and educational. What we collectively identified were at least six possibilities. For the two communities themselves (Native and non-Native members of Burns Lake and the Southside of Francis Lake), the film could be an opportunity to look through fresh eyes at their tragic past, conflicted present and potential future of a healthier co-existence. For other communities (small towns) with similar demographics and histories in non-metropolitan British Columbia and, indeed, across the whole of Canada (as we gradually came to realize), communities still stuck in history's tragic antagonisms, there could be the possibility of learning from the experience of the two communities in our story, and being able to see a way forward. For schoolchildren, who for the most part were still not being exposed to any of this dark side of Canadian history, we could perhaps devise a curriculum around the film. And for the great majority of adult non-Native Canadians, we, as non-Natives ourselves, could present a story which would hopefully unsettle the settler society. As we began to screen the film in its rough-cut versions to various audiences in small workshops and conference settings, two further audiences emerged. There is a wider audience (not specifically Canadian) who deal with the same archetypal issues: colonization, land conflicts, dispossession and cultural genocide across the 'New World' and in the Israeli–Palestinian conflict. And there is the audience of planners. Our story provides a microcosm of the planner's world and of planning history, which is founded on the very act of colonization, on the superimposition of a colonizing project on an allegedly 'empty land', and at the same time there is an attempt to find new ways through which planning can work today in such contexts.[12] Those became our target audiences and intentions, and we proceeded with the editing always with these purposes of intervention in mind.

Two-and-a-half years later, with the editing process completed, we moved into the action stages of the project for which we had been carefully preparing the ground through our relationship-building during the research and filming. Our first challenge was to take the completed film back to the community and attempt to use it as a catalyst for a new kind of cross-cultural dialogue. Partnering with the Social Planning and Research Council of British Columbia, we applied for and received provincial government funding to organize such a dialogue, revolving around the screening of the film. This required three months of careful planning, which happened in four stages, during which we were also working behind the scenes, as planners, trying to build support across the community for moving the Gathering Place forward as a facility for the entire community, and for generating interest in some kind of capacity-building, leadership training and facilities management training for youth.

Step 1

We convened an advisory group in the town, comprising the mayor, two new Village councillors, the two chiefs, the senior policy adviser to the Cheslatta Nation, the high school principal, the drama and dance teacher at the high school (who has a prominent role in the film), the staff sergeant of the Royal Canadian Mounted Police (RCMP)[13] and one of his First Nations officers, alongside our own project team.[14] We convened a full-day meeting with this advisory group, which began with the screening of the film. Half the people in the room were in the film as interviewees and had seen its evolution through the various rough-cuts, but others were seeing it for the first time, so it was a test of sorts about

---

[12] For an outstanding discourse on these issues see Libby Porter (2010).

[13] Staff Sergeant Mike Kisters intends to use our film in training his new recruits to the region.

[14] Our project team at this point expanded beyond ourselves to include Scott Graham, the Director of Community Development at SPARC, who in addition to community development brings a knowledge of the region as well as facilitation and curriculum development skills; Nathan Edelson, a former senior planner with the city of Vancouver with a track record of collaborative approaches to community economic development in a fractured inner city neighbourhood; Norma-Jean McLaren, an exceptional cross-cultural facilitator; and Pauline Goertzen, now heading the economic development division of Community Futures, a provincial NGO based in Smithers, 100 miles west of Burns Lake.

its likely impact. The question in the minds of everyone in the project team was, would this film further polarize existing conflicts or could it start to shift the discourse? We were literally holding our breath waiting for their responses.

The first person to speak was one of the new Village councillors, Lianne Olson. She was visibly shocked, and began to describe how as a teenager, when there were race riots in the main street of the town, her father locked her indoors and told her that the Indians were trying to take over the town. When the water and sewer dispute erupted, she had automatically assumed that it was those darn Indians expecting something for nothing again. But, having just watched the film, she said that she finally understood now why the town had always been so divided, and how people like herself had always been misinformed. This very honest confession of ignorance and pre-judgement set the tone for comments that followed. Chief Leween spoke about how, finally, their (Cheslatta) truth had been told, and that this would not be an easy film for the wider community to watch, as it is not 'sugar-coated'. Here are some other reactions that we recorded, as each person revealed their own insights and epiphanies.

Mayor Bernice Magee:
The leaders gathered here today are demonstrating good will and taking an important step for the future for our communities. We do need to move forward. The old guard is moving out and new leaders are moving in . . . I am so glad to have two of our younger Councillors with me today so they can be part of this change . . . This film is important and sometimes difficult to watch and I think it will help us address some of the challenges that hold us back.

Chief Rob Charlie:
We need to use this film to make a positive change in our community and we need to show that this process is going to move things ahead . . . We need to build on our strengths and create a process that involves people in moving forward together.

Chief Corrina Leween:
This film is very refreshing for me to see as a leader because it connects me and will connect others to the story of our people. There is lots in this film that is not sugar-coated – we need a film like this to make the truth plain to see. The presence of people here today – watching this film together – demonstrates a willingness to move forward together and I am glad to be a part of this.

Councillor Lianne Olson:
I came here in my teens and this film makes sense of many of the divisions that I have seen in this community. It helps me see the truth of what has happened here. It explains the causes for the division and differences at play in our community.

Councillor Quinten Beach:
We are experiencing a lot of changes in our community at the moment. We are in a season of change and this film holds important pieces of information that can help us improve cross-cultural relationships. There are stories in this film that show us what it takes to work together. We need true partnerships.

The conversation that unfolded surprised us all. Instead of resisting the film, the non-Native community leaders were embracing it, yet recognizing that it would be challenging for many in the community to face the account of past injustices and give proper acknowledgement to that, and use it as an occasion to move forward together. So this advisory group then came up with their own idea of how to lead this change process. The mayor and the chiefs first agreed to issue a joint press release urging the community to come and watch and discuss the film. Then, mindful of the likely strong emotions that could be aroused in an audience (from anger and denial to guilt and shame, as well as hope and inspiration), Chief Rob Charlie suggested that he and Chief Leween and the mayor should stand up together just before the screening, and speak to the community about keeping an open mind and being prepared to learn and to discuss.

Attention then turned to the question of designing the dialogue that would follow the screening. We explained that we envisaged two workshops (comprising a screening plus dialogue circles): one for youth, the other for the community at large. Further, we imagined breaking the audience into small groups, and facilitating dialogue circles with no more than eight people per circle. We also wanted to train local youth as well as adults as facilitators, and the advisory group suggested pairs of facilitators, each pair comprising a First Nations person and a non-Native person. The project team felt that this session was a huge success in getting (hitherto antagonistic) community leaders on board with us. Leonie went directly from this meeting to an interview with the local newspaper, the *Lakes District News*, and at the end of the hour with the new owner of the paper, Laura Blackwell, we had a commitment from her of free advertising for our event and at least two articles covering it.[15]

Step 2

We returned to the community a month later to spend two evenings training the facilitators whom we had recruited from the community,

---

[15] Historically the paper had been very biased against the Native population. The new owner, who is often mistaken as being First Nations herself and had been on the receiving end of racist behaviour because of that (she has some Chinese heritage), seems determined to change that.

thanks to the help of an energetic and charismatic young First Nations woman. We had eight youth and five adult volunteers, of whom six were First Nations. Again, we began by showing them the film and having a dialogue circle to discuss their responses to it. And again we were surprised at the profundity and honesty of the responses. Some of the non-Native youth spoke with heavy hearts and tears about their own ignorance of the town's history of relations between Native and non-Native peoples. There was also anger that this was being kept from them in the school text books. They wanted to take the film home and show their parents, and have family discussions. Among the Native youth, some spoke of growing up ashamed of being Native but now, with the existence of this film, they could finally be proud of who they are, and they wanted to show the film to all their friends, immediately. Others spoke of growing up not wanting to hear their parents' stories of pain, especially the pain of the Residential School experience, but now they understood why it was important to hear and discuss those stories and understand the intergenerational impact.

Each person in the circle spoke in these deeply felt ways. At the end of the first evening, everyone was energized to take the film out into the community. By the end of the second evening, this group had bonded and was galvanized (we felt) to become a future leadership cadre for the town.

Step 3

In the wake of the advisory group meeting, Leonie had side conversations with the high school principal about the importance of doing a special screening for the teachers, before the community screenings, so that they could be prepared for the conversations that the high school youth might want to have about the content of the film. That screening took place immediately after our facilitator training. It was 'professional development' day at the high school, and teachers had a variety of activities to choose among, but twenty-two of the twenty-nine teachers came to our screening, along with the principal, and stayed for 90 minutes of discussion. And again, we witnessed people reaching into places of profound honesty, displaying emotions from shame to anger to relief. The relief expressed was that finally 'the veil of silence about what's been going on in this town has been lifted'. One male teacher spoke of trying to imagine how he would feel if his children were forcibly removed from his family and taken away for ten months of the year to a place where they were not allowed to speak their own language or engage in their own cultural practices. Women teachers nodded in agreement. The principal acknowledged that the school had been part of the problem, that it had indeed been 'redneck high [school]', that fights between Native and non-Native students had been ubiquitous, and that the school had in fact lost its accreditation ten years earlier and ever since had been struggling to re-invent itself (as the film in fact depicts). The overall response from the teachers was, 'how soon can we have this for classroom use?' And seven teachers volunteered on the spot to help us facilitate the community dialogues, as well as to recruit youth for the youth screening.

Step 4

In the weeks leading up to the community screenings on 3 and 4 June 2010, we worked to attract the interest of the two politicians who represent the region in the provincial and federal parliaments. Both committed to taking part, but at the last minute the provincial member cancelled. The federal member came and stayed the whole 5 hours, participating in a dialogue circle himself. Each of the two events began with music (local musicians who are on the film soundtrack, Native and non-Native playing together) and food, followed by the mayor and the two chiefs standing up together and speaking about the importance of the film to the community and asking people to watch with an open mind, emphasizing that the intent of the workshops was to move from a reflection on and hopefully new understanding of the past, to a tough look at the present, culminating in a concrete conversation about how to move forward together. Then we launched into the 90-minute screening, followed by an intermission (more live music) while we re-arranged chairs into dialogue circles. The facilitated dialogues then ran for 90 minutes and focused on two questions: what was the most significant impact the film had on you?; and, how might this community move forward together now and on what?

During the dialogue circles, the project team along with the mayor and two chiefs were moving about the room as witnesses, listening to what was being said, but not speaking.

Notes were being taken by the second facilitator in each group, and one of our project team was responsible for absorbing what was being said in all groups and summarizing at the end, after which the mayor and chiefs had the final closing words. These words from the leaders were inspiring, as the mayor acknowledged the past mistakes made by the village and Chief Rob Charlie publicly buried his resentment, noting that four years ago he had given up on this town, but now he was filled with hope, in seeing the young people energized for change and the spirit of hope for moving forward reflected in the dialogues.

Even more inspiring were the comments made within dialogue circles, which became the subject of an editorial in the *Lakes District News* the following week.

Strikingly, people who attended were so engaged that they stayed for 5 hours, including an extra 15 minutes very late in the evening to fill out evaluations. Fifty youth attended the youth screening, roughly half of whom were First Nations, and forty remained for the dialogue, twenty-one of whom completed the evaluation. In response to the first question, 'How well did this screening and dialogue help your community address racism?', seventeen of twenty-one replies gave the highest possible score for this answer. In response to the second question, 'How well did this screening and dialogue help your community identify pathways to working together across cultural differences?', twenty of twenty-one replies circled very good or good. These responses were similar in the community-wide screening. Additionally, there were very positive answers to a question inquiring about people's overall awareness of historical and present-day relations between Native and non-Native peoples before and after the workshops, with many respondents noting a significant increase in awareness. Approximately 150 people attended the community-wide screening, which began at 5.30 pm and ran for 5 hours. Eighty people stayed on for the dialogue circles, and forty-five stayed to complete the evaluation, with thirty-seven of them noting a significant shift in awareness.

Qualitative answers, from both youth and adults, to the question 'How will you act on what you have learned through the screening and dialogue?' contained many expressions of the desire to volunteer to work on community projects such as the Gathering Place. And the two most common answers to the question 'What other types of activities or events that bring people together would you recommend for anti-racism projects?' were either, 'more films or plays like this one' or 'take this film on the road'.

Perhaps the final word on this event should be drawn from the editorial (entitled 'Inspiring') in the local paper:

The youth that viewed the documentary were so inspiring . . . Some felt ashamed, some felt sad, but the consensus with them all was that they felt that what had happened to the First Nations in our community was not right and they are determined to do what they can now to make it right from here on. (Blackwell 2010)

During the months of organizing the community screenings, our project team also worked with the Burns Lake Band and the Village to develop a strategic plan for moving the Gathering Place forward as a venue for youth, and discussing the possibility of leadership training for some of the youth who had volunteered as facilitators or who had expressed a desire during the workshops to get involved in community development projects. This is ongoing work for us, as is helping to maintain the momentum we have created through our intervention, especially with the youth, but also with the town's leadership. It is our ethical responsibility. It is an involving project. And we need ongoing evaluations, in six months' time, in several years from now and beyond, so as not to delude ourselves with the initial wave of energy that we have generated.

Next steps

These workshops were both an end in themselves (as per our original hopes for the project) and also a pilot for a further series of workshops in other towns in this region. There were a number of people from these towns who came to the Burns Lake workshop and have now requested similar events in their communities. Once we have evaluated this first set of workshops, we will refine the approach before applying for further grants to continue the process of community dialogue in the region, and then beyond it.

Simultaneously, we are working strenuously to promote screenings of the film in strategic venues. The film was featured on the opening night of the annual conference of the Planning Institute of British Columbia in early June 2010, with an audience of planners from all over the province. It was screened for 100 community development folks from all over British Columbia who were in Vancouver for a conference on creative approaches to community development.[16] It was used in a series of cross-cultural dialogues in four different cultural centres in Vancouver during the spring of 2010 with the intent of raising awareness among different immigrant cultures of the plight of First Nations in Canada. We now have a distributor for the film *Moving Images*, which specializes in accessing schools and universities. And we have built a Facebook website to spread the word and create discussion about the film.[17]

On yet another front, we are working with politicians (as above), NGOs (Social Planning & Research Council of British Columbia) and funders to strategize how to access funds to support new planning projects in the region that will benefit the whole community. In other words, our

[16] Organized by the Social Planning & Research Council of British Columbia, 18 May 2010.
[17] See: www.facebook.com/FINDING.OUR.WAY.thefilm.

research strategy is to put as much effort into communication, dissemination and follow-on planning as we put into the research and making of the film. The completion of the film is just the beginning of a much longer engagement with these communities and with this set of policy issues.

Are we dreamers?

Will the film succeed in being not only a catalyst for dialogue, but also in mobilizing commitment and resources around future planning projects? Like all good stories, ours must end on a note of suspense. We can say that the first community screenings were definitely successful as a catalyst for apparently transformative dialogue. But we don't know yet whether the result will be the mobilization of resources around community development projects. We have a responsibility to continue to be engaged, to help maintain the momentum and to help the community to access resources.

But, more reflectively, no researchers can precisely predict whether the tool or approach they are using will be an effective catalyst for social change. The analysis of the outcomes of such a process can only be done retrospectively. The field of social interaction and political action is constantly characterized by uncertainty. In this field we do not have a mechanical algorithm in which we insert some initial inputs and after that we can predict how audiences will react, interact, engage in dialogue and possibly provoke changes. The field of social interaction is full of surprises and unintended effects, which do not need to be seen as an obstacle but certainly as a structural dimension. The only things we can be sure of are what happened in the past, things we can now make sense of. We can affirm from our first experience in using film in this way that it was very successful both in provoking dialogue and in instigating policy changes (see Sandercock and Attili 2009, 2010a). But there are no general rules. Everything depends on the specificities, including our own attention to detail, and to relationship-building (as phronetic social science teaches).

But there are some things of which we can be sure. One thing, and this is the reason we are exploring this digital ethnographic approach, is the new post-modern epistemological consciousness and the story (or narratological) turn in planning research and action. We know from past experiences that some issues cannot be understood through mechanistic or quantitative languages. We know, looking at the literature dealing with the anthropology of performance as well as at our own past experiences, recent rough-cut and community screenings of this film, that the languages we are using have the potentialities to provoke dialogue and interaction. And we know that in order to pursue this goal we must not only create the film, but also the *space* in which this interaction can take place, and that is both relational space as well as workshop space. And that is the process we are building right now, which is linked with the potentialities that ethnographic films can develop in the planning field (Sandercock and Attili 2010b).

While our film tells a definitive story of injustice and struggles for justice, it does not have a definitive ending. The intent is to create an 'open space' in which audiences can debate the stories themselves and the lessons they should take away. We, as researchers, are in a dialogue with a polyphony of voices, both in the film (our narration juxtaposed with interviews) and in the subsequent dissemination process. No one voice, including ours, claims final authority. As Flyvbjerg (2001: 139) has argued, 'the goal of phronetic research is to produce input into the ongoing social dialogue and praxis in a society, rather than to generate ultimate, unequivocally verified knowledge'.

In this chapter we have provided a detailed narrative and concrete examples of how power works and with what consequences, and we have suggested (through the stories portrayed in the film) how power might be changed and work with other consequences. We have worked collaboratively to create new meanings as well as new understandings. In these ways, we become actors in the flow of history, rather than bystanders.

REFERENCES

Attili, G. 2007. 'Digital Ethnographies in the Planning Field', *Planning Theory and Practice* 8(1): 90–8.

2008. *Rappresentare la Citta dei Migranti*. Milan: Jaca Books.

2010a. 'Beyond the Flatlands: Digital Ethnographies in the Planning Field', in Sandercock and Attili (eds.), *Multimedia Explorations in Urban Policy and Planning*, pp. 39–56.

2010b. 'Representations of an Unsettled City: Hypermedial Landscapes in Rome', in Sandercock and Attili (eds.), *Multimedia Explorations in Urban Policy and Planning*, pp. 177–208.

Attili, G. and Sandercock, L. 2007. *Where Strangers become Neighbours: The Story of the Collingwood Neighbourhood House and the Integration of Immigrants in Vancouver*. Montreal: National Film Board of Canada (50-minute documentary).

Blackwell, L. 2010. 'Inspiring', editorial, *Lakes District News*, 10 June.

Bourdieu, P. 1990. *In Other Words: Essays Towards a Reflexive Sociology.* Cambridge: Polity.

Churchman, C. W. 1971. *The Design of Inquiring Systems.* New York: Basic Books.

Eckstein, B. and Throgmorton, J. (eds.) 2003. *Story and Sustainability.* Cambridge, MA: MIT Press.

Flyvbjerg, B. 1996. 'The Dark Side of Planning: Rationality and Realrationalität', in S. Mandelbaum, L. Mazza and R. Burchell (eds.), *Explorations in Planning Theory.* New Brunswick, NJ: Center for Urban Policy Research Press, pp. 383–94.

2001. *Making Social Science Matter: Why Social Inquiry Fails and How it can Succeed Again.* Cambridge University Press.

Forester, J. 1989. *Planning in the Face of Power.* Berkeley, CA: University of California Press.

Freire, P. 1970. *The Pedagogy of the Oppressed.* New York: Herder & Herder.

Friedmann, J. 1973. *Retracking America.* New York: Doubleday Anchor.

Geertz, C. 1988. *Works and Lives: The Anthropologist as Author.* Stanford University Press.

hooks, b. 1984. *Feminist Theory: From Margin to Center.* Boston, MA: South End Press.

Kelly, J. G. 1984. *Women, History, and Theory.* University of Chicago Press.

Landry, C. 2000. *The Creative City.* London: Earthscan.

2006. *The Art of City Making.* London: Earthscan.

Lerner, G. 1997. *Why History Matters.* Oxford University Press.

Mandelbaum, S. 1991. 'Telling Stories', *Journal of Planning Education and Research* 10(1): 209–14.

Porter, L. 2010. *Unlearning Planning's Colonial Cultures.* London: Ashgate.

Rabinow, P. and Sullivan, W. M. (eds.) 1987. *Interpretive Social Science: A Second Look.* Berkeley, CA: University of California Press.

Royal Commission on Aboriginal Peoples (RCAP) 1998. vols 1–5.

Said, E. 1979. *Orientalism.* New York: Vantage Books.

Sandercock, L. 1998. *Towards Cosmopolis: Planning for Multicultural Cities.* Chichester: John Wiley.

2003a. *Cosmopolis 2: Mongrel Cities of the 21st Century.* London: Continuum.

2003b. 'Out of the Closet: The Importance of Stories and Storytelling in Planning Practice', *Planning Theory and Practice* 4(1): 11–28.

2005a. 'A Planning Imagination for the 21st Century', *Journal of the American Planning Association* 70(2): 133–41.

2005b. 'A New Spin on the Creative City: Artist/Planner Collaborations', *Planning Theory & Practice* 6(1): 101–3.

Sandercock, L. and Attili, G. 2009. *Where Strangers become Neighbours: The Integration of Immigrants in Vancouver, Canada.* Dordrecht: Springer.

2010a. 'Digital Ethnography as Planning Praxis: An Experiment with Film as Social Research, Community Engagement and Policy Dialogue', *Planning Theory and Practice* 11(1): 23–46.

(eds.) 2010b. *Multimedia Explorations in Urban Policy and Planning: Beyond the Flatlands.* Dordrecht: Springer.

2010c. *Finding Our Way.* Vancouver: Moving Images, 90-minute documentary.

Sarkissian, W. and Hurford, D., with Wenman, C. 2010. *Creative Community Planning: Transformative Engagement Methods for Working at the Edge.* London: Earthscan.

Stretton, H. 1969. *The Political Sciences.* London: Routledge & Kegan Paul.

Trinh, Minh-ha T. 1989. *Woman Native Other.* Bloomington, IN: Indiana University Press.

9   Phronesis and critical policy analysis:
     Heathrow's 'third runway' and the politics of
     sustainable aviation in the United Kingdom

Steven Griggs and David Howarth[1]

In recent years, air travel has become increasingly associated in the public domain with a set of negative externalities and frustrations. Where once airports were the symbolic gateways to freedom, modernity and greater economic growth, today they are synonymous with global warming, noise and air pollution, congestion, security checks and delays. Seen against this background, the Labour government's decision in January 2009 to give the go-ahead for a third runway and a sixth terminal at Heathrow Airport was another bold step designed to deal with the issue.[2] But it provoked widespread condemnation, exposed splits in the Cabinet, and triggered another high-profile protest campaign against expansion by local residents, environmental and conservation lobbies, direct action environmentalists, as well as celebrities and even members of the government's own parliamentary majority.

Shortly after its election in May 1997, New Labour had resolved to deal decisively with the historical legacy of incremental planning and ongoing protest in the field of aviation. Accepting the need for firm leadership in this domain, it thus prepared the ground for the development of new legislation that would set out a strategic plan for airports for the next twenty or thirty years. In 2003, a new aviation White Paper, *The Future of Air Transport*, came down firmly on the side of expanding airport capacity and bolstering the aviation industry (DfT 2003).

---

[1] We would like to thank the editors and an anonymous reader for their helpful comments on this chapter. The chapter draws upon ongoing empirical research undertaken by the authors, some of which will be presented in a forthcoming book entitled *Reframing 'Sustainable Aviation' in the UK* (Manchester University Press, 2012).

[2] The proposed plans would have potentially increased the number of flights at Heathrow to more than 700,000 per annum (from the current level of 473,000), although there would have be an initial limit of 605,000 flights. Carbon emissions were predicted to rise to 23.6 million tonnes by 2030 from the current level of 17.1 million tonnes and an estimated 700 homes in the nearby village of Sipson would have been destroyed to make way for the new runway and terminal. See *The Telegraph*, 15 January 2009 and *Financial Times*, 16 January 2009.

But rather than setting the conditions for consensual deliberation and rational policy-making, the consultation process and the resultant national plan heightened the antagonisms dividing various stakeholders. In fact, subsequent attempts to implement its plans met with heightened contestation and resistance, especially as this conjuncture coincided with the growing political salience of the dangers of climate change. These dangers prompted the emergence of a broader and more intense climate-change coalition, which managed to construct global civil aviation as an exemplary case of its wider war against productivism. In short, for commentators on both sides of the aviation divide, New Labour singularly failed to achieve authoritative governance (Hajer 2009), either in support of the runway or in leading opposition to expansion. Just days after entering office in May 2010, the Conservative–Liberal-Democrat coalition abandoned New Labour's plans to expand Heathrow Airport, signalling a new round of consultation and policy formulation.

These continuing tensions over airport expansion in the United Kingdom, and the failure of the New Labour government to resolve them, testify to the difficulties facing governments when they seek to address and resolve 'wicked' policy issues. These controversies often galvanize multiple actors and agencies into action under conditions of policy ambiguity and sharp value conflict. But they also raise important analytical questions. How is government to demonstrate effective political leadership? How can it deal with the various and often competing demands that are articulated by different actors and groups? How can government strive to build legitimate coalitions for change that bring together multiple and unstable publics? These questions have to be seen in the light of an arguably more pressing question: how is it possible for governments and public agencies to mediate between the desire for increased economic growth and effective environmental protection?

This chapter responds to such questions by examining the UK government's decision to grant approval for the expansion of Heathrow Airport. New Labour continued to support the proposed third runway (and other airport expansions), even though there was mounting political opposition, and despite the fact that this policy exposed the growing contradiction between its commitment to unbridled economic growth *and* environmental protection. By critically explaining this decision, we show how New Labour altered its tactics and strategies in an attempt to deal with increasingly intense demands and grievances. We also address how and why it continued to over-invest in the expansion of Heathrow. Our conclusion explores the degree to which progressive governments might forge a 'partial equilibrium' in the complex policy domain of aviation.

We begin our analysis by outlining our approach to these questions, and then problematizing the decision to expand Heathrow Airport once again. We then focus on the political and ideological practices through which the UK government endeavoured to deal with the conflicting demands voiced by rival stakeholders and citizens. In particular, we draw attention to the logics of framing and New Labour's attempts to shape the terrain of argumentation throughout and beyond the consultation over the third runway. Having established the failures of New Labour's attempt to displace contestation, we discuss the weaknesses of its 'managed consultation'; the absence of 'ideological cover' for government to expand Heathrow; and the limited resonance of its fantasmatic narrative[3] of 'sustainable aviation' in the context of the changing politics of climate change. This leads us to assess critically why and how New Labour continued to invest so heavily in the third runway. Here we draw attention to the importance of the productivist ideology of New Labour; the structural power of the aviation industry; the hold over policy of Gordon Brown; and the continued fantasmatic appeal of aviation.

Discourse, practice and power

In his remarkable book *Making Social Science Matter*, Bent Flyvbjerg (2001) issues a call to arms to those who wish to re-animate the project of critical political theory. He eschews the practice of a normalized social science, which seeks to imitate the natural sciences in the name of law-like explanations, by developing a different ethos and method of social science that is based on the quest for phronesis or practical wisdom. Flyvbjerg thus grounds his approach on a search for 'practical knowledge' and 'practical ethics' (2001: 56), rather than the ideal of a predictive science (epistemé) that promises greater social and technical control of the world (techné). In fleshing out this method, Flyvbjerg brings together the concepts of power and value so as to provide a meaningful alternative to positivist and rationalist models of social science.

---

[3] Fantasmatic narratives are integral elements of what Glynos and Howarth have termed the logic of fantasy, in which the latter refers to the way subjects are gripped by certain ideas and signifying forms. In this approach, fantasmatic narratives promise a fullness-to-come once a named or implied obstacle is overcome (the beatific dimension of fantasy) or alternatively they foretell of disaster if the obstacle proves to be insurmountable (the horrific dimension of fantasy), although in any particular instance the two work hand-in-hand. In so doing, they bring a form of ideological closure to the radical contingency of social relations, thereby naturalizing the different relations of domination within which a subject is enmeshed. In this conception, fantasy is not simply an ideological illusion or a form of false consciousness that comes between a subject and social reality, but actively structures the way a subject perceives and experiences the world (see Glynos and Howarth 2007). In the case of UK aviation policy, as we discuss below, the New Labour government and supporters of expansion sought (but ultimately failed) to 'rhetorically redefine' the question of airport expansion in terms of 'sustainable aviation', thus articulating a beatific fantasy in which aviation expansion and environmental sustainability could be linked in a harmonious and mutually reinforcing fashion.

Drawing on Machiavelli and Foucault, rather than Hobbes, Habermas and Lukes, in Flyvbjerg's approach power is not understood as a question of 'possession, sovereignty, and control' – that is, the idea of power as entity – but in its concrete application in various strategies and tactics. Rather than endorsing a juridical model of sovereign power that simply represses, limits and excludes, power consists of dispersed 'force relations' that can constitute relations and practices (2001: 116). By linking the work of Aristotle, Nietzsche and Heidegger, Flyvbjerg also shows how the investigation of power must be connected to questions of knowledge and value. He thus folds the need to critically evaluate social practices from a particular point of view into his specific studies of power and rationality. These insights are evident in his careful empirical analyses of Aalborg (1998) and megaprojects (Flyvbjerg, Bruzelius and Rottengatter 2003; see also Flyvbjerg, Chapter 6, above).

We agree with the general thrust of Flyvbjerg's reworked project for a re-enchanted and engaged social science. Critical theorists and policy analysts of various hues ought to focus on pressing issues in the present, and should strive to elaborate interpretations that can enable us to intervene sensitively in particular contexts with a view to bringing about greater democracy and freedom. Flyvbjerg is also right in our view to stress the role of empirical case studies as the means to develop meaningful knowledge of the social world, while developing the requisite skills for conducting social science research. Knowledge of 'little things' or exemplary cases, such as the ongoing contestations around the expansion of Heathrow Airport, thus help us to cast light on similar cases, while foregrounding the tension between continued economic growth and environmental protection. Intensive explorations of particular cases can indeed lead to significant insights and understandings that carry a more universal and general import. (In fact, in our view, they carry such implications better than those studies that are *designed* to make statements on a more universal level.)

Yet in elaborating our approach to the critical explanation of aviation politics in the United Kingdom during the last decade or so, there are a couple of theoretical and methodological remainders that call for further clarification. To begin with, there is the tricky split between facts and values, which has marked our modern sensibility at least since Kant. The question is reasonably easy to pose, but not so easy to resolve. How can we avoid a naive positivism and scientism that excludes values, and an overbearing partisanship that is not tempered by the protocols of the scientific method and its values of objectivity and truth? In our view, it is clear that any useful characterization of a complex social process or practice *presupposes* some normative stance, which inevitably shapes our descriptions of phenomena in certain ways. This stance affects both our selection of research objects, as well as the construction of particular interpretations and the evaluations they make possible. At the same time, our interpretations are still accountable to the tribunal of other researchers and practitioners, who will scrutinize the consistency, empirical grounds and plausibility of the interpretations we proffer.

What is more, in our view, critical interpretations also require a passage through the conflicting self-interpretations (and thus values) of the social actors we study, even if they are not reducible to these contextualized self-interpretations. A number of questions present themselves here. What is the relationship between a hermeneutical project that seeks to interpret and understand the meanings of practices, on the one hand, and a project of explaining such processes without simply reproducing the actor's point of view, on the other? How can such explanations be critical? What is the relationship between what we might call negative or demystificatory critique, which exposes the 'hidden' biases and exclusions of particular policies, and the construction and projection of alternative and more positive values and norms? In short, what are the conditions of possibility of critical explanation in the social sciences?

In seeking to furnish answers to these epistemological and methodological questions, our approach is based on what we call the 'logics of critical explanation' (Glynos and Howarth 2007). But we begin with a more ontological question. What is the relationship between discourses and practices? In one important line of thinking in *Making Social Science Matter*, Flyvbjerg rightly prioritizes the role of practices in his approach, and he seeks to build his interpretations on their characterization and critique. But in so doing he relativizes the role of discourse to a more secondary position (2001: 134–5). If his main objective in this regard is to establish some distance from the kinds of interpretation that people express about their actions, then he is evidently on the right track here, though it is not entirely clear how this translates into precise methodological postulates.

However, his relegation of discourse to a secondary position is more problematic, for his reliance on Foucault leads him to develop other sorts of argument in his text that push in a different direction. For example, when he discusses the relationship between power, rationality and truth, his approach is less clear-cut. Paraphrasing Foucault, he argues that 'discourses can be both an instrument of power and its effect, but also an obstacle, a point of resistance or a starting point for a counterposing strategy. Discourses thus transfer and produce power.' He goes on to stress that rationality and power, knowledge and power, reason and power, truth and power, are not externally related, for 'power produces rationality and truth; rationality and truth produces power' (2001: 124).

He thus endorses Foucault's claim 'that power and knowledge directly imply one another' (2001: 125). Discourses in this perspective are thus not just separate and secondary linguistic elements, as suggested in other arguments by Flyvbjerg, but are imbricated in the production of power relations and political practices.

How, then, are we to conceptualize the relationship between discourse, power and practice? In our conception, discourse is not reducible to language, if the latter is seen to consist simply of concepts, words and sentences. It is the equivalence between language and discourse that seems to inform Flyvbjerg's desire to look at practice *before* discourse (2001: 134). But in one straightforward sense, as philosophers such as J. L. Austin and John Searle have argued, linguistic utterances like 'I promise' are not just words, signs or even assertions, but *acts* that carry a certain force and consequence. They are *discursive practices* that can be investigated in the same way that Foucault analysed the social production of scientific statements in his *Archaeology of Knowledge* (1972).

But perhaps these practices are just a particular *subset* of practices, which can and ought to be distinguished from other activities like kicking an object on a field? In a crucial respect, the answer to this question is negative, for it is important to note that the latter activity is not without meaning. Kicking an object in a particular context is an action, but it acquires its meaning and significance only within the context of playing a football match, for example. Its meaning thus differs from the angry response of a football supporter, who kicks the ball into a nearby street after his team has conceded a late goal. At the same time, different social practices are themselves meaningful entities. They are thus instances of playing football or explosions of anger and frustration. At the same time, critical researchers also seek to characterize these practices in terms of their meaning, import and significance. They wish to render them intelligible in terms of rules and meanings. In short, language, actions and objects are intertwined in what we shall call discourse.

Discourse theory offers a fruitful way to conceptualize these various distinctions. In our view, discourse is an *articulatory practice* that constitutes social relations and formations, and constructs their meaning. It is articulatory in that it links together contingent elements into relational systems, in which the identity of the elements are modified as a result of the articulatory practice. In accounting for the formation of discourses we stress the primacy of politics and power. Discourses are thus constituted by the drawing of political frontiers between social subjects via the exercise of power. In this model, one force endeavours to impose its values and norms by winning the consent of its allies and by securing the compliance of its others, though force may be required to subject its opponents. The logic of hegemony captures this complex set of processes. An important condition for any articulatory practice (including hegemonic practices) is the radical contingency of all social and natural elements, which can always be constructed in different ways (Howarth 2000, 2009).

The radical contingency and historicity of the different elements that are located in particular fields of meaning is captured by the *discursive* character of social relations and processes. It is thus possible to disaggregate two key aspects of discourse theory: the discursive and discourse. We shall take the *discursive* to be an ontological category – that is, a categorical presupposition for our understanding of particular entities and social relations – whereby every object or any symbolic order is meaningful, that is, situated in a field of significant differences and similarities. But equally in this approach, following thinkers like Heidegger, Lacan and Derrida, it also means that such entities are *incomplete* and thus *radically contingent.* Each system of meaningful practice is marked by a lack, and their meaning or objectivity depends on the way they are socially and politically constructed. By contrast, the concept of *discourse* refers to particular systems of meaningful or articulatory practice. Thatcherism or New Labour in the United Kingdom, or the different forms of the apartheid system in South Africa, or the radical environmentalism associated with social movements in contemporary societies, can all be classified as discourses in this sense of the term. It follows from our rendering of the discursive that these systems are finite and contingent constructions, which are constituted politically by the construction of social antagonisms and the creation of political frontiers. Every discursive formation thus involves the exercise of power, as well as certain forms of exclusion, and this means that every discursive structure is uneven and hierarchical.

The logics of critical explanation

Yet these basic ontological assumptions of discourse theory are not sufficient for the conduct of discourse analysis. What Glynos and Howarth (2007) have termed 'logics of critical explanation' enables us to translate these ontological coordinates into a set of research strategies. It also offers a way of addressing the relationship between understanding and explanation, as well as the connection between ethics and normativity. Very schematically, our approach to critical explanation consists of five connected steps.

First, following Foucault (and in line with the phronetic approach), it begins by *problematizing* a particular practice or regime. As Flyvbjerg correctly argues, one of the most difficult and yet vital tasks is thus to construct a set of phenomena as a problem: the way 'being gives itself to be, necessarily, thought', as Foucault once put it (1985: 11). This problematization is related both to the field of academic questions, and to the social and political issues that confront us in a specific historical conjuncture (Foucault 1984a).

Second, the *form* of explanation is retroductive, rather than just inductive or deductive. The explanatory task begins with an anomalous or wondrous phenomenon, which must then be constructed as a tractable *explanandum*, and then rendered intelligible, if, and only if, a putative *explanans* were to hold (Peirce 1957; Hanson 1961). Critical explanation thus proceeds by seeking to render a problematized phenomenon more intelligible. This involves the production of an hypothesis that is tested through a to-and-fro movement with the available empirical data until we are persuaded that the putative *explanans* clears away the confusion and properly fits the phenomenon under consideration.

Third, the *content* of any putative *explanans* is couched principally in terms of logics, rather than laws, causal mechanisms or cultural interpretations. The logic of a discourse captures the *rules* that govern a practice or regime, as well as the *conditions* that make such rules possible and impossible. *Social logics* enable one to *characterize* practices and regimes in different contexts by discerning the rules and norms that govern them. While their discernment relies to some extent on the self-interpretations of actors involved in the practice, they are not sufficient to explain and evaluate such practices. *Political logics* enable the researcher to critically explain the emergence and formation of a practice or regime by exploring the intersecting logics of equivalence and difference. They can help us to show other possibilities of social organization when the 'ignoble origins' of rules and norms are reactivated, contested and instituted. Put like this, it is no coincidence that the concept of political logics is intimately related to Foucault's method of genealogy, which enabled Foucault to chart the complex lines of descent and emergence in the formation of an identity or a rule, and to disclose alternative paths and possibilities. *Fantasmatic logics* disclose a particular *way* in which subjects identify and are gripped by a discourse, and they enable us to detect the particular narratives that provide ideological closure for the subject. But it is important to remember that these fantasmatic identifications constitute only one mode of enjoyment and identification.

Fourth, any putative *explanans* comprises a plurality of logics, as well as other causal mechanisms, which have to be linked together in order to render a problematic phenomenon intelligible. Here we stress the practice of *articulation*, which involves linking together different elements in a logic that modifies each, while producing a synthesis comprising 'a rich totality of many determinations and relations' (Marx 1973: 100).

Finally, each of these logics thus enables the critic to render visible the *contingent* character of a practice, policy or institution by showing the role of power, exclusion and closure in its formation and reproduction. What is more, as Foucault made explicit in his later writings, exhibiting the *contingency* of a practice or identity provides a vital inroad into its critique and evaluation. His genealogical studies were thus carried out in part to 'separate out, from the *contingency* that has made us what we are, the possibility of no longer being, doing, or thinking what we are, do, or think' (1984b: 46). Constructed around different responses to radical contingency, social, political and fantasmatic logics endeavour to formalize these intuitions and tactics.

In advancing our arguments, we concentrate principally on the 'official public discourses' of the opposed forces engaged in the struggle about the future of Heathrow. We thus focus on a carefully selected set of media statements made by key agents and groups; interviews given by elite actors; articles and reports that appeared in major national newspapers; and a series of in-depth semi-structured interviews that were conducted with important social actors. We also analyse the consultation processes about aviation expansion, which took place between December 2000 and December 2003, and during the attempts to implement the new legislation proposed in 2009. Informing these practices of data collection and analysis is an interpretive approach to the identification and study of different communities of meaning. This means that alongside our observation and characterization of the discursive practices of the different forces, we examine the linguistic and non-linguistic practices of the actors involved by seeking to discern the different logics of their practices; their construction of equivalential relations between disparate demands; and the role of metaphors and empty signifiers in their articulation of specific discourses (see, for example, Yanow 2000; Howarth 2004).

Our use of semi-structured interviews has generated one particular 'space' for dialogue with primary stakeholders. We first made contact with stakeholders during the consultation for the 2003 Air Transport White Paper, and our engagement with them continued throughout the consultation, as well as the campaign against the third runway at Heathrow. Indeed, during our ongoing investigation of the case we have sent draft reports and papers to stakeholders for their comment and discussion, and have used these exchanges to modify our interpretations. (In fact, our overall interaction with relevant actors and groups goes back to our analyses of the ways in which various groups and coalitions sought to prevent the expansion of Manchester Airport during the mid-1990s;

see Griggs and Howarth 2002, 2004.) This longitudinal engagement, especially evident in our in-depth interviews, has offered the opportunity for us (and the stakeholders) to engage in practices of critical reflection; to 'test' our emerging interpretations of the case; and to assess ongoing strategies and tactics.

Bearing this in mind, we need to say a few words about our involvement with different stakeholders, as well as the status we attribute to their accounts in our explanation of events and processes. While we support the ethnographic impulse that is evident in numerous interpretive approaches, which takes seriously the way involved social actors make sense of their situations, we reject a descriptive approach that merely reports the views of social agents in an unmediated fashion. An overweening emphasis on the 'contextualized self-interpretations' of multiple stakeholders runs the risk of downplaying the critical explanation of practices and regimes, in which the task of *explanation* is often to go beyond the way actors interpret their worlds by furnishing concepts, logics and narratives that are not necessarily available to them. *Critical* explanation also involves the practice of highlighting the contingent emergence and subjective grip of various practices and regimes, thus foregrounding the exclusion of certain identities and possibilities through the operation of power and hegemony. In addition, this means that our dialogue with stakeholders has sought to avoid an overstretched normativism that too hastily endorses an *a priori* set of norms and principles against which to evaluate existing institutions, policies and practices. We shall explore the relationship between ethics, critique and normative evaluation in more concrete detail when we conclude our overall account of the Heathrow struggles.

Problematizing the politics of megaprojects: the decision to expand Heathrow

The building of large infrastructure projects poses particular difficulties for governments. They are inherently risky affairs, which engage multiple actors with conflicting interests, and which often rely on poorly informed cost–benefit analyses. They are often undertaken with a limited consideration of alternatives, as particular project concepts are 'locked in' or 'captured' early on by producer interests (Flyvbjerg 2009). Taking office in 1997, the New Labour government of Tony Blair faced a growing number of competing and intensely felt demands in the field of aviation policy. Those favouring more expansion charged the government with 'dithering' and 'piecemeal development', and of failing to take the lead with respect to the adequate provision of airport capacity (Caves and Gosling 1997: 320). Airlines, airport operators, trades unions, air users, organized business and sections of the tourist industry thus called on the UK government to support an increase in airport capacity, especially Heathrow, which was widely perceived to be the 'jewel in the crown' of British aviation. They also campaigned vigorously for the government to continue supporting the aviation industry with tax subsidies. Initially couching their demands and claims in terms of 'the freedom to fly', they have more recently expressed their demands in the rhetoric of 'responsible' and 'sustainable growth' in aviation. At the same time, local residents and environmentalists demanded more stringent regulation of air travel, especially with respect to its negative environmental impacts on noise and air pollution. In fact, when Labour entered office, local residents at Heathrow were in the midst of what turned out to be the longest public inquiry ever in British history over Terminal 5, while residents at Manchester had joined with direct action environmentalists to oppose the building of the second runway at Manchester Airport in what was coined to be a 'Vegans and Volvos' alliance (Griggs and Howarth 2002).

Yet despite the contradictory nature of these pressures, they all coalesced around the single universal demand for a national aviation strategy, which most parties felt had been lacking since the saga of the third London airport in the 1960s and 1970s. In the absence of any national strategy on aviation since 1985, New Labour deflected immediate pressures for change by signalling its intention to issue a new aviation White Paper, which would set out a long-term strategy for British airports. In December 2000 it opened the public consultation on such a strategy. By June 2003, when the consultation period ended, more than 400,000 responses and representations had been registered. The subsequent White Paper, *The Future of Air Transport*, outlined a strategic plan for the development of air transport over the next thirty years. It came down firmly on the side of promoting expansion to meet projected demand for air travel, with environmental concerns relegated to a relatively subsidiary role. New runways were proposed for Stansted, Edinburgh and Birmingham, with approval for another runway at Heathrow dependent on the meeting of new environmental conditions. Indeed, despite claims by the Labour government to have delivered a 'balanced approach' to airports policy, its strategy of 'therapeutic consultation', which sought to engineer some form of policy settlement between competing demands, backfired, as rather than setting the conditions for consensual deliberation over the future of UK airports, the consultation process, and the resulting White Paper, heightened the antagonisms dividing stakeholders (Griggs and Howarth 2007).

Outside the fairly narrow confines of the 'public deliberations', the consultation process pitted two hegemonic projects against one another. On the one hand, AirportWatch, moving away from the traditional politics of single-issue sectional lobbying towards the new movement politics of multi-issue coalitions and the repertoire of direct action, brought together local airport protest groups with national environmental and conservation lobbies such as the Council for the Protection of Rural England, Friends of the Earth and Transport 2000. It advocated a policy of 'demand management' in aviation, arguing that airport growth across the United Kingdom is unnecessary whilst working for the removal of the tax concessions enjoyed by airlines. On the other hand, Freedom to Fly drew together airport companies, airlines and trades unions, air users, organized business and sections of the tourist industry around a rhetoric of 'sustainable growth'. Its proponents implored the government to increase runway capacity to meet rising demand, while deploying the language of sustainability and environmental responsibility to offset damaging criticisms from those opposed to expansion. Indeed, it sought to provide 'ideological cover' for New Labour to launch a programme for expansion of UK airports (Griggs and Howarth 2004; Howarth and Griggs 2006).

In short, no sooner had the Transport Secretary, Alistair Darling published the 2003 White Paper, than he and his government became embroiled in the repeated failings of successive administrations to manage UK airports policy. First, despite extensive consultation, the limits of New Labour's attempts at 'therapeutic consultation' had left local residents and environmentalists excluded from the deliberative exercise. Political debate was polarized between competing coalitions. Indeed, as Flyvbjerg, Bruzelius and Rothengatter (2003: 5) suggest, this polarization was exacerbated by the clash of competing 'truths' and rival constructions of social reality. Second, its efforts to communicate 'authoritative claims' (Hajer 2009) via the White Paper were blighted by an unconvincing identification of the public interest, especially with respect to issues of environmental sustainability, as well as its commitment to expansion as a part of a discourse of 'sustainable aviation'. Finally, and of particular importance for this study of expansion at Heathrow Airport, New Labour had slipped into the trap set by previous governments, by also seeking to act as both the 'promoter' of the aviation industry *and* the 'guardian' of the public interest (Flyvbjerg, Bruzelius and Rothengatter 2003: 138).

On top of this, the White Paper had set in place only the general conditions for expansion at Heathrow, as well as other airports. The implementation of these projects still had to be navigated and the go-ahead for the third runway at Heathrow granted. How did New Labour subsequently seek to extricate itself from the conflicting tensions surrounding the decision to expand Heathrow? How did it lead in constructing the public interest? And how did it strive to communicate authoritative claims to governance? It is to these questions that we now turn. We begin by first examining the events that characterized the run-up to the decision before turning to examine the political and ideological logics of New Labour.

Preparing for take off

The Labour government accepted that final approval for expansion at Heathrow would have to meet environmental conditions on air quality, noise pollution and public transport access to the airport. In early 2004, the Department for Transport (DfT) thus established the Project for the Sustainable Development of Heathrow (PSDH), a set of technical working groups to evaluate whether an expanded Heathrow could meet the environmental conditions imposed by the 2003 White Paper. In June 2005, while awaiting the conclusions of the PSDH, the British Airports Authority (BAA) released for consultation its interim master plans for Heathrow, which set out its further proposals for a third runway and a sixth terminal (BAA 2005). The New Labour government continued to signal its public commitment to expansion. In his 2005 and 2006 Pre-Budget reports, the Chancellor of the Exchequer, Gordon Brown, emphasized the contribution of Heathrow to the economic productivity and competitiveness of the UK economy (HM Treasury 2005: 73, 2006: 175). These arguments were reiterated in the 2003 *Air Transport White Paper Progress Report*, which was published just a few days after Brown's Pre-Budget Report in December 2006. The Report confirmed the government's commitment to the expansion at Heathrow, as long as environmental conditions could be met, because the airport was in an 'increasingly uncompetitive position' and because demand was 'far in excess of runway capacity'. Investing in Heathrow would offer 'a higher economic value than at any other UK airport', with a third runway 'worth £5 billion' (DfT 2006: 45–6).

This first round of public declarations triggered intermittent skirmishes in the media between supporters and opponents of the third runway. Indeed, during this 'phoney war', competing coalitions once again positioned themselves to articulate their rival demands on government. Future Heathrow, an industry-based expansionist lobby, of which BAA was a founding member, thus formed in early 2005, just before the launch of BAA's interim plan for Heathrow. It was followed in June 2007 by the formation of Flying Matters, a broad pro-aviation coalition that brought together the aviation industry, businesses and trade unions. It soon established itself as a less aggressive and less high-profile successor to Freedom to Fly, which had emerged during the initial consultation process.

Opposing these expansionist lobbies was a broad climate-change coalition, which, in the wake of a wave of scientific and expert studies on the contribution of aviation to climate change, targeted aviation as part of its wider fight against climate change. This broad coalition brought together local residents, environmental lobbies, conservation groups and direct action environmentalists, such as Plane Stupid, which was a non-violent direct action anti-aviation network that hit the headlines after a number of high-profile media actions.[4] It typified the new movement politics of airport protest. Indeed, the Camp for Climate Action took place at Heathrow in August 2007, with protesters occupying a site near the airport and calling upon the public to 'remember, we cannot stop climate change without stopping airport expansion'.[5]

The Public Consultation on the expansion of Heathrow began on 22 November 2007, only to close on 27 February 2008. In fact, the DfT held a series of eleven public exhibitions in the communities surrounding Heathrow, though there was no exhibition in the communities whose homes were directly threatened by expansion, allegedly due to the absence of 'suitable venues'.[6] As came to be expected, the opening of consultation was marked by a heightening of public demonstrations and direct action protests. On the final day of the formal consultation, Plane Stupid activists unfurled two banners on the roof of the Houses of Parliament, one saying 'No Third Runway', and the other declaring Parliament to be 'BAA HQ'.[7] Allegations of collusion between New Labour, the DfT, BAA and British Airways (BA) had figured prominently in the campaign against expansion. Gaining access to minutes of departmental meetings released under the Freedom of Information Act, Justine Greening, the Tory MP for Putney, publicly condemned BAA's involvement with the DfT, focusing particularly on its provision of air and noise pollution data to the ministry.[8] Indeed, *Panorama*, the prime-time BBC news programme, further aired these allegations in its own investigation into the connections between New Labour and the aviation industry.[9]

With the official closure of consultation, there followed almost a year in which the government repeatedly delayed the public announcement

---

[4] See, for example, *The Sunday Times*, 'Focus: The New Swampy', 8 October 2006.

[5] *Response to injunction*: www.climatecamp.org.uk/injunction.php, accessed 28 August 2007.

[6] *The Guardian*, 22 November 2007.

[7] BBC News at: http://news.bbc.co.uk/1/hi/uk_politics/7266512.stm, accessed 28 November 2008.

[8] *The Observer*, 18 November 2007.

[9] The BBC programme entitled 'Friends in High Places' was aired on 21 July 2008.

of its decision over the third runway, blaming the initial delay on the requirement to evaluate the 70,000 responses to the consultation. But a wider set of uncertainties surrounded the future of the third runway. After its takeover by the Spanish transport group Ferrovial, BAA was persistently dogged by boardroom shuffles and growing publicity over its financial troubles, not to mention the fiasco of the opening of Terminal 5 at Heathrow.[10] At the end of August 2008, the Competition Commission called for BAA to sell off three of its seven airports, including two in London from Heathrow, Stansted and Gatwick.[11] Indeed, the opposition Conservative Party also declared itself against expansion at Heathrow, promoting a 'better not bigger Heathrow', which tapped into growing criticisms of the regulation of British airports and business demands to address the so-called 'Heathrow hassle'.[12] At the same time, the European Union (EU) warned that the third runway would breach European air pollution limits, to be joined over time by the Environment Agency, the Sustainable Development Commission and Sir David King, former government climate change adviser, who all came out publicly against the third runway.[13] More importantly, the UK banking crisis and ensuing economic recession further undermined calls for expansion, at least in the short term, as airlines were hit by the economic slowdown and began to cut flights.[14]

Such doubts were compounded by the increasing electoral pressures faced by the Labour government. Tony Blair resigned as Prime Minister in June 2007 as part of a negotiated transfer of powers to his chancellor, Gordon Brown, with whom he had modernized the Labour Party. By the autumn of 2008, Brown's premiership was under increasing attack as his electoral popularity waned, and as he faced allegations of a sexist-macho leadership, as well as persistent rumours over challenges for the leadership of the party. Amid one such crisis of leadership at the end of September 2008, Ruth Kelly, the Secretary of State for Transport, resigned.[15] The decision over the third runway was thus further postponed when Geoff Hoon replaced Kelly at the DfT.

What is more, by late October and early November 2008, reports were circulating about growing Cabinet and backbench opposition to

[10] See, for example, *The Times*, 'BAA takeover by Ferrovial as Bad as Rover Deal', 23 April 2008; and for the fiasco of the opening of Terminal 5, see http://news.bbc.co.uk/1/hi/uk/7314816.stm, accessed 2 April 2008.
[11] *The Guardian*, 18 and 21 August 2008.   [12] *The Times*, 17 June 2008.
[13] See, for example, *The Guardian*, 18 August 2008; *The Independent*, 21 December 2008 and 21 May 2008; *The Observer*, 21 December 2008.
[14] See, for example, *London Evening Standard*, 3 November 2008.
[15] *The Guardian*, 24 September 2008.

the expansion of Heathrow, which was deemed to threaten the green credentials of the Labour Party, especially its capacity to deliver planned reductions in carbon emissions, and marginal seats in the south-east.[16] In the Cabinet, opposition to expansion was led initially by Hilary Benn at the Department for Environment, Food and Rural Affairs, and Ed Miliband at Energy and Climate Change, as well as Harriet Harman, the Leader of the House, and David Miliband, the Foreign Secretary.[17] Outside the Cabinet, forty-one Labour MPs gave their support to an early day parliamentary motion calling for a rethink on the third runway.[18]

At the beginning of December 2008, Hoon announced the suspension of any decision on expansion at Heathrow until January 2009.[19] Opposition within the Cabinet and the ranks of the Labour Party continued in what was increasingly portrayed in the media as a battle between Ed Miliband and Peter Mandelson, the Business Secretary.[20] Indeed, Hilary Benn publicly intervened in the campaign, declaring in an interview with *The Sunday Times* on 14 December 2008 that Britain was not able to breach EU air pollution limits – the key issue at stake in the government decision over Heathrow. Equally, backbench MPs prepared for a cross-party revolt, tabling in mid-December a motion for a vote in the Commons on the third runway at Heathrow.

The New Year was marked by the public support of the Transport Minister, Lord Adonis, for a £4.5 billion international rail exchange for Heathrow Airport, although this support was somewhat publicly distanced from the impending third runway decision.[21] On 12 January, Nick Raynsford, the former Labour government minister, announced the formation of a cross-party group in support of a London estuary airport.[22] Brown again met with Labour MPs, and the press carried reports that Labour whips were ringing around to ensure support for the expansion of Heathrow. To make matters worse for Brown, Conservative Party leader David Cameron proposed to use one of the Opposition days in the Commons to debate the third runway amid rumours that the government were on the verge of announcing its support for the third runway and sixth terminal.[23]

---

[16] *New Statesman*, 29 October 2008; *The Guardian*, 3 November 2008; *Financial Times*, 10 November 2008.

[17] They were later to be joined by John Denham, see *The Telegraph*, 14 December 2008; *The Guardian*, 21 December 2008.

[18] *The Guardian*, 3 and 6 November 2008.

[19] See C. Ames, 'Labour "Dithering" over Third Runway', *New Statesman*, 4 December 2008; *Financial Times*, 5 December 2008.

[20] *London Evening Standard*, 15 December 2008.

[21] *Financial Times*, 4 January 2009; *The Guardian*, 5 January 2009.

[22] *The Guardian*, 12 January 2009.   [23] *The Guardian*, 14 January 2009.

On 15 January 2009, Hoon announced to the Commons the government's approval of the expansion at Heathrow. Lobbying by Benn and Miliband had forced concessions from the Transport Secretary. Indeed, Miliband, in his allegedly 'bruising encounters with Hoon' had delivered what was termed a 'half runway' with additional capacity being open only to what was deemed to be 'green slots'.[24] However, on the announcement of the decision to the House of Commons, John McDonnell grabbed the mace, the symbol of the office of the Speaker, and was asked to leave the Commons.[25] There was no formal vote on the decision. The Opposition did devote one of its parliamentary Opposition days to expansion at Heathrow, but any such vote had no direct consequence on government policy. Ultimately, twenty-eight Labour MPs voted with the opposition and the government successfully defended its majority in the Commons. The concessions announced by the government and the Conservatives' inability to rule out future expansion in the south-east were allegedly sufficient to ensure the government's majority.[26]

New Labour strategies and tactics

Throughout this protracted battle of claim and counter-claim, the Labour government pursued various strategies and practices in order to advance the implementation of its 2003 White Paper. At the same time, it sought to ward off the growing grievances and demands that accompanied the proposed expansion of Heathrow. In this section, we first identify the logics of managed consultation and framing, before turning to the discussion of the logics of deferred responsibility or individualization, incentivization and brokerage. We shall begin with what we shall call the logic of 'managed consultation'.

New Labour's earlier attempts to engage in a process of 'therapeutic consultation', in which it sought to create the apparent conditions for a consensual dialogue, had backfired amid the formation of competing coalitions and the construction of various social antagonisms. In the case of the third runway at Heathrow, the Brown government endeavoured to impose clear boundaries on the process of consultation through what we term the logic of managed consultation. As we have noted, only eleven public exhibitions were organized during a consultation process that ran for just three months, including, as widely reported, the national slowdown of the Christmas and New Year festivities. Importantly, the New Labour government had earlier excluded communities from the

---

[24] *The Guardian*, 16 January 2009.   [25] *The Telegraph*, 15 January 2009.
[26] *The Daily Mail*, 29 January 2009; *The Guardian*, 28 and 29 January 2009.

development of the Project for the Sustainable Development of Heathrow (PSDH), which brought together the likes of BAA, National Air Traffic Services (NATS), Civil Aviation Authority (CAA), DfT Rail and the Highways Agency, as well as external scientific experts.

It is striking that this initiative did not include representatives from local communities or environmental lobbies. Indeed, the PSDH was an initial attempt to anchor the decision over Heathrow within the technical and scientific realms, rather than the political domain, thus legitimizing the processes of decision-making through the mobilization and appeal to scientific discourse. More fully, the Aviation Environmental Division of the DfT thus coordinated three technical panels of air-quality experts and academics, which were lauded by the DfT for their 'balanced membership' and methods of 'independent peer review', as well as their stakeholder involvement of 'representatives from recognized best practice working groups' (DfT 2007a: 2–3). In fact, the consultation process did not formally offer the opportunity to question the case for the expansion of the third runway. At no point during the consultation period were participants directly questioned about the need to build the new runway. From the government's point of view, the case for expansion had already been decided in the consultations that led to the 2003 White Paper. This consultation focused on whether or not the new infrastructure would meet the environmental conditions previously laid down in the 2003 White Paper (DfT 2007b: 3 and 114–18).

This framing of the issue thus privileged the role of environmental expertise, especially claims over future levels of air quality and noise at Heathrow, while paradoxically excluding broader environmental questions about carbon emissions and global warming (DfT 2007b: 18). Commenting on the particular boundaries imposed on the consultation process, John Stewart, the chair of HACAN ClearSkies, argued that 'if Ruth Kelly wanted to ruin the opposition, this is a good way to do it. If we had to spend millions of pounds on research, we could not spend any money on campaigning'.[27] These views were shared by a *Guardian* leader, which suggested that the process was 'not a consultation, nor even an attempt at conversion', but 'a lecture'. This editorial prompted a response from the Secretary of State for Transport, in which she defended the 'consultation' as an integral 'part of a transparent public process. This is not a "closed debate", this is democracy.'[28]

However, when local campaigners quickly picked up on the technical findings of the DfT's own November 2007 report, *Attitudes to Noise from Aviation Sources in England* (ANASE), such expertise was summarily

[27] *The Guardian*, 22 November 2007.   [28] *The Guardian*, 23 and 26 November 2007.

dismissed. HACAN ClearSkies, the anti-Heathrow expansion local residents' group, argued that the ANASE report proved that people complain of aircraft noise at lower thresholds than previously believed by government (levels of 50 rather than 57 decibels). Local campaigners were quick to suggest that this finding scuppered the government's assertion that expansion at Heathrow would not increase numbers of people affected by noise pollution (based on 2002 estimates). Indeed, campaigners argued that 'about 10 times as many people – over 2 million – are affected by a 50 decibel cut-off point than the Government's favoured 57 decibels'.[29] The government responded by denying the credibility of its own report, praising the work of the 'independent consultants' who undertook the study on their behalf, but citing peer reviewers to denounce the evidence of the ANASE study as 'unclear, partial or subject to different interpretations' (DfT 2007b: 47). At the same time, the DfT thus proffered the fantasy of 'neutral scientific evidence' and disclosed its limits, making visible the political logics of the naming of 'evidence' (or not as the case may be).

These disputes about the practices and process of the public consultation, as well as the role of government, reveal the limits of New Labour efforts to create a legitimate terrain of argumentation, which could frame certain demands as acceptable and tractable, while excluding and concealing others. Government ministers and officials repeatedly stressed the economic importance of Heathrow, and its role in generating jobs and maintaining the economic competitiveness of the United Kingdom. For example, a few days after the launch of the consultation, in a speech to the Confederation of British Industry (CBI), Gordon Brown returned to well-known claims that aviation was a crucial motor of economic growth. He argued that the government had 'to respond to a clear business imperative and increase capacity at our airports . . . Our prosperity depends on it: Britain as a world financial centre must be readily accessible from around the world.'[30]

These assertions and aspirations were important ingredients of a continuing narrative that plotted various 'threats' to economic well-being, as well as affective appeals to the 'joys' and 'freedoms' associated with flying. It was repeatedly stated that economic benefits would be threatened if the government stalled its plans for expansion. The White Paper Progress Report conjured up the 'horrific' fantasy of the United Kingdom's declining economic competitiveness, coupled with the growing

[29] HACAN ClearSkies, press release, 6 November 2007: www.hacan.org.uk, accessed 20 November 2007.
[30] For a transcript of the speech, see www.cbi.org.uk/ndbs/press.nsf, accessed 20 April 2010.

threats of European competitors, who have expanded capacity to meet rising demand, and the inexorable rise of China, which according to the Report 'plans to invest $17.5 billion on launching 71 airport expansion projects, relocating 11 airports and building 49 new airports' (DfT 2006: 10). The threat of international competition was thus invoked to undermine any attempts to constrain expansion at Heathrow. In a speech to London business leaders, just a day before the launch of the consultation process, Ruth Kelly declared that 'if Heathrow is allowed to become uncompetitive, the flights and routes it operates will simply move elsewhere. All it will do is shift capacity over the Channel. It will make us feel pure, but with no benefit to the rest of the planet.'[31]

More importantly, the Brown government sought to reframe expansion at Heathrow as a sustainable response to aviation. This was part of an ongoing rhetorical practice of redescribing airport expansions as consistent with a form of 'sustainable' and 'responsible aviation'. At the same time, the DfT sought to reinscribe the various elements of the Air Transport White Paper into the emergent discourse of sustainable and environmentally sensitive development. It thus identified the expansionist White Paper as a precursor to the *Stern Review*, which inquired into the economics of climate change, as it allegedly followed the 'same approach Sir Nicholas Stern recommended right across our economy' (DfT 2006: 7). Equally, expansion at Heathrow was represented as a type of 'demand management' in which the DfT confirmed that the third runway 'would only be satisfying around 70 per cent of the unconstrained demand forecast for 2030' (DfT 2007b: 44). In fact, over the consultation period, Brown and his colleagues regularly sought to redefine expansion at Heathrow as a 'green response'. These rhetorical redescriptions relied in part on the success of appeals to the threat of international competition, which it was argued would immediately absorb any fall in capacity at Heathrow. However, it came increasingly to rest on the argument that the third runway would ease congestion, such as the stacking of planes over London. When questioned about the environmental impacts of airport congestion at Heathrow, Gordon Brown declared that 'it's not simply a decision about the number of passengers, it's also a decision about the ways that we actually operate our airlines'.[32]

The Brown government thus came to rely upon the articulation of fantasmatic narratives, in which aviation expansion and environmental protection were presented as compatible objectives, in order to justify its decisions and policies. For example, during the consultation over the third runway, the DfT released its strategy paper, *Towards a*

---

[31] *The Guardian*, 21 November 2007.   [32] *The Observer*, 6 January 2008.

Sustainable Transport System in which it described economic growth and carbon reduction as 'both essential and mutually consistent' objectives. It thus dismissed the 'stark choice between being "rich and dirty" or "poor and green" as a "false dichotomy"' (2007c: 7–8). These fantasmatic appeals were designed to mask over the contradictions of New Labour's expansionist policy, though they cannot be divorced from appeals to highly contested claims about the supposed benefits of future techno-logical changes, which were alleged to include 'a higher proportion of twin-engined, as opposed to four-engined aircraft, with lower emissions' (DfT 2007b: 67 and 115). In fact, it was the availability of these 'tech-nological fixes' that ultimately provided the conditions for New Labour to grant approval for the third runway without 'the need for radical mit-igation measures' (DfT 2007b: 36 and 60–1).

These various strategies of reframing co-existed with – and indeed relied upon – a wider logic of deferred responsibility or individualization. What we characterize as the logics of deferred responsibility or individ-ualization captures the way the New Labour government endeavoured to incorporate multiple stakeholders into the shared ownership or man-agement of a desired policy outcome. In other words, it sought to priv-ilege the mutual dependencies that hold government and stakeholders together, while at the same time shifting responsibility for outcomes away from the sole ownership of the Labour government, and on to the indus-try and citizens. The White Paper Progress Report thereby notes how the Labour government's Climate Change Programme underlines 'the role that Government, industry and individuals have to play in order to lessen the UK's environmental impacts' (DfT 2006: 16). Indeed, in June 2005 the Blair government offered its support for the formation of the Sustain-able Aviation Strategy, which was a network that brought together leading airlines, airports and aerospace manufacturers, and which in response to the 2003 White Paper set out targets to reduce CO_2 and nitrogen oxide emissions of new aircraft, and to lower the perceived external noise of aircraft, with airports engaging in community-related noise limitations. Its launch was firmly endorsed by the government, with the aviation minister, Karen Buck, declaring 'we look to the industry to take their strategy forward energetically so that aviation contributes to a sustain-able society'.[33] Indeed, in the foreword to the 52-page strategy, the Prime Minister, Tony Blair, offered his own support to the initiative, stating that by 'working with Government, and society to tackle the environ-mental issues associated with aviation, the industry can demonstrate that

---

[33] Department for Transport news release 2005/0067, 20 June 2005: www.dft.gov.uk, accessed 28 June 2005.

economic success, social progress and respect for the environment can go hand in hand' (Sustainable Aviation 2005: 3).

However, the Labour government also extended the chain of responsibility in to the international arena, where it claimed that many of the difficulties faced by the government in tackling the contribution of air transport to climate change have their origins in the international arena. Here the government echoed the rhetoric of the *Stern Review*, in which it problematizes the non-inclusion of international aviation emissions in its Kyoto targets; the 'out of date' Chicago Convention on international air routes, which 'stands as a barrier to action'; and the limited progress within the International Civil Aviation Organization (ICAO) on aviation emissions since 1998. What is more, the government questioned the failure of international actors to address the impact of aviation on climate change, stating that 'many countries still see aviation only as a very minor part of the global problem of climate change and are concerned about the potential impact on the industry of measures such as emissions trading'. Ultimately, therefore, it shifted responsibility for limited progress on to various international actors. The Progress Report claimed that 'while we have obtained formal recognition for our view that provisions such as fuel tax exemptions are anomalous, it has not yet been possible to reach consensus within ICAO with regard to specific economic instruments'. The problem of aviation was thus transformed into an international problem, which attributed blame and responsibility on to international partners. This construction has the added advantage of drawing attention to the less environmentally friendly aviation policies of international competitors (DfT 2006: 13).

The logic of deferred responsibility operated in tandem with what we might call the logics of incentivization and brokerage. Practices of incentivization capture the various ways in which government adopts a hands-off approach to the environmental regulation of the air transport industry by proposing and supporting the development of an emissions trading scheme. This is not to say that the logic of incentivization does not have recourse to 'sticks' and disincentives in some instances. For example, the 2006 Pre-Budget Report announced the doubling of Air Passenger Duty from the beginning of February 2007. Nonetheless, the recourse to practices of emissions trading became the nodal point for the Labour government's response to aviation's impact on climate change. References to the inclusion of aviation in emissions trading are peppered throughout the government's policies on the environment, notably in the 2005 sustainable development strategy and its 2006 UK climate change programme (DEFRA 2005: 86, 2006: 71–2). The policy measure is partly legitimized because it resonates with the *Stern Review* on the economics of climate change, especially 'his strong belief that market mechanisms are the most effective way of reducing carbon emissions' (DfT 2006: 14).

However, it is in its construction as a policy instrument that marries economic competitiveness, the regulation of demand and environmental protection that it became pivotal in the maintenance of the fantasy of sustainable aviation. For example, the Progress Report argues that the inclusion of aviation in the EU Emissions Trading Scheme 'is the most efficient and cost-effective way to ensure that the sector plays its part in tackling climate change', because 'it avoids artificial targets for each sector which would distort economic decision-making' (DfT 2006: 8). Emissions trading is thus contrasted by the Progress Report to 'the alternative of industry-specific carbon targets which can constrain growth and be arbitrary and inflexible'. It is extolled as one of the most 'cost-effective ways of reducing carbon emissions while responding to the strong demand for air travel' (DfT 2006: 15). Practices of incentivization thus enable government to assume a 'distance' from the market for aviation, while establishing steering mechanisms that favour particular policy outcomes. In short, it provides a solution that promises to square the circle of 'sustainable aviation'.

Finally, in what we term the logic of brokerage, government rearticulates its attempts to position itself as an 'honest broker' that seeks to accommodate and balance the various interests and demands, so as to produce a partial and acceptable equilibrium. Here, once again, the White Paper is portrayed as the embodiment of 'honest' brokerage. The Progress Report thus stresses how the White Paper 'rejected a predict and provide approach and instead provided a comprehensive strategy', which itself 'rejected proposals for new capacity at several airports and at new greenfield locations, and instead promoted making much better use of existing airport capacity' (DfT 2006: 7). Strategies and practices of brokerage thus support the articulation of government demands in the Progress Report (DfT 2006: 16) for the better management of existing airport capacity through improvement and modernization; new decision processes based on emissions cost assessments; investment in new technology to offset the noise and pollution of jet aircraft; and the funding of research into aviation and the environment (see, for example, the commitment of £5m to the new knowledge transfer network called OMEGA or Opportunities for Meeting the Environmental challenge of Growth in Aviation).

But one important consequence of the logic of brokerage is that it reproduces the fantasy that competing demands for growth and environmental protection are in some way reconcilable, and that, through appeals to the 'sustainable development of aviation capacity' (DfT 2006: 21), it is possible to reach a policy solution that simultaneously and satisfactorily addresses the demands of those stakeholders who are seeking to combat climate change and protect local environments, on the one hand, while delivering further capacity for air travel, on the other. Yet it also exposes contradictions in the arguments articulated by government. The privileging of brokerage as a means of finding a 'balance' between competing demands frames the work of government, not as an elimination of the negative impacts of air transport, but more in terms of a mitigation of the environmental impact of aviation on climate change. Most importantly, this logic of brokerage, as against those of deferred responsibility, individualization and incentivization, presents government as the ultimate arbitrator of the public interest and the defender of the common good.

Assessing the outcome

What are we to make of the Labour government's strategies and tactics during this period? At the outset, it is important to stress that throughout the twists and turns of the decision and its aftermath, the authority of the Labour government suffered a number of setbacks. Its political leadership came under attack from both supporters and opponents of expansion, as it became ensnared in its own efforts to position itself as an 'honest broker', while effectively abdicating its directing function by employing logics of steering and incentivization, and by deferring or decentring responsibility to other groups, individuals and constituencies. In fact, despite the decision to approve the third runway, expansion at Heathrow remained in doubt and Labour's aviation policy was increasingly discredited, having for many observers been effectively 'murdered' by the Committee on Climate Change's judgement that the predicted doubling of passenger numbers was not compatible with wider commitments to keep CO_2 emissions from commercial aviation in 2050 no higher than they were in 2005.[34] At the end of March 2010, campaigners subsequently won a High Court ruling that the government had not sufficiently addressed the issue of climate change in its deliberations over the construction of the third runway. Although this judgment did not

---

[34] AirportWatch, press release, 8 December 2009: www.airportwatch.org.uk, accessed 9 May 2010. However, the Committee did suggest that a 60 per cent growth in demand for air travel would still be possible, achieved through technological improvements, air traffic management and operational efficiencies, and 80 per cent reductions in emissions across other sectors (Committee on Climate Change 2009).

reverse the decision to expand Heathrow, the High Court judge did call upon government officials to carry out a further policy review of aviation in the near future.[35]

However, by the spring of 2010, the decision to expand Heathrow had become embroiled in a closely fought general election campaign, in which the main opposition parties remained committed to reversing any plans for expansion. In the first few days of taking office in May 2010, the new Liberal–Conservative Coalition quickly abandoned proposals for the construction of a third runway and sixth terminal at Heathrow Airport, as well as the planned second runway at Stansted. At least in the short term, this decision reversed over a decade of New Labour's sponsorship of aviation expansion. Indeed, it is difficult to deny that the Labour government, while recognizing the challenge of reducing carbon emissions from commercial aviation, failed decisively in its efforts to constitute a legitimate policy consensus around what might be termed sustainable aviation. Yet, at the time of writing, it remains to be seen whether the decision of the Liberal–Conservative Coalition government actually marks a weakening of the grip of aviation expansion on British politicians and policy-makers. In a speech to the Airport Operators' Association on 25 October 2010, the new Secretary of State for Transport, Philip Hammond, confirmed that the priority for government was the more efficient use of existing airport capacity, thus making airports 'better, not bigger'. He promised that the government's commitment to this new strategy would be written into a forthcoming Airport Economic Regulation Bill. However, at the same time, he also announced that the government would begin consultation on a new aviation policy framework in early 2012.[36] This announcement followed closely on the heels of the creation of the South East Airports Task Force in June 2010 to 'review and understand the existing runway, terminal and other capacity constraints at Heathrow, Gatwick and Stansted, taking account of demand for air travel and the Government's commitment to a low-carbon and eco-friendly economy'.[37] Indeed, in March 2011, the Coalition also launched its own broad consultation exercise, publishing a scoping paper for the development of a sustainable framework for aviation (DfT 2011a), which was to run alongside the production of a report from the South East Airports Task Force. The

---

[35] BBC News at: news.bbc.co.uk/1/hi/england/london/8588220.stm, accessed 10 April 2010.
[36] www.dft.gov.uk/speeches, accessed 5 November 2010.
[37] www.dft.gov.uk/pgr, accessed 5 November 2010.

latter was duly prepared and submitted to government in July 2011 (DfT 2011b).

That the strategies and tactics of the Labour government ultimately failed to ward off growing grievances and demands owes much to its political management of the decision surrounding the third runway. The Labour government repeated its failings of the consultation process and formulation of the 2003 White Paper. The legacy of the hardening of opposition in the 2003 consultation exercise cannot be divorced from the political dynamics of the decision over the third runway at Heathrow. Nonetheless, Labour's 'managed consultation' over Heathrow reduced the consultation process to a technocratic window-dressing exercise, which generated further exclusions and frontiers. Indeed, such framings further polarized political debates over the third runway, mobilizing as in 2003 competing coalitions and hardening opposition, rather than providing an arena for dialogue and consensus formation. Its attempts to frame the consultation process fuelled allegations of exclusion and 'capture' by aviation insiders whose structural power was arguably reflected in the government's proposals and discourse. Once again, as those opposing expansion noted, many of the key players advocating growth on behalf of the airline and airport companies had close relationships with the New Labour government. These personal and symbolic linkages reinforced the perception of a powerful set of structural and institutional connections between the state and big business. Rather than the development of agonistic pluralism whereby actors regard each other as adversaries rather than 'enemies', there developed closed and exclusionary forms of antagonistic politics.

Most importantly, Labour failed in its efforts at rhetorical redescription, which attempted to reframe the zero-sum game of airport expansion *or* environmental protection as a positive-sum game where both growth in aviation *and* environmental protection were achievable. The creation and acceptance of an empty signifier such as 'sustainable aviation', which would be underpinned by a beatific fantasy in which aviation expansion and environmental sustainability could be linked in a harmonious and mutually reinforcing fashion, might have proved an astute strategic manoeuvre to displace environmental concerns and stabilize the meaning of aviation policy. However, it proved much more difficult to achieve and it rendered the government vulnerable to further critiques and challenges, especially from those who questioned the scientific evidence and empirical basis upon which New Labour's public policy was meant to have been grounded.

In fact, in its efforts to deploy such fantasmatic narratives, New Labour was hampered by the changing political and policy context. First, it suffered from the absence of 'ideological cover' for expansion, which was provided throughout the formulation of the 2003 White Paper by the likes of the Freedom to Fly coalition for expansion. In the case of the third runway at Heathrow, such a coalition as Flying Matters was unable to fulfil that role for the Labour government. In the second place, and partly explaining the failure of the aviation industry to offer Labour the requisite 'ideological cover' for expansion, the changing political salience of climate-change politics formed a new terrain of argumentation. This new terrain disclosed untenable contradictions in the government's policy discourse.

More fully, a peculiar set of events and intellectual interventions in the period following the publication of the new White Paper in 2003 heightened the problem of climate change for the government and public alike. First, there was a publicized set of natural phenomena and events – dramatic temperature rises, extreme events like melting glaciers, droughts and flooding, all of which were symbolized in the media by events such as Hurricane Katrina and the destruction of New Orleans in August 2005 – that began to be taken as evidence of rapid climate change. The understanding that these natural phenomena were closely linked to climate change was bolstered by a growing scientific consensus that the events and phenomena associated with climate change was a human creation. In early January 2004, Sir David King, the UK government's chief scientific adviser, declared that climate change was a far greater threat than international terrorism; in fact, it was declared 'the most severe problem we are facing today'.[38] These linkages were strengthened in the wider popular imagination by a series of political and cultural interventions. In 2006, the former US Vice-President Al Gore presented the documentary film *An Inconvenient Truth*, which detailed the threat of climate change, and became the fourth highest grossing documentary film to date. Closer to home, in September 2004 Tony Blair gave a highly publicized speech on climate change, in which he argued that 'the emission of greenhouse gases, associated with industrialization and strong economic growth from a world population that has increased six-fold in 200 years' was 'causing global warming at a rate that began as significant, has become alarming and is simply unsustainable in the long term'. Blair's speech made it clear that the scientific and anecdotal evidence of global warming and climate change was indisputable. In fact, he extolled the virtues of the United Kingdom's excellence in science, especially in the environmental field where 'the world-renowned Hadley and Tyndall centres for

---

[38] BBC News: http://news.bbc.co.uk/1/hi/sci/tech/3381425.stm, accessed 3 April 2009.

climate change research' were singled out for praise; the very scientists and centres that were soon to question important aspects of the Blair government's aviation policy.[39] These claims were to be reiterated in the *Stern Review* (2006), which was published some two years later (see above).

In short, the Labour government failed ultimately in its efforts to constitute a legitimate terrain of argumentation, which could frame certain demands as acceptable and tractable, while excluding and concealing others. Thus, its main response to the crises and deficiencies surrounding Heathrow was to retreat back to the construction of fantasmatic narratives – 'cake-and-eat-it' forms of justification and representation – such as 'sustainable aviation'. These ideological representations ultimately betray its inability to shape the policy agenda and exude a leadership function. And in the case of Heathrow, they were quickly scuppered by their lack of credibility and resonance in the changing policy environment. In fact, rather than concealing demands, they opened government up to increasing challenge and critique. Why, then, did Labour continue in its support for Heathrow? Why did it continue to over-invest in its defence of expansion? It is to these final questions that we now turn.

Critical explanation: Heathrow and the logics of UK aviation expansion

There is little doubt that the ongoing struggles over the future expansion of Heathrow Airport, and the aviation industry more generally, constitute a 'wicked problem' for policy-makers, politicians and all those citizens differentially affected by the decision and its long-term implications. The problem is about ongoing power struggles between rival political forces, and seemingly intractable clashes of values. What does our particular interpretation tell us? How does it enable us to explain critically the events and processes under investigation?

At the outset, it is important to connect the competing forces working to determine the future of Heathrow Airport to the broader set of social, political and fantasmatic logics within which they operate. Commercial and military aviation has been of high strategic importance to most industrial states since its invention at the beginning of the twentieth century. Yet the decisive triggering of post-war aviation occurred during the Second World War, as the United States and Britain rapidly expanded the manufacture of aircraft, constructed additional runways,

---

[39] For a full transcript of the speech, see http://webarchive.nationalarchives.gov.uk and http://www.number10.gov.uk, accessed 3 April 2009.

secured international air routes and quickly developed new aircraft technologies. Expansion in the thirty or so years following the war was mainly
directed by the state via the nationalization of leading airlines, as well as
the state provision of airports and other transport infrastructure. The
UK aviation industry and transport provision was thus an integral part
and parcel of the Fordist mode of development, which structured the
regime of accumulation and mode of governance during this period.
However, under the Thatcher governments of the 1980s, the initial role
of the state in advancing UK aviation gave way to the role of the market and private enterprise in spearheading growth. Route entry barriers
were lowered on domestic and international routes and new low-cost
scheduled airlines such as Ryanair, Go and easyJet entered the market
to compete against the newly privatized national carrier, British Airways. This latter privatization was accompanied by that of the British
Airports Authority (BAA), which then owned the three largest London
Airports – Heathrow, Gatwick and Stansted – and four regional airports
in the United Kingdom.

More precisely, then, in this schema, the logic of aviation expansion
was both brought about by, and partly constitutive of, the emergence
and consolidation of Thatcher's neoliberal model of capital accumulation. In February 1987, for example, BA and BAA were privatized
and floated on the London Stock Exchange amid great media fanfares.
Both privatizations were heralded as major success stories in breaking
with the restrictions of nationalization and state regulation by inject-
ing healthy competition and by stimulating consumption. At the same
time, the Thatcher government presided over the opening of a fourth
terminal at Heathrow, while initiating the eventual decision to build a
fifth terminal at Heathrow and the decision to expand Stansted Airport. But the strong bond between the Thatcher government and the
aviation industry went even deeper than that. The growth of air travel
and global tourism was a symbolic indicator of the rising affluence and
increased consumerism promoted by the Thatcher government and its
successors. It gave greater credence to the latter's belief in popular capitalism and individualized consumption, and was intimately connected
to the Thatcher government's support for finance capital and economic
globalization. There is a clear connection between the logic of finan-
cialization and the need for improved global transport infrastructure.
This was epitomized, for example, in the continuing plans to expand
and pour resources into Heathrow and other airports in the south-east
of England. Airlines and airports were an integral part of the growing service industry, which the government sought to protect from the
threat of foreign competition, and were intimately connected to high-tech

industries such as BAE Systems and the military–industrial complex more generally.

Support for the aviation and tourist industries, and their insatiable demand for greater and improved airport infrastructure, continued unabated during the Major years. BAA announced its proposals to build Terminal 5 at Heathrow Airport in May 1992, while Manchester Airport opened its second terminal in 1993 and gained approval for a second runway in 1997. It continued under New Labour, with the official approval of a fifth terminal and third runway at Heathrow, as well as a second runway at Stansted (see above). Indeed, if anything, the demands for expansion were encouraged and intensified during this period. With the advent of aviation deregulation in the United Kingdom and Europe, the emergence of low-cost carriers further stimulated consumer demand for air travel and put even greater pressure on airport capacity. The economic boom that coincided with, and was strongly encouraged by, the first ten years of New Labour led to even greater consumer demand for air travel, a massive growth in passenger numbers, both business and tourist, and added more pressures to expand airport capacity, as well as the retail and business opportunities that followed in its wake.

But if the basic post-Fordist regime of accumulation that was promoted by the Thatcher government was also bolstered by subsequent governments, then it was articulated with different modes of regulation and new forms of ideological justification. Initially, the Major government sought to attenuate the more strident and exclusionary dimensions of Thatcherism with a new rhetoric of classlessness and inclusivity. But though its style of statecraft was less abrasive than that of Thatcherism, the basic policies that had fostered the neoliberal regime of accumulation were left intact. The same was true of New Labour. Though elaborating a new Third Way rhetoric, which would transcend the 'New Right' and the 'Old Left', and while there was more concern with social inclusion, which was to some degree backed up with new policy initiatives and programmes (such as the widely trumpeted windfall tax and the minimum wage), the Blair government remained committed to the Thatcher policies of privatization and deregulation, coupled with political and ideological support for the City of London.

One important difference with Thatcherism was the refashioning of the state to improve global economic competitiveness, and the development of a new mode of network governance in selected policy domains. As Jessop (2002) and others have correctly shown, drawing on regulation theory, the post-Fordist regime of accumulation in the post-Thatcher era has been accompanied by a new kind of state, which he calls the

'Schumpeterian competition state'. This notion can be used to characterize a state that

> aims to secure economic growth within its borders and/or to secure competitive advantages for capitals based in its borders, even where they operate abroad, by promoting the economic and extra-economic conditions that are currently deemed vital for success in competition with economic actors and spaces located in other states . . . As such, the competition state prioritizes the pursuit of strategies intended to create, structure, or reinforce – as far as it is economically and politically feasible to do so – the competitive advantages of its territory, population, built environment, social institutions and economic agents. (Jessop 2002: 96)

As Finlayson points out, New Labour sought 'to deploy the state in the name of the market' (2003: 179), thus changing cultures and identities so as to 'develop a way in which wealth creation and moral cohesion [can] be maintained' (2003: 198).

The 'competition state' has emerged in the wake of various efforts by different political forces to engineer a post-Fordist solution to the crises and contradictions associated with the 'Fordist compromise'. The idea of a competition state is helpful in explaining the way in which successive governments, ministers and high-ranking civil servants in the Department for Transport have continued to support the expansion of airports and the aviation industry. Of course, this is not the only reason. It is also explained by New Labour ideology, which was built around the idea of continuing economic growth making possible the more equitable distribution of resources. If anything, the election of Gordon Brown as Prime Minister, with his commitment to productivism and his acquiescence to the demands of the City and finance capital more generally, exacerbated these tendencies. It was Brown who prioritized expansion at Heathrow over Stansted when he clashed with Tony Blair over the issue. As chancellor he made repeated statements in support of the economic contribution of Heathrow and aviation more generally. Indeed, at the opening of consultation over the third runway, his support for expansion and for industry was brought into the public domain as a means of delegitimizing the consultation process. In a typical assessment, Simon Jenkins, a political commentator for *The Guardian*, wrote that 'the word "business" still mesmerizes Brown . . . If business wants a new runway at Heathrow, Brown orders one. If business wants the planning regime collapsed, he will collapse it . . . Never was the maxim, what is good for General Motors is good for the nation, so enshrined in one man. Any theory that Brown is not a real Thatcherite is rubbish.'[40]

[40] *The Guardian*, 28 November 2008.

Critical evaluation

As we have suggested, our understanding of the practice of critical evaluation is internally connected to the logics of characterization and explanation, though the latter must acknowledge the radical contingency of social processes, as well as the contestability of the interpretations that arise. This in turn makes it possible to stress the primacy of political practices in the construction and reproduction of various social forms, as well as the role of ideologies in their maintenance. Our interpretation of the ongoing struggles to shape the future expansion of Heathrow Airport in relation to the contradictory logics of aviation expansion is thus partly designed to expose the role of structural power, political exclusion and ideological deception in the various practices of deliberation and consultation initiated by successive UK governments. It has also sought to underline the fantasmatic quality of the ideology of 'sustainable aviation' and 'responsible growth', and other attempts by the government and pro-aviation groups to have their cake and eat it.

Our narrative has thus highlighted the lack of democratic consultation and negotiation in the formation and implementation of public policy on this issue, while foregrounding the various modes of co-optation and window-dressing that appeared in the various deliberations and consultations thus far convened. At the same time, we have endeavoured to frame these issues in different perspectives so as to highlight the underlying value conflicts they epitomize. One framing of the conflict highlights the tension between unfettered economic growth and environmental protection. Another framing of the struggle foregrounds the torsions between democratic consultation and negotiation, on the one hand, and technocratic and so-called evidence-based forms of decision-making, on the other. Both axes of contestation go to the heart of this problem, and they raise crucial issues for democratic politics in advanced industrial societies. Part of this practice of critique and evaluation involves the making visible of contradictions, false claims and exaggerations on both sides of the political division. Yet in making these critical evaluations we should not simply dismiss notions like 'sustainable' and 'responsible' aviation expansion, nor should we dismiss out of hand the various governmental practices of deliberative evaluation. We should instead take these commitments at their word, and then use them as one set of yardsticks with which to measure and evaluate the objects that we investigate. The immanent and genealogical critique of practices can work in this way.

Yet, at the same time, the development of this evaluation also presupposes the articulation and clarification of those norms and values that can be projected into our problematizations both to render aspects of our objects of inquiry more visible, and because they are the inevitable presuppositions of any critical inquiry into power. Where do such values, norms and ideals come from? In part, as Nietzsche would put it, they are the inevitable presumptions of any 'perspective seeing', though in our case they are embodied in our commitment to the project of radical democracy and the possibility of an eco-egalitarian system of social relations. As a minimum, this project involves the extension of democratic values such as freedom, equality, popular accountability, responsibility and pluralism into wider and wider spheres of society. In addition, our concept of radical democracy is also linked to the values and ethos of political ecology, which include the ideas of solidarity, autonomy and our responsibility to nature (see, for example, Lipietz 1995). Finally, its commitment to an ethos of radical contingency, which acknowledges its own precariousness and contestability, leaves the articulation of such a project open to the role of difference and the construction of new subjectivities. In our view, this democratic ethos should also inform the construction and transformation of various institutional forms.

The articulation of these elements is thus predicated on the affirmation of certain values and ideals, though the latter is tempered by an acknowledgement of the tensions and torsions in the ideals, values and prospective norms, as well as the various institutional embodiments associated with this project. These values and norms have also to be tested and clarified in the production of critical evaluations. But though this is a vital source for the critique and normative evaluation of a set of problematized practices, it does not suffice. This is because our critical evaluation of a problematized phenomenon like airport expansion in the United Kingdom can and should also build upon the values, norms and ideals of those forces that compose the struggle being investigated. Notions like 'sustainable aviation', 'demand management' and 'evidence-based policy-making' feed into our normative schemas for evaluating and justifying practices and regimes. We should thus take them seriously by both testing and evaluating their claims, while using them to measure and evaluate the objects that we investigate.

What is to be done?

Echoing pragmatists like William James, it is an axiomatic feature of Flyvbjerg's innovative approach to social science that our critical explanations should make a difference to the real world. What should be done about airport expansion and the growth of the aviation industry in Britain more generally? Are there any policy prescriptions and strategic implications that emerge from our story? It goes without saying that these

200 Steven Griggs and David Howarth

are complex and controversial questions that require much reflection and deliberation. Nonetheless, there are some general remarks that arise from our analysis.

In an important respect, the ecological maxim 'Think Globally, Act Locally' is tailor made to think about possible solutions to the problems of unsustainable aviation (for a broader discussion of the environmental impact of aviation, see Gössling and Upham 2009). To operationalize this idea, each of us has to think carefully before pressing 'Confirm' when booking our next flight. Are our journeys necessary? Are there realistic alternatives to flying? Can our purposes be achieved in different ways? At the very least, we should seek to offset the environmental impacts of our 'binge flying'. We can also work on forging connections between different struggles aiming to bring about more sustainable forms of aviation. In recent years, the dislocatory effects of aviation expansion have resulted in new assemblages on both sides of the argument. On the one hand, coalitions like Freedom to Fly and Flying Matters have linked airport companies, airlines and trades unions, air users, organized business and sections of the tourist industry around the rhetoric of 'responsible' and 'sustainable growth' in aviation. They have called on government to take a lead in *increasing* airport capacity, while continuing to support the aviation industry with tax subsidies.

But they have been opposed by groups like AirportWatch, HACAN ClearSkies, Stop Stansted Expansion and the Aviation Environment Federation, which have elaborated a policy of demand management. They have called on governments to regulate the expansion of aviation in an effective fashion, while bringing together local airport protest groups with national environmental and conservation lobbies, such as the Council for the Protection of Rural England, Friends of the Earth and Transport 2000. At times, they have gone beyond the 'normal' modes of campaigning and local protest by forging tactical links with more radical environmental activists and movements such as Plane Stupid and the Camp for Climate Change. Direct action has been threatened and used effectively. Their proposals for greater environmental regulation, coupled with the management of aviation growth, argue that unfettered airport growth across the United Kingdom is unnecessary. They have demanded the removal of the tax concessions and subsidies enjoyed by airlines and the need for more sustainable transport networks, such as high-speed rail links.

Finally, we need to think more carefully about the role of government. Many radicals and progressives are wary of government and state interventions. Yet on an issue like aviation, governments of a progressive hue have an important part to play in constructing a clear line – an ecologically defensible balance between economic growth and environmental protection – and then seeking to lead, educate and legislate. They must strike appropriate balances and then forcefully articulate the case for such proposals among key opinion-makers and the wider public. In the case of UK aviation, they should maintain an immediate moratorium on the expansion of airports and end aviation tax breaks on fuel and airline tickets (Green Alliance 2010). They should also introduce emissions charging for airplanes to encourage the use of cleaner technology (aviation will be included in the EU Emissions Trading Scheme from 2012), while promoting high-speed rail routes to reduce short-haul aviation (Juniper 2007: 141–51), although questions are increasingly raised over high-speed rail's environmental impact. But governments and states can only go so far. It is only the concerted efforts of responsible individuals, the forging of red–green coalitions in different sites, plus pressures for governmental action at the national, regional and global levels, which can begin to tackle this pressing issue.

REFERENCES

British Airports Authority (BAA) 2005. *Heathrow Airport Interim Master Plan. Draft for Consultation.* Hayes: BAA Heathrow.
Caves, R. E. and Gosling, G. D. 1997. *Strategic Airport Planning.* Oxford: Pergamon.
Committee on Climate Change (CCC) 2009. *Meeting the UK Aviation Targets – Options for Reducing Emissions to 2050.* London: CCC.
Department for the Environment, Food and Rural Affairs (DEFRA) 2005. *The UK Government Sustainable Development Strategy.* Cm 6467. London: HMSO.
2006. *Climate Change. The UK Programme 2006.* Cm 6764. London: HMSO.
Department for Transport (DfT) 2003. *The Future of Air Transport.* White Paper, Cm 6046. London: HMSO.
2006. *The Future of Air Transport.* Progress Report. Cm 6977. London: Department for Transport.
2007a. *Executive Summary. Project for the Sustainable Development of Heathrow.* London: Department for Transport, available at www.dft.gov.uk, accessed 9 March 2009.
2007b. *Adding Capacity at Heathrow Airport.* Consultation Document. London: Department for Transport.
2007c. *Towards a Sustainable Transport System. Supporting Economic Growth in a Low Carbon World.* Cm 7226. London: HMSO.
2011a. 'Developing a Sustainable Framework for UK Aviation', Scoping document. London: Department for Transport, March.
2011b. South East Airports Taskforce, Report. London: Department for Transport, July.
Finlayson, A. 2003. *Making Sense of New Labour.* London: Lawrence & Wishart.

Flyvbjerg, B. 1998. *Rationality and Power: Democracy and Power*. Chicago University Press.

2001. *Making Social Science Matter: Why Social Inquiry Fails and How it can Succeed Again*. Cambridge University Press.

2009. 'Survival of the Unfittest: Why the Worst Infrastructure gets Built – and What We can do About It', *Oxford Review of Economic Policy* 25(3): 344–67.

Flyvbjerg, B., Bruzelius, N. and Rottengatter, W. 2003. *Megaprojects and Risk: An Anatomy of Ambition*. Cambridge University Press.

Foucault, M. 1972. *The Archaeology of Knowledge*. London: Tavistock.

1984a. 'Nietzsche, Genealogy, History', in P. Rabinow (ed.), *The Foucault Reader*. Harmondsworth: Penguin, pp. 76–100.

1984b. 'What is Enlightenment?', in P. Rabinow (ed.), *The Foucault Reader*. Harmondsworth: Penguin, pp. 32–50.

1985. *The Use of Pleasure*. New York: Pantheon.

Glynos, J. and Howarth, D. 2007. *Logics of Critical Explanation in Political and Social Theory*. London: Routledge.

Gössling, S. and Upham, P. (eds.) 2009. *Climate Change and Aviation. Issues, Challenges and Solutions*. London: Earthscan.

Green Alliance 2010. *Making Aviation Pay its Way: The Case for Raising More Revenue from Plane Journeys*. London: Green Alliance.

Griggs, S. and Howarth, D. 2002. 'An Alliance of Interest and Identity? Explaining the Campaign against Manchester Airport's Second Runway', *Mobilization* 7(1): 43–58.

2004. 'A Transformative Political Campaign? The New Rhetoric of Protest Against Airport Expansion in the UK', *Journal of Political Ideologies* 9(2): 167–87.

2007. 'Airport Governance, Politics and Protest Networks', in M. Marcussen and J. Torfing (eds.), *Democratic Network Governance in Europe*. Basingstoke: Palgrave Macmillan, pp. 66–88.

Hajer, M. A. 2009. *Authoritative Governance. Policy Making in the Age of Mediatization*. Oxford University Press.

Hanson, N. R. 1961. *Patterns of Discovery*. Cambridge University Press.

HM Treasury 2005. *Britain Meeting the Global Challenge: Enterprise, Fairness and Responsibility*. Pre-Budget Report 2005, Cm 6701. London: HMSO.

2006. *Investing in Britain's Potential: Building Our Long-Term Future*. Pre-Budget Report 2006, Cm 6984. London: HMSO.

Howarth, D. 2000. *Discourse*. Buckingham: Open University Press.

2004. 'Applying Discourse Theory: The Method of Articulation', in D. R. Howarth and J. Torfing (eds.), *Discourse Theory in European Politics. Identity, Policy and Governance*. Basingstoke: Palgrave Macmillan, pp. 316–50.

2009. 'Discourse, Power, and Policy: Articulating a Hegemony Approach to Critical Policy Studies', *Critical Policy Studies* 3(3–4): 309–35.

Howarth, D. and Griggs, S. 2006. 'Metaphor, Catachresis and Equivalence: The Rhetoric of Freedom to Fly in the Struggle over Aviation Policy in the UK', *Policy and Society* 25(2): 23–46.

Jessop, B. 2002. *The Future of the Capitalist State*. Cambridge: Polity.

Juniper, T. 2007. *Saving Planet Earth: What is Destroying the Earth and What You can do to Help*. London: Collins.

Lipietz, A. 1995. *Green Hopes*. Cambridge: Polity.

Marx, K. 1973. *Grundrisse*. London: Allen Lane.

Peirce, C. S. 1957. *Essays in the Philosophy of Science*. New York: The Liberal Arts Press.

Stern, N. 2006. *The Economics of Climate Change. The Stern Review*. London: Cabinet Office/HM Treasury.

Sustainable Aviation 2005. *Sustainable Aviation, A Strategy Towards Sustainable Development of UK Aviation*. London: Sustainable Aviation, available at www.sustainableaviation.co.uk, accessed 12 December 2005.

Yanow, D. 2000. *Conducting Interpretive Policy Analysis*. Thousand Oaks, CA: Sage.

Amnesty in the age of accountability: Brazil
     in comparative context

Tricia D. Olsen, Leigh A. Payne and Andrew G. Reiter

A childhood disrupted by military dictatorship. This is how Janaina and
Edson Teles might describe growing up in São Paulo, Brazil in the 1960s
and 1970s. The military police raided their house one night, apprehended
their parents and took them to the notorious Department of Operations
of Information–Centre for Internal Defence Operations torture centre.
The children at first remained at home in the care of their 'nanny'.
When the military realized the nanny's identity – the children's aunt,
their mother's sister – she too ended up in the detention centre. A prison
guard took the children into her home, bringing them to the detention
centre during the day where they could see their parents. Rather than
contributing to the family's well-being, these visits tortured the Teles
parents and children. The parents saw their children's presence as a
threat; their failure to provide the information the military desired would
bring harm to their children. The visible signs of physical and emotional
abuse of their parents, without having any capacity to stop it, tormented
the children.

   The military detained and tortured the Teles family for their involvement in a political movement in Araguaia. In the early 1970s, members
of the Communist Party of Brazil fled urban centres and the military
dictatorship to form a resistance community in the Amazon. Once the
military discovered the enclave, it tortured, killed and disappeared nearly
all of the members of the group and community sympathizers. The massacre in Araguaia accounts for nearly 80 of the estimated 436 dead and
disappeared during military rule (Comissão de Familiares de Mortos e
Desaparecidos Políticos/IEVE 2009: 19).

   Brazil's Amnesty Law, passed in 1979, protects the military regime and
its members from prosecution for murder, disappearances and torture.
No perpetrator has faced investigation or trial for human rights abuses
during the authoritarian regime. Brazil is unique in Latin America for its
failure to prosecute past atrocities. Most of the countries in the region
have found legal loopholes in their amnesty laws or deemed the laws
unconstitutional, thereby creating pathways for human rights trials. In

addition, most countries have implemented some form of official truth process to investigate past violence.

The relatively low level of dead and disappeared in Brazil might explain the strength of the Amnesty Law. Four hundred dead and disappeared in a populous country like Brazil does not compare with the estimated 9,000 to 30,000 deaths and disappearances in the much smaller Argentina. Although the military regime tortured an estimated 30,000 Brazilians (Fávero 2009: 214), the size of the country population density results in a relatively lower rate of torture. Uruguay has the reputation as the country with the largest per capita prison population in the world with a much smaller number of torture victims, estimated at 4,000 (Pion-Berlin 1993). The weakness of Brazil's human rights community or its comparatively more gradual transition to democracy could further explain the absence of justice for human rights crimes. The target of the regime's repression – armed militants – may have elicited less sympathy from Brazilian society than the mobilization in defence of 'innocent victims' in neighbouring countries. A particular feature of the Amnesty Law also generated support for it: immunity from prosecution for all political violence (on the part of the mobilized left and the military regime right), liberation of political prisoners and the return of exiles. The Amnesty Law's financial reparations to victims, survivors and their families further weakened opposition to it, since recipients feared that they might lose these funds with the erosion of the law (González 2005).

Many would argue that Brazil has defied the worldwide trend to hold perpetrators accountable for past violence. Evidence of a global justice norm exists in every region of the world at the domestic, international and hybrid court level. The ad hoc International Criminal Tribunal for Yugoslavia famously put former President Slobodan Milosevic on trial. A hybrid international and domestic court in Cambodia has prosecuted the Khmer Rouge leaders. The use of universal jurisdiction nearly succeeded in extraditing to and trying in Spain the former Chilean dictator Augusto Pinochet, and succeeded in convicting, sentencing and imprisoning Argentine perpetrators. Domestic courts convicted and imprisoned former Peruvian president Alberto Fujimori in 2008. Most recently, the International Criminal Court has issued an arrest warrant for Sudanese President Omar al-Bashir. Despite these transformations around the world, Brazil's Amnesty Law remains firmly entrenched.

The unfolding of the Brazilian transitional justice story has multiple implications. First, what should be done to address past atrocities, such as those that the Teles family suffered? Would Brazil be in a better situation today, in terms of human rights and democracy, if it had implemented the internationally promoted transitional justice mechanisms? We ask the key phronetic question of 'Who wins and who loses?' when particular transitional justice paths are taken. And in what ways are these different paths desirable?

Brazil's failure to adhere to the global justice norm has come at some cost. Its reputation as a regional leader faces challenges when other countries in the region and the world have adopted the norm and it has failed to do so. Victim-survivors have raised awareness of Brazil's defiance of international law in the Inter-American Commission on Human Rights (*Gomes Lund v. Brazil* case in 2010). Blocked in criminal courts, the Teles family attempted, without success, to highlight the absence of justice by filing a civil suit in Brazilian courts against their torturer. At the end of 2009, a petition circulated internationally demanding justice for the past military regime's atrocities in Brazil. Little progress on the justice front has occurred despite pressure on Brazil; the Brazilian Supreme Court upheld the Amnesty Law in April 2010.

To understand the transitional justice pathway in Brazil, this chapter first presents some background regarding the scholarship on the justice norm. We then turn to our own research, which challenges the conventional wisdom regarding the norm and its global strength. We show that Brazil may actually represent a more typical pattern of transitional justice adoption in which amnesty, and *not* accountability, remains a central mechanism. We use a statistical approach, or techné, to demonstrate the continued use of amnesties despite the norm of accountability and the prevailing view in the transitional justice literature that trials have begun to replace amnesties. The transitional justice literature assumes that the continued use of amnesties in Brazil and elsewhere has negative consequences for democracy and human rights prospects. Our research suggests, however, that even Brazil has an opportunity to develop value-rational transitional justice policies.

Our justice balance approach contends that transitional justice mechanisms – specifically trials and amnesties – complement each other to bring positive results for human rights and democracy. We use the phronetic approach not only to give meaning to this finding, which some consider counter-intuitive, but also to consider the values and interests behind the existing scholarship on transitional justice. We argue that the phronetic approach values not only the knowledge claims made possible through this particular study, but how those claims are successful (or not) in confronting and challenging existing power relations, which in the case of Brazil are deeply and historically embedded. In addition, our justice balance approach challenges conventional wisdom that amnesties necessarily block improvements in human rights and democracy. We show, instead, how amnesties may contribute to advancing those goals when used in a particular context.

Brazil and the justice norm

Questions of values and interests pervade research on transitional justice. Justice 'entrepreneurs' have promoted human rights trials and truth commissions as an alternative to *de facto* and *de jure* amnesties. Scholars have identified a justice 'cascade' or revolution, or the adoption of trials and truth commissions to replace amnesties (Lutz and Sikkink 2001; Sriram 2005; Sikkink and Booth Walling 2007). International non-governmental organizations promote the norm; international treaties, covenants and laws have institutionalized it; and international, regional and national courts increasingly enforce it. The justice cascade suggests that few countries can transition from authoritarian rule or civil war today without investigating and putting perpetrators of human rights violations on trial, due to the prevalence of this norm. This argument further asserts that human rights trials deter future human rights violations, and the failure to prosecute past violations perpetuates a culture of impunity.

Regarding trials, scholars and international human rights advocates have assumed three positive roles. First, criminal actions – even when carried out by state or military officials – that face investigation and prosecution signal an end to the culture of impunity and establish equality under the law; key principles of democratic rule. The courts become a legitimate and powerful check on the state, and a mechanism by which citizens can defend their rights and seek protection. Second, putting the authoritarian regime's officials on trial demonstrates a clear break with the former regime and establishes a new political and legal democratic regime with respect for human rights. Third, holding individuals accountable for past human rights violations delegitimizes certain justifications of past violence, specifically 'due obedience' and 'just war' theses. By prosecuting past acts, courts make the likelihood of prosecution for future violations visible, and thereby contribute to deterrence (Orentlicher 1991; Méndez 1997).

Truth commissions establish an official version about past political violence that combats authoritarian efforts to minimize or justify human rights violations (Landman, Chapter 3, above). Exposure to perpetrators of past violence through truth commissions holds them publicly accountable. A truth commission, moreover, allows victims, survivors and perpetrators to participate in a public and democratic process of restorative justice, with the prospect of reducing violence and strengthening democratic processes (Zalaquett 1992; Hayner 2001).

Advocates of trials and truth commissions suggest that amnesties, in contrast, perpetuate the culture of impunity by failing to hold perpetrators accountable. Opponents of amnesty argue that 'impunity for the most heinous acts – war crimes, genocide and crimes against

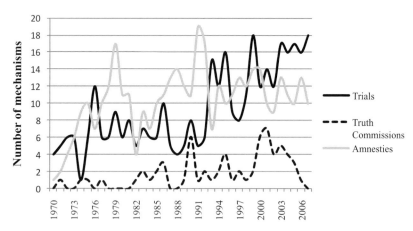

Figure 10.1 Mechanisms employed, by year, 1970–2006 (all countries)

humanity – should not be tolerated under any circumstances', and that the practice of amnesty is akin to 'letting the guilty get away with murder, literally, scot-free' (Joyner 1998: 593–4). They reject the assumptions made by some scholars that amnesties could play a positive role. Even if amnesties safeguard transitions by providing stability (Snyder and Vinjamuri 2003), advocates of trials and truth commissions view them as too costly for democratic and human rights goals. These scholars contend that societies that choose amnesty over trials are destined to experience cycles of retributive violence or vigilante justice (Borneman 1997; Bass 2000). The transitional justice scholarship tends to view accountability as a moral, legal and political imperative for overcoming authoritarian legacies.

In this global justice norm context, Brazil's Amnesty Law seems anachronistic. Adopted in 1979, it would appear to reflect an earlier method of dealing with the past; a method the justice cascade would argue has become obsolete. Our research contradicts that view, however, by demonstrating that the increase in the use of trials and truth commissions has not coincided with a corresponding decrease in the use of amnesties. Instead, amnesties as a mechanism to deal with the past have thrived despite the justice cascade and the spread of a global justice norm. Rather than an anachronism, Brazil represents the continued use of amnesties as a mechanism for dealing with past authoritarian state violence in the contemporary era. Figure 10.1 shows that amnesties have persisted despite an increase in trials and truth commissions around the world.

While Brazil has not implemented mechanisms consistent with the global justice norm, the norm has had an impact on discussions within the country. Twice in 2009, Brazilian policy-makers and shapers invited us to present our findings from the Transitional Justice Database Project. These invitations – from the Ministry of Justice's Amnesty Committee and a scholarly advocacy group endorsing a truth commission – reflect heightened concern within Brazil over its transitional justice image. The conferences included policy-makers who had not previously endorsed accountability mechanisms and who, instead, had defended the 1979 Amnesty Law and subsequent reparations laws for victims and their families. These policy-makers now link transitional justice to international reputation. The interest in the topic in Brazil has provided a forum for scholars, policy-makers, victims and human rights groups who have steadfastly advocated accountability. They use this forum to promote the value of trials and truth commissions.

Brazil thus represents an interesting puzzle for the justice norm. On the one hand, the norm seems to have had its intended effect. It has brought dialogue to Brazil about transitional justice and challenges to the Amnesty Law. President Luis Inácio 'Lula' da Silva favoured a truth commission to investigate past atrocities until military leaders resisted its establishment and threatened to resign in protest. Human rights groups had renewed optimism for some form of accountability with the election of Lula's successor, President Dilma Rousseff. President Rousseff, jailed for two years during the military dictatorship, advocated a review of the 1979 Amnesty Law prior to her election. In office, Rousseff declared a truth commission could be established by the end of 2011 and has repeatedly urged Congress to pass legislation to create a truth commission. Rousseff's efforts paid off and the truth commission was legally established in November 2011 (Monteiro 2011).

Despite the adoption of the truth commission, Brazil still represents the persistence of amnesty in the era of accountability. It further challenges the claim that amnesties necessarily undermine democracy and human rights. It shows that much of the research on transitional justice has rested on normative assumptions, rather than on careful analysis. Our analysis, however, does not swing to the other side of the pendulum and embrace an entirely positivist paradigm. Rather, the phronetic approach requires both techné (know-how) and epistemé (knowledge that is abstract or universal) to reach practical wisdom, or phronesis.

Our Transitional Justice Database (TJDB) Project attempts to provide that analysis. Containing data on transitional justice mechanisms implemented in all countries of the world from 1970 to 2006, it explores what types of transitional justice processes advance democracy and human rights. Findings from the project contribute to a more nuanced understanding of important political processes and outcomes. While existing research tends to characterize those who advocate trials and truth commissions as idealists and advocates of amnesty as realists, our research shows this to be simplistic. When employing a value-rational phronetic approach we find compatibility across this justice–amnesty divide. The TJDB provides the information, episteme and case-specific, contextual information to emphasize values and interests. Based on techné, we find that prudent decision-makers exercising practical wisdom, or phronesis, would not depend on one particular mechanism (e.g., trials, truth commissions or amnesties) in achieving the goals of improving human rights and democracy. Instead, they would combine mechanisms to balance justice with stability. We examine 'winners' and 'losers' in this justice balance.

The justice balance

The justice balance approach developed in our research considers Brazil's transitional justice as a dynamic rather than a static process. Its amnesty and reparations decision does not preclude the adoption of accountability mechanisms. Amnesty and reparations thus served particular stability functions, but the demand for justice prevails. Our research shows that Brazil's democracy and human rights profile could be greatly strengthened by heeding that demand.

The justice balance emerges from the TJDB Project. The TJDB includes three main types of transitional justice mechanisms used by all countries of the world from 1970 to 2006: trials, truth commissions and amnesties.[1] In this chapter, we limit our analysis to countries making a transition from authoritarian rule, excluding those that have neither begun the transition nor have consolidated democracies. Using Polity IV's 'Regime Transition Variable', we establish that there have been

---

[1] The source of the data on transitional justice is Keesing's World News Archives, including Keesing's Contemporary Archives (1931–87) and Keesing's Record of World Events (1987–Present). A team of researchers closely analysed 24,599 pages (from p. 23,733 to p. 48,332) of the Keesing's archive, a catalogue of world events, for information on transitional justice mechanisms. Keesing's provides the coverage – geographically and temporally – necessary to develop a cross-national data set of transitional justice over a period of nearly four decades. Utilizing news sources from around the world, including newspapers and wire services, and government reports, Keesing's provides an unparalleled source of unbiased summaries of world events. Finally, Keesing's focuses its coverage on political, social and economic events, and is a respected, reliable source for this type of data, making it an ideal source for information on transitional justice mechanisms. For others who have used this as a primary source for data collection see, for example, Walter (2002), Doyle and Sambanis (2006) and Engene (2007).

ninety-one transitions in seventy-four countries during this period (Marshall and Jaggers 2005).[2] These transitional countries have adopted forty-nine trials, thirty truth commissions and forty-six amnesties.[3]

The database allows us to measure the effect of transitional justice mechanisms on political outcomes by including standard indices of human rights – Cingranelli and Richards (2008); Political Terror Scale (Gibney, Cornett and Wood 2007) – and democracy – Polity IV (Marshall and Jaggers 2005); Freedom House (2008).[4] We statistically

---

[2] Polity provides several methods for identifying transitions: a three or more point increase in the democracy (Polity) score; a move from autocracy (a negative or zero Polity score) to either a partial democracy (a 1–6 Polity score) or a full democracy (a 7–10 Polity score); and particular scores on the regime transition (Regtrans) variable (i.e., 97 for state transformation or 99 for state creation) when the first year of the new polity is a partial or full democracy and the previous polity was autocratic. For a similar use of Polity IV's data to determine transitions and regime types see, for example, Epstein *et al.* (2006) and Sikkink and Booth Walling (2007).

[3] The TJDB Project defines trials as situations in which a court of law holds alleged perpetrators of human rights violations criminally accountable. To be counted in the data set, a verdict must conclude the trial. In addition to domestic courts, the TJDB also includes judgments in international or hybrid courts, jointly administered by international and domestic actors. The TJDB defines truth commissions as newly established, temporary bodies officially sanctioned by the state or an international governmental organization to investigate a pattern of human rights abuses and that issue a report. We exclude pre-existing government institutions that investigate past human rights violations as part of their official duties. We further exclude commissions created to investigate corruption, embezzlement, fraud and similar crimes. Amnesties are defined as situations in which a state officially declares that those accused or convicted of human rights violations, whether individuals or groups, will not be prosecuted, further prosecuted and/or will be pardoned for their crimes and released from prison.

[4] 'Polity', from the data set Polity IV, is a weighted score derived from coding the competitiveness of political participation, the regulation of participation, the openness and competitiveness of executive recruitment, and constraints on the executive. This measure is especially attractive because of its comprehensive temporal and geographical coverage. The second measure of democracy comes from the Freedom House project, which provides measures of political rights (focused on participation) and civil liberties (institutional aspects of democracy and freedom of expression). One limitation of this data source for the proposed project is that it begins in 1980. Despite the limitations on the number of cases that can be included, and the criticisms of the Freedom House project, it provides a measure of the specific aspects of democracy (rights and freedoms) that transitional justice is most likely to affect. We also use the two most respected measures of human rights in our analysis. The Physical Integrity Rights Index (PHYSINT) generated by Cingranelli and Richards and the Political Terror Scale (PTS) use the same sources for their data: Amnesty International Reports and the US State Department Country Reports on Human Rights Practices. Despite these similarities, the two databases measure human rights in different ways. Cingranelli's and Richards' PHYSINT provides a scale to measure government protection against specific human rights violations, including torture, extrajudicial killing, political imprisonment and disappearance. The Cingranelli–Richards database is somewhat limited since it begins in 1980 and its coverage is rather sporadic during democratic transitions; it nonetheless remains a widely accepted measure of human rights violations. PTS provides a 'terror scale' indicating whether terror has expanded to the entire population or citizens are

analyse the effect of particular mechanisms and mechanism combinations on changes in democracy and human rights measures. We estimate a series of regressions, using standard ordinary least squares, while also controlling for several alternative explanations for those changes, specifically wealth, timing of transitions, level of repression and region.[5] Our results, summarized in Table 10.1, show that transitional justice has a positive relationship with changes in human rights, as well as democracy measures. These findings affirm that dealing with past violence is better for these political outcomes than alternative paths. Our other findings, however, pose a conundrum for existing assumptions about transitional justice and its impact on democracy and human rights.

We find, for example, that none of the single mechanisms advocated by policy-makers and scholars has a positive effect on changes in democracy and human rights measures. When used alone, neither trials nor amnesties have a statistically significant relationship with those particular political objectives. Truth commissions by themselves, moreover,

relatively safe and protected from wrongful imprisonment and torture. PTS begins in 1976, which limits the observations we include in our analysis, although not to the same degree as the Cingranelli–Richards data. Using a variety of human rights measures is essential. Davenport (1996) has shown that democracy affects physical integrity and civil liberties differently, and it may also be the case that transitional justice mechanisms do not have the same effect across different measures.

[5] Because democratic theory often assumes that the wealthier the country, the more democratic it will be and the lower its level of human rights violations, we include GDP per capita to control for economic explanations (see Przeworski *et al.* 2000). This also follows previous work that finds that economic development decreases human rights violations (Poe, Tate and Keith 1999). The World Bank's World Development Indicators provides those measures to control for this factor. Timing may also influence democracy and human rights measures. The more time that has passed since transition, regardless of the mechanism adopted, the greater the likelihood that the country's democracy and human rights protections will improve. Furthermore, Davenport (1996) has shown that democratization itself significantly improves human rights, particularly in the first few years. Thus, a country that transitioned in the 1970s is more likely to have had the time to firmly establish democracy and improve its human rights record, compared with one that transitioned in the 1990s. Therefore, we also control for countries beginning their transitions at different points. The prior level of repression may also be an important factor to consider. Studies have shown that high levels of abuses in previous years are an extremely strong predictor of the level of repression in a given year. The prior level of repression, therefore, and not the transitional justice mechanism may affect the levels of improvements. As such, we also include Polity IV's Polity2 score, a measure of the level of repression prior to the transition of democracy. Region may also explain human rights and democracy outcomes. Some scholars assume that transitional justice and its success result from its concentration in Latin America, and to a lesser extent Europe. Success, in this view, has little to do with transitional justice mechanisms, but instead with historical patterns and cultural attributes of the regions in which transitional justice has penetrated most successfully. Moreover, many scholars believe transitional justice has a contagion effect, whereby mechanisms spread to countries due to geographical proximity. To avoid measuring the effect of regional differences, rather than transitional justice mechanisms, we use regional indicators as control variables.

Table 10.1 *Effect of transitional justice on human rights and democracy*

	TJ overall	Only trial	Only amnesty	Only TC	Trials and amnesties	Amnesties and TCs	Trials and TCs	Trials, TCs and amnesties
Polity	0	0	0	0	+	0	0	0
Civil liberties (Freedom House)	+	0	0	0	0	–	0	+
Political rights (Freedom House)	0	0	0	0	0	0	0	0
Physical integrity	+	0	n/a	–	n/a	n/a	n/a	0
Political Terror Scale (Amnesty International)	+	0	0	–	+	0	0	+
Political Terror Scale (US State Department)	+	n/a	n/a	–	+	n/a	n/a	+

Note: 'n/a' signifies that the model itself with the specified dependent variable was not meaningful; '+' and '–' mean statistically significant positive or negative relationships; '0' means that we found no evidence of a statistically significant relationship. The dependent variable in each model is measured as the difference between the year before transition to democracy and ten years after the transition. The model specifications are consistent; the only changes are the independent and dependent variables of interest, as shown above (Olsen, Payne and Reiter 2010).

generate a statistically significant, but negative, relationship with human rights. These findings suggest that the trial versus amnesty debate is irrelevant, since neither mechanism by itself advances the goals of democracy and human rights, and using truth commissions alone to resolve past violence will likely harm, rather than improve, human rights and democracy scores. Our research, in other words, challenges the normative claims in the literature that accountability mechanisms prove more successful than amnesties in bringing desired political change. From a policy-oriented perspective, advocating single mechanisms – particularly truth commissions – does not provide a demonstrated pathway to strengthening human rights or democracy.

The focus on single-mechanism adoption, moreover, does not reflect the empirical reality of state choices. In the transitions to democracy since 1970, states have demonstrated a tendency to do nothing at all (thirty-four of ninety-one transitions) or adopt multiple mechanisms (thirty-five transitions). Only one-fourth of the cases (twenty-two transitions) involve a single mechanism, and amnesties, not trials or truth commissions, constitute the most common single mechanism adopted (nine transitions). Brazil's amnesty process, therefore, falls into the modal category of transitional countries that adopt a single mechanism. Based on contemporary transitional justice practices around the world, Brazil's amnesty may reflect a partial, rather than a complete, process. The current discussion about additional accountability mechanisms fits the standard pattern of multiple mechanisms to deal with the authoritarian past. Indeed, in October 2011, Brazil approved the adoption of a new transitional justice mechanism: an official truth commission.

The transitional justice literature has not yet captured this empirical reality, focusing on trade-offs between mechanisms rather than the effect of combining them. The International Center for Transitional Justice has recognized the limitations of single-mechanism policies and advocated an 'holistic' approach that includes multiple mechanisms (ICTJ 2010). This claim only somewhat concurs with our own findings. We do not contend that 'more is better'; instead, we find that particular combinations of mechanisms improve human rights and democracy. Specifically two combinations – trials and amnesties, or trials, amnesties and truth commissions – have a positive effect on democracy and human rights measures.

In sum, our findings cannot confirm existing transitional justice claims. The statistical analysis summarized in Table 10.1 suggests that amnesties and trials complement and balance, rather than contradict, each other. Truth commissions, moreover, overcome their negative impact and contribute to democracy and human rights when combined with trials and amnesties. These findings may fill in some of the gaps in the transitional justice story. They provide possible explanations for the continued use of amnesties during the global justice norm era that do not jeopardize democracy and human rights outcomes.

Our findings further suggest that these mechanisms may not occur at the same time. Instead, countries may sequence, rather than trade-off, particular mechanisms. Amnesties tend to occur in the early years of the transition. Those transitions that occurred earlier in our sample (1970–89) adopted amnesties, on average, about three years post-transition. More recently (1990–2004), state leaders have adopted amnesty more quickly, just eighteen months after transition. Trials, alternatively, tend to occur later in the transition: about five-and-a-half years, on average, post-transition for the earlier sample and about three-and-a-half years post-transition for the more recent transitions. Scholarship on 'delayed' or 'post-transitional' justice in Latin America illustrates the sequencing of trials sometimes long after the amnesty process (Sikkink and Booth Walling 2007; Collins 2010). In other words, the persistence of amnesties may reflect democratic leaders' decisions to adopt stability mechanisms during the early period of the transition, followed by later trials and truth commissions to address the demand for accountability.

The political economy of transitional justice may further explain the combining and sequencing of trials after amnesties. Our analysis shows that countries with contracting economics are most likely to avoid trials and opt for the less expensive amnesty mechanism. Given the economic crises that tend to accompany transitions, and the instability generally experienced after transition, it is not surprising that governments in these countries might adopt amnesties. As their economies improve, however, we would expect a shift to the more expensive trial option. Figure 10.2 illustrates this relationship graphically. The probability line for granting amnesties peaks somewhat earlier than the truth commissions curve. This indicates that amnesties prove more likely choices for poorer countries and truth commissions prove more likely in countries with moderate growth. The adoption of trials shows sharp increases in probability just shortly after a country's economy begins to grow. The probability a country will do nothing increases sharply with low or negative growth. If we assume that economies will tend to grow in the later stages of transition, we would expect trials also to follow the amnesties implemented in earlier and more economically unstable transition years.

Our research does not consider amnesty and trials as separate or unrelated processes. Paying specific attention to context, we suggest that they work together in two ways. First, where transitions from authoritarian rule require negotiations with the former authoritarian regime or where

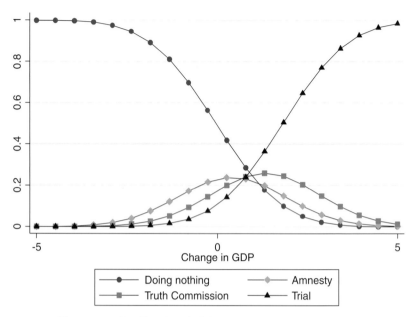

Figure 10.2 Predicted probability that a country will adopt a TJ mechanism as GDP changes

economies are struggling, amnesties provide necessary stability. If in these cases new and fragile democracies attempted to put perpetrators on trial, they might threaten that transition by catalysing authoritarian forces to halt the advance towards democracy. Amnesties may pave the way for the transition by overcoming authoritarian legacies in the judicial system, securing democracy and later allowing for successful human rights trials to occur without prompting negative reactions from former regime forces and society.

In addition to this sequential approach, we suggest that a complementary approach may explain the success of these combined mechanisms. New democracies may not prove to be capable of trying all of the perpetrators of past human rights crimes. They may not have the financial or human resources to do so. They may worry that such an act could provoke spoilers. As such, they may attempt to limit the number or scope of trials in some way. To do so, they would put a select number of perpetrators on trial, while allowing amnesties for others. Such a practice could ensure stability and accountability.

The most effective strategies of combining and sequencing transitional justice mechanisms imply that there will always be winners and losers.

Scholars, advocates and policy-makers who support trials and truth commissions, and reject amnesties as an acceptable mechanism for dealing with the past, would have to recognize the value of amnesties in complementing trials or trials and truth commissions to achieve the desired political goals. When we presented our work to advocates of Peruvian trials, they referred to our project, only half facetiously, as 'the work of the devil'. Nonetheless, they agreed that the Peruvian transition, as well as many others, would not have occurred without the assurance of amnesties. Scholars and policy-makers who advocate amnesties would have to recognize that amnesties alone would be unlikely to improve democracy and human rights, and that trials have not threatened transitions. Bruce Ackerman, for example, notes a key danger of trials: 'if backward-looking faultfinding spirals out of control, the bitter divisions that ensue may divert the community from its main tasks, which is to prevent the recurrence of an arbitrary dictatorship . . . ' (Ackerman 1992: 71). Proponents of truth commissions would have to acknowledge the negative consequences of adopting this single mechanism to substitute trials and amnesties. One truth commission advocate, for example, argued that our negative findings 'reflect bad truth commissions, and not the good ones'. We contend that truth commissions alone – whether good ones or bad ones – are too limited to bring improvements in democracy and human rights.

By adopting a more analytical approach, scholars, advocates and policy-makers would focus on winning strategies rather than mechanism preferences. Combining and sequencing trials and amnesties, or trials, amnesties and truth commissions is more likely to improve democracy and human rights than adopting a preferred single mechanism. Rather than assuming that their desired mechanisms have positive results, scholars, advocates and policy-makers must consider the limitations of these mechanisms and their possible positive interaction with those mechanisms they previously ignored or condemned.

Viewed in this context, Brazil's amnesty process looks less anachronistic and more partial. It is a crucial case for understanding transitional justice and its impact. Amnesty provided a mechanism for the military to withdraw its political rule. The initial negative reaction by the military to recent discussions regarding a truth commission, even thirty years after the Amnesty Law, suggests that an earlier move might have derailed that transition.[6] The sustained demand for accountability,

---

[6] 'Jobim diz que preparou pedido de demissão por discordar de caráter unilateral da comissão da verdade', *O Globo*, 2 March 2010, available at: http://oglobo.globo.com/pais/mat/2010/03/02/jobim-diz-que-preparou-pedido-de-demissao-por-discordar-de-carater-unilateral-da-comissao-da-verdade-915976129.asp, accessed 2 July 2010.

reflected in the cases brought to the Inter-American Commission on Human Rights, Brazil's Supreme Court, domestic civil courts and an international petition, may finally render results. Our findings further support the demand for trials or the combination of trials and truth commissions, by showing the positive impact on democracy and human rights from combining these mechanisms with the Amnesty Law.

A first look at Brazil's democracy score might suggest that the Amnesty Law has worked in strengthening the political process. Brazil's Polity score – an index measuring the competitiveness of political participation, the regulation of participation, the openness and competitiveness of executive recruitment, and constraints on the executive – improved during the ten years following the transition to democracy. The Freedom House scores, however, show more ambiguous results. Political rights scores, or political participation, improved during the ten years post-transition. Civil liberties, or institutional aspects of democracy and freedom of expression, however, fell during the same period. In other words, certain democratic processes improved, while others deteriorated. Human rights measures showed even less improvement. Neither the Political Terror Scale nor the Cingranelli–Richard Physical Integrity Index showed any improvement in Brazil's human rights record ten years after the transition. In addition, some of those measures declined during this period. While we cannot show a causal link to the Amnesty Law in the Brazil case, our findings from the TJDB would suggest that combining amnesty with trials or trials and truth commissions might bring positive results for both democracy and human rights in Brazil.

Brazil also offers some explanation as to why combining trials or trials and truth commissions might bring this positive change. The continued criminal violence and police abuses in the country may result from a culture of impunity. The legacy of the Amnesty Law justifies violence as a mechanism for establishing order and national security. Sectors within Brazilian society endorse violent, rather than judicial, responses to criminality. This includes support for vigilante justice because of the absence of successful legal mechanisms (Caldeira 2006). It also reflects attitudes within the police force about the effective use of torture and execution of criminals (Paoli and Telles 1998; Pereira 2000; Huggins, Haritos-Fatouros and Zimbardo 2002; Arias 2004). The Brazilian case thus suggests the limits of amnesty. It provides stability, but fails to build trust in the rule of law or deterrence of human rights abuses. On the other hand, without the stability provided by amnesty, Brazil may not have achieved the minimal level of democracy it has enjoyed.

The justice balance would therefore provide a strategy by which Brazil might advance democracy and human rights. By retaining some aspects of the Amnesty Law, but adding trials or trials and a truth commission, Brazil should see improvements in these political measures. Brazil, however, also shows the difficulty of overcoming resistance to the justice balance approach.

Resistance to the justice balance

Our value-rational phronesis approach to transitional justice would recommend advocacy of balancing amnesty with trials or trials and truth commissions. This finding is the result of recognizing both what *ought* to be done and *what is possible*, given inherent power structures and struggles within countries going through significant transitions. It represents a step beyond purely normative research, purely positivist research and Kuhnian 'normal science' by contextualizing our findings – relying on situational ethics, as the phronetic approach recommends – to answer this problematic for post-transition countries with a diversity of methods. Yet these normative, practical, legal and social resistances do exist and thus limit the possibility of the justice balance in Brazil and elsewhere. Brazil, for example, experienced a pacted transition and a relatively slower transfer of power. Human rights groups were also less active than their Argentine or Chilean counterparts. There were relatively fewer deaths during Brazilian military rule than in neighbouring countries. All of these factors suggest the necessity of a focus on situational ethics.

Much of the existing theoretical literature on transitional justice represents the normative challenge to the justice balance. A strong preference for trials and truth commissions condemns amnesties. While we share the normative commitment to justice for past atrocity with victims, other scholars and advocacy groups, our research pushes such claims and also considers the possibility that justice is compatible with some amnesty. Acceptance of amnesty does not preclude trials. Indeed, together these two mechanisms offer the most likely pathway to improved political outcomes. The justice balance includes both a normative endorsement of trials complemented by a pragmatic strategy of amnesties. Despite our findings, advocates of trials see amnesties as obstacles to overcome, not useful mechanisms to advance democracy and human rights. Only by assessing what is possible – based on other interests and power mechanisms – are we able to understand that balancing amnesty and trials also facilitates balancing who 'wins' and 'loses'.

Advocates of truth commissions may have the most to lose from the justice balance approach, since it considers this mechanism innocuous only when combined with trials and amnesties. These advocates resist the justice balance, finding that truth commissions alone will undermine human rights. Their normative commitment to truth commissions considers them benign, not harmful. They consider some truth commission models flawed, but not risky mechanisms that negatively affect the processes of human rights advocated in transitional justice. Our research does not yet explain why truth commissions have a negative impact. We suspect, however, that they raise expectations for justice by investigating past atrocity. They may also create resentment and open old wounds that provoke more violence and state crackdown. Unless justice accompanies those processes, therefore, they undermine efforts to deter human rights violations. In other words, amnesties may still prove to be necessary in order to provide enough stability for truth commission investigations into the past. Trials will meet the demand for accountability raised by the investigations. A normative preference for truth commissions attempts to perfect them on their own terms, but fails to consider their dependence on other mechanisms for success on democracy and human rights fronts.

The normative resistance to the justice balance shows how the interests and values of advocates, scholars and policy-makers reflect the topics they study and the results they report. Stakeholding becomes apparent among not only the directly affected victims, survivors or perpetrators, but also among scholars and practitioners advocating particular mechanism preferences. We have used the phronetic approach to examine the direction of transitional justice policies and the research on those policies. It explores the weakness of that direction in promoting particular policies and outcomes.

Advocates of amnesties, for example, would raise practical objections to the justice balance. They might raise a moral hazard question. If transitional countries effectively complement amnesties with trials, what function will amnesties perform in negotiating transitions in the future? That is, if perpetrators recognize the trend of sequencing trials after amnesties, they will be unlikely to trust amnesties to protect them from future prosecution. Such recognition would reduce the capacity of democratic forces to negotiate the withdrawal of authoritarian regimes, the capacity of new democracies to appease potential spoilers, and the strength and stability of the transition process.

Consistent with a value-rational, phronetic approach, our research does not provide the final, 'correct' answer. We are able to share, given current political and power structures, only what is currently happening (that is, where we are going) and which mechanisms create more 'winners' than 'losers' as conceptualized in terms of democracy and human rights. The justice balance, therefore, usefully describes past effective practices, but might have grave long-term consequences for future transitional justice processes.

We also recognize that our own findings are, in part, the result of others' values inherent in data generation. The outcome variables we use measure a particular version of democracy and a unique (and quite limited) conception of human rights that may not be shared by all. Indeed, with the myriad of transitional justice goals, it is quite possible that the justice balance positively affects only these *types* of democracy and human rights and could either have no effect or a negative effect on other interpretations. We are fully aware that scholars' views and perspectives are intrinsically incorporated in generating this knowledge.

Legal resistances also threaten the justice balance. The global justice norm rests on the assumption that amnesty for past human rights violations often violates international law. The justice balance endorsement of amnesty could be viewed as violating international law. This argument is derived from multiple international conventions. The Convention on the Prevention and Punishment of the Crime of Genocide (CPPCG), for example, stipulates that states must enact domestic legislation to punish perpetrators of genocide and penalize those found guilty. Likewise, the International Convention Against Torture and Other Cruel, Inhuman or Degrading Treatment or Punishment (ICAT) compels countries to make all acts of torture offences under their laws and requires state parties either to prosecute or to extradite alleged torturers. These agreements, as well as the Rome Statute, treat certain human rights as non-derogable and require countries to prosecute violations. Legal interpretations of other international treaties – including the International Covenant on Civil and Political Rights, the European Convention for the Protection of Human Rights and Fundamental Freedoms, and the American Convention on Human Rights – also suggest that prosecutions and punishments are the only means of ensuring protection of the rights enumerated within the treaties. Both the European Court of Human Rights and the Inter-American Commission on Human Rights have also ruled that only criminal accountability is an effective remedy for violations of the European and American Conventions (Roht-Arriaza 1990; Orentlicher 1991).

Scholars of amnesty, however, have challenged this interpretation of international law. They contend that international law covers only blanket amnesties that prohibit all prosecutorial activity. Partial amnesties, in contrast, allow governments to determine which cases to pursue without jeopardizing the country's stability. Indeed, these scholars contend that amnesties always exist in some form since governments are not willing or capable of prosecuting every violation (Pensky 2008). Some of the amnesty laws following authoritarian rule fall into a grey area. They were intended as blanket amnesties to prevent prosecutions for past human rights violations. Human rights groups, victims and survivor advocates, and the legal community found loopholes in these amnesties that allowed for some trials. In these cases, therefore, trials followed amnesties. The original law did not intend to complement the amnesty with trials.

The specific transitional justice contexts, therefore, reflect different top-down or bottom-up strategies. Rather than policy design, the adoption of trials after amnesties may reflect a robust civil society capable of fighting for rights in the face of amnesty and encouraged by a global justice norm. The improvement in democracy and human rights resulting from the use of combined mechanisms may emerge not from government efforts to combine or sequence mechanisms, but the capacity of civil society actors to challenge prevailing limitations on rights and freedoms. That capacity, in turn, may not depend alone on the historical strength of social movements, but also on strategic opportunities presented to them. Even then, however, they may not succeed in introducing trials and truth commissions to complement amnesties.

Our presentations in Brazil provided insights into this process. While victims, survivor groups and the human rights community have struggled for justice during and after the dictatorship, the government has only recently considered complementing amnesty with accountability. These long-term advocates for justice seemed surprised, and somewhat distrustful, of government officials' endorsement of transitional justice. What explains this change in attitude thirty years after the amnesty law? Government officials hinted at an explanation in their conference presentations; they expressed a shared commitment to the global justice norm. Compliance to the norm required Brazil to move beyond its Amnesty Law. A truth commission provided the means by which Brazil could simultaneously protect the military from prosecution, while adopting a modern transitional justice mechanism. Brazil, therefore, would keep up with nations throughout the world that have embraced the global justice norm, without provoking the military, victims or survivors.

Or so government officials assumed. In fact, the decision provoked widespread social resistance. The military initially rattled its sabres to prevent even investigation into its authoritarian past. Amnesty, in other words, not only protected the military from prosecution, it protected the military's untarnished reputation. There are no documents, bodies of the disappeared or public confessions by perpetrators to challenge the military's heroic past. The truth commission potenially threatens that image. Phronetic analysis and forensic investigation into the past thus challenges the military's institutional power, its reputation, and its ability to control history and memory of the authoritarian past.

Brazilian human rights lawyers and the victims and survivor groups have challenged the truth commission for not allowing justice. The truth commission might overcome the Amnesty Law's limitations on the basic right to know the fate of victims, to bury them and to mourn them. It is unlikely to allow individuals their right to redress for such injustices committed by the authoritarian regime. Justice, moreover, is not only for individuals directly affected by the military dictatorship. Overcoming the legacy of authoritarianism, the culture of impunity and passivity in the face of injustice depends on strengthening the judiciary. One mechanism for doing so is to show that the courts can and will prosecute past state crimes, that no one in the country is above the law.

Despite the normative, legal and social challenges the justice balance faces, it provides concrete and empirical evidence to support advocates of justice. It shows that a dynamic process is underway around the world in which amnesties continue to exist, but trials and sometimes truth commissions can accompany those amnesties and strengthen democracy and human rights. We had an opportunity to discuss these findings with the advocates of a truth commission in Brazil, encouraging them with our findings to pursue justice as well as truth. We had an opportunity to talk to the Ministry of Justice's Amnesty Committee about the possibility of adhering to the global justice norm by adding trials to the amnesty process.

Not all of the reaction to our work in Brazil has proved to be positive, revealing interesting sets of transitional justice constituencies. Some of the advocates of truth commissions seem to view them merely as a mechanism for modernizing Brazil and boosting its global leadership role. In this way, they respond to the global justice norm strategically, rather than normatively. They have no intention of considering the justice option along with the existing amnesty and the new truth commission. Our findings thus perplex these groups and individuals. They show that simply adding a truth commission does not necessarily meet the global justice norm, or enhance Brazil's international leadership or address the local or international demand for justice for past atrocities.

On the other hand, our research matches the demands of the mobilized victims and survivor groups we encountered at these meetings. While this sector of Brazilian society supports a truth commission, they see it as complementing rather than as substituting legal accountability for past crimes. Their demand for retributive justice to accompany the amnesty and the new truth commission is entirely consistent with our findings. As an illustration, to the 'Right to Truth' name tags used at one conference, victims and survivors added the words 'and Justice'. Our research provided them with the data and analysis to show that justice does not topple democracies, but can complement amnesties to build stronger democracies and human rights profiles. Based on our conversations with the victims and survivors, they understood that our research demonstrates that a truth commission may not be enough by itself to bring improvements in human rights and democracy. Truth commissions 'and justice', or with trials, would be more likely to complement the existing amnesty law to bring about these improvements. Yet not all of the organizers or truth commission advocates in the audience shared this perspective on our research; some accused our research of 'sabotaging the truth commission'.

Our research has also resonated outside Brazil. The Inter-American Commission on Human Rights has asked for our input to consider the positive aspects of trials when added to amnesties in the region. When we presented our findings at the Korean Truth and Reconciliation Commission, we made it clear that a truth commission there would complement the existing trials and amnesties to strengthen human rights and democracy. This presentation occurred at the same political moment in which the government hoped to stop or weaken the truth commission, due to the uncomfortable truths it had begun to reveal. Our work has the potential to bolster the accountability norm around the globe by promoting trials that complement existing amnesties. We hope it will be used in that way.

Conclusion

Based on our analysis, we find that prudent decision-makers exercising practical wisdom, or phronesis, would not depend on one particular mechanism (e.g., trials, truth commissions or amnesties) to achieve the goals of improving human rights and democracy. Instead, they would combine mechanisms to balance justice with stability. Our research began with the question of whether transitional justice fulfils its objectives and whether advocates should continue pressuring states to employ transitional justice mechanisms. Happily, we find that it is worth defending. Combining amnesty with trials or trials and truth commissions increases democratic strength and human rights protections.

These findings should bolster justice advocacy. They demonstrate that amnesties do not necessarily constitute an anachronistic response to past authoritarian state violence, but may form part of a dynamic process of establishing some democratic stability before adding accountability. The results for democracy and human rights provide a practical argument that advocates can use to enhance normative, legal and social ones.

Ideas and interests, in other words, need not pose obstacles to the justice balance approach. The combinations of mechanisms show that each one contributes to the desired outcomes: stability and accountability. Our value-rational approach involves acknowledging the practical necessity, and the legality of amnesties, *as long as they accompany trials*. The results of our research also endorse truth commissions, specifically when used in combination with trials and amnesties.

Brazil's reluctance to undermine its thirty-year-old amnesty and allow for justice in the case of the Teles family and many others reflect strong ideas and interests. But those ideas and interests are dynamic, not static. The global justice norm has begun to transform behaviours around the world. This shift does not necessarily mean a reduction in amnesties. It does appear to involve adding accountability mechanisms to existing amnesties. The global norm has created a new domestic context in which the amnesty appears to hold Brazil back, and accountability would advance its international leadership and reputation. Victims, survivors and justice advocates may not share the government's ideas and interests regarding accountability. Nonetheless, the convergence of these views may mean that Brazil, for the first time since the dictatorship, may begin to judge the military regime's violence. To do so is not only to recognize that the country is safe for justice, but also to demonstrate that the country's democratic strength and human rights record may depend on justice.

REFERENCES

Ackerman, Bruce 1992. *The Future of Liberal Revolution*. New Haven, CT: Yale University Press.

Arias, Desmond 2004. 'Faith in our Neighbors: Networks and Social Order in Three Brazilian Favelas', *Latin American Politics and Society* 46(1): 1–38.

Bass, Gary J. 2000. *Stay the Hand of Vengeance: The Politics of War Crimes Tribunals*. Princeton University Press.

Borneman, John 1997. *Settling Accounts: Violence, Injustice, and Accountability in Postsocialist Europe*. Princeton University Press.

Caldeira, Teresa 2006. 'I Came to Sabotage Your Reasoning! Violence and Resignifications of Justice in Brazil', in J. Comaroff and J. L. Comaroff (eds.), *Law and Disorder in the Postcolony*. University of Chicago Press, pp. 102–49.

Cingranelli, David and Richards, David 2008. 'Cingranelli–Richards Human Rights Dataset', available at: http://ciri.binghamton.edu.

Collins, Cath 2010. *Post-transitional Justice: Human Rights Trials in Chile and El Salvador*. University Park, PA: Pennsylvania State University Press.

Comissão de Familiares de Mortos e Desaparecidos Políticos/Instituto de Estudos sobre a Violência do Estado (IEVE) 2009. *Dossiê ditadura: Mortos e desaparecidos políticos no Brasil, 1964–1985*. São Paulo: Imprensa Oficial.

Davenport, Christian 1996. 'The Weight of the Past: Exploring Lagged Determinants of Political Repression', *Political Research Quarterly* 49: 377–403.

Doyle, Michael W. and Sambanis, Nicholas 2006. *Making War and Building Peace: United Nations Peace Operations*. Princeton University Press.

Engene, Jan Oskar 2007. 'Five Decades of Terrorism in Europe: The TWEED Dataset', *Journal of Peace Research* 44: 109–21.

Epstein, David L., Bates, Robert, Goldstone, Jack, Kristensen, Ida and O'Halloran, Sharyn 2006. 'Democratic Transitions', *American Journal of Political Science* 50: 551–69.

Fávero, Eugênia Augusta Gonzaga 2009. 'Crimes da ditadura: iniciativas do Ministério Público federal em São Paulo', in I. V. P. Soares and S. A. S. Kishi (eds.), *Memória e Verdade: a justiça de transição no estado democrático brasileiro*. Belo Horizonte: Editora Fórum, pp. 213–32.

Freedom House 2008. 'Freedom in the World 2008', available at: www.freedomhouse.org.

Gibney, Mark, Cornett, Linda and Wood, Reed 2007. 'Political Terror Scale 1976–2006', available at: www.politicalterrorscale.org.

González, Eduardo 2005. 'Brazil: Between the Politics of Memory and Transitional Justice', International Center for Transitional Justice, New York.

Hayner, Priscilla 2001. *Unspeakable Truths: Facing the Challenge of Truth Commissions*. New York: Routledge.

Huggins, Martha K., Haritos-Fatouros, Mika and Zimbardo, Philip G. 2002. *Violence Workers: Police Torturers and Murders Reconstruct Brazilian Atrocities*. Berkeley, CA: University of California Press.

International Center for Transitional Justice (ICTJ) 2010. 'What Is Transitional Justice?', available at: www.ictj.org/en/tj/780.html.

Joyner, Christopher C. 1998. 'Redressing Impunity for Human Rights Violations: The Universal Declaration and the Search for Accountability', *Denver Journal of International Law and Policy* 26: 591–624.

Lutz, Ellen and Sikkink, Kathryn 2001. 'The Justice Cascade: The Evolution and Impact of Foreign Human Rights Trials in Latin America', *Chicago Journal of International Law* 2: 1–33.

Marshall, Monty and Jaggers, Keith 2005. 'Polity IV Project: Political Regime Characteristics and Transitions 1800–2004', available at: www.systemicpeace.org/polity/polity4.htm.

Méndez, Juan 1997. 'Accountability for Past Abuses', *Human Rights Quarterly* 19: 225–82.

Monteiro, Tânia 2011. 'Dilma defende aprovação da Comissão da Verdade', *O Estado de Sao Paulo*, 23 March 2011, available at: www.estadao.com.br/noticias/nacional,dilma-defende-aprovacao-da-comissao-da-verdade, 696303,0.htm, accessed 2 July 2010.

Olsen, Tricia, Payne, Leigh and Reiter, Andrew 2010. *Transitional Justice in Balance: Comparing Processes, Weighing Efficacy*. Washington, DC: United States Institute of Peace Press.

Orentlicher, Diane 1991. 'Settling Accounts: The Duty to Prosecute Human Rights Violations of a Prior Regime', *Yale Law Journal* 100: 2551–92.

Paoli, Maria Cecilia and Telles, Vera da Silva 1998. 'Social Rights: Conflicts and Negotiations in Contemporary Brazil', in S. Alvarez, E. Dagnino and A. Escobar (eds.), *Cultures of Politics/Politics of Cultures: Re-visioning Latin American Social Movements*. Boulder, CO: Westview Press, pp. 64–92.

Pensky, Max 2008. 'Amnesty on Trial: Impunity, Accountability, and the Norms of International Law', *Ethics & Global Politics* 1: 1–40.

Pereira, Anthony W. 2000. 'An Ugly Democracy: State Violence and the Rule of Law in Post-authoritarian Brazil', in P. R. Kingstone and T. J. Power (eds.), *Democratic Brazil: Actors, Institutions, and Processes*. Pittsburgh, PA: University of Pittsburgh Press, pp. 217–35.

Pion-Berlin, David 1993. 'To Prosecute or to Pardon? Human Rights Decisions in the Latin American Southern Cone', *Human Rights Quarterly* 15: 105–30.

Poe, Steven C., Tate, Neal and Keith, Linda Camp 1999. 'Repression of the Human Right to Personal Integrity Revisited: A Global Cross-National Study Covering the Years 1976–1993', *International Studies Quarterly* 43: 291–313.

Przeworski, Adam, Alvarez, Michael E., Cheibub, Jose Antonio and Limongi, Fernando 2000. *Democracy and Development: Political Institutions and Well-being in the World, 1950–1990*. New York: Cambridge University Press.

Roht-Arriaza, Naomi 1990. 'State Responsibility to Investigate and Prosecute Grave Human Rights Violations in International Law', *California Law Review* 78: 451–81.

Sikkink, Kathryn and Booth Walling, Carrie 2007. 'The Impact of Human Rights Trials in Latin America', *Journal of Peace Research* 44: 427–45.

Snyder, Jack and Vinjamuri, Leslie 2003. 'Trials and Errors: Principle and Pragmatism in Strategies of International Justice', *International Security* 28: 5–44.

Sriram, Chandra Lekha 2005. *Globalizing Justice for Mass Atrocities: A Revolution in Accountability*. New York: Routledge.

Walter, Barbara F. 2002. *Committing to Peace: The Successful Settlement of Civil Wars*. Princeton University Press.

Zalaquett, José 1992. 'Balancing Ethical Imperatives and Political Constraints: The Dilemmas of New Democracies Confronting Past Human Rights Violations', *Hastings Law Journal* 43: 1425–38.

11　Feminist phronesis and technologies of citizenship

Virginia Eubanks

When I first read Bent Flyvbjerg's work, I was struck with a kind of profound gratitude. 'Ah,' I thought, 'now here's something I can actually *use*.' For those of us undertaking collaborative research with our neighbours or with social movements, phronesis can feel like a longed-for ally, a companion in a struggle that can sometimes feel isolating. The questions he raises are familiar to engaged academics trying to bridge analysis, social action and a commitment to scholarship for social change: how do we develop 'wisdom that works' in specific social contexts, while tackling complex global problems?; how do we create mechanisms for uncovering and validating collective, real-world knowledge?; how do we make informed and democratic decisions about critical issues in the face of contingency, dissent, difference and change? Phronesis is useful because it gives us permission to finally abandon the failed project of producing a social science focused on universal truth, broad generalizability, prediction and a stance of disinterested neutrality. Better yet, it challenges us to invent a better social science, one that connects research to practical reasoning and social action. I am inspired by the challenge levied by *Making Social Science Matter* (2001), and the wealth of thoughtful scholarship it has generated. Flyvbjerg's reinterpretation of phronesis opens up intellectual room in crowded disciplinary halls, providing vital public space to explore knowledge that matters.

One aspect of phronetic social science that has been underexplored, however, is its close links to feminist epistemology and sociology of knowledge. After getting over the initial pleasure of recognition, my next response to Flyvbjerg's work was puzzlement. I felt like I was standing between two beloved friends at a party, gaping, wondering, 'how is it possible that the two of you haven't met?' The resonances between phronetic social science and current feminist scholarship into how knowledge is created and legitimated are obvious, varied and powerful.

Feminist epistemology and sociology of knowledge focus on the ways that social location – that is, each individual and group's position in contextually specific yet enduring networks of power and privilege – affects how we know, how we think about ourselves as knowers and how knowledge is institutionally created and validated. While representing the breadth of thirty years of work in this exciting and vibrant field is beyond the scope of this chapter, there are three significant contributions that bear mention as we begin to develop a relationship between phronesis and feminism. The first is Dorothy E. Smith's generative work on sociology for people and her explanation of how the ruling relations shape what and how knowledge is produced (Smith 1987, 1990, 1993, 1999, 2006). The second is the contribution of Black feminist thought, particularly the immensely productive concept of intersectionality as suggested by the Combahee River Collective ([1977] 2000) and Barbara Smith (1998), and elaborated by Kimberlé Crenshaw and Patricia Hill Collins (Crenshaw 1991; Collins 1998, 2000). The third is the contribution of feminist studies of science and technology, particularly Sandra Harding's standpoint theory (Harding 1991, 1998, 2003, 2006; Harding *et al.* 2008) and Donna Haraway's situated knowledges (Haraway 1990, 1991, 1997; Haraway and Goodeve 2000).

Phronetic and feminist social inquiry are both interested in placing power at the centre of analysis. Both accept the bounded nature of rationality, insist on reflexivity and engage in *praxis*. But between phronesis and feminist epistemology and sociology of knowledge, there are more specific and significant resonances. Like feminist sociologists of knowledge, phronetic social scientists are interested in integrating the resources and perspectives of the oppressed and marginalized into scholarly analysis. Like Dorothy Smith's sociology for people, phronesis helps us to explore how knowledge arises from ordinary people, embedded in their everyday/everynight lives, and relies on the world to 'complete the sense' that social science can make (Smith n.d.). Like Donna Haraway's situated knowledges, phronesis acknowledges that all of our understandings, shaped by our social locations, are partial and incomplete. Finally, phronetic social science is dedicated, like Sandra Harding's strong objectivity, to producing *better* knowledge, that is, knowledge that is both more true and more just. In addition, there are also important lessons that phronetic researchers can learn from feminist thinkers who they may have overlooked. The work of Black feminist thinkers to articulate the concepts of social location and intersectionality, particularly, can complement the focus on values and conflict in phronesis with theoretical and methodological tools for understanding difference, oppression and domination.

The conversation between feminist epistemology and sociology of knowledge and phronetic social science is long overdue. Like anyone who has ever made a good match, I want to introduce two dear friends because I know how much they have in common. Better, I know they have much to learn from each other. In this chapter, I hope to put the two in conversation by exploring a case study of developing technologies of citizenship through participatory research, collective action and sustained community organizing. The case is drawn from nearly a decade of participation in two grassroots organizing groups – Women at the YWCA Making Social Movement (WYMSM) and Our Knowledge, Our Power: Surviving Welfare (OKOP) – both of which attempt to create a high-tech equity agenda that protects the economic human rights of women struggling to meet their basic needs in the Capital Region of New York.[1] These examples illustrate how feminism and phronesis, together, can be a powerful force in scholarship for social change.

Building technologies of citizenship

In 2001, as a graduate student in science and technology studies at Rensselaer Polytechnic Institute, I entered into a relationship with the YWCA of Troy-Cohoes. The Troy-Cohoes YWCA is a fascinating organization, both part of a women's membership movement dedicated to empowering women and girls and eliminating racism by any means necessary, and home to ninety poor and working-class women seeking to craft the lives they want for themselves. At the YWCA, I helped found a participatory action, research and design group that consisted of women who lived at the YWCA, students and faculty members from Rensselaer, and other community members from Troy. The group was called WYMSM (Women at the YWCA Making Social Movement – we pronounced it *wim-sim*), and was made up of myself, Nancy D. Campbell, 'Coffee',[2] Jes Constantine, Cuemi Gibson, Ruth Delgado Gutzman, Cosandra Jennings, Julia Soto Lebentritt, Chitsunge (Chris) Mapondera, Patty Marshall, Zianaveva Raitano and Jennifer Rose.

WYMSM undertook nearly a dozen ambitious technology and social justice projects between January 2001 and September 2003. These projects were designed to make visible the role information technology plays in economic and social justice concerns in a region increasingly dedicating itself to high-tech growth. Our initial projects tended to focus on technological skill, understanding and capacity-building. WYMSM was central, for example, in creating the YWCA Community Technology Laboratory, an internal technology resource collaboratively designed, administered, maintained and programmed by WYMSM, YWCA

---

[1] The Capital Region is in upstate New York, and consists of the areas around three small cities: Albany (the state capital), Schenectady and Troy.
[2] A pseudonym.

residents, staff and volunteers. WYMSM members were also vital to producing the YWCA Online Women's Resource Directory, a 'woman-to-woman' technology mentorship programme focused on researching and designing a web-based database of community programmes and resources in Albany, Schenectady and Rensselaer counties.

Originally, my goal was to close the 'digital divide'[3] by providing situated technology training, asset-based community development and workforce preparation for low-income women. But WYMSM members and other women in the YWCA community repeatedly disputed and disrupted the central assumption of the digital divide frame: that they were information technology 'have nots'. As my relationships with them developed, they described their struggles to meet their basic needs in the high-tech economy, and their significant, often troubling, interactions with the tools of the information revolution. Women in the YWCA community did *not* lack interaction with information technology. As I describe in detail elsewhere,[4] the women I worked with had a great deal of interaction with IT in their everyday lives, particularly in the low-wage workforce and the social service system.

Given time and resources to interpret their own experiences, WYMSM members articulated broadly structural critiques of the high-tech economy, local politics and regional development schemes. They expressed concerns about increasing social and economic inequality in our hometown; high-tech economic development initiatives that increased these inequalities, while delivering benefits to a few college-educated professionals; deterioration of public benefits; economic exploitation of poor and working-class women, especially in their role as familial and community caretakers; and political marginalization of people struggling to meet their basic needs at the local, regional and national levels. WYMSM members were concerned with economic and political oppression in the region's high-tech future. They were interested in justice, not access. As WYMSM member Ruth Delgado Gutzman insisted, 'It's not technology that will make our lives better. That will make us "haves". It's social conditions, financial conditions, the environment. Technology is just a little part of it . . . it's not *justice.*'

As our shared understanding of the relationship between technology and inequality deepened, WYMSM's focus began to shift and broaden. Over time, rather than focusing solely on making technological products

---

[3] The putative divide that separates technology 'haves' from technology 'have nots' in the United States.

[4] See Virginia Eubanks, *Technologies of Citizenship: Women, Inequality and the Information Age* (2011).

or learning technological skills, WYMSM created collective practices for analysing – and intervening in – the interlocking issues that make up a high-tech equity agenda. Out of this new focus, we took on an array of new projects, including a community education exercise called Beat the System: Surviving Welfare, a nine-part workshop exploring women's economic justice issues, and a welfare simulation held for 100 community members in honour of Hunger Awareness Day. Insights that arose from these projects upended traditional understandings of the relationship between technology and women's poverty in the United States, and resulted in a focus on the hidden inequalities of the information economy, the relationship between technology and state violence, and the role that information rights play in supporting or undercutting economic human rights. Over time, WYMSM came to believe that the goal of high-tech equity programmes should not be producing technological products *per se*, but rather on producing 'technologies of citizenship'[5] that helped participants meaningfully engage and critique the technological present and respond to the citizenship and social justice effects of information technology.

Focusing on citizenship rather than technical proficiency opened up space for women in the YWCA community to learn skills in terms of concrete needs and on their own terms; to understand and claim political identities; and to express core values like justice, recognition, self-determination and solidarity. Thus, perhaps the most important outcome of WYMSM was an increased sense of entitlement to political articulation and action among members. Though many began with an abiding distrust of the formal political process, members began to define politics for themselves, and claim a right to grassroots power. WYMSM created personal, organizational and political change, and catalysed several other vital community projects. The most significant for my ongoing work is a welfare rights and economic justice organization called Our Knowledge, Our Power: Surviving Welfare (OKOP).

OKOP, made up of women and families currently receiving public assistance and their allies, has produced several innovative projects, including a set of 'Welfare Information Cards' that help individuals seeking public assistance claim their rights and receive their entitlements in the social service system. More recently, we have been working with a national anti-poverty organization, the Poor People's Economic and Human Rights Campaign (PPEHRC), to take testimony of economic human rights violations in the Capital Region (see Figure 11.1). We are

---

[5] This phrase comes from Barbara Cruikshank's wonderful book, *The Will to Empower: Democratic Citizens and Other Subjects* (1999).

If you have **power** then you fight to prove it or you get other kids to fight for you.

Power means you get enough to eat and you have friends to stay with if you can't go home. If you don't fight then you get beaten up.

This is the truth that no one talks about.

I am smart and I mostly like learning but I can't stand the other kids. They are always looking at me and starting trouble. Teachers don't see it. They only see what they want to see and what happens last. They don't know that there is a whole other life that is all about who has the power in the room.

I was a survivor and refused to get beaten up so I got sent to a detention facility on a PINS-JD petition. First, I was close to home and it was non-secure so I ran all the time. Five facilities and four months in jail later, I am in OCFS and can't run.

I am starting now to see how I can avoid fighting but that is only because everything is so controlled. In the meantime, I lost a *whole year* of school.

Figure 11.1 An excerpt of Joe's story of the violation of his economic human right to education (OKOP 2010)

currently producing a set of five 'zines that document violations of the rights to freedom of expression; a living wage; the well-being of a person and his or her family, including food, clothing, housing, healthcare and necessary social services; education; and the equal protection of women and children.

My work with WYMSM and OKOP has also catalysed a new research agenda in my 'other life' as a faculty member in the Department of Women's Studies at the University at Albany, SUNY. One of the most profound lessons I learned by listening to my collaborators was that poor and working-class women, particularly when they seek to access public assistance, are increasingly hypervisible as subjects of information technology-driven administration systems: management information systems (MIS) in the child protective and public assistance systems; closed-circuit television and other security and surveillance devices in their schools and neighbourhoods; and work process tracking systems in the low-wage workplace. With the support of the National Science Foundation, I have spent the last three years studying the lessons about citizenship, decision-making, and the political process that social service clients and front-line caseworkers take from their interactions with welfare administration technologies.

Points of conversation for a feminist phronesis

The work of WYMSM and OKOP provides several important lessons about joining phronetic and feminist social science. As multiracial, cross-class women's organizations, WYMSM and OKOP faced unique challenges that *Making Social Science Matter* does not explicitly anticipate. First, broader cultural 'texts' mediated members' understandings of our context and experience, requiring us to explore the link between our local experiences and the extra-local and global forces that influence them. Second, the reality of members' very deep differences in class, race, power, and access to resources called for specific and sustained attention to difference and identity, an approach that Flyvbjerg and others have suggested, but do not always adequately explain. Third, members' different social locations created different forms of knowledge, which provided incredible resources for collaborative research and action, but also required translation and conversation to create a robust, strongly objective account of the world. These experiences suggest that putting feminist epistemology and sociology of knowledge in conversation with phronesis can produce a vigorous social science, create valid knowledge about our shared social worlds, produce personal transformation in participants, and foster progressive social change in communities.

Based on my experience in WYMSM and OKOP, I would like to highlight three points of conversation that I believe can enrich both feminist and phronetic social science:

(1) The relationship between the local micro-practices of the people being studied and the 'ruling relations' and discourses that shape their experience.

Flyvbjerg insists that phronetic social researchers study values and power by getting closer to reality: emphasizing 'little things', paying primary attention to practice, studying cases and contexts, and engaging in ongoing dialogue with a polyphony of voices.[6] To escape social science's increasing irrelevance, Flyvbjerg argues, phronetic researchers should begin their projects by concerning themselves with the 'minutiae' and local micro-practices, studying concrete case studies embedded in their contexts. But a focus on power is also central to Flyvbjerg's methodology. This focus requires a scaling up from local micro-practices to the structural level, and he specifically calls on phronetic researchers to join agency and structure and to reject approaches that dichotomize macro-level and micro-level explanations for social phenomena (Flyvbjerg 2001: 137–8).

It is instructive to put Flyvbjerg's dual focus on the minute and the global in dialogue with Dorothy Smith's *sociology for people*. Her work is

---

[6] He writes, 'Phronetic researchers seek to transcend [the] problem of [ir]relevance by anchoring their research in the context studied ... one gets close to the phenomena or group whom one studies during data collection, and remains close during the phases of data analysis, feedback, and publication of results' (Flyvbjerg 2001: 132).

particularly complementary, as it offers suggestions for understanding both the everyday/everynight experience of women and the 'ruling relations', the extra-local forces that coordinate and shape our subjectivities, understandings and agency (Smith 1999). However, for Smith, texts and discourse remain central to understanding women's concrete activities, unlike Flyvbjerg, who counsels focusing first and primarily on practice. Texts are the mechanism through which ideological codes – pieces of discourse with real, concrete impacts, such as 'standard North American family', 'political correctness' or 'personal responsibility' – order and organize practice and understanding across a variety of sites and settings. Her method for uncovering ideological codes and the operation of the ruling relations, called *institutional ethnography* (Smith 2006, 2007; Campbell and Gregor 2004), explores the ways in which our unique life experiences are standardized across contexts. Institutional ethnography uncovers local perspectives and also explores how institutions *produce* those perspectives across local sites.

In our work with WYMSM and OKOP, it was crucial to both 'meet people where they are at' and to get beyond many participants' initial understandings of their own experience. We began by creating forums in which a diverse group of women could get together, form bonds of trust and mutual respect, and explore their everyday experiences with technology, the social service system and the community. But it became rapidly apparent that the group needed to develop resources for framing our experiences within the broader forces that shape our lives. Women in the social service system, in particular, faced serious challenges in recognizing their experience as valid, socially important and collective in nature. Under the 1996 Personal Responsibility and Work Opportunity Reconciliation Act (commonly called welfare reform), the social service system in the United States has become increasingly punitive and disciplinary, rhetorically committed to creating individual self-sufficiency, while unable or unwilling to provide the resources women need to be truly self-determining. Women in the welfare system thus learn that they should be able to make it on their own, but face serious – and unacknowledged – structural barriers that constrain their ability to make decisions that positively impact their lives and their families. This creates a situation in which women internalize – or project onto others – the failures of a broken and dysfunctional social system.

It was common for women to come to WYMSM programmes blaming themselves for failing to 'make it'. They would say that they just had trouble balancing their cheque books or that they made bad financial decisions. The lesson that the failure of women to get by combining low-wage work, parenting and public assistance is an *individual* failure was learned and reinforced in a variety of contexts: community organizations solely focused on job training and budgeting, social service programmes that interrogate and control every dime recipients spend, and media that portrays people receiving public assistance as lazy, unintelligent and fraudulent. If we had stopped after gathering 'local knowledge', many participants' first interpretations of their experience would have simply confirmed these widely held opinions.

Instead, we developed a variety of resources to compare, validate and expand our understandings. For example, the academic members of WYMSM trained other members in interview techniques, and we performed interviews about problems in the social service system. We then collectively analysed the data, uncovering common themes across a variety of experiences, which formed the basis for our Beat the System popular education exercise. WYMSM also created programmes – like the Women's Economic Empowerment Series – that helped us to frame our experiences within larger political and economic developments. The series, in fact, created one of my favourite moments in all my years at the YWCA. At a session about the self-sufficiency wage, participants were asked to estimate the true cost of living in Rensselaer County, collaboratively estimating expenses for housing, food, childcare, utilities and other basic needs on a flip-chart at the front of the room. We then calculated what a truly self-sufficient wage would be for our families. Cosandra Jennings, who later became a WYMSM member, on finding that her self-sufficiency wage as a single parent of one toddler was nearly $15 an hour, looked up and said, 'I just realized that my economic problems are not my economic problems. They're *society*'s economic problems.'

(2) An understanding of how social location is shaped by race, class, gender, sex, age, ability and nationality, and other vectors of difference. An analysis of power is central to Flyvbjerg's work, and, he argues, critical to the study of social and political phenomena. Following Foucault's 'power analysis and ethics', Flyvbjerg's is a truly democratic social science willing to accommodate – even make use of! – conflict, difference and dissent. This is infinitely more useful than a discursive ethics that requires us to strive for consensus by bracketing our differences and behaving as if we live in an equitable world. This stance should make phronetic social science a great friend and resource to feminist epistemology and sociology of knowledge. Still, Flyvbjerg and his allies have not been terribly specific when it comes to *how* phronetic researchers should deal with race, class and gender, and other vectors of identity.

This lack of specificity gives me pause, as I've been at far too many academic conferences and workshops where well-intentioned attempts to deal with difference fizzled because of a lack of shared interpretive tools and frameworks. These conversations become especially frustrating when they involve 'additive' frameworks for oppression. Additive frameworks imply that each oppression or privilege an individual or group experiences is combined on a linear scale; that is, if you are a white, heterosexual man, you are a +3, and if you are an Asian lesbian, you are a –3. This is simply not how oppression and domination work. Each of us inhabits a *specific* location in a dense, interconnected web of privilege and domination, where oppressions are interwoven and mutually reinforcing. This is not to say that all oppressions are somehow equal, but rather to insist that scholars pay serious and sustained attention to the social and historical contexts in which oppression occurs. Additive frameworks, on the other hand, quickly devolve into ineffectual, abstract conversations such as 'who's more oppressed: White women or Black men?'

The feminist literature can be of enormous use in forestalling such ridiculous arguments, and in opening up what it means to do phronetic social science in a world marked by enormous disparities in power. Intersectional analysis, as articulated by a variety of Black feminist scholars and activists, may help us meaningfully operationalize Flyvbjerg's call to attend to difference, diversity and the politics of identity in our phronetic work. The Combahee River Collective first articulated intersectionality when they wrote, 'The most general statement of our politics at the present time would be that we are actively committed to struggling against racial, sexual, heterosexual, and class oppression, and see as our particular task the development of integrated analysis and practice based upon the fact that the major systems of oppression are interlocking' ([1977] 2000). Intersectionality has since been expanded to connote 'an analysis claiming that systems of race, social class, gender, sexuality, ethnicity, nation, and age form mutually constructing features of social organization' (Collins 2000: 299). Rather than assuming an additive framework, intersectional analysis attends carefully to the ways that different vectors of oppression work together – homophobia is used to buttress sexism, for example, and vice-versa – to produce specific social locations from which individuals and groups experience their daily lives.

Kimberlé Crenshaw, a critical race scholar exploring how interconnected forms of oppression make it difficult for the law to respond fully to the experience of Black women with domestic and sexual violence, explains:

Intersectionality grew out of trying to conceptualize the way the law responded to issues where both race and gender discrimination were involved. What happened was like an accident, a collision . . . if you're standing in the path of multiple forms of exclusion, you are likely to get hit by both . . . [but] when the race ambulance and the gender ambulance arrive at the scene, they see these women of color lying in the intersection and they say, 'Well, we can't figure out if this was just race or just sex discrimination. And unless they can show us which one it was, we can't help them.' (Crenshaw and Thomas 2004: 2)

In her generative 1991 article, 'Mapping the Margins: Intersectionality, Identity Politics, and Violence Against Women of Color', Crenshaw levied an important challenge to both dominant conceptions of social justice that see difference and social location as intrinsically negative hold-overs of bias that should be eliminated (as in the Habermasian ideal speech situation), and to identity politics that too often elide intragroup differences in the service of solidarity. Both of these political strategies are of limited use to people who experience the convergence of systems of race, class and gender domination. 'For example,' she writes, 'racism as experienced by people of color who are of a particular gender – male – tends to determine the parameters of antiracist strategies, just as sexism experienced by women who are of a particular race – white – tends to ground the women's movement' (Crenshaw 1991: 1252). Intersectional analysis is now largely, if incompletely, mainstreamed into Women's Studies, and provides an important corrective to Second Wave feminist frameworks that posited the common experience of 'women' as a group without attending to intragroup differences.

Intersectional analysis is extremely useful for producing sophisticated understandings of both oppression and privilege. For example, where people are located in relationship to the power structures of society – their social location – has an enormous impact on how they encounter and relate to the tools of the information revolution. In my own life, for example, information technology fulfils high-tech economy boosters' most ambitious promises. It enriches the democratic process and expands my opportunities for a fulfilling and prosperous career. Online databases and web-based portals ease my relationship with government, increase transparency and accountability, and simplify my daily tasks.

Women in the YWCA community had a more complicated relationship with IT. Though they valued technological access and skills, they also directly experienced the more exploitative face of IT as workers in low-wage high-tech occupations such as data entry and call centres, as clients of increasingly computerized government services, and as citizens surveyed by technologies in public institutions and spaces. It was not so much that they lacked access to technology, but that their everyday experiences with it are invasive, intrusive and extractive. Partly because of my own racial and class privilege – my unique social location – I failed to recognize or adequately appreciate women in the YWCA community's experiences with IT. My understandings of digital inequity had been so colonized by digital divide frameworks, which posit that poor and working-class people simply lack 'access' to technology, that it was difficult for me to see past my own presumptions to the reality of the day-to-day 'minutiae'. Intersectional analysis helped me better understand my own blind spots, as well as the interaction between social location, practice and knowledge.

In WYMSM's and OKOP's work on technologies of citizenship, intersectional approaches have been critical to studying how social location impacts *all* people's experience with technology in their everyday lives. Non-intersectional analyses of IT privilege the experiences of wealthy and educationally advantaged people in the global North, and view technology as merely a consumer product, access to which is an unmitigated social good. But this approach to high-tech equity focuses on relatively privileged people, which makes it difficult to understand and account for the experiences of those who inhabit vastly different social locations – and thus have vastly different experiences with information technology – due to their class, ethnicity, race, sexuality, ability and nationality. Non-intersectional analyses overlook the significant role low-wage workers in wide variety of jobs – such as industrial and product assembly, packaging and delivery, customer service, data entry, and the caring occupations – play in the high-tech economy. Non-intersectional approaches also tend to discount the vast experience most women have with IT as the subjects of technologies of state administration. These are significant, everyday experiences of the information age, shared by millions of women the world over. These are, in fact, *the great majority* of women's experiences with information technology, both abroad and here at home. Intersectional analysis can correct the myopia that often hampers our ability to see beyond our own experience and imagine a truly just technological future.

(3) The relationship between social location and knowledge production.

Our social location does not only influence our access to resources and power; it also impacts how we see and understand the world. While Flyvbjerg's separation of episteme from phronesis clarifies the ideal role of social science as aiding in deliberation about values and goals rather than achieving universal prediction, it is less useful to try to separate epistemology from practical reasoning. 'How do we come to know what we know?' is as important a question to studying power and values as 'what should be done?'

Feminist epistemologists and feminist sociologists of knowledge insist that robust knowledge is created when investigators refuse to produce unlocatable, irresponsible knowledge claims under the guise of neutrality. In her path-breaking article, 'Situated Knowledges: The Science Question in Feminism and the Privilege of Partial Perspective', Donna Haraway argues 'for politics and epistemologies of location, positioning, and situating, where partiality and not universality is the condition of being heard to make rational knowledge claims. These are claims on people's lives . . . only the god-trick [of seeing everything from nowhere] is forbidden' (Haraway 1991: 195). According to feminist epistemology, all social locations provide *both* uniquely clear vision (in some areas) and specific barriers to insight (in others).[7] While none of us are perfect interpreters of our own experience, the gaps in the knowledge of the powerful are systemic and significant. Socially or culturally sanctioned ignorances and silences supporting the status quo are created and maintained by institutions such as schools, workplaces, families and neighbourhoods.

The standpoints of the marginalized, the knowledge that is generated from their unique and particular social locations, thus offer important epistemological resources in any quest to create a more just world. As Sandra Harding has written, 'Marginalized groups have interests in asking questions [about power], and dominant groups have interests in not hearing them' (1998: 151). We must be cautious when making claims for epistemological privilege, however, as they can quickly become arguments for epistemological superiority: re-inscribing a hierarchy of knowledge that is profoundly anti-democratic.[8] Knowledge that arises from a particular social location – what feminist scholars call a 'standpoint' – is relational and learned, fought for and won. Standpoints are not demographic, biological or otherwise 'natural' positions we inhabit (Wylie 2003). All social locations are partial, non-innocent and complicated – the danger lies in losing the specificity of socially located knowledge by collapsing complex relationships onto simple demographic categories of identity.

Feminist epistemologists have not simply replaced the neutral scientific gaze with the interested observer, the man in the white coat with the woman struggling in the trenches. Rather, we have developed techniques

---

[7] In *Making Social Science Matter*, Flyvbjerg makes a similar point, writing that 'phronetic research explicitly sees itself as not having a privileged position from which the final truth can be told and further discussion stopped. We cannot think of an "eye turned in no particular direction", as Nietzsche says' (2001: 139).

[8] Knowledge that arises from a particular social location – what feminist scholars call a 'standpoint' – is an incredibly useful resource when it is seen as akin to W. E. B. DuBois' 'double consciousness'. For marginalized people, understanding the world is characterized by multiple points of view: those that arise from your counter-hegemonic subject position, as well as those that arise from the subject position you must inhabit in order to exist successfully in dominant society. Standpoint is less useful when it is seen as essential knowledge that adheres to a particular kind of person 'women's knowledge', for example.

for achieving what Sandra Harding calls *strong objectivity*.[9] Strong objectivity – rather than weak neutrality – provides 'a kind of method for maximizing our ability to block "might makes right" in the sciences' (Harding 2003: 129). Strong objectivity is best achieved when a number of different standpoints are put in conversation with each other in the context of social justice-oriented research and action.[10] This process develops oppositional consciousness, locatable political commitments, and strategies for alliance- and coalition-building within the context of (post)colonial domination and globalization. Rather than seeing difference as divisive, current feminist sociologists of knowledge emphasize that 'the ability to make new coalitions across new kinds of alliances by translating "knowledges among very different – and power-differentiated – communities"... is the form that love takes in the postmodern world' (Sandoval 1995: 410–17).

WYMSM's and OKOP's participatory approach created a context of trust, reciprocity, accountability and transparency in which members' feelings of entitlement to political articulation grew and strong bonds within the group were forged. Participatory process also created rich, robust, timely knowledge: both practical knowledge that helped us plan political action in specific contexts, and more abstract, generalized theories about the relationship between technology and politics, the information age and inequality. By integrating the points of view of multiple analysts, triangulating between the standpoints of participants from a wide variety of social locations, and increasing accountability and transparency in research, we produced knowledge that was not neutral, but was in fact highly objective, rigorous and generalizable.

The technologies of citizenship developed by WYMSM and OKOP call for engaged, collective inquiry, across difference, because every standpoint can produce important information for analysing our shared world.[11] Insights were strengthened each time they passed through the

---

[9] For more on strong objectivity and socially situated knowledge, see Sandra Harding's work, including *The Feminist Standpoint Theory Reader: Intellectual and Political Controversies* (2003), particularly chapter 8, 'Rethinking Standpoint Epistemology: What is "Strong Objectivity"?', and *Is Science Multicultural? Postcolonialisms, Feminisms, and Epistemologies* (1998).

[10] Again, Flyvbjerg echoes this debate in the feminist literature when he, quoting Nietzsche, argues, 'There is *only* a perspective seeing, *only* a perspective "knowing"; and the *more* affects we allow to speak about one thing, the *more* eyes, different eyes, we can use to observe one thing, the more complete will our "concept" of this thing, our "objectivity", be' (Flyvbjerg 2001: 139, quoting Nietzsche 1969: 119, emphasis in original).

[11] This insight comes primarily from the work of Donna Haraway. For Haraway, there simply are no innocent powers with which, or positions from which, to represent the world. Rather, 'objectivity turns out to be about particular and specific embodiment... only partial perspective promises objective vision' (Haraway 1991: 190). For Haraway, objectivity is always 'a local achievement... [concerned with] holding things together

mind of another analyst; interpretations were validated each time the results of research were tested in action in the real world. For WYMSM member Julia Soto Lebentritt, what worked best about WYMSM was the cooperative process we developed to create collective knowledge across difference. It is in the collaboration of a diverse group of participants that she feels true individual *and* social empowerment lie. She remarked in an interview, 'It was beautiful that we were from different walks. We had different ages, different experience. But we were all on the same level. It was really across different cultures, diversity . . . interacting positively . . . almost like a family gathering of . . . what we were passionate about, and what we felt should be done.'

The incredible richness of the YWCA community offered important resources for creating robust knowledge. Far from typifying some kind of monolithic culture of poverty, the YWCA community offered vibrancy, diversity and resourcefulness. YWCA residents are aged 17 to 70, have a fifth grade education and multiple Masters' degrees, live at the YWCA for six weeks or twenty-six years. They work as nurses, data specialists, cooks, counsellors and artists, as well as being mothers, lovers, wives, sisters and friends. The walls of the YWCA are highly permeable – in the years I spent embedded in the community, I interacted with residents, staff and administrators, as well as local artists, activists, community organizers, day-care parents, board members and others. Women in the YWCA community have absorbed more than their fair share of the stresses and strains produced by the collision of hypercapitalism and neoliberalism. Because of this position and their experiences with the extractive and exploitative faces of information technology, women in the YWCA community were able to develop incredibly insightful analyses of the relationship between technology, politics and poverty in the United States.

Conclusion: on not losing the epistemological address

Like any matchmaker, I do not know how the relationship between phronesis and feminist epistemology and sociology of knowledge will work out. But before I send them on their way to get to know each other a little better, I have a few insights that I hope will help them build a lasting bond. First, objectivity is too powerful to be abandoned. A renewed, phronetic social science must abandon the stance of the neutral and disinterested observer, but objectivity is far too valuable to leave solely in the hands of the natural sciences. Second, while attention to the local

well enough so that people can share in that account powerfully' (Haraway and Goodeve 2000: 161).

and locatable may fill an important gap in mainstream social science, the reality of transnational politics and flows demands that we understand and account for both micro-level practices *and* the global processes and discourses that shape our experiences. Third, we must plan for diversity, not 'add in' frameworks for dealing with difference after the intellectual agenda has been set. Grounding phronetic research in feminist understandings of race, class, gender, sexuality and nation should help make it a robust and accountable force for social justice.

Finally, I suggest to both feminist analysts and phronetic social scientists that we cannot give up on theory in our rush to attend to practical reasoning. We must engage in praxis, the iterative cycle of action and reflection. The problem is not that academics make theory; it is that we too often think that we are the *only ones* who make theory. As Paulo Freire remarked in 1987, at the end of a public schooling workshop at the Highlander Research and Education Center in New Market, Tennessee:

Look. I am also an academic. I am not trying to diminish the value of the academy. What I would like is that the academy also recognizes the value of those who are not inside of it, who are also creating knowledge, and doing beautiful things. Now, you [teachers from the community] have demonstrated you also do that. Your action becomes the object of your curiosity, and getting distance from the object of your curiosity, it becomes an object of knowledge. Then you exercise the act of *knowing*. You are reknowing what you already knew yesterday, and this permanent reflexive act makes possible . . . better practice . . . Unfortunately, this is not what happens inside of the academy, because in the academy, *we get such distance from concreteness, . . . from reality, . . . that at some moment, we lose the epistemological address* . . . But it is not theory that is wrong. What is wrong in theoreticism. Theory is fantastic! Today we had theory here. (Highlander Research and Education Center 1998, emphasis added)

We must have both theory and practice. If we are ever to reshape social relations, we must use theory to dig to the roots of our understandings, explore underlying reasoning, systems and structures. But in so doing, we must never cast ourselves adrift from the experience of everyday practice, 'losing the epistemological address', cutting the tether that connects us to our compatriots, and thus, the reality of our shared social world.

REFERENCES

Campbell, Marie Louise and Gregor, Frances Mary 2004. *Mapping Social Relations: A Primer in Doing Institutional Ethnography*. Walnut Creek, CA: Rowman Littlefield AltaMira.
Collins, Patricia Hill 1998. *Fighting Words: Black Women and the Search for Justice*. Minneapolis, MN: University of Minnesota Press.
    2000. *Black Feminist Thought: Knowledge, Consciousness, and the Politics of Empowerment*, 2nd edn. New York: Routledge.

Combahee River Collective [1977] 2000. 'A Black Feminist Statement', in Manning Marable and Leith Mullings (eds.), *Let Nobody Turn Us Around: Voices of Resistance, Reform, and Renewal: An African American Anthology*. New York: Rowman & Littlefield, pp. 524–9.

Crenshaw, Kimberlé 1991. 'Mapping the Margins: Intersectionality, Identity Politics, and Violence against Women of Color', *Stanford Law Review* 43: 1241–99.

Crenshaw, Kimberlé and Thomas, Sheila 2004. 'Intersectionality: The Double Bind of Race and Gender', *Perspectives: The Quarterly Magazine For and About Women Lawyers*. Spring, available online at: www.abanet.org/women/perspectives/Spring2004CrenshawPSP.pdf, accessed 26 March 2010.

Cruikshank, Barbara 1999. *The Will to Empower: Democratic Citizens and Other Subjects*. Ithaca, NY: Cornell University Press.

Eubanks, Virginia 2011. *Digital Dead End: Fighting for Social Justice in the Information Age*. Cambridge, MA: MIT Press.

Flyvbjerg, Bent 2001. *Making Social Science Matter: Why Social Inquiry Fails and How it can Succeed Again*. Cambridge University Press.

Haraway, Donna 1990. *Primate Visions: Gender, Race and Nature in the World of Modern Science*. New York: Routledge.

1991. *Simians, Cyborgs and Women: The Reinvention of Nature*. New York: Routledge.

1997. *Modest_Witness@Second_Millennium.FemaleMan_Meets_OncoMouse: Feminism and Technoscience*. New York: Routledge.

Haraway, Donna and Goodeve, Thyrza Nichols 2000. *How Like a Leaf: An Interview with Thyrza Nichols Goodeve*. New York: Routledge.

Harding, Sandra G. 1991. *Whose Science? Whose Knowledge? Thinking from Women's Lives*. Ithaca, NY: Cornell University Press.

1998. *Is Science Multicultural? Postcolonialisms, Feminisms, and Epistemologies*. Bloomington, IN: Indiana University Press.

2003. *The Feminist Standpoint Theory Reader: Intellectual and Political Controversies*. New York: Routledge.

2006. *Science and Social Inequality: Feminist and Postcolonial Issues*. Champaign, IL: University of Illinois Press.

Harding, Sandra, Grewal, Inderpal, Kaplan, Caren and Wiegman, Robyn 2008. *Science from Below: Feminisms, Postcolonialities, and Modernities*. Durham, NC: Duke University Press.

Highlander Research and Education Center 1998. Myles Horton, Paulo Freire and Friends Gather at Highlander, video-recording.

Nietzsche, Friedrich 1969. *On the Genealogy of Morals*. New York: Vintage Books.

Sandoval, Chela 1995. 'New Sciences: Cyborg Feminism and the Methodology of the Oppressed', in Chris Hables Gray (ed.), *The Cyborg Handbook*. New York: Routledge.

Smith, Barbara 1998. *The Truth That Never Hurts: Writings on Race, Gender and Freedom*. New Brunswick, NJ: Rutgers University Press.

Smith, Dorothy E. 1987. *The Everyday World as Problematic: A Feminist Sociology*. Hanover, NH: Northeastern University Press.

1990. *The Conceptual Practices of Power: A Feminist Sociology of Knowledge*. University of Toronto Press.

1993. *Texts, Facts and Femininity: Exploring the Relations of Ruling*. New York: Routledge.

1999. *Writing the Social: Critique, Theory and Investigations*. University of Toronto Press.

2006. *Institutional Ethnography as Practice*. New York: Rowman & Littlefield.

2007. 'Institutional Ethnography: From a Sociology for Women to a Sociology for People', in Sharlene Nagy Hesse-Biber (ed.), *Handbook of Feminist Research: Theory and Praxis*. Thousand Oaks, CA: Sage, pp. 409–16.

n.d. 'Dorothy Smith.' From Institutional Ethnography: Online Resources and Discussion, available at: http://faculty.maxwell.syr.edu/mdevault/dorothy_smith.htm, accessed 26 March 2010.

Wylie, Alison 2003. 'Why Standpoint Matters', in R. Figueroa and S. Harding (eds.), *Science and Other Cultures: Issues in Philosophies of Science and Technology*. New York: Routledge, pp. 26–48.

Author's note

This work would be inconceivable without the remarkable generosity and resourcefulness of the women of the YWCA of Troy-Cohoes community and of my activist colleagues in Our Knowledge, Our Power: Surviving Welfare. I would especially like to thank my research collaborators in WYMSM, including: Nancy D. Campbell, 'Coffee', Jessica Constantine, Cuemi Gibson, Ruth Delgado Gutzman, Cosandra Jennings, Chitsunge Mapondera, Patty Marshall, Christine Nealon, Zianaveva Raitano, Jennifer Rose and Julia Soto Lebentritt. Special thanks to Isaac and Mark, who kept us smiling through long afternoon meetings. My thanks also go to the members of OKOP, including Linda Adams, Aalim Ammar, Anne Bink, Devona Brown, Hee Jeong 'Robyn' Chung, Jes Constantine, Roberta Farrell, Mishel Filisha, Deborah Ford, Cuemi Gibson, Catherine Gordon, Kenneth and Kenny Harris, Kizzy Howell, Molly Hussey, Victoria Kereszi, Penny Lane, Nadya Lawson, Tiffany Lherisson, Andrew Lynn, Patty Marshall, Shihoko Nakagawa, Christine Nealon, Ibi Oduyemi, Mary Pimble, Denise Roe, Glen Taylor, Donna Tenney, Shaneeka Thrasher, Maggie Torres, Kristin Turano, Jennifer Vasquez, Dametriss Walker and Kim Wheeler. My academic colleagues and students at both Rensselaer Polytechnic Institute and the University at Albany, SUNY have been equally generous. This research was funded, in part, by a HUD Community Outreach Partnership (COPC) grant and a National Science Foundation dissertation improvement grant (NSF-0322525). Mistakes, omissions and conclusions are, of course, my own.

12   Making the teaching of social justice matter

William Paul Simmons

In *Making Social Science Matter*, Bent Flyvbjerg deconstructs the dominant hierarchy that privileges the natural sciences over the social sciences by offering a third way out of the 'science wars' debate; one that carves out a significant place for *both* the natural sciences and the social sciences. As he writes, 'where natural science is weak, social science is strong and vice versa' (2001: 53). Social science, Flyvbjerg argues, should be recast based largely upon Aristotle's conception of phronesis or practical wisdom mixed with a healthy dose of Foucault's understanding of power. This reinvigorated social science trumps natural science in the understanding of social phenomena by emphasizing contexts, interpretations and an in-depth understanding of existing power relations. In short, it is 'an intellectual activity aimed at . . . contributing to social and political praxis' (2001: 4). His call for a phronetic social science is a useful antidote to the hegemonic position of formal modelling and other positivistic approaches that had come to dominate the social sciences, especially American political science. Of course, much, if not all, of social science, including the formal modelling that has dominated the *American Political Science Review*, claims to be 'contributing to social and political praxis' (2001: 4). Flyvbjerg though harkens back to Aristotle to show the necessity of an in-depth understanding of context and the ability to make political judgements within these contexts. What is not as clear is the extent to which Flyvbjerg is calling on social scientists to get involved and *do* politics in lieu of merely *studying* politics. For Aristotle, phronetics as an intellectual virtue was not gained by stepping back and contemplating reality from an objective distance, as if that was possible, but it came from getting one's hands dirty by actively confronting the problems of the day. To what extent is Flyvbjerg urging social scientists to be social and political beings, to strive to be, in Bourdieu's terms, virtuoso social actors?

Here, I reconsider the role of praxis in phronetic social science using the creation of Arizona State University's innovative new Masters programme in Social Justice and Human Rights as an example. I follow

Flyvbjerg's lead and journey back to Aristotle and Foucault, but I develop a more critical phronetic social science based upon a more radical interpretation of the inter-relationships between power and phronesis. I will argue that a phronetic social science, *to the extent that it is concerned with questions of social justice*, must get involved in doing politics, especially in the deconstruction of predominant ideologies that serve to marginalize and oppress. I call this approach *anti-hegemonic phronetics*. Since our academic knowledge is infused with hegemonic power structures, phronetic social scientists must work with marginalized communities to call into question academic knowledge itself through the co-generation of new knowledge. To do otherwise would risk perpetuating current power structures and their oppressions. Such an approach would call for a radical re-thinking of the way social scientists are taught, especially at the graduate level. I will briefly discuss the ways that the faculty and students in our Masters programme work with affected communities in the co-generation of knowledge, especially through participatory action research.[1]

Flyvbjerg's phronetic social science

Flyvbjerg joins a chorus of recent thinkers who have explicitly called for a revival of Aristotelian phronesis to counter the privileging of scientistic or technological thinking, including, *inter alia*, Jean-François Lyotard, Hans-Georg Gadamer, Martin Heidegger, Hannah Arendt, Jürgen Habermas and Richard Bernstein (see Tabachnick 2004). Additionally, according to Flyvbjerg, many others in a wide variety of disciplines already conduct research that can be labelled phronetic or 'phronetic-like' (2001: 162), ranging from Pierre Bourdieu and Clifford Geertz to Robert Bellah, Alisdair MacIntyre, Robert Putnam and Wendy Brown. Flyvbjerg also mentions several feminist scholars who combine a Foucauldian understanding of power with 'progressive praxis' (2001: 164) including Judith Butler, Nancy Fraser and Naomi Wolf.[2] Of course, numerous other scholars have argued for a theoretically informed

---

[1] Flyvbjerg briefly mentions action research, implying that it is a subset of phronetic social science where 'researchers take on the perspective and goals of those under study and use research results as part of an effort to achieve these goals' (2001: 192n.6). Leading proponents of action research have been split on Flyvbjerg's work. Greenwood (2008), who advocates a more pragmatic and all-encompassing approach, sees it as a 'treatise on action research' (192) while Eikeland (2006) is frustrated by what he sees as Flyvbjerg's inexplicable dismissal of action research.

[2] Landman (2008) and Schram (2004) add such works as Scott's *Moral Economy of the Peasant* and Payne's *Uncivil Movements* as well as the works of Cynthia Enloe, Frances Fox Piven and Richard A. Cloward.

praxis supplemented by a Foucauldian understanding of power, including feminist scholars, critical race theorists, cultural anthropologists, critical geographers and critical pedagogy scholars. Flyvbjerg's work has
much in common with many of these, but it can be distinguished by its
sustained call for using phronesis to re-orient the overall project of social
science research.

He harkens back to Aristotle's three intellectual virtues of epistemé,
phronesis and techné to carve out a niche for the social sciences. While
epistemé or abstract knowledge can be known with certainty and is an
appropriate *telos* for the natural sciences, and techné or applied skills is
appropriate for the arts (writ large), Aristotle argues that the human sciences (ethics and politics) should aim for phronesis or practical wisdom.
This phronesis will be learned through immersion in, and the studying
of, real-world examples, what Kant called the 'go-carts of judgement'.
Flyvbjerg urges social scientists to focus more on case studies and the
involvement in applied problems in the political sphere, instead of aiming for theories and data with the certitude of the natural sciences and
epistemé.

Methodological guidelines for phronetics

Near the end of *Making Social Science Matter*, Flyvbjerg develops nine
methodological guidelines for phronetic social science research. Several
of these aim for more in-depth understandings of specific contexts such as
'emphasizing little things', 'getting close to reality', 'studying cases and
contexts' and 'looking at practice before discourse'. More importantly
for my theoretical argument, several of the guidelines call for an embrace
of communal validity supplemented by extensive analyses of power and
power relations.

Two of the methodological guidelines urge the researcher to embrace
communal validity and discourse. For instance, phronetic research is
value laden, but it is not based upon any sort of foundational ethics.
Instead, it embraces a situational ethics that is firmly rooted in 'the
socially and historically conditioned context' with sets of validity claims
that can be judged by a 'community of social scientists'. Phronetic
research also involves 'dialoguing with a polyphony of voices' where the
researcher's voice should not claim 'final authority' (Flyvbjerg 2001:
139). Here, Flyvbjerg appears on the surface to be very close to embracing the ideal speech situation of Habermas, where truth is determined by
full dialogue in the community with each validity claim tested 'in competition with other validity claims and other interpretations' (2001: 139).

Nonetheless, Flyvbjerg learned, *pace* Habermas, while working with the Regional Planning Authority of Aalborg, Denmark, that knowledge or communal validity claims cannot be divorced from power relations. Those who held political power often did not embrace what appeared to be the rational solution, and they were often willing to manipulate the knowledge that was disseminated in order to fit their political agendas:

I had seen knowledge being marginalized by power, and power producing the knowledge that served its purpose best. I concluded that knowledge about the phenomena which decide whether economic, social, geographic or other knowledge gets to count as important is at least as important as that knowledge itself. If you are not knowledgeable about the former, you cannot be effective with the latter. (Flyvbjerg 2001: 142)

Flyvbjerg labels this power-infused rationality *Realrationalität* or 'real rationality' (1998: 6; cf. Flyvbjerg and Richardson 2002), as opposed to formal or abstract rationality. Knowledge cannot be divorced from power relations. As Foucault writes:

We should abandon the belief that power makes mad and that, by the same token, the renunciation of power is one of the conditions of knowledge. We should admit rather that power produced knowledge (and not simply by encouraging it because it serves power or by applying it because it is useful) that power and knowledge directly imply one another; that there is no power relation without the correlative constitution of a field of knowledge. (1979: 27)

In response, Flyvbjerg calls for researchers to put 'power at the core' in their analyses. This is not the relatively centralized political power that has been studied for centuries by political theorists, but Foucault's analyses of 'governmental rationalities' which are 'omnipresent' and continuously caught in a web with knowledge. As Flyvbjerg writes, 'power produces knowledge and knowledge produces power' (2001: 132). It is crucial to note that the researcher and his or her knowledge are also already always caught up in a web of power relations. This becomes clearer when we consider his guideline of 'joining agency and structure'. Following Bourdieu, Flyvbjerg urges researchers to seek to understand how external power relations are internalized within subjects, while keeping in mind that subjects are simultaneously exercising agency in relation to social structures. In conducting research, the social scientist, too, exercises agency, but this agency will be constrained by the dominant social structure and its concomitant power relations which are internalized by the researcher.

Despite some scathing critiques,[3] Flyvbjerg's work has resonated with many scholars, especially those seeking a useful antidote to the over-scientistic ways of conducting social sciences. His work is often cited as a key text in the struggle for methodological pluralism, including those in the Perestroika movement in political science (see Monroe 2005), but his work does much more. It sums up an ethos that moves productively beyond the stale either/or debates of the 1990s and serves as a useful prolegomena to a revitalized social science. Flyvbjerg though is offering only one possible path from this starting point. As he writes, his work is 'only a first step that will undoubtedly need further theoretical and methodological refinement' (2001: 5). I would like to push his interpretations of Aristotle and Foucault to suggest a more radical path, especially for researchers studying social justice. To show the necessity of this path, I will return to Aristotle and Foucault and the inter-relatedness between phronesis and power, especially its importance in relationship to social justice work.

Back to Aristotle: power and phronesis reconsidered

In the *Nicomachean Ethics* (1962), Aristotle famously distinguishes the moral virtues from intellectual virtues such as phronesis, but what is often overlooked is their interconnectedness. The moral virtues require phronesis to be realized and phronesis rests upon a prior ground in moral virtues. The moral virtues such as courage, generosity, justice and gentleness are initially learned through habits that are inculcated by education and through feelings of pleasure and pain. They are realized (*hexis*) by the performance of actions, but only those in accordance with phronesis (1144b26). For instance, a person becomes courageous by performing courageous actions, but only when they are performed by choosing it for its own sake, and from 'a firm and unchangeable character' (1105a33).

At the same time, phronesis requires the moral virtues for its actualization. Since phronesis is the ability to deliberate and then act 'rationally

---

[3] Many reviewers take Flyvbjerg to task for oversimplifying or caricaturing the social and natural sciences (Sent 2002: 733; Hawkesworth 2006: 153) or too quickly dismissing the progress of the social sciences (Langbein 2002: 496; McIntyre 2004: 419; Laitin 2006) with such breezy comments as: 'after more than 200 years of attempts, one could reasonably expect that there would exist at least a sign that social science has moved in the desired direction, that is, toward predictive theory. It has not' (2001: 32). We would expect such a work to draw strong opposition from a range of fields as it challenges 'disciplinary fiefdoms, protected research communities and structures of power in the hierarchies of universities and research funding organizations' (Landman 2008: 181). It has touched some nerves.

in matters good and bad for man' (1140b5), it rests upon a prior under-standing of what is good, and this is, for the most part, determined by the moral virtues. Aristotle writes, 'virtue makes us aim at the right tar-get, and practical wisdom [phronesis] makes us use the right means' (1144a7). Further, those who lack self-control (*sophrosyne*; etymologi-cally, the saving of phronesis), those who have not realized the moral virtues, will also be 'corrupted by pleasure or pain' to know what is best in a given situation. Only those like Pericles who 'have the capacity of seeing what is good for themselves and for mankind' (1140b7) and then have knowledge of the proper means to achieve it can be deemed to have phronesis. Those who are proficient at deliberating for bad ends merely possess cleverness (*deinos*) and not phronesis (1144a25).

Two points need to be stressed from this sketch of Aristotle's theory. First, phronesis for Aristotle is not merely a form of knowing, but it is realized through action. 'To be a man of practical wisdom, one must not only know [what one ought to do] but he must also be able to act accordingly' (1152a7). Practical wisdom is realized in its 'supreme and comprehensive form' through the 'art of legislation' (1141b25), but it can also be achieved in lesser forms of action, such as looking after oneself, household management or engaging in deliberative and judicial politics. Second, young people do not attain phronesis because it 'is concerned with particulars as well [as with universals], and knowledge of particulars comes from experience' (1141a8). Young people have not been immersed in enough experiences to understand all of the nuances of particular contexts to understand how best to act. Moreover, their ability to exercise phronesis will be limited by their lack of actualized moral virtues. Since young people tend to follow their emotions, they cannot reliably know what target to aim for.

Phronesis and power revisited

We now begin to see that in Aristotle's polis phronesis will be ascribed only to a select few. Only those who attain the moral virtues, and know how best to act, *and* are able to act, will realize phronesis. After all, most people 'do not even have a notion of what is noble and truly pleasant' (1179b15). Only a select few will know what is best for themselves and for the polis. Only these few should practise the art of legislation and rule the polis. These few will be bound by what Aristotle calls *homonoia* or like-mindedness. This homonoia, which appears to be the highest level of political friendship is 'not merely agreement of opinion' and it is not just agreement 'about any subject', but it is an agreement among good men about the fundamentals of a society, 'the realm of great matters' (*ta en megethei*) (1167a27). 'They are of the same mind each with himself and all with one another' (1167b5). This like-mindedness about great matters will be presumably developed through a common upbringing, which will inculcate the same habits and moral virtues. This is the role of the Aristotelian lawmaker. Indeed, it is the most important task of the lawmaker. 'To obtain the right training for virtue from youth up is difficult, unless one has been brought up under the right laws' (1179b33). Like-mindedness is possible only among the good men who have shed personal interest as much as possible. 'The base [*faulos*] on the other hand are incapable of homonoia except in some small degree, as they are of friendship, since they try to get more than their share of advantages, and take less than their share of labours and public burdens' (1167a10–15). Lacking phronesis, the proper moral virtues, and the common understanding of the fundamentals of a society, the base should be excluded from the political sphere and its debates.

Phronesis, cauterization and justice

The polis will reproduce itself by training lawmakers with similar conceptions of virtues and reason, and by excluding the opinions of those who are deemed faulos and beneath phronesis because they have not shed self-interest. Here we see the fatal flaw of most theories of discursive democracy that aim for communal validity; namely, many voices will be excluded from the discourse.[4] The Aristotelian polis now begins to resemble groupthink more than an ideal speech situation. In turn, without these voices present in the debate, the polis will not question who has been excluded and what human cost was incurred in establishing the polis. For instance, one of the costs of establishing the Athenian empire was the vast production at the Laurium silver mines with thousands of slaves working in horrendous conditions leading to greatly reduced life spans. These slaves were *aneu logou* (without a voice), in Aristotle's terminology, and excluded from the polis, and their suffering seemed to have been ignored by Aristotle (1932), who relegated some men to be natural slaves.

I use the term 'cauterization' to describe the systematic way that these individuals are marginalized. The three aspects of cauterization nicely correspond to the term's three inter-related meanings (cf. *Oxford English Dictionary*). The first meaning comes from its roots in the Greek verb

---

[4] Sanders calls this the 'primary' problem of discursive democracy: 'how more of the people who routinely speak less . . . might take part and be heard and how those who typically dominate might be made to attend to the views of others' (1997: 352).

kauteriazein, which means to burn with a kauter or a branding iron. Such branding was historically done to physically mark a slave or criminal as having no rights. Second, cauterization refers to a medical procedure in which burning is used to seal off or remove part of the body. This procedure is most often used to stop bleeding, but it can also seal a wound to stop the spread of infection. Finally, in its most metaphorical meaning, cauterization means to deaden feelings or make one callous to the suffering of another. Many philosophical theories often cauterize the 'Marginalized Other'. The 'Other' is branded as beneath humanity, below those who deserve rights as are the 'base' in Aristotle's works. Then, those that are deemed inferior or without rights are sealed off from the polis or the courtroom, in effect, treating the voice of the rightless as an infection that must be stopped from spreading. As the political philosopher Hannah Arendt held, drawing on Aristotle, the political man must 'protect the island of freedom they have come to inhabit against the surrounding sea of necessity' (Arendt 1963: 280). That is, political men must decide which individuals are capable of entering the political realm; that is, they must cauterize or seal off the polis from those who are unable to shed their selfish interests or lack the necessary homonoia about the great matters of the polis. Finally, those with rights, the full members of the polis, deaden their feelings towards the suffering of those who are branded as rightless, such as the slaves at Laurium.

To avoid perpetuating the continued cauterization of the marginalized, a phronetic social science must constantly interrogate current conditions to determine who is excluded by the omnipresent 'governmental rationalities'. However, the relationship between power and knowledge is so insidious that we must constantly interrogate all forms of knowledge, all sciences, even our own, to understand how they reproduce current power structures. As Bourdieu argues, the rules of the game, what Aristotle called the realm of great matters, are too often taken for granted, tending towards the reproduction of objective conditions. We are all enmeshed in power relations, even the researcher. To what extent is our knowledge, and the deliberations it is based upon, already cauterizing the Other?

Flyvbjerg holds that the phronetic social scientist should focus on the 'classic value-rational questions', and engage in 'deliberation about such values and interests' (2004: 402). As he writes, when one interpretation 'demonstrates the previous interpretation to be "merely" interpretation, this new interpretation remains valid until another, still better interpretation is produced' (2001: 131). This dialogue appears to occur within 'a community of social scientists' (2001: 131; cf. 2004: 408). But, this procedure is more likely than not reproducing the existing power structure with its 'governmental rationalities', and will not call into question the various ways that peoples are cauterized. Based upon the analysis above, we must constantly question who is included in the community or validity group. Who is part of the polyphony of voices? What steps are we taking to deconstruct existing power relations?

Nonetheless, as Flyvbjerg and those in the Perestroika movement have detailed, most social scientists lack meaningful social and political expertise and experience, and this is especially true when considering marginalized populations. Unless researchers are immersed in a context we will not possess the 'context-dependent' skills and judgement to satisfactorily understand the 'rules of the game' (2001: 42–3). If we are studying social justice and human rights, it is highly unlikely that the marginalized peoples, those who are in the best position to understand their predicament, will be part of the deliberative community that determines the answers to the 'classic value-rational questions' about what is best socially and politically. As Upendra Baxi (n.d.) wrote of the urgent need to reform human rights education (HRE) from the perspective of the Other: 'perhaps, the first step in the activist journey of hyper solidarity is for HRE activists to learn from the victims of the perfidies of power rather than to presume to educate them in the struggle for survival and justice'.

If we seek informed action, if we seek a plurality of voices, the disruption of power, to do social justice in a real democratic debate, then we must privilege the voices of the marginalized, even in relation to our own voices as researchers. I echo Schram's call for a 'problem-driven, contextually sensitive approach to enable people on the bottom working in dialogue with social researchers to challenge power' (2004: 419).

Doing justice with the marginalized: towards an anti-hegemonic phronetics

What does it mean to do justice and how is that to be taught? Systematic cauterization or marginalization means that to do justice we must not only create discursive communities, but anti-hegemonic communities where the voices of those marginalized by predominant discourses are privileged. We must resist the temptation where we believe that we have included all voices – we must continuously deconstruct how we continue to privilege or stage certain voices. Or, in a Spivakian vein, we must ask whether we are speaking for our own representations of – basically ventriloquizing – the marginalized voices. To do justice for the marginalized would require suspending our own voices in humility. Spivak describes this nicely as a 'no holds barred self-suspending leap into the other's sea – basically without preparation' (Spivak 2004: 207–8). This is what she aptly calls 'learning to learn from below'. To continuously deconstruct the hegemonic system requires access to a different epistemé, one that is resistant to appropriation and manipulation, and one that resists becoming the new hegemonic system. This 'fundamental epistemic transformation' (Ray 2003: 44), or what Rancière calls 'a novel perceptual universe' (1999: 5), is accessed by a patient listening to the voice of the marginalized.

The teaching of anti-hegemonic phronetics

As for teaching phronetics, or at least for better understanding the relationship 'between knowledge and context' (2001: 9), Flyvbjerg turns to the well-known Dreyfus model of skill acquisition. Ironically, this model was originally applied by Dreyfus in the context of teaching fighter pilots what most would call a techné. Dreyfus derived five stages for learning skills: novice, advanced beginner, competent performer, proficient performer and expert. He quickly noticed that even in the early stages a learner knows all the rules and knows what to do. Only in the latter stages does a learner move 'beyond analytical rationality' and react intuitively. At the expert or virtuoso level, 'intuitive, holistic, and synchronous action is now at the centre' (Flyvbjerg 2001: 17). Experts intuitively understand a context and can act to take advantage of it. Therefore, a virtuoso social actor who is able to effectively create social change is not a detached observer as in the epistemic model, but someone who can intuitively address the given social context.

To teach such intuitive and holistic expertise the understanding of context and judgement are crucial, so Flyvbjerg touts the pedagogical advantages of the case method made famous in the Harvard Business School. 'Such business schools may be called Aristotelian, whereas schools stressing theory and rules may be called Platonic. We could do with more Aristotelian schools of political science' (2004: 403). In such an Aristotelian school, Flyvbjerg's budding social scientists should also engage in experiential learning through internships, study abroad and summer jobs (2001: 72).

Teaching an anti-hegemonic phronetics would also entail case-based education and experiential learning. After all, phronesis would still be privileged over techné and episteme and it would still require a deep understanding of context and power, but we would stress a host of new questions, such as who is *aneu logou* (without a voice, Aristotle's term) in the political community?; what does it mean to speak for the Other?; are our attempts at representation and empowerment actually perpetuating the hegemonic discourse? The telos would no longer be producing virtuoso social actors proficient in understanding sociopolitical contexts and adept at marshalling political power, but rather the facilitation of anti-hegemonic discourses based on local or indigenous knowledges. Virtuoso teachers and practitioners of phronesis would now be those who can learn to learn from below through Spivak's 'no holds barred self-suspending leap into the other's sea' (Spivak 2004: 207–8). In a way, a graduate programme in social justice would be creating knowledge capital (cf. Chatzkel 2003: 4), but instead of creating knowledge in order to generate material wealth, we would be co-creating knowledge with the marginalized to leverage against existing power relations, including the more insidious 'governmental rationalities'. Knowledge would not be created on behalf of the marginalized, but would be co-created by the marginalized for their use. I argue below that participatory action research as it is increasingly employed in our Social Justice and Human Rights programme is ideal for bringing about such a transformation.

Action research in the social justice and human rights curriculum

In 2008, after enduring years of organizational chaos and bureaucratic bumbling that had stymied our planning, we finally had the green light for the implementation of our new MA programme in Social Justice and Human Rights. The curriculum had basically been set for almost three years, but now, of all times, a faculty member new to the planning process urged us to revisit the research methods sequence, which had already been the subject of much debate, research and tinkering. But, I had to agree, something was not quite right. We had designed a one-of-a-kind curriculum from the ground up. We were going to be a truly interdisciplinary, truly community-embedded, truly globally engaged MA programme that we hoped would attract students from around the United States and across the globe. Our curriculum features problem-based seminars, community-embedded seminars, grant-writing and development, and other courses unique for a human rights programme. Almost all our courses were designed to have students working hand-in-hand with community groups near and far.

I had to admit that the methods sequence was one of the last vestiges of a standard graduate curriculum. The only feature that set it apart was its accelerated pace, with students in a 33-credit Masters programme moving from basic research methods to advanced methods in either a qualitative or quantitative track in just a couple of semesters. We envisioned the programme being methodically rigorous enough to prepare students for PhD programmes in the social sciences, and even to be prepared for conducting research for governmental and non-governmental organizations if they wished. The faculty wanted students who could assist them with their research projects through research assistantships or independent studies. What was the alternative to the traditional methods sequence? When the new faculty member finally mentioned the idea of an action research course – a term that was unfamiliar to many faculty, it came across as a perfect way to teach the qualitative methods track, and little more. As we read more about action research it became clearer that action research is not a type of research, nor is it limited to qualitative research. It is a way of doing research or, more accurately, an ethos for doing research, one that dovetails perfectly with the rest of our curriculum. After further discussion we decided that we would offer only one advanced research course on a regular basis and that would be Action Research for Social Justice and Human Rights. The course would apply mixed-methods research to a variety of current social justice issues in the community.

I see those discussions as a gift, as I now believe the action research course is a perfect fit for our programme. It epitomizes the ethos of our faculty and students, and it seems to be the perfect type of methods course for any social justice and human rights programme.

Action research means many things to many people. For many, the way our course has developed will not be 'pure' enough; for others, it will appear as something too heterodox. As I see it, our action research course is always seeking to reach an ideal that is never attainable; it is in 'Derridean' fashion forever *a-venir* (to come), and this ideal continuously haunts the rest of our curriculum and our programme as a whole.

Action research: towards a definition

The term 'action research' describes a wide range of approaches, with the meaning varying greatly across disciplines. In the field of education, where the term is most widely used, it generally refers to teachers conducting research in the classroom in order to better inform their pedagogical practices. In health psychology, it is most known as community-based health research, mainly employing quantitative methodologies. In anthropology, it almost solely refers to a type of qualitative and ethnographic research. In development studies, it mostly goes under such acronyms as PRA (participatory rural appraisal) or RRA (rapid rural appraisal). Action research seems to fall along something of a continuum from minimal involvement with the community (perhaps in the field of education), thus, being almost another name for applied social research, to a fully participatory model that involves the most patient and sophisticated of ethnographic methods. Greenwood and Levin (2007), in their wonderful introductory textbook on action research, advocate 'pragmatic action research', where the amount and type of community engagement varies over time and depends upon the context. For me, though, action research in the more ethnographic mode remains something of an ideal towards which all action research should strive.

At its most basic, level action research, or what many call participatory action research (PAR), is a collaborative research effort between academic researchers and community stakeholders to address a current community problem. In ideal participatory action research, community stakeholders are involved in all aspects of the research process with all research decisions determined in part by the community problem and the stakeholders. The researcher 'works with' the community members to 'co-generate knowledge', and thus the researcher's main task becomes that of facilitating learning arenas where the researcher and community members can learn from each other (Greenwood and Levin 2007).

It is important to note that action research is not necessarily qualitative or quantitative. Research decisions, such as selecting the appropriate methodology, are determined by the academic literature, relevant theories, the researcher's expertise, the community problem and the community (cf. Flyvbjerg 2001: 196n.7). The community is involved in all decision-making, including what type of methodology to choose. If the community desires a large-scale survey to address the problem, then quantitative methods would most likely be necessary. Indeed, as problem-based and community-based, action research is inherently multidisciplinary, with a problem leading the community/researchers to possibly explore several disciplines within a specific research project.

As opposed to more traditional ways of conducting research, the action researcher does not see the community members as subjects to be studied. Instead, the researcher actively works with the community, seeing them as full partners in the research project. As such, the researcher does not 'orchestrate' the process, but allows it to develop as the relationship with the community grows. Greenwood and Levin aptly describe the action researcher as a 'friendly outsider' (2007: 115ff.), who is more of a coach than an expert or boss. Indeed, the experts in the subject matter at hand are often the community members themselves. Instead of the lone researcher working on their own in their office, social skills become crucial, including the interconnected abilities to build rapport in a short period of time, empathy and the ability to listen. Working hand-in-hand with the community requires the respect of the community members, which will be earned only through ethical integrity. Other necessary skills include being a risk-taker who is willing to adapt as the project unfolds, someone who is confident that they will be able to adjust in mid-stream, and learn new areas of knowledge or new methodologies as needed. Perhaps, most importantly a good action researcher will be patient, having tolerance for diverse points of view, including those they think are wrong, and have a good sense of humour, with self-deprecating humour often being crucial.

The final research report is a product of the entire group, and the intended audience includes the community stakeholders as well as other researchers. The work of the Sangtin Writers and Richa Nagar (2006) perhaps exemplifies this ideal of co-generating knowledge and co-publishing results. Their work on the politics of development among NGOs and activists in India was originally co-written by nine women – one American scholar and eight Indian activists – and originally published in Hindi. After sparking much controversy in India, the work was published in the United States by a university press with additional personal reflections.[5] The US-based researcher took the lead on editing the book, but it is a collection of autobiographies and reflections by each of the women, and it was published with the collective listed as 'first author'. As they worked together in development politics, some group members took on more of the work of community organizing and others would take on more of the task of formal writing. Neither was privileged. Indeed, through this division of labour they were 'deconstructing the idea of the scholar or writer as an expert in this kind of collaboration', causing the formal scholar to 'reflect on the extent to which I had internalized the very definitions of "expert" that I was ostensibly interested in dismantling through collaboration' (Sangtin Writers and Nagar 2006: xxxix–xl). Working with community members aided in the deconstruction of the hegemonic governmental rationalities in which she was enmeshed.

Action research in the social justice and human rights curriculum

The students in the MA programme in Social Justice and Human Rights have quickly embraced these ideals emanating from action research. However, logistical obstacles often prevent the students from fully implementing an action research project in a single course. These obstacles include the length of the academic semester, the diachrony between academic and community calendars, the need to teach so many other

---

[5] I am thankful to Raymond Duvall for recommending this wonderful work. I have just co-written a book chapter on art and social justice at the US–Mexico borderlands with eight other authors including community activists, artists and students (two of whom are undocumented) (see Albarran *et al.* n.d.).

research skills, and the shifting needs of the community. I cannot claim that the students in our Masters programme have become virtuoso social actors through our action research courses or the rest of our curriculum. Aristotle would hold that their relative youth and inexperience would prevent them from attaining such a level of phronesis. Dreyfus would probably add that they are merely in the first stages of acquiring the skills needed to be accomplished action researchers, especially the necessary intuitions and holistic understanding. Nonetheless, they have been exposed to a research ethos that teaches them to be involved with marginalized communities in the co-creation of knowledge. Under the tutelage of faculty co-researchers, students working with action research experience a 'deep kind of participative knowing' where 'validity is measured by the depth of relationship, plurality of knowing, practical significance, and enduring nature of inquiry' (Burgess 2006: 424, 432). The faculty, in this course and throughout the programme, must also provide the students with the necessary theoretical and substantive background to draw upon as they work with the community, including solid foundations in international human rights law, social movements and NGO management; as well as the tools to conduct good quality scientific research that is reliable and valid.

Meanwhile, the ideals based upon the philosophical analyses above and the more 'ethnographic' modes of action research will continue to haunt our research and our programme. The students and faculty will continue to ask in what ways they are privileging certain voices and cauterizing others. Are we perpetuating the marginalization of those that we must serve in a social justice programme? To do justice means to constantly ask whether we are just enough. Justice thus can never be attained, or in Levinas' succinct formulation: 'justice is always a justice which desires a better justice' (Levinas 1988: 178).

Conclusion

Flyvbjerg argues for a phronetic social science where 'the goal is to help restore social and political science to its classical position as a practical, intellectual activity aimed at clarifying the problems, risks and possibilities we face as humans and societies and at contributing to social and political praxis' (2004: 400). Such a social science will focus on such questions as:
(1) Where are we going?
(2) Who gains and who loses, and by which mechanisms of power?
(3) Is this development desirable?
(4) What if anything should we do about it?

The anti-hegemonic phronetics that I develop, based upon the inter-relationship between phronesis and power asks Flyvbjerg's questions and others including:

(1) Who is *aneu logou* (without a voice; Aristotle's term) in the political community?
(2) What does it mean to speak for the Other?
(3) Are our attempts at empowerment actually perpetuating the hegemonic discourse?

These questions will be best addressed through a social science that not only deconstructs the hierarchy between natural and social sciences, but also deconstructs the privileging of the researcher's voice over those in the community. It will account for power politics as Flyvbjerg showed in his excellent study of Aalborg and the more insidious modes of power that Foucault discussed. The researcher must 'learn to learn from below'; that is, must work with marginalized populations in the creation of anti-hegemonic knowledge communities that take on all types of existing power relationships. Such an anti-hegemonic phronetics is ideal for pro-grammes like ours where students learn to 'do' social justice and human rights. And, to the extent that they seek to do social justice, it would be ideal for graduate programmes in many other disciplines.

REFERENCES

Albarran, Marco, Butzine, Judy, Coplan, Rebecca, Daniels, Grace, Garcia, Francisco, Juarez, Dulce, Ohm, Melanie, Rodriguez Vega, Silvia and Simmons, William n.d. 'I'm Migration: Evolving Principles and Practices in Social Justice and the Arts from Diverse Voices in Campus–Community Spaces', unpublished manuscript.

Arendt, Hannah 1963. *On Revolution*. New York: Viking Press.

Aristotle 1932. *Politics*, Book I. Cambridge, MA: Loeb Classical Library.
     1962. *Nicomachean Ethics*, trans. Martin Ostwald. New York: Macmillan.

Baxi, Upendra n.d. 'Random Reflections on the [Im]possibility of Human Rights Education', available at: www.pdhre.org/dialogue/reflections.html.

Burgess, Judy 2006. 'Participatory Action Research: First-Person Perspectives of a Graduate Student', *Action Research* 4(4): 419–37.

Chatzkel, Jay L. 2003. *Knowledge Capital: How Knowledge-based Enterprises Really Get Built*. Oxford University Press.

Eikeland, Olav 2006. 'Making Political Science Matter: Debating Knowledge, Research, and Method', *International Journal of Action Research* 4(3): 314–19.

Flyvbjerg, Bent 1998. *Rationality and Power: Democracy in Practice*. University of Chicago Press.
     2001. *Making Social Science Matter: Why Social Inquiry Fails and How it can Succeed Again*. Cambridge University Press.

2004. 'A Perestroikan Straw Man Answers Back: David Laitin and Phronetic Political Science', *Politics & Society* 32(3): 389–416.

Flyvbjerg, Bent and Richardson, Tim 2002. 'Planning and Foucault: In Search of the Dark Side of Planning Theory', in P. Allmendinger and M. Tewdwr-Jones (eds.), *Planning Futures: New Directions for Planning Theory*. London: Routledge, pp. 44–62.

Foucault, Michel 1979. *Discipline and Punish: The Birth of the Prison*, trans. Alan Sheridan. New York: Vintage Books.

Greenwood, Davydd J. 2008. 'Schram, Sanford F. and Brian Caterino (eds.) Making Political Science Matter: Debating Knowledge, Research, and Method', *Systematic Practice and Action Research* 21: 191–6.

Greenwood, Davydd J. and Levin, Morten 2007. *Introduction to Action Research: Social Research for Social Change*. Thousand Oaks, CA: Sage.

Hawkesworth, Mary 2006. 'Contesting the Terrain: Flyvbjerg on Facts, Knowledge, Values, and Power', in Schram and Caterino (eds.), *Making Political Science Matter*, pp. 152–70.

Laitin, David D. 2006. 'The Perestroikan Challenge to Social Science', in Schram and Caterino (eds.), *Making Political Science Matter*, pp. 33–55.

Landman, Todd 2008. 'Paradigmatic Contestation and the Persistence of Perennial Dualities', *Political Studies Review* 6: 178–85.

Langbein, Laura 2002. 'Making Social Science Matter: Why Social Inquiry Fails and How it can Succeed Again by Brent Flyvbjerg', *Public Choice* 113: 495–9.

Levinas, Emmanuel 1988. 'The Paradox of Morality: An Interview with Emmanuel Levinas', in *The Provocation of Levinas*, eds. Robert Bernasconi and David Wood. London: Routledge.

McIntyre, Lee 2004. 'Making Social Science Matter: Why Social Inquiry Fails and How it can Succeed Again', *Philosophy of Science* 71(3): 418–21.

Monroe, Kristen Renwick 2005. *Perestroika! The Raucous Rebellion in Political Science*. New Haven, CT: Yale University Press.

Rancière, Jacques 1999. *Dis-agreement: Politics and Philosophy*, trans. Julie Rose. Minneapolis, MN: University of Minnesota Press.

Ray, Sangeeta 2003. 'Ethical Encounters: Spivak, Alexander and Kincaid', *Cultural Studies* 17: 42–55.

Sanders, Lynn 1997. 'Against Deliberation', *Political Theory* 25: 347–76.

Sangtin Writers and Nagar, Richa 2006. *Playing with Fire: Feminist Thought and Activism Through Seven Lives in India*. Minneapolis, MN: University of Minnesota Press.

Schram, Sanford F. 2004. 'Beyond Paradigm: Resisting the Assimilation of Phronetic Social Science', *Politics & Society* 32(3): 417–33.

Schram, Sanford F. and Caterino, Brian (eds.) 2006. *Making Political Science Matter: Debating Knowledge, Research, and Method*. New York University Press.

Sent, Esther-Mirjam 2002. 'Making Social Science Matter: Why Social Inquiry Fails and How It Can Succeed Again' (Book Review), *Southern Economic Journal* 68(3): 732–4.

Spivak, Gayatri Chakravorty 2004. '"On the Cusp of the Personal and the Imper-
  sonal": An Interview with Gayatri Chakravorty Spivak by Laura Lyons and
  Cynthia Franklin', *Biography* 27: 203–21.
Tabachnick, David E. 2004. 'Phronesis, Democracy and Technology', *Canadian
  Journal of Political Science* 37: 997–1016.

13 Spatial phronesis: a case study in geosurveillance

Ranu Basu[1]

Introduction: towards an ethics of discomfort

In his essay 'For an Ethic of Discomfort', Foucault provocatively reminds us:

> Never consent to being completely comfortable with one's own presuppositions. Never to let them fall peacefully asleep, but also never to believe that a new fact will suffice to overturn them; never to imagine that one can change them like arbitrary axioms, remembering that in order to give them the necessary mobility one must have a distant view, but also look at what is nearby and all around oneself. To be very mindful that everything one perceives is evident only against a familiar and little-known horizon, that every certainty is sure only through the support of a ground that is always unexplored. The most fragile instant has its roots. In that lesson, there is a whole ethic of sleepless evidence that does not rule out, far from it, a rigorous economy of the True and the False; but that is not the whole story. (1994a: 448)

To engage with an ethic of discomfort, as described by Foucault, is to engage in an act of phronesis. In other words: how does one challenge one's own presuppositions and never let them fall peacefully asleep?; how does one cultivate a sense of mindfulness that challenges the certainty of ground unexplored?; how can one address the roots of this fragile instance? In this chapter I will argue that the art of phronesis, with its variants of value rationality, practical rationality and dialogical significance offers a particular kind of understanding to the governance of spatial practices: an approach we can define as *spatial phronesis*. Phronesis inherently privileges practical wisdom and intuitive understanding alongside the realities of power relations in the construction of knowledge (see Flyvbjerg 2001, 2004). This particular perspective provides powerful ammunition against the hegemonic discourse of neoliberal

[1] Thanks to Rob Fiedler for his invaluable comments and feedback on an earlier draft. Special thanks to Rohan Basu and Katie German for their able research assistance. Funding from Social Science and Humanities Research Council 410-2005-2452 is gratefully acknowledged.

rationality. Cloaked in the language of efficiency, accountability, competition and scientific logic, the discourse of neoliberal policy insidiously purports a mantra of progress and change. In this way the neoliberal rationale continually moulded, reconfigured and celebrated, as most recently through its Third-Way logics, normalizes an essence of individual freedom, self-interest and entrepreneurial governance, strategically converting along the way a broad populace to its utopian rhetoric (Basu 2009: 482). The centrality of space in the process of poverty management and social planning is opportunistically placed within this broader governmentality framework. Its instrument of articulation is the advent of neoliberal cartographies, where the city is sifted and sorted, classified/declassified/reclassified according to the whims and fancies of budgetary clawbacks and constraints. Spaces of representation are technocratically produced through diverting mapping exercises of exclusion and inclusion, while planners and advocates of social policy inadvertently become players in the game of 'rationing the rationed'. It is in this way that power morphs or migrates, and pre-existing privilege insinuates itself in new technologies of surveillance, even when those technologies are ostensibly designed to allow for positive social change.[2] Yet paradoxical spaces sometimes emerge and rupture these paradigms through acts of phronesis. Dissent and contradictions within the multiplicity of governing structures and community agents complicate and challenge static understandings of spatial neoliberal reasoning in sophisticated ways. This chapter will argue that such acts of spatial phronesis allow for a particular kind of 'movable thought' for space – to make it live and breathe – and, as Foucault might argue, in a way that it is able to present the realities and complexities of spatial logics in a structural, intuitive, emotive, but eventually political manner. This transgressive understanding of space as non-Euclidean, heterotopic and multiple challenges the singularity and fixity of neoliberal cartographic space and re-centres the political and relational into the analysis. This chapter provides a case study for spatial phronesis as a transformative methodology that builds into its foundation a critical spatial dimension and relational dynamics. As I have argued earlier (Basu 2009) and will demonstrate through the case study below, the art of spatial phronesis is devoid of disengaged rationality; but is, instead, multifaceted, reciprocal and complex; socially and politically engaged; reflexive and retrospective throughout the research process; and wary of power relations and rationalities that rapidly become dominant interpretations. Through this process it produces new subjects

---

[2] Personal communication, Bent Flyvbjerg, 2010.

and subjectivities that become enmeshed in a particular relationality – in tandem or opposed to neoliberal governmentalities.

In the wake of rapidly deteriorating conditions of schools during the past decade, the Learning Opportunities Grant was established to provide funding for schools in dire need across the province of Ontario. In Toronto, reports such as *Poverty by Postal Code* have become guiding doctrines for poverty recognition and alleviation. Localized spaces of poverty and marginality in such documents are efficiently identified, territorially demarcated and labelled as 'at risk' and 'priority areas' where resources and opportunities to support the needs of the most vulnerable populations should be directed. With its progressive and pragmatic discourse, attention is strategically diverted from underlying structural factors and the neoliberal strategies that had originally led to such conditions in the first place. Instead, attention is focused on measuring and labelling communities that have failed; and to the further sifting and sorting of vulnerabilities. How, then, can the techniques of identification reflect a spatially contingent redistributive justice system that can coherently combine with the social politics of equality? This chapter provides a case study for spatial phronesis as a transformative methodology that builds into its foundations a critical spatial dimension and relational dynamics. Using the case study of the Model Inner City School Initiative, adopted by the Toronto District School Board in 2006–7, the logics, politics and ethics of a redistributional funding allocation process is traced and explored.

Cartographic representation of spatial policy: the *problématiques* of space

Questions of space have been accorded a great deal of attention beyond geography. As a social construct, space is closely bound with social reality. In his discussion on the social production of space, Lefebvre (1991) notes that space does not exist in itself but is produced. Therefore, in and of itself, it can never serve as an epistemological starting point. Space, in other words, is relational, historical and ideological and can be understood only in the context of specific societies. Lefebvre's trialectics combining the 'perceived', 'conceived' and 'lived dimensions' in the production of space constitute a contradictory dialectical unity: space emerges only in the interplay of all three. Lefebvre's understanding of space in an active rather than static, absolute sense, highlights the intricate web of relationships that is continuously produced and reproduced. Thus, space understood in this way is seen not as an *a priori* or ontological entity, but rather emphasis is placed on the processes and strategies of producing space. Yet a neoliberalized understanding facilitates a static, absolute and abstract conceptualization of space as it serves to simplify its inherent complexities and internalized contradictions. Universal truths render space as bounded and fixed, an entity that is apolitical, ahistorical and agency free. And therein lies the dilemma and contradictions of the problématiques of space and much of how social spatial policy is conceptualized and put into practice. For example, strategies of neoliberal poverty 'management', regulations and governmental technologies have led to contradictory understandings of the city and its disciplinary mechanisms through symbolic orderings.

In *The Rule of Freedom*, Patrick Joyce (2003: 20) noted that, in order for the liberal state to operate, it was first necessary for it to identify those it sought to govern. Geosurveillance – or the art of governance through the workings of space – is one such strategic activity used to know those who are governed; and often, *though not always* as I have argued (Basu 2005), operationalized through the use of geographic information systems (GIS). In recent years, with the proliferation of software and census data availability, GIS has allowed the explosion of mapping techniques into the realm of public policy (PPGIS). Graham (2005: 563) similarly discusses how contemporary capitalist societies are continuously brought into being through code. GIS has been criticized as a powerful planning tool that often perpetuates power differentials. These criticisms are largely centred on, for example, GIS's role in interfering with privacy (see Pickles 1995), in its facilitation of military usage (Smith 1992), and its sometimes improper categorization and representations of social space, segmentation and construction of consumer identity (see Goss 1995). On a descriptive level, the simple visual display of colour-coded stratifications through choropleth mapping involves demarcating the everyday living and carving up and making sense of a disordered urban environment through neighbourhood categorizations. The images have powerful and alluring impacts on a wider public and uncritically become inscribed in the representational landscape of the city through its disciplining techniques. The consequential territorialized identities of places so produced (i.e., at risk) conjoin with the subjectivities of residents inherently constituted through such localizations. As I have argued in earlier work (Basu 2005), the release of such indicators, particularly at the residential level, creates a *landscape of perpetual spectacle*: hierarchical spaces that are under constant observation, scrutiny and judgement. The production of such constructed truths create criteria, indices and other regulatory mechanisms to form threshold levels that are normalized and thereby amenable to a larger public in a climate of neoliberal governance. As de Certeau (1984: 102) argues:

Their rhetorical transplantation carries away and displaces the analytical, coherent proper meaning of urbanism; it constitutes a 'wandering of the semantic' produced by masses that make some parts of the city disappear and exaggerate others, distorting it, fragmenting it, and diverting it from its immobile order.

However, during the past few years works by *critical GIS* scholars have actively engaged in these critiques and continue to find creative and constructive ways of dealing with these various limitations (see Schuurman 2000). The work by feminist scholars (Kwan 2002; McLafferty 2004), Public Participation GIS (Sieber 2003) and critical GIS (Crampton 2003, 2004) users, among others, has seriously attempted to re-envision (Kwan) and re-appropriate (Crampton) GIS in an attempt to re-establish its role as a powerful critical tool. While exploring notions of governmentality through GIS, Jeremy Crampton powerfully argues, 'it is not technologies of surveillance – mapping or GIS *per se* – that are problematic, but rather the underlying political rationality of normalization which constituted people and the environment as threatened resources under risk or hazard' (2003: 137). In his analysis of the representational challenges of mapping the suburbs, Fiedler has argued:

The question of who's doing the representing matters. Certainly, where you live may be a reflection of who you are; but how this is understood and represented also tends to reflect where the person doing the interpreting and representing lives. (2011: 82)

How, then, can a critical GIS work to incorporate a more phronetic approach? The errors associated with flawed and exaggerated representations can be noted to be technical, philosophical and political. On the *technical* side Miron (1998) affirms GIS's univariate, descriptive and exploratory perspective as useful, but also warns of the problems that are frequently overlooked in the mapping process: mainly problems related to spatial autocorrelation, aggregation effects as a result of the modifiable area unit problem (MAUP), edge effects, sullied sample, error propagation, and the identification–testing paradox, among others. From a more *philosophical* perspective the 'view from afar', 'governing from a distance' and abstract instrumental reasoning in the 'knowledge of the aggregates' (see Joyce 2003) often obfuscates the local stories and the rich texture of everyday life. And *politically*, the inherent structural inequities caused historically by decades of neoliberal reform are lost and focus is instead based on discussions of localized descriptive presents. All of these limitations apply to the reports previously discussed. As I have argued earlier (Basu 2009), the art of spatial phronesis would actively attempt to counter these limitations and be devoid of disengaged rationality; instead, it would be multifaceted, reciprocal and complex; socially and politically engaged; reflexive and retrospective throughout the research process; and wary of power relations and rationalities that rapidly become dominant interpretations.

Using the case study of the Model Inner City School Initiative adopted by the Toronto District School Board in 2006–7, the logics, politics and ethics of a redistributional funding allocation process are traced and explored. Strongly enmeshed in the logics of the *Poverty by Postal Code* guidelines, a social policy report produced in 2004 for the city of Toronto by the United Way,[3] the spatial containment of neighbourhoods experiencing dire poverty became the strategic focus. Through an elaborate mapping exercise the social polarization of neighbourhoods experiencing concentrated poverty was identified. The geography of poverty was highlighted across the city as a series of 'priority neighbourhoods' where infrastructure and resources needed to be targeted. The report generated much interest in both public and academic circles, especially with regard to the novelty and allurement of mapping outcomes. The social and economic implications of the report's findings created a consensual vision highlighting the unjust and inequitable conditions of the city. Yet such strategies, as Swyngeouw argues, produce a consensual vision of the urban environment that presents a clear and present danger that '*annuls the properly political moment* and contributes to the emergence and consolidation of a postpolitical and postdemocratic condition' (Swyngeouw 2009: 601, emphasis added). Attention is strategically diverted from underlying structural factors and the neoliberal strategies that had led to such conditions in the first place. Instead, attention is focused on technocracies: measuring and labelling communities that have failed, and to the further sifting and sorting of vulnerabilities. Neighbourhood identities very rapidly translate into the politics of stigmatization, individuation and stern accountability. Yet this form of policy reform, readily received by social planning and general public discourse, lacks a fundamental critical dimension in the process of its formulation. The redistributive system very rapidly develops into a strategy of geosurveillance that relies on scientific rational planning models. The view from afar excludes the complexities and contradictions of everydayness itself. To counter this delinquent narrative, we can draw from de Certeau's (1984: 130) discussion on matters of space that 'begins with the inscription of the body in the order's text' and is articulated by an 'enunciatory focalization' where 'space becomes a practiced place'.

---

[3] A non-profit agency and largest funder of the voluntary sector and social services in Canada.

Spatial phronesis would thus engage with space theoretically, politically and experientially, and would offer another kind of spatiality: a kind de Certeau (1984: 93) would endorse that would entail an 'anthropological, poetic and mythic experience of space'.

Step 1. Learning Opportunities Grant: a political ethic of *progressive* rationalities?

In the wake of rapidly deteriorating conditions of schools during the past decade, the Learning Opportunities Grant (LOG) was established as a new system of funding for schools in dire need across the province of Ontario. Originally instituted in 1997 under the regime of Mike Harris' Progressive Conservative Party (1995–2002) and the rubric of the 'Common Sense Revolution', the rationalized educational restructuring model found itself in a dire state of 'crisis'. As Mackenzie's (2007: 5) genealogy on educational funding implemented during the Harris era demonstrates, the centralized funding formula implemented in 1997 provided much less than that which was required at all levels to fund the basic elements of the education system. He notes, first, that the formula provided less to school boards for teachers' salaries, yet the boards were mandated to maintain the salary levels stipulated by contractual agreements. Second, less money was provided to boards for school operations and maintenance. Third, adult secondary school credit courses were funded at only half the amount. Fourth, there were funding cutbacks for children in special education and children at risk. Fifth, local priorities were ignored. Last, but not least, Mackenzie notes, the formula provided less than half the amount under the LOG recommended by the expert panel convened to study programming for students at risk (2007: 6). The funding was driven primarily by enrolment levels causing inflexibility in the system, which led to inequitable and unreasonable demands for school closures across the province.

The LOG funding constituted a mere 1.41 per cent of the total budget (approximately $200 million, which was less than half the amount recommended by the task force). At this time four indicators were used based on the 1991 census including low income cut-off rates (LICO), low education, recent immigration and aboriginal status. In the final year of Progressive Conservative Party rule under Ernie Eves (2002–3), based on information retrieved from the 1996 census, the LOG had increased to 2.02 per cent. The increase was based primarily on the demographic component, with lone status included in the index calculated. With the defeat of the Progressive Conservatives, the Liberal government (2003–present) captured public opinion with its campaign and promise to include LOG investment in public education. By the end of 2006, the LOG had peaked at just over 3 per cent of the budget of over $500 million. Over the next few years, however, the LOG was reduced, and by 2009–10 had been brought down to 2.09 per cent ($414 million), of which $100 million was mostly used to cover the gap in funding for teachers' salaries.[4]

The ministry web site,[5] on the other hand, ensures the grant's maximum instrumental efficacy in that it purports that all school boards, whether falling under urban or rural jurisdictions, are eligible for LOG funding. Further, it claims that the funding will allow school boards to put in place a wide range of supports and programmes for students who come from disadvantaged socioeconomic backgrounds to improve the educational achievement of these students. The LOG incorporates three components into its model to determine the allocation of the funding: demographic; early literacy; and literacy and maths. The first component, and central to this chapter, is guided by 'community data on risk factors'. The *risk factors* included in this model are low family income, low parental education, recent immigration, and aboriginal status – foundational certainties, Foucault would argue, that guarantee the constitution of subjectivities through power relations. The ministry suggests that some of the programmes and services that boards may use to help these students include reading programmes, adapted curriculum, tutors, counsellors, mentoring, classroom assistants, before- and after-school programmes, homework clubs, breakfast and lunch programmes, and reduced class size. The second component focuses its resources on improving the early literacy of primary-level students with greatest need (junior kindergarten to grade 3). The third component focuses on students in grades 7–10. Additional resources provided by the LOG include summer school programmes, transportation aid and parental support. Other initiatives described provide numerous opportunities including:

- lower pupil/teacher ratios, educational assistants, adapted curriculum, extra tutors and expanded kindergartens;
- counsellors, social workers, early assessment, mentoring, orientation and life skills, parenting classes, home/school linkages, stay-in-school and school re-entry programmes;
- augmented literacy and numeracy programming, intensified remedial reading programmes and summer school programmes;

[4] Data kindly provided by Toronto Social Planning Council (March 2010).
[5] See: https://ozone.scholarsportal.info/html/1873/7560/10297220.htm, accessed 16 February 2010.

- breakfast/lunch programmes, extracurricular activities, before- and after-school programmes, and recreation and sports activities; and
- homework help, computer-aided instruction, arts and culture programmes and outdoor education.

The LOG as outlined above suggests a softer, more conducive form of neoliberal governance that is predicated on targeted and instrumental reasoning. Rhetorical persuasions aside, more realistically educational policies for the disadvantaged have been designed by neoliberal regimes to deflect the repercussions felt by a decade of systematic cutbacks to the system. Schram *et al.* (2009: 398) note that welfare policies for the poor have been redesigned in recent years to reflect the idea that the state has a legitimate interest in ensuring that socially marginal groups practise appropriate behaviours. 'New paternalist' welfare programmes, they argue, use a variety of incentives, surveillance mechanisms and restrictive rules to modify client behaviours (2009: 398). Yet the language and script of such progressive funding discourse readily filters into the dialogue of progress and change. Mackenzie's work through the Ontario Alternative Budget Working Group (1998) carefully traces the funding recourse that preceded the LOG. Mackenzie argues that despite government claims to be motivated by a concern for equity among students there is a widening gap between actual and adequate educational funding. The funding, he argues, has instead addressed the inadequacies for some students by imposing inadequacies on others. The total level of funding for education in Ontario, he notes, was insufficient to ensure an adequate level of resources for all students. Further, the funding formula evolved into thirty-four separate grant components that were inextricably more complicated. Mackenzie notes, for example, that for the LOG (one component of the larger fund) the total amount allocated is already far short of what is required. How these funds are then used and distributed by the school boards across the province is regionally contingent.

Step 2. From the province to the board: Toronto Model Inner City School Initiative – quarantining geographies of 'risk'

Neoliberal regimes are deeply contradictory and these contradictions are increasingly evident in the education sector (Robertson and Dale 2002; Basu 2005; Hill 2009). Robertson and Dale (2002) note how states are faced with the dilemma about how best to manage these tensions and contradictions within the framework of political rationality itself. They identify two main elements of neoliberal governance or strategies where local states of emergency are created: states of *neoliberal localisms*. First, there is an exercise in decentralization, where there is greater responsiveness to the needs of the intended recipients and a fragmentation in the provision of services. Second, a marketized culture is created between schools that draws institutions and workers into competition with each other. Polarization of school populations along social class lines results in some schools experiencing *delocalization* (usually among successful schools), while others experience *intensified localization* (usually among unpopular schools). As a result of neoliberal policies over the years, schools have suffered a great depletion of resources and some areas have been rendered less capable of responding to problems and risk from their own resources. As Robertson and Dale note, the solutions therefore need to be isolated and quarantined in order to differentiate them from the mainstream and avoid any possibility of further 'backsliding'. By quarantining the problems within the system, rather than quarantining the structural problems, makes the management of poverty amenable for neoliberal regimes to promote a 'softer and more compassionate' state of governing affairs. These, they note, are not strategies to be applied across school boards and must be managed within a frame separate from the hegemony of neoliberalism.

Translating the LOG to individual school boards is regionally contingent, based on the way the funds are allocated locally. In Toronto, the Model Inner City School Initiative was undertaken as one response to the funding received from the LOG. 'Inner City Schools' (not necessarily an inner city phenomenon, but interestingly a term that is still of rhetorical relevance in the collective imagination of the school board) are identified by the Toronto District School Board (TDSB) as schools with a large concentration of students living in poverty. In November 2004, the TDSB established a task force with a mandate to identify up to five inner city elementary schools based on criteria presented in research and to look carefully at resources already in the community. The vision of the task force was to achieve fairness and equity, establish schools as the heart of the community, build an exclusive culture, and establish high educational expectations; in other words, to promote the ideal school-self as enterprise. The funding of such a school would include $1.03 million based on a selection criteria and advice of the task force. The task force identified seven inner city neighbourhoods in Toronto, based on United Way's *Poverty by Postal Code* Report and the TDSB Learning Opportunities Index, which is based primarily on test scores of individual schools. By 2006–7, approximately $125 million or 5 per cent of the money allocated from the LOG for the TDSB went to fund the first three participating schools. In the second phase, five more schools were funded.

Step 3. From spatial fixity to spatial phronesis: transforming space theoretically, politically and experientially

The selection process is a spatial process, and, as I will argue, an inherently contradictory one in the way that school spaces are transformed from an object of analysis (spatial fixity) to ascertain an agency of its own (spatial phronesis). This transformative nature of spatial phronesis is outlined below.

The task force is guided by a methodology that constructs poverty cluster maps in the city: a neoliberal technique of creating 'equality within inequality' (Fiedler 2011). The geographic data are drawn from seven sources, including: results from poor test scores based on the learning opportunities index; *Poverty by Postal Code: The Geography of Neighbourhood Poverty, 1981–1991*, prepared by United Way and the Canadian Council on Social Development; and the *Strong Neighbourhoods* Task Force Report, prepared by United Way of Greater Toronto in cooperation with the city of Toronto, members of the provincial and federal levels of government and the private sector. In Toronto, as discussed earlier, reports on sociospatial polarization, such as *Poverty by Postal Code* and *Strong Neighbourhoods*, have become guiding doctrines for poverty recognition and alleviation. Localized spaces of poverty and marginality in such documents are efficiently identified and labelled as 'at risk' and 'priority areas' where resources and opportunities to support the needs of the most vulnerable populations should be directed. Robertson and Dale (2002) note that these 'zones of emergency' are particular types of rupture that require more systematic interventions by the state. The Model Inner City School Initiative draws on these reports to replicate the spaces of vulnerability.

There are a number of critiques and cautionary tales that must also be brought to the forefront of these discussions. First, despite the reformist language of progress and change, the danger presented in the 're-and-continual' representation of poverty and displacement through such mapping discourse results in a particular and powerful form of spatial fetishism. Spatial identities of poverty, displacement, marginality and 'risk' become inscribed into the landscape and its people – *willingly or not.* The objective scientific rationale of the view from afar triumphs the subjective agency and experiential understandings and meanings of place. Second, and as argued earlier, the focus and broader debate is quickly diverted into best practices of identification and policy fixes, rather than the underlying structural reasons of deficiency. Consequently, the spatial unevenness caused by decades of neoliberal clawbacks and change is ameliorated through neighbourhood branding and labelling of school communities. Such discursive framing inherently involves reconceptualizing how communities and cities are understood, how schools and communities are thereby represented, and how these relations become deeply embedded in the terrain of social policy discourse. As Robertson and Dale note, these frames must be managed separately from the hegemony of neoliberal dictates in order to compensate for market failures and market inadequacies. In other words, the state must intervene, *but* not in a way that undermines the premise of neoliberalism. Finally, as Swyngedouw (2009) argues, the discourse produced in such a way annuls the proper political moment and contributes to the emergence and consolidation of a post-political and post-democratic condition.

Yet through acts of spatial phronesis these limitations and static understandings of space can be ameliorated and even transgressed. Thinking through such mapping processes critically and ontogenetically within an ethic of discomfort, the following section demonstrates how static understandings become fluid: the singular perspective becomes multiple; the apolitical viewpoint becomes political; and, ideally, the reformist agenda becomes radical. This exercise of spatial phronesis originated within the community of schools themselves, though *paradoxically* within the competitive framework of the neoliberal model itself. As the following section demonstrates, despite its representational reproductions as 'at risk' communities, simultaneous contestations were taking place negating those perceptions.

Localized consultation: towards spatial phronesis

In December 2006, I was invited to participate in the Inner City Model School Initiative. The two-month process involved visiting a number of schools in specific clusters of the city to determine the allocation of a large sum of money for its further development. Four cluster teams were established in this phase of the project, with seven members in each cluster. The consultation process itself involved a number of practitioners who were associated with the school board, community groups and university, but primarily from the education sector, determined to improve the deteriorating conditions and low morale affecting their school community and beyond. Five schools were included in each cluster and on the recommendation of the team, in consultation with the board, *only one school* would be eligible to receive the model school funding of $1 million. It is important to note at this point that only schools that had actively had the time to draft detailed proposals were included in the selection process. Thus, proactive principals who were able to mobilize their local

Table 13.1 *Inner City Model School Initiative*

	School A	School B	School C	School D
Demographics	677 students. Thirty different language groups. 89% primary language other than English.	666 students. Thirty different language groups. 85% primary language other than English.	243 students. 74% primary language other than English.	387 students. 91% primary language other than English.
School programmes	Special needs with ESL resource reception area. Resource teacher for each grade. Learning disability teacher. SEPT. KELI. Welcome to kindergarten. Three reading recovery teachers. Curriculum cafes twice a month for teacher PD. Curricular enhancement. Leadership development (DPA leaders, lunch monitors). Safe and caring schools (Eco schools, TPS liaison officer). Equity initiatives (anti-racist education, Equity Committee). Student success programmes (Later Literacy, Reading Recovery).	Storie Wing with five specialized classrooms for students with developmental disabilities, including a Snoezelen Room. SEPT. Model Schools for Inner Cities Cluster. KELI. Welcome to kindergarten. Nutrition programme. Peer mediation. Second Step. Equity initiatives.	Outdoor classroom: Millennium Garden. Gold Eco schools certification. School-wide equity initiatives. Remedial numeracy and literacy activities. Leadership development programmes. Safe and caring schools programmes. Curricular enhancement programmes. Special education (intensive support behavioural programmes).	Welcome to kindergarten. Member of Toronto Schools on the Move. Safe and caring schools programmes (Let's Stop Bullying, Safe Arrival Programme). Snack programme. Social skills programmes (Adopt a Grandparent, Social Skills Group). Early reading intervention. Reading recovery. Curricular enhancement programmes (Borrow a Book, Scientists in School).

Community links	School is open seven days a week to outside groups (piano lessons, Tai Chi, a Pentecostal church). Liaison with Toronto Public Health, Toronto Parks and Recreation, Parkway Forest Daycare, Dairy Farmers of Ontario.	Houses YMCA Before and After School programme. School open to community groups (adult ESL, sports activities, international language classes). Programmes with Toronto Public Library, Toronto Public Health, Toronto Police Services, Parks and Forestry.	YMCA Before and After School programme. Basketball 4 Life programme. Partnership with local high school that helps with Homework Club, Student Leadership Council and coop placements. Big Brothers and Big Sisters in school mentoring.	Grandparents programme established between S. Lodge and grade 5 class. Visits to library. Support for and from Community Services. After School programme.
Clubs and co-curriculars	Twenty-nine clubs and co-curriculars. Seven athletics teams.	Fourteen clubs and co-curriculars. Four athletics teams.	Twelve clubs and co-curriculars. Eight athletics teams.	Thirty clubs and co-curriculars. Thirteen athletics teams and intramural events. Participates in maths and speech competitions.
Parent involvement	Parent volunteers at information centre and in classrooms. Parent 'experts' for planning celebrations unit. 'Parents and Partners' evening in each grade. Evening parenting courses.	School Council meetings. Parent volunteers in classrooms and on excursions. Daily nutrition programme uses parent volunteers. Monthly workshops for parents.	Twice weekly early years drop in programme for parents. Volunteers in library, classrooms and snack programme. Families participate in Family Maths, Literacy Night, Family Fitness Night and Science Night.	Volunteers in classrooms and library. Participates in Community cafe. Parenting programmes put on by Community agencies (like SEPT).

community and teachers were critical in initiating the process. This was the difficult exercise of choice, where each school was equally deserving of the grant, but due to budget constraints and the politics of targeted-funding only one school would be eligible to access the grant. In order to assist the Cluster Team members to gather information in a consistent way and report on key findings, a list of guidelines was recommended by the evaluators. These included two main sections:

(A) Existing conditions/needs:
- general characteristics of the school;
- parent/caregiver/family involvement;
- community links; and
- strengths and challenges of the school community.

(B) Potential for becoming a successful model school as indicated by:
- the school's vision;
- the school's readiness to embrace the project;
- indicators of commitment to the five Inner City Model School essential components; and
- proposal preparation process.

Despite the labelling of schools and the challenges faced by decades of cutbacks, all the schools presented creative and alternative ideas for radical reformulations and personal visions for change. The summaries of these rich details (tangible and intangible resources) are briefly outlined in Table 13.1. Within a context of multicultural diversity where over 80 per cent of students speak a primary language other than English, the schools were in dire need of maintaining and further building settlement programmes, English as a Second Language programmes and support services. Breakfast programmes, outreach to libraries and senior homes and reading recovery programmes were fostered by the principals and through a network of engaged and committed social service agencies. Parental participation was also a key element in the determining process, and this proved to be a complex and contradictory procedure. Parents with minimum language skills might have felt reticent to participate, or might not have had the time to volunteer based on their work schedules, yet the Model School Initiative and selection criteria largely depended on an active participatory parent body. In other words, for the first phase to be successful for the rationalization and success of the programme, the school's earlier initiative and accomplishments were integral. Being labelled as a neighbourhood at risk, on the one hand, but with an active social and cultural capital community context, on the other hand, would work in tandem.

During the consultation process, a deep phronetic understanding of space (both its challenges and strengths) was conveyed by residents and supporters to a broader audience. The pressing need to build on more local resources, they argued, would allow schools to provide more equitable opportunities from a level playing field (such as ESL classes, special educational opportunities, breakfast programmes, after-school recreational and homework clubs). These were emphasized as essential components of a public education system and necessary for transformative change. The detailed narratives and engagements (such as described in Table 13.1) illustrate the lived experience and complex everydayness that escape the normal route of analysis portrayed by the poverty cluster maps with which they had so clearly been identified. Instead, alternative phronetic mappings were collectively produced using *their* collective spatial knowledge, which in turn aided much critical discussion. These strong emotive connections to place through cross-cultural alliances and friendships re-envisioned these places in alternative ways, thus producing alternative cartographic engagements. A deep sense of place and belonging textured the maps in new and innovative ways, which in turn were able to challenge the dominant representations of their neighbourhoods. For example, spatial claims were made through local narratives that changed preconceived meanings. Further, these discussions ruptured incomplete and biased understandings of their communities and allowed for comparative discussions *across the board* (and city) to take place (discussed further below). This collusion of abstract space (formulated by the planners through mapping indices), representational space (by the communities, evaluators and residents), and lived space (by the residents' and teachers' understandings of the school spaces), provided interesting collations and contradictions of understandings. Providing a fertile ground for political consciousness could later be cultivated for much needed social and political change. These initial seedlings of the Model School Initiative were later used as poster cases for further funding initiatives.

Why phronesis? As Flyvbjerg (2001) has argued, phronesis allows practical wisdom, intuitive knowledge and dialogical perspectives to thrive. The multiplicity of viewpoints are meshed together to form new power–knowledge relations. *Why then is spatial phronesis critical within this context?* Imbued with this kind of knowledge, space comes alive with lived reality and transformative action is a possibility, especially when structural inequities become more transparent. For example, during our discussions we frequently reverted to drawing on a number of 'ontogenetic' maps (see Kitchin and Dodge 2007) and alternative GIS outputs (more locally specific, less aggregated and comparative) that we had produced to contextualize the discussion further through the exercise of spatial phronesis. As I have argued earlier (Basu 2009), this tacking back and forth – *the blending of scientific/GIS and phronetic reasoning* – from the micro-localized merging of voices, experiences, data, maps/counter-maps and stories, strategies, charismatic leaders and politics, along with a theoretical and practical understanding of the wider neoliberal process of rational decision-making itself, cumulatively built from previous years of research and theoretical understandings, led to a much more complicated, textured and deeper understanding of how the complex process of neoliberalization produces educational spaces, states and subjects in various and contradictory ways. This is a research process, as Richard Bernstein (1982) notes, which builds towards all moments of the single process of understanding. In this particular case study, spatial phronesis – exemplified through value rationality, practical rationality and dialogical voices – was consciously allowed to thrive through the voices of practical experience, commitment, passion and political wisdom of the various individuals and groups involved in the process. Yet it imbued (and was in turn imbued by) the relational and fluid process of critical GIS: with *power relations as its central concern* in contextualizing and grounding inner city school realities. As de Certeau (1984) notes, these intertwined paths give their shape to spaces as they weave places together. Flyvbjerg (2001) argues that phronesis is marginalized in the intellectual scheme of things in current research, as scientific and technological development often takes place without ethical checks and balances. The justification of such arguments is of increasing relevance in the critique of the larger project of neoliberalism. Neoliberalism's emphasis on instrumental rationality as a governmental technology rather than value rationality is apparent and well documented.

Thus, spatial phronesis as a transformative methodology that is engaged in practical wisdom, reflexive practices, hidden knowledge and unorthodox sources, combined with the contextual, fluid and even emotive dimensionality of a critical and community-engaged GIS, provides a useful starting point in understanding the structural barriers in place and develops a sensitivity to the political and ethical implications involved in the conflicting spaces of education (Basu 2009). This study of concrete, materialized, spatial negotiations through which individual and collective subjectivities are constituted by means of the art of spatial phronesis dispels neoliberal abstractions and hard fixities inscribed in the city and replaces it with a more textured understanding of its everyday practices and peoples. As Rose notes:

therefore the question of the state that was central to earlier investigations of political power is relocated – simply as one element whose functionality is historically specific and contextually variable in multiple circuits of power, connecting a diversity of authorities and forces, within a whole variety of complex assemblages. (1999: 5)

Yet the battles to maintain resources and grants and build on the strengths of the community with dwindling resources remain. The LOG money used by the boards for the benefit of other vulnerable schools must maintain care and tread carefully to avoid the public perception that it has not been well spent by an undeserving class, lest it irk a middle-class neoliberal sensibility. Acutely aware of this political dilemma, especially among long-standing members with a well-honed phronetic wisdom of the educational negotiating process, the initiators of this programme face a fine balancing act. Gathering wider public support, producing informed statistical analysis and accessible reports, outreach programmes and media communications, the success stories of the schools over the three-year period of the initiative are now being celebrated and publicized by the community. The increased test scores, decline in drop-out rates, better attendance and increased parental participation are acknowledged indicators of success that the neoliberal state cannot contest. Such strategies justify the continual maintenance and provide the basis to rally for increased funding from the province and boards. Yet, at the same time, programmes and resources for middle-class parents must not fall from the radar of wider public perception. Rationing the rationed is a fine balancing act of politicking within the neoliberal state.

Conclusion

Neoliberal governmentality entails a particular kind of spatiality; that is, governing at a distance. Governmental technologies of power, such as the carving out of spaces of poverty as a disciplining exercise, help construct a particular kind of neoliberal subjectivity. As Leitner, Peck and Shephard (2007) have noted, neoliberal programmes are rarely imposed in a pure form; rather, they are always introduced within politico-institutional contexts that have been moulded significantly by earlier regulatory arrangements, institutional practices and political compromises. Graham (2005: 564) argues that software codes actively shape and structure geographical inequalities within and between places in a wide variety of ways, and states that 'these are particular topological spaces within sociotechnical systems through which actors have to "pass" in order that the system actually functions in the way that dominant actors desire' (2005: 565).

As argued in this chapter, reports such as *Poverty by Postal Code* and *Strong Neighbourhoods*, which have become guiding doctrines for poverty recognition and alleviation, are also epistemic discussions abstracted from everyday realities. Localized spaces of poverty and marginality in such documents, which are efficiently identified and labelled as 'at risk' and 'priority areas' where resources and opportunities to support the needs of the most vulnerable populations should be directed, simultaneously become spaces of surveillance and spectacle. But most importantly, despite its progressive and pragmatic discourse, attention is strategically diverted from underlying structural factors and the neoliberal strategies that had led to such conditions in the first place. Instead, attention is focused on measuring and labelling communities that have failed, as well as on the further sifting and sorting of vulnerabilities depending on indices that change and mutate from census year to census year. Placing in or out of these categorizations then becomes a game of rationing the rationed. Neighbourhood identities very rapidly translate into the politics of stigmatization, individuation and stern accountability: neoliberal strategies and technologies that shape, guide and direct what Foucault would refer to as the 'conduct of conduct' (Rose 1999). Yet this form of policy reform, which is readily received by social planning and general public discourse, lacks a fundamental critical dimension in the process of its formulation. The redistributive system, a process with predetermined outcomes, very rapidly develops into a strategy of geosurveillance that relies on scientific rational planning models.

At the beginning of the chapter we asked the question: how can the techniques of identification reflect a spatially contingent redistributive justice system that can coherently combine with the social politics of equality? This chapter provides a case study for spatial phronesis as a transformative methodology that builds into its foundations a critical spatial dimension and relational dynamics. Using the case study of the Model Inner City School Initiative adopted by the Toronto District School Board in 2006–7, the logics, politics and ethics of a redistributional funding allocation process was traced and explored. Spatial phronesis allowed for the collusion of space, where the abstract, utilitarian and epistemological space of the planners, negotiated through the representational space of the school workers and lived space of the community residents themselves, produced a more holistic understanding of the everydayness of the model inner city school experience. Using the preordained space that was constructed as a normalizing and abnormalizing device through the reification of neighbourhood profiles, some myths were dispelled, others emphasized, and yet others negated through the social and political game of the evaluation process. As Brenner and Theodore (2002) have argued, the effects of neoliberalism must be understood in contextually specific ways, as neoliberalism reproduces and intensifies uneven spatial development within and between cities using space as its privileged instrument. The act of spatial phronesis, as an ideological transformation with its inherent understanding of the tensions, conflicts and contradictions within the game of neoliberal practices, is able to disrupt these strategies of political economic restructuring by allowing the emotive and political to intercept through its value rationality (rather than instrumental rationality), practical rationality (rather than static and fixated rationality) and dialogical significance (rather than a hegemonic neoliberal discourse) with *power relations at the centre of all analysis*. Neoliberalism reframes power in insidious ways and the act of politicking through strategies of spatial phronesis attempts to illustrate the negotiation through this process in variegated ways. As planners, academics and activists, spatial phronesis builds into our ethics of discomfort – it helps us gain a phronetical understanding of space that intimately reflects space as dialogical, symbolic and value laden rather than rational, detached and representational – and as Foucault (1994b) would heed us, 'ascertaining the possibility of constituting a new politics of truth'.

REFERENCES

Basu, R. 2005. 'Geo-surveillance through the Mapping of "Test" Results: An Ethical Dilemma or Public Policy Solution?', *ACME: An International E-journal for Critical Geographies* 3: 87–111.

2009. 'Phronesis through GIS: Exploring Political Spaces of Education', *Professional Geographer* 61: 481–92.

Bernstein, R. 1982. 'From Hermeneutics to Praxis', *The Review of Metaphysics* 35: 823–45.

Brenner, N. and Theodore, N. 2002. 'Preface: From the "New Localism" to the Spaces of Neoliberalism', *Antipode* 34: 341–7.

Certeau, M. de 2002. *The Practice of Everyday Life*. Berkeley, CA: University of California Press.

Crampton, J. W. 2003. 'Cartographic Rationality and the Politics of Geosurveillance and Security', *Cartography and Geographic Information Science* 30: 135–48.

2004. 'GIS and Geographic Governance', *Cartographica* 39: 41–53.

Fiedler, R. S. 2011. 'The Representational Challenge of the In-between', in D. Young, P. Burke Wood and R. Keil (eds.), *Between Infrastructure: Urban Connectivity in an Age of Vulnerability*. Praxis (e)Press, Critical Topographies Series, e-edition, available at: www.praxis-epress.org/availablebooks/inbetween.html.

Flyvbjerg, B. 2001. *Making Social Science Matter: Why Social Inquiry Fails and How it can Succeed Again*. Cambridge University Press.

2004. 'Phronetic Planning Research: Theoretical and Methodological Reflections', *Planning Theory and Practice* 5: 283–306.

Foucault, M. 1994a. 'For an Ethic of Discomfort', in *Power*, eds. J. D. Faubion and P. Rabinow. New York: The New Press.

1994b. 'Truth and Power', in *Power*, eds. J. D. Faubion and P. Rabinow. New York: The New Press.

Goss, J. 1995. 'We Know Who You Are and We Know Where You Live: The Instrumental Rationality of Geodemographic Systems', *Economic Geography* 71: 171–98.

Graham, S. 2005. 'Software-sorted Geographies', *Progress in Human Geography* 29: 562–80.

Hill, D. 2009. *The Rich World and the Impoverishment of Education: Diminishing Democracy, Equity and Worker's Rights*. New York: Routledge.

Joyce, P. 2003. *The Rule of Freedom: Liberalism and the Modern City*. London: Verso.

Kitchin, R. and Dodge, M. 2007. 'Rethinking Maps', *Progress in Human Geography* 3: 331–44.

Kwan, M. P. 2002. 'Feminist Visualization: Re-envisioning GIS as a Method in Feminist Geographic Research', *Annals of the Association of American Geographers* 92: 645–61.

Lefebvre, H. 1991. *The Production of Space*. Oxford: Blackwell.

Leitner, H., Peck, J. and Shephard, E. S. (eds.) 2007. *Contesting Neoliberalism: Urban Frontiers*. New York: Guilford Press.

Mackenzie, H. 2007. 'Missing the Mark: how Ontario's Education Funding Formula is Shortchanging Students', Canadian Centre for Policy Alternatives, Ontario.

McLafferty, S. 2004. 'The Socialization of GIS', *Cartographica* 39: 51–3.

Miron, J. R. 1998. 'Causal Model Building and Analysis using GIS', paper presented at the 38th European Congress of the Regional Science Association in Vienna, Austria, 31 August 1998. Paper available from author.

Pickles, J. 1995. *Ground Truth*. New York: Guilford.

Robertson, S. L. and Dale, R. 2002. 'Local States of Emergency: The Contradictions of Neo-liberal Governance in Education in New Zealand', *British Journal of Sociology of Education* 23: 463–82.

Rose, N. 1999. *Powers of Freedom: Reframing Political Thought*. Cambridge University Press.

Schram, S. F., Soss, J., Fording, R. C. and Houser, L. 2009. 'Deciding to Discipline: A Multi-method Study of Race, Choice, and Punishment at the Frontlines of Welfare Reform', *American Sociological Review* 74: 398–422.

Schuurman, N. 2000. 'Trouble in the Heartland: GIS and its Critics in the 1990s', *Progress in Human Geography* 24: 569–90.

Sieber, R. 2003. 'Public Participation GIS Across Borders', *The Canadian Geographer* 47: 50–61.

Smith, N. 1992. 'History and Philosophy of Geography: Real Wars, Theory Wars', *Progress in Human Geography* 16: 257–71.

Swyngedouw, E. 2009. 'The Antimonies of the Postpolitical City: In Search of a Democratic Politics of Environmental Production', *International Journal of Urban and Regional Research* 33(3): 601–20.

14 Important next steps in phronetic social science

Bent Flyvbjerg, Todd Landman and Sanford Schram

Applied phronesis

The term 'phronetic social science' was coined in *Making Social Science Matter* (Flyvbjerg 2001). However, as pointed out in that volume and by Schram (2006), phronetic social science existed well before this particular articulation of the concept, but it was just not organized, recognized or named as such. Rather, it occurred here and there as scholars had adopted phronesis-like methods for their own purposes. The present title is the first organized volume of empirical–practical work in phronetic social science. Before *Making Social Science Matter*, phronesis, as a critical term of Aristotelian philosophy, had been theorized and its continuing importance as a key concept in Western thought had been convincingly argued by distinguished philosophers like Hans Georg Gadamer, Hannah Arendt, Alasdair MacIntyre and Richard J. Bernstein, among others. But no one had developed the theory and philosophy of phronesis into a practical methodology that could be applied by researchers interested in actually practising a phronetic social science. *Making Social Science Matter* developed such a methodology. Its implications were discussed and developed further in *Making Political Science Matter* (Schram and Caterino 2006). After these two theoretical–methodological contributions, it was evident that an important next step in demonstrating the usefulness of phronetic social science would be to illustrate, with concrete examples, how applied phronesis works in practical, empirical social science research. The contributions on applied phronesis contained in the present volume make clear that this next step has now been taken.

We use the term 'applied' in this book with some reluctance and with a different meaning than is usual in the natural and social sciences, where it typically means applying theory that has been developed *a priori*. The conventional view holds that theory precedes action in a top-down movement, where one arrives at the right action by first choosing the right theory and then applying that theory properly to the practical question at hand; for example, like engineers applying the laws of physics to construct a bridge. Phronetic social scientists are sceptical of this view, at least as it pertains to social and political action, as such action requires a knowledge of context that is simply not accessible through theory alone. In phronetic social science, 'applied' means thinking about practice and action with a point of departure not in top-down, decontextualized theory and rules, but in 'bottom-up' contextual and action-oriented knowledge, teased out from the context and actions under study by asking and answering the value-rational questions that stand at the core of phronetic social science (Schram 1995). What is applied is not theory, but a philosophy of engagement that recognizes that phronesis is a skill and that *having* phronesis is iteratively dependent on *practising* phronesis, as emphasized by Frank in Chapter 4, above.

Phronetic social scientists are also sceptical of the type of expert-based, social engineering that typically follows from the practice-as-applied-theory point of view. Phronetic social scientists see such social engineering as not only problematic, but also as dangerous, since historically it has led to massive human suffering, especially when applied to large-scale social phenomena and ignoring what Scott (1998) calls *mētis* – local, practical knowledge. Instead of relying on social engineering and experts for social action, phronetic social scientists rely on public deliberation and the public sphere, not because these set-ups are perfect, but because they are the best we have for collective decision-making. From a phronetic perspective, social science works best not when it tries to give us the unrealizable perfection of expert knowledge, such as that which comes from abstract models, but instead when it strives for the 'adequation' of what works for any collective as it struggles to decide things for itself. In the public sphere, expert testimony – including the research results of phronetic social scientists – is explicitly seen as only one voice among many and as being balanced by other voices and other knowledge in deliberating about and acting on the specific social and political issues at hand.

The phronetic conception of social research returns social science to society and its politics, to concern itself with society's improvement and to enter into public dialogue and praxis, as observed by Schatzki (2006: 133). Each of the eight case studies presented above is an example of how this return to praxis may be carried out in actual research. Each study contains the type of grounded, contextual knowledge that may be used for making better decisions in the policy areas concerned, where 'better' is defined as being more inclusive of values and groups that are legitimate and pertinent to the issues at hand, but that may have been marginalized by other more powerful values and groups, had the former not achieved a voice through phronetic research.

Simmons writes in Chapter 12 above that, 'What is not as clear is the extent to which [*Making Social Science Matter*] is calling on social scientists to get involved and *do* politics in lieu of merely *studying* politics... To what extent is Flyvbjerg urging social scientists to be social and political beings, to strive to be, in Bourdieu's terms, virtuoso social actors?' (emphasis in original). Simmons rightly points out that for Aristotle phronesis as an intellectual virtue is not obtained by stepping back and contemplating reality from an objective distance, but comes from getting one's hands dirty by actively confronting the problems of the day. Aristotle's definition of phronesis as 'reason capable of action' means that phronetic research results ('reason') are results only to the extent that they have an impact on practice ('action'). Reason is made capable of action by effectively having reason enter practice; for instance, via the work on 'tension points' described below. The unequivocal answer to Simmons' question is therefore that the phronetic call to social scientists is exactly to become virtuoso social actors in their chosen field of study and to *do* politics with their research, as Bourdieu recommended and himself did, instead of writing yet another paper or book with little or no practical import. Phronetic social science challenges the current metric approach of measuring the impact of academic work by its citations in other academic work. Phronetic social science offers a way forward by showing that a more important type of impact exists for social science; namely, its impact on policy and practice. The case studies above demonstrate in detail how such impact may be achieved in practical phronetic research.

What the case studies show

Each case study is summarized in Chapter 1 and will not be further summarized here. Instead, we observe that seen as a whole the case studies show that:

- Claims made by theoreticians of phronetic social science that applied phronetic research is well suited for effectively influencing policy and practice are verified by the case studies.
- Phronetic research and phronetic impact are replicable across different problematics, geographies and time periods. If properly adapted to context the phronetic approach may therefore be used across the social sciences, in different countries and covering both contemporary and historical studies.
- Phronetic social science scales well. It is suitable both for the type of community study reported in Chapter 8 by Sandercock and Attili on racism in rural Canada and for more global concerns like those covered

in Chapter 10 by Olsen, Payne and Reiter in their worldwide study of transitional justice in emerging democracies. The focus on power in phronetic research also requires a scaling up from local micro-practices to the structural level, as pointed out by Eubanks in Chapter 11.

- Local problems have global import, when seen through the lens of phronetic social science, be they the fight over London Heathrow's third runway as analysed by Griggs and Howarth in Chapter 9, which pinpoints a growing global concern over economic growth versus the environment, or the design of a new curriculum for social justice and human rights at Arizona State University as described by Simmons in Chapter 12, which deals with the problem of how elitist university education may help empower disadvantaged groups.

- Phronetic research adds a 'bottom-up' perspective that can tilt a policy process most often dominated by experts towards alternative policy responses that are neglected, as described by Shdaimah and Stahl in Chapter 7 about the development of the Philadelphia Housing Trust Fund and an unexpected focus on low-income home repair.

- In societies governed by less than democratic institutions, phronesis is a way of making empirical research subversive by producing 'inconvenient' truths that challenge existing power relations, as seen in Chapter 3 by Landman on narrative analysis and Chapter 12 by Simmons on teaching social justice, in particular the attention to the complexities of the US–Mexican border.

- Problematization of 'tension points' is emerging from the case studies as a particularly important theme for phronetic research, because a focus on tension points appears to be especially effective in generating the type of change in policy and practice that is the hallmark of phronetic social science. We therefore conclude the book by taking a closer look at what tension points are and how researchers may work with them in phronetic social science.

Tension points in phronetic social science

The last finding is perhaps the most politically suggestive of our survey of current phronetic research projects. In phronetic research, tension points are power relations that are particularly susceptible to problematization and thus to change, because they are fraught with dubious practices, contestable knowledge and potential conflict. Thus, even a small challenge – like problematization from scholars – may tip the scales and trigger change in a tension point. It is interesting to note that each of the case studies presented above identifies important tension points and problematizes them in attempts to influence social and political action.

The focus on tension points was not orchestrated by the editors of the book or otherwise coordinated. We take this to mean that such a focus is intrinsic to applied phronetic social science. We explain the focus on tension points by the attention paid by phronetic researchers to issues of power and especially researchers' commitment to challenge the abuse of power.

Specifically, the following tension points were identified by the eight case studies:

- *Flyvbjerg*: more and larger megaprojects are being built versus the poor performance of projects.
- *Shdaimah and Stahl*: the American homeownership dream versus homeownership reality for low-income owners.
- *Sandercock and Attili*: First Nations (indigenous) Canadians versus modern settler society.
- *Griggs and Howarth*: economic growth versus environmental protection in aviation.
- *Olsen, Payne and Reiter*: transitional justice versus stability in emerging democracies.
- *Eubanks*: oppressive versus liberating uses of information technology for poor, working-class women.
- *Simmons*: elite university education versus the needs of marginalized communities.
- *Basu*: how techniques of social policy generate the very problems they were designed to solve.

As examples of dubious practices found in these tension points, consider Flyvbjerg's uncovering of the routine use of deceptive cost–benefit analyses, with falsely inflated benefits and falsely deflated costs, used to get megaprojects approved and funded (Chapter 6); or the attempt by the UK government to launch the concept 'sustainable aviation' – a godsend of an oxymoron for phronetic problematization – to justify airport expansions, as recounted by Griggs and Howarth (Chapter 9); or the overselling by the US federal government of the homeownership dream to low-income households, problematized by the research project in which Shdaimah and Stahl participated long before society at large caught on to just how destabilizing this policy would turn out to be for the global economy when the housing bubble burst in 2007–8 and the dream resurfaced as a nightmare of bad debt and foreclosures (Chapter 7).

As mentioned by Flyvbjerg in Chapter 6, problematizing tension points may be compared with hitting a rock with a hammer. If you hit the rock at random it seems unbreakable, even if you hit it hard. If you hit the rock strategically at the small, near invisible fault lines that most rocks have, the rock will fracture, even if you hit it gently. Tension points are the fault lines that phronetic researchers seek out; that is where researchers hit existing practices to make them come apart and create space for new and better ones, where 'better' is defined by the values of phronetic researchers and their reference groups (see below). Michel Foucault was a master at identifying and problematizing tension points, most notably in psychiatry, prisons and sexuality, but also in social welfare, architecture and urban planning. Foucault said that the purpose of problematizing the dubious social and political practices found in tension points is:

> precisely to bring it about that practitioners no longer know what to do, so that the acts, gestures, discourses that up until then had seemed to go without saying become problematic, difficult, dangerous. (Michel Foucault quoted in Miller 1993: 235)

In phronetic social science, and in the case studies above, the following three-step procedure is involved in working with tension points. For their specific field of interest, researchers strive to:

(1) actively identify dubious practices within policy and social action;
(2) undermine these practices through problematization; and
(3) constructively help to develop new and better practices.

As an example, consider the case study by Sandercock and Attili in Chapter 8. Here tension, problematization and action are evident already in the felicitous title of their study, 'Unsettling a settler society'. The dubious practice identified by the authors is the treatment of First Nations (indigenous) Canadians by non-native Canadians, the latter constituting modern settler society. The case study kicks off by describing an incident in 2000, when the municipality of Burns Lake shut off water and sewer services to a local First Nations reservation as part of a dispute over land and taxation. The authors show that such attempts by settler society at disenfranchising and disciplining First Nations is nothing new, it has been going on for almost two centuries of colonization and is happening in many places in Canada. It is mainly about expropriating land and it effectively undercuts the lives of First Nations and violates their human rights. The authors do not mince words when they describe settler practices as 'blatant racism' and the outcome of such practices as 'pure cultural genocide'. They then up the ante – and increase tension in an already highly tense tension point – by pointing out that Canada has a first-rate record of defending human rights abroad, but is evidently not very good at doing so at home for its own First Nations. We might add that the dubious practices pointed to by Sandercock and Attili are pertinent not only to Canada, but also to the United States, Australia,

Brazil, Denmark (Greenland), China (Tibet) and other societies that marginalize and violate the rights of indigenous people.

Next – after having identified and documented the dubious practices of settler society – Sandercock and Attili decided to try and undermine these practices through problematization. They resolved to present their research as a 'story which would hopefully unsettle the settler society'. For impact, their chosen medium was film used as digital ethnography, in addition to more conventional scholarly media like their chapter in the present book. The first showing of their film was for audiences at Burns Lake. The result was exactly as described by Foucault above, that 'the acts, gestures, discourses that up until then [the showing of the film] had seemed to go without saying bec[a]me problematic, difficult, dangerous'. The non-native mayor of Burns Lake described the film as 'difficult to watch' but 'important'. One of the native chiefs said that the film 'is not sugar-coated [but] we need a film like this to make the truth plain to see'. After the practices of settler society were exposed on the silver screen for all to see, it became clear that such practices could not be justified in twenty-first-century Canada. The film triggered the mayor to acknowledge past mistakes and there was general agreement that the community now had to move on to a different *modus operandi*.

Third, and finally, Sandercock and Attili explicitly saw it as part of their research to help to develop new and better practices to constructively replace the dubious ones uncovered through problematization. As phronetic researchers, they were not satisfied with simply identifying problems and analysing them; they also wanted to help to develop solutions and become 'actors in the flow of history, rather than bystanders', as they put it. The authors are explicit that it was tempting, and would have been easier, to make a pure advocacy film on behalf of First Nations, given the scale of historic injustices. But they felt that such a film might exacerbate the existing polarization, which was the last thing Burns Lake needed. Instead, what was required was 'healing across the cultural divide', in the words of the authors – across the tension point, in effect – and for this to happen dialogue was needed, not attack. How that dialogue was established and how it has affected people at Burns Lake – making one of the First Nations chiefs publicly bury his resentment, noting that he had previously given up on the town but was now filled with hope again – is the most inspirational part of Sandercock's and Attili's study. In many ways, they provide Foucauldian problematization better than Foucault by infusing it with a healthy dose of compassion and proaction, setting a high and meaningful standard for other phronetic researchers to follow. At the same time, Sandercock and Attili are clear that they must not delude themselves with the initial wave of enthusiasm and change they have triggered with their research. Lasting phronetic impact will likely take longer to establish, and the authors are committed to such impact and plan to go back and evaluate the results of their research periodically to ensure a durable contribution.

Sandercock and Attili seem to trust dialogue and consensus a bit more than some of the other authors in the book, including Flyvbjerg in Chapter 6, who warns that tension points might bite back at researchers and that conflict may be more characteristic of phronetic research than consensus, since phronetic research is power research. If phronetic research triggers change, it is likely to gain both friends and enemies for researchers, argues Flyvbjerg. If nobody is against a specific piece of phronetic research, it may be because the research is unimportant as regards its implications for practice. Consensus cannot be ruled out, Flyvbjerg concedes, but *a priori* it should be considered with caution, since power research shows that too often consensus is an illusion created by disregarding power, as in Habermasian discourse ethics or by marginalizing groups who are inconvenient to the supposed consensus (Flyvbjerg 2001: 104–9). Nevertheless, phronetic social science is sufficiently accommodating and experimental – scientific – to allow different views to exist and to decide between them on the basis of empirical test instead of on account of *a priori* normative assumptions. Whether consensus or conflict is more characteristic for phronetic research – or in which types of situations each best apply – is thus an open empirical question to be decided by further research.

Above we concluded that the phronetic approach can be used across different problematics and geographies. It should be remembered, however, that phronesis works on the basis of context-dependent knowledge and that therefore the approach must always be adapted to context. When a group of African scholars invited Flyvbjerg to teach them, on their home turf, how to do phronetic social science, he first used his Aalborg study as teaching material (Flyvbjerg 1998), because that was all he had available at the time. The reaction from his African colleagues was unequivocal: 'We'd get killed if we did this kind of research here [in Africa]!' Similarly, Landman, Simmons and Smith engaged in long-term human rights research methods training in China in which a cohort of Chinese academics identified substantive research questions that were in need of solid methodological solutions, well aware that 'human rights' are politically a highly controversial subject in China. In cases like these you adapt, needless to say. Different cultures and political regimes have different tolerance levels for how far scholars are allowed to go in identifying and problematizing tension points and dubious practices. In the relatively advanced democracies of northern Europe and North America, tolerance for such work is high and problematization and critique may even be encouraged as a way of improving democracy. In non-democratic societies and emerging democracies, tolerance is typically lower and critique may be seen as controversial or even criminal; for instance, in countries that see critique of their governments as attempts at undermining the state. Clearly, phronetic research must be adapted to such differences of context. In the African case, over a period of several years Flyvbjerg and his local colleagues developed phronetic research adapted to the local context, by developing local case studies. The impact on practice was even more profound than in the North, with enduring national policy changes for the management of land and water in an emerging democracy (Flyvbjerg 2001: 164–5; Lerise 2005; Nnkya 2008). In the Chinese case, by putting method first and having the Chinese define the content of the human rights issues they wanted to work on, the programme remained politically 'neutral' while building capacity and challenging dominant institutions and culture in China. 'Methods' became a subversive tool to enter into China to conduct human rights research, and the results of the different analyses provided a number of inconvenient facts that went beyond opinion and advocacy in addressing significant areas in need of redress by Chinese authorities (Landman, Simmons and Smith 2010).

It should also be noted that the normative basis for applied phronesis, and for problematizing tension points, is the attitude among those who problematize and act, and this attitude is not based on idiosyncratic moral or personal preferences, but on a context-dependent common world view and interests among a reference group, well aware that different groups typically have different world views and different interests, and that there exists no general principle by which all differences can be resolved, no view from nowhere. For phronetic social scientists, the socially and historically conditioned context, and not fictive universals, constitutes the most effective bulwark against relativism and nihilism and is the best basis for action. Our sociality and history is the only foundation we have, the only solid ground under our feet. And this sociohistorical foundation is fully adequate: it is the foundation that makes the adequation of phronetic social science an important resource for democratic deliberation about shared concerns.

Flyvbjerg, for example, in his work on megaprojects and city management, defines his reference group as people who champion the values and rules that citizens and parliaments of democratic societies have decided should apply to governance, truth, ethics, economics, the environment, safety, social affairs and so on – as opposed to bending and misusing these values and rules to serve special interests. The latter is what usually happens, and what problematization uncovers again and again, as documented by the case studies above. Flyvbjerg deliberately defines the normative and social basis for his work this widely, and this uncontroversially, in order to make it as difficult as possible for those opposed to his work to topple it on grounds of idiosyncrasy. The strategy of Sandercock and Attili seems similar, but other reference groups and values are possible for other phronetic research with other purposes, needless to say, as illustrated by Eubanks (Chapter 11), Simmons (Chapter 12) and Basu (Chapter 13) above.

For people who take democracy and scholarship seriously – and phronetic social scientists typically do – problematization of tension points is among the finest and most productive things one can do. Open and constant critique is the core mechanism for making the age-old institutions of democracy and scholarship work, and such critique must be constantly practised to keep these institutions effective and improving, as pointed out by social thinkers as different as Socrates, Karl Popper and Pierre Bourdieu. Those who practise such critique are part of a millennia-long project that, although it has had its setbacks and is not perfect by any means, is remarkably successful. In our view, then, the future for phronetic research is very bright indeed.

Important next steps

As a way of closing, we see the following important next steps in phronetic social science, directed at consolidating and further developing this particular approach to social science research:

- Further theorizing and teasing out of methodological lessons from the case studies presented above: for instance, regarding similarities and differences between the case studies; what does and does not work well, theoretically and methodologically, in and across cases; and a comparative study across cases of how phronetic impact is achieved most effectively.
- Clarification of similarities and differences between phronetic social science and other types of social science research. A key question would be, where is phronetic social science uniquely 'phronetic', and where does it overlap with other types of social science, for instance, policy research, action research and collaborative research?
- Exploration of the subpolitical 'dark power' identified by Luke (2006: 267), that is, the real rationalities at work in actual governance, public and private, as opposed to the 'light power' of the state, civil society and markets studied by conventional social science. Flyvbjerg (1996) and Yiftachel (1998) have pioneered this type of work in planning

research. Linstead, Maréchal and Griffin (forthcoming) have similar work underway in organization research.

- Using phronetic social science as a subversion of dominant practices within democratic and non-democratic countries, where empirical research and the methods that underpin them provide a lever for uncovering inconvenient facts whose articulation can bring about positive change.
- Further research on 'tension points'. As mentioned above, the case studies show that a focus on tension points appears to be particularly productive in triggering social and political change with phronetic social science. We should therefore try to refine our understanding of how tension points work and how we may best study them. As a general rule of thumb, the tension between what is *said* and what is *done* in specific policy areas forms an excellent point of departure for phronetic research, because it gets us straight to the rationality–power nexus and to issues of accountability. At present, the following are obvious tension points, but many more less conspicuous ones exist: economic growth versus climate change; authoritative versus democratic governance; globalization versus localized social and economic life; what corporations say about social and environmental corporate responsibility and what they actually do; human rights violations; and tensions in the global financial system. For the latter, it is interesting to note that one of the most outspoken critics of the global financial system, Nassim Taleb, recently found it pertinent to develop explicit 'phronetic rules' to increase robustness and avoid repetition of the type of global financial disaster seen in 2007–9 (Taleb 2010: 370). Thus, phronetic social science is finding its way into finance in addition to many other areas of social science.
- Further clarification of a number of tenacious misunderstandings about phronetic social science, including, but not necessarily limited to: phronetic social science is less insistent on strong methodology and strong validity than other social science; relativism is more of an issue for phronetic research than for other research; the fact–value dichotomy has special import and consequences for phronetic social science compared with other social sciences; phronetic social science must take the point of view of marginalized communities; phronetic social science is action research or collaborative research; phronetic social science is at odds with action research and collaborative research. A common misunderstanding about phronetic social science that should finally have been laid to rest with Chapters 2 and 3 by Schram and Landman above is that the widespread and recommended use of narrative and case study research in phronetic social science renders it a qualitative

methodology. Schram and Landman demonstrate that this is not the case, as does Flyvbjerg (2001, 2006: 57–60).

- Implementation of more phronetic case studies aimed at impacting policy and practice, and at generating material for further theorizing of phronetic social science.

Social science is at a critical juncture. The momentum lies with alternatives to the dominant scientistic social science that unreflectively seeks to apply the models of the natural sciences to the social world. The foregoing chapters amply demonstrate the power of a phronetic social science to contribute to the revitalization of democratized public decision-making. The future is open to connecting research to policy-making in ways that prior configurations only imagined. Now those dreams can become reality, but not in some grandiose vision of the abstract modellers who reduce social relations to causal relationships between variables, but in more contextually sensitive ways, case by case, here and now, as citizens and publics allow – and as researchers respond. The challenge is whether they will. The researchers whose work is presented in this book have responded in compelling ways. We await the responses of others.

REFERENCES

Flyvbjerg, Bent 1996. 'The Dark Side of Planning: Rationality and *Realrationalität*', in S. Mandelbaum, L. Mazza and R. Burchell (eds.), *Explorations in Planning Theory*. New Brunswick, NJ: Center for Urban Policy Research Press, pp. 383–94.
  1998. *Rationality and Power: Democracy in Practice*. University of Chicago Press.
  2001. *Making Social Science Matter: Why Social Inquiry Fails and How it can Succeed Again*. Cambridge University Press.
  2006. 'A Perestroikan Straw Man Answers Back: David Laitin and Phronetic Political Science', in Schram and Caterino (eds.), *Making Political Science Matter*, pp. 56–85.
Landman, Todd, Simmons, Paul W. and Smith, Rhona 2010. *Human Rights in Our Time: Multidisciplinary Perspectives*. Beijing: China Legal Publishing House.
Lerise, Fred S. 2005. *Politics in Land and Water Use Management: Study in Kilimanjaro, Tanzania*. Dar es Salaam: Mkuki na Nyota Publishers.
Linstead, Stephen A., Maréchal, Garance and Griffin, Ricky W. (eds.), forthcoming. 'The Dark Side of Organization', special issue of *Organization Studies*.
Luke, Timothy W. 2006. 'Finding New Mainstreams: Perestroika, Phronesis, and Political Science in the United States', in Schram and Caterino (eds.), *Making Political Science Matter*, pp. 252–68.
Miller, James 1993. *The Passion of Michel Foucault*. New York: Simon & Schuster.
Nnkya, Tumsifu J. 2008. *Why Planning Does Not Work: Land-use Planning and Residents Rights in Tanzania*. Dar es Salaam: Mkuki na Nyota Publishers.

Schatzki, Theodore 2006. 'Social Science in Society', in Schram and Caterino (eds.), *Making Political Science Matter*, pp. 117–33.

Schram, Sanford F. 1995. *Words of Welfare: The Poverty of Social Science and the Social Science of Poverty*. Minneapolis, MN: University of Minnesota Press.

2006. 'Return to Politics: Perestroika, Phronesis, and Post-paradigmatic Political Science', in Schram and Caterino (eds.), *Making Political Science Matter*, pp. 17–32.

Schram, Sanford F. and Caterino, Brian (eds.) 2006. *Making Political Science Matter: Debating Knowledge, Research, and Method*. New York University Press.

Scott, James C. 1998. *Seeing Like a State: How Certain Schemes to Improve the Human Condition Have Failed*. New Haven, CT: Yale University Press.

Taleb, Nassim Nicholas 2010. *The Black Swan: The Impact of the Highly Improbable*, 2nd edn. London: Penguin.

Yiftachel, Oren 1998. 'Planning and Social Control: Exploring the Dark Side', *Journal of Planning Literature* 12(4): 395–406.

Index